THE STRUGGLE
FOR INDOCHINA

THE INSTITUTE OF PACIFIC RELATIONS

The Institute of Pacific Relations is an unofficial and nonpartisan organization founded in 1925 to facilitate the scientific study of the peoples of the Pacific area. It is composed of autonomous National Councils in the principal countries having important interests in the Pacific area, together with an International Secretariat. It is privately financed by contributions from National Councils, corporations, and foundations. It is governed by a Pacific Council composed of members appointed by each of the National Councils.

The Institute as such and the National Councils of which it is composed do not advocate policies or express opinions on national or international affairs. Responsibility for statements of fact or opinion in Institute publications rests solely with the authors.

THE STRUGGLE
FOR INDOCHINA

ELLEN J. HAMMER

WITH A PREFACE BY RUPERT EMERSON

*Published under the auspices of the
Institute of Pacific Relations*

STANFORD UNIVERSITY PRESS
STANFORD, CALIFORNIA

1954

STANFORD UNIVERSITY PRESS, STANFORD, CALIFORNIA
Published in Great Britain, India, and Pakistan by
Geoffrey Cumberlege, Oxford University Press
London, Bombay, and Karachi

The Baker and Taylor Company, Hillside, New Jersey
Henry M. Snyder & Company, 440 Fourth Avenue, New York 16
W. S. Hall & Company, 457 Madison Avenue, New York 22

The author wishes to thank the following for permission to quote
briefly: The Macmillan Company for material from *No Peace for
Asia* by Harold R. Isaacs (copyright 1947); Charles Scribner's Sons
and Jonathan Cape, Ltd., for material from *A Dragon Apparent*
by Norman Lewis.

Printed and bound in the United States of America

Library of Congress Catalog Card Number: 54-6815

TO MY MOTHER AND FATHER

NOTE

THIS book forms part of a group of studies prepared under the auspices of the Institute of Pacific Relations on the nationalist movements of Southeast Asia since World War II. Other volumes in this series include *Nationalism and Revolution in Indonesia* by George McT. Kahin, *Japan's Role in Southeast Asian Nationalism* by Willard H. Elsbree, *Asian Nationalism and the West* edited by the undersigned, *Malaya: Communist or Free* by Victor Purcell and forthcoming volumes on the Viet Minh regime by Bernard B. Fall and on representative government in Southeast Asia by Rupert Emerson and others.

For advice and assistance in the preparation of the present book the Institute and the author are indebted to many people—more than can be listed here—but special mention should be made of Professor Rupert Emerson, Dr. Virginia Thompson, Professor Nathaniel Peffer, Professor Walter Sharp, and Professor Paul Mus, and also of Mrs. Helen Wall for assistance in preparing the index. Particular thanks are due to the author herself for so expeditiously handling the difficult trans-Atlantic task of simultaneously revising chapters and proofs in order to meet a publisher's deadline and take account of a complex and rapidly developing situation.

Though the book is issued under the auspices of the International Secretariat of the Institute of Pacific Relations, it should be noted that responsibility for opinions expressed in it rests solely with the author.

WILLIAM L. HOLLAND
Secretary-General

New York
March, 1954

NOTE ON THE SECOND PRINTING

THE recognition accorded the timeliness of this book has made it necessary to order a second printing while the Geneva Conference is in progress. There has not been time for the author to revise the text in order to take account of the discussions, still inconclusive, which have taken place at the conference, or of the numerous official statements made by the various governments. This second edition, which will be distributed through the History Book Club as well as through bookstores, therefore appears without any revision of the text of the first edition except for a few minor typographical corrections.

W.L.H.

May 24, 1954

PREFACE

Professor of Government, Harvard University

IT WOULD BE difficult to find any corner of the world in which the major problems of our troubled times come more acutely to a focus than in Indochina. Despite the fact that only the French and the Indochinese are direct participants in it, the global and symbolic significance of the conflict is so great that, as in Korea, the sufferings of the millions of people whose land has been the battleground are almost lost to sight. For a decade colonialism, Communism, and nationalism have battled here for predominance, in so confused and tangled a fashion as to baffle the efforts of either active statesman or armchair analyst to reduce the issues to simple and orderly coherence. East and West, in both senses of those geographical terms, have met in an open and head-on conflict whose world-wide implications have been obscured but not concealed by the unreadiness of the powers in the background—the United States, Communist China, and the Soviet Union—to commit themselves fully to the sides they champion. The ending of the fighting in Korea has thrown more sharply in relief the complex nature of the Indochinese problem and the stark fact that here is a long-continued and brutal war to which no answer has been found.

The more the conflict has come to involve the United States, the more it has served as a testing ground for the grand strategy of American policy and for the relations of the United States both with her allies and with the peoples of Asia, neutralist as well as partisan. Of the significance attached to Indochina by Moscow and Peking we have less direct evidence than for the United States, but it is possible that their attitudes will be more clearly revealed at the forthcoming Geneva conference which was virtually the sole fruit of the recent meeting of the Foreign Ministers of the Big Four at Berlin. The continuance and outcome of the struggle profoundly involve the role of France in the world at large, in her relations with NATO and with Germany, and in her hold over the remainder of her great colonial empire. In the opinion of many, looking back to Japan's use of Indochina as a springboard for further attack, the fate of the country may prove the determining factor in the destiny of all of southern Asia.

The scene of bitter warfare since 1946 and one of the potential breeding grounds of the dreaded third World War, Indochina has been the constant concern of the Foreign Offices of the powers—and yet, paradoxically and almost inexplicably, it has never made a full-dress appearance on the stage of the United Nations.

The one outstanding element which most significantly distinguishes the

vii

situation in Indochina from that which has existed in the other countries of
Southeast Asia and, indeed, everywhere else in the world, is that nationalism
has come to be largely identified with Communism. When this is combined
with the fact that Viet Nam shares a considerable frontier with China, which
since 1950 has been in Communist hands, the makings of the present dilemma are evident.

In all the neighboring countries, despite the efforts of the Communists to
put themselves forward as the only true spokesmen for national aspirations,
the nationalist leaders and groups have not only distinguished themselves
from the Communists but have, either continuously or from time to time, engaged in active warfare with them. In Indonesia, between the two colonial
wars which the Dutch euphemistically labeled police actions, the Indonesian
Republic met a Communist rising by force and successfully put it down. In
the Philippines the Hukbalahap, however justifiable its grievances in terms of
land tenure and poverty, never represented more than a relatively small minority, and was dealt with as an enemy of the Philippine state. Thailand, apparently only slightly infiltrated by the Communists, has exhibited no tolerance for the movement, and the Burmese government has battled with the
Communist factions which threatened the nationalist regime in that country.
To seek to draw more than the most superficial parallel between the state of
affairs in Indochina and the lengthy struggle in Malaya is grossly to misread
the situation. Virtually all observers agree that in the former country even at
the present day the forces headed by Ho Chi Minh have a wide hold among
the Vietnamese, whereas in Malaya the Communist guerrillas represent only
some fraction of the Chinese community and have achieved no significant
standing among either the Malays or the Indians.

It is only since the end of 1949 or the beginning of 1950, as Miss Hammer
points out, that the leadership of the Communists in the Vietnamese nationalist movement has come to have much more than local importance. The key
turning point was presumably the dramatic advance of the Red forces in
China, reaching the Tonkinese border in December 1949. With China in
Communist hands a total reassessment of the situation was in order for all
concerned—and there were few who were not. Particularly for the United
States, this shattering of a principal plank in the American foreign policy
platform meant that, even before the dust had settled, new lines of policy
must be worked out which, given the centrality of the United States as the
leader of the shaping free-world coalition, could not help having vast effects
for everyone else. As far as Indochina was concerned, the outbreak of war in
Korea only served to harden and extend decisions which had already been
taken in the preceding months.

The detailed account of the events of these months is contained in Miss
Hammer's lucid narrative; but in summary fashion it may be said that the

most important results were the explicit lining up of the great powers on the two contesting sides, and the decision of the Viet Minh to leave no doubts as to its attachment to the Communist camp. The Viet Minh's recognition of the new Chinese government was followed by the return recognition of the Viet Minh by the People's Republic of China, the Soviet Union, and other members of the Communist bloc; while, on the other side, the United States and Great Britain extended their recognition to the French-sponsored government of Viet Nam and to Cambodia and Laos. So far as the French themselves were concerned, no major change was involved since they were already committed to the Bao Dai experiment, but they could now expect both that they would receive American aid in the war and that their opponents would be able to derive substantial benefits from the existence of a friendly government across the border. Furthermore, the French were now in a better position to make use of the contention, hitherto little developed by them, that this was no colonial campaign in which they were engaged, but one of the fronts on which the free world was holding back the onslaughts of Communism. At a little later stage, the Korean analogy, slim as it was in some aspects and dangerous as it was in others, could serve the French well for propaganda purposes. It should, however, be noted in passing that one of the more recent and significant twists given it lies in the argument that if a cease-fire without full victory were possible in Korea, why might not the French with equal justification seek a negotiated settlement in Indochina?

The alignment of forces which was shaped in 1950 has held firm up to now, but there are deep and perplexing contradictions within each of the coalitions which has been formed. At least on the free-world side none of the parties has been happy with its role and with the company it is obliged to keep. Such discomfiture as may have been felt by the two major Communist powers has at all events been more adequately concealed than that of their adversaries, who habitually allow their disagreements to be aired in public. All those involved are in one sense or another trapped by the commitments they have entered into; the end result is the perpetuation of a conflict which can neither be decisively ended without running the gravest risks nor compromised without sacrificing basic positions of one or more of the contestants.

In the case of Ho Chi Minh and the group surrounding him it is difficult to conceive that they can be wholly satisfied with their intimate dependence upon a foreign regime which is both Communist and Chinese. In the earlier years of the struggle it was a point of strength for Ho that, whatever his past record as a Moscow Communist, he now put himself forward as a nationalist heading a national government in which a number of groups and parties were represented. There can be no doubt that Ho retains much of his former national stature, but the drift away from the Viet Minh since 1950—although it has swelled the ranks of the *attentistes* rather than of the backers of Bao Dai

—must in part be attributed to the fears of many concerning both Communism and China. On the latter score, however, it is well to keep in mind that while the Vietnamese share the general Southeast Asian antipathy to the Chinese, against whom they boast of having defended their independence for a thousand years, it is also true that the Vietnamese culture is closely related to that of China, and that the Vietnamese nationalist leaders and groups have repeatedly over the last decades based themselves in China and established friendly working relations with corresponding Chinese parties and movements.

Whatever political disfavor Ho Chi Minh may have suffered from his association with China is presumably slight as compared with the antagonism inevitably faced by Bao Dai when, his checkered career having led him to part from the Japanese and from Ho, he returned to Viet Nam under the explicit patronage of the French. Given the almost universal determination of the Vietnamese to get out from under French rule, the one essential condition for the success of Bao Dai was that he establish himself as an independent national leader; yet it is only plausible to assume that the French turned to him because they believed that they would, at least in the long run, have to make lesser concessions to him than to the Viet Minh. Whatever the protestations of both Bao Dai and the French, it was all too evident that his return to power rested almost wholly on the troops with which France controlled the areas it had been able to regain. Bit by bit, the logic of events has forced the two uneasy partners—on one side to seek, on the other to grant—increasing increments of substantive independence; but it still appears to be the fact that a Bao Dai unsupported by French arms would be doomed to a short and troubled reign. The still unresolved difficulties which he has had in drawing into his government men with national standing and a broad popular following are irrefutable evidence of his own lack of national appeal and of his failure to break down the suspicion that he is tied to French apron strings.

Of all the parties to the conflict—save, always, the Indochinese peoples themselves—it is the French who are most gravely trapped. Even apart from the deep cleavages within France and the inability of any recent French government to come to firm and clear-cut decisions, the dilemmas by which France is confronted in Indochina are peculiarly painful and unpalatable. To read into the French public mind a unity of purpose which is actually non-existent, it may be surmised that by now the goal most likely to secure general adherence would be a speedy ending of the war in such fashion as to leave the formally independent states of Viet Nam, Cambodia, and Laos, members of a French Union in which France would play the leading role and be able to safeguard her cultural, economic, and other interests. But no one has yet been able to conceive the terms or conditions under which such a termination of the war could be brought about.

There is no need to amplify what has already been said of the relations between Bao Dai and the French: if he is to be effectively useful as a national
rallying point against the Viet Minh, he must be endowed with real independence; and if he is endowed with real independence, much of his charm
for the French necessarily evaporates. Since no third force of major consequence appears to have arisen, the alternative to Bao Dai is the Viet Minh,
and here the failure to capitalize on the agreements of 1946 and the redefini-
tion of positions in 1950 render very dim the prospects of any lastingly satisfactory arrangement. There remains the possibility of working out some type
of Viet Minh–Bao Dai coalition regime, but there is scant reason to think
that Bao Dai could hold his own in such a deal.

Internationally, the French position is as equivocal as it is in relation to the
internal affairs of Indochina, and for much the same reasons. Carrying on an
exhausting and inconclusive war which has been increasingly portrayed as
devoted not to the French colonial interest but to the preservation of freedom
against Communist imperialism, France has been highly reluctant to invoke
the international collaboration which such a cause might seem to deserve. Although particular reasons can be found to cover each stage of the argument,
it seems not improbable that the root cause of the French hesitations is to be
sought in a perpetuation of the feeling that Indochina is a French colonial
problem to be dealt with under French sovereignty. Any real opening of the
international doors would weaken the French claim to regard the country as
a more or less private preserve within the Union. As far as submission of the
conflict to the United Nations is concerned, the French are well aware of the
hostile reception they would receive in a number of quarters and are also
disinclined to do anything which would further an expansion of international
jurisdiction in the colonial sphere. If Indochina, why not Morocco, Tunisia,
Madagascar, and who knows what else?

Within the more restricted family of the NATO powers France could
count on a more sympathetic response because of the much greater immediate
concern with the Indochinese drain on French military strength and the con-
sequent intensification of French opposition to German rearmament. From
these powers France has sought and received moral and diplomatic endorsement of her role in Indochina. In addition she has made it plain that she
would welcome financial and material aid, but she has desired no direct military participation by others, in part because she wants to retain sole command of the situation and in part because of fears that Peking might respond
by throwing Chinese troops into the battle.

Aside from possible token contributions, it is only the United States which
has felt itself in a position to meet the French pleas, and a large and growing
share of the costs of the war have in fact been met from the American treasury; but on neither side is the relationship a very satisfactory one. The French

no doubt have lingering memories of the American hostility in the course of World War II to a restoration of French rule in Indochina and, with greater relevance to the present state of affairs, they view with somewhat contradictory dismay both the American pressure for larger independence for the Indochinese peoples and the possibility that the United States might end by squeezing out France as the leading economic and political power in the area. American aid is desperately needed and sought, but if the price to be paid for it includes the necessity of surrendering the determination of policy and strategy to Washington there would be many who would regard it as too dearly bought.

By all accounts the war in Indochina is, thoroughly understandably, a vastly unpopular one in France, but the difficulty of ending it is as great as the difficulty of stirring up any popular enthusiasm for it. Year by year military victory has been postponed to the following year, and there has never been assurance that military victory could be translated into a political decision compatible with French desires and ambitions, however they may be defined. Here again the tie-up with the United States complicates matters because it seems unquestionable that the French ability to work out a negotiated settlement is hampered by the rigorous American opposition to any deal which would have the look of appeasement of Communism.

The American dilemma is compounded of a number of different elements. The United States has entangled itself in a war in a distant corner of Asia in which it resolutely does not want to participate and from which it equally resolutely cannot abstain. It has committed itself to the cause of France and of Bao Dai, but enough of the old spirit of anticolonialism is left to make this a somewhat unsavory commitment: it cannot bring itself wholly to ignore the fact that the free world looks less than free to a people whose country is being fought over by a foreign army. Aware that a lasting peace can be built only on satisfaction of the national aspirations of the Indochinese, the United States must at the same time conciliate a France reluctant to abandon her colonial past. At a further remove, the United States, as a champion of the right of peoples to self-determination, backs the claim of the Vietnamese to make their own free choice in the world; but if they should choose Communism, as seems not unlikely, is it then also the American obligation to save them from themselves?

The United States has declared the stalemated Indochinese war to be a vital part of the defense of the free world, but it is well aware that the only remaining step of sending American combat forces would be opposed by France and by much of home opinion, would rouse the wrath of neutralist Asia, and would not improbably bring similar Chinese aid to the Viet Minh, with the grave risk of provoking World War III. It would like to channel the massive American aid direct to the Indochinese states, but it has been met by French obstruction on this score, and it cannot evade the fact that these states remain weak instruments. On any realistic view it is the French command which dominates the scene. If there were to be direct and overt Chinese intervention in the war, the American position would in a sense be simplified, although at an appalling cost; but as it is, the United States is deeply involved in a war in which it does not want to fight.

With the ending of the fighting in Korea, Indochina was left as the one area in which Communist and anti-Communist forces were engaged in open warfare and as the principal specific barrier to an approach to the general Far Eastern settlement which it was hoped might emerge from the Korean cease-fire. In consequence, during recent months there has been increasing concern over the actual military progress and intensified efforts to secure an international solution.

Even the procedural questions involved in working toward an agreement on Indochina were far from simple. No agreement which lacked the approval of Communist China and the United States was likely to be of lasting significance or to lessen tensions in the Far East. These two powers, however, were not formally participants in the war and were also not on speaking terms with each other, even though they had met to transact business in Korea. Responding principally to strong French pressures, the Foreign Ministers of the Big Four, meeting in Berlin in February, found an answer to this phase of the controversy in their decision to hold a further conference in Geneva in April, this time including the Chinese People's Republic, at which, as the official communique stated, "the problem of restoring peace in Indochina shall also be discussed." This decision came at a time when the United States was already reexamining its commitments in Indochina and the implications of the New Look in American policy announced by Secretary of State Dulles on January 12.

Despite optimistic assertions by high American officials, it was obvious that things were not going well either in France, where there were growing demands for an end to the war on almost any terms, or in Indochina, where the military initiative seemed to rest with the Vietminh rather than with the French. To bolster French morale and avert the possibility of serious reverses in the field, the flow of American military aid was speeded and increased, and, most significantly, a substantial number of Air Force technicians were rushed to Indochina to train French ground crews in the servicing of American military planes which had been made available. With the Geneva conference looming ahead, it appeared imperative to deny the Communists the prestige of even minor victories, yet American public and Congressional opinion was deeply alarmed at the prospect that the United States might shortly find itself plunged into the war.

The Indochinese war provided an unhappy testing ground for the new

American doctrine of "massive retaliatory power" to be applied at places and with means of our own choosing, which the Secretary of State had proclaimed. In Indochina, the United States was committed in a place obviously not of its own choosing to an assistance program which was strictly limited, even though in its latest formulation it involved a pledge to supply whatever equipment might be needed for victory. Massive retaliation seemed wholly inapplicable within Indochina itself and would probably mean bringing in China and perhaps the Soviet Union as active belligerents—an eventuality which few, if any, could desire. Furthermore, the Geneva conference necessarily involved a recanvassing of the embattled issue of American recognition of Communist China, or of the seating of its representatives in the United Nations, without which agreement on Indochina might prove impossible.

American anxiety mounted toward the end of March as the beleagured garrison of Dienbienphu was heavily assaulted by Vietminh forces. On March 29 Secretary Dulles in an important policy speech asserted that "the imposition on Southeast Asia of the political system of Communist Russia and its Chinese Communist ally, by whatever means, would be a grave threat to the whole free community. The United States feels that that possibility should not be passively accepted, but should be met by united action." Acknowledging the risks involved, he said that these were "far less than would face us a few years from now, if we dare not be resolute today." He went on to reaffirm the opposition of the United States to recognition of Communist China and to its admission into the United Nations.

The recent intensification of activity strongly suggests that the struggle for Indochina is shaping toward a climax which cannot be long postponed, but the nature of that climax still remains obscure. Whatever the ultimate resolution of the conflict may be, one stark fact must accompany the statesmen to the conference tables of Geneva: the incalculable human tragedy of a war fought with savagery and brutality on both sides. Although Indochina has been spared the horrors of the atom or hydrogen bomb, it has known the grim effects of air strafing and napalm incendiary bombing, which strike both soldiers at the front and civilians in the villages. In France today the war is justly termed *la sale guerre;* but the French loathing for it can be only a pale shadow of that of the people of Indochina. Be the issue colonialism, nationalism, or Communism, a staggering price has already been paid in human misery.

March 30, 1954

CONTENTS

AUTHOR'S FOREWORD

THIS STUDY of a valiant people and of the tragic situation in which they find themselves has been undertaken with humility by the writer, aware of the presumptuousness of trying to analyze and interpret an experience so remote from her own. It is all too easy to read alien habits of thought into circumstances where they can have no meaning, or to confuse scholarship with the collection and tabulation of the errors made by other foreigners. Coming from an academic environment imbued with respect for the printed word, I have reluctantly had to recognize in the course of preparing this book how inadequate, inaccurate, and often untrue the printed word has been in regard to Indochina and its people. For this reason I have had to make a special effort to discriminate among sources, and to search for authorities among the men who know most about their country although they have rarely had the time or the inclination to put down their knowledge on paper.

I have tried to depict a segment of living history abstracted from its past, without the benefit of the perspective which the passage of time allows to the historian of the past. My only justification for such an attempt is that I have had the privilege of personal conversations and, in some instances, friendship with a number of the people, both Vietnamese and Frenchmen, who have played leading roles in the events described here. To translate the experience and spirit of one country into those of another is a difficult task indeed, and if I have made errors in the process, I can blame no one but myself. To all those, Vietnamese and Frenchmen, who have been so kind, and without whose generous aid this book could never have been written, I can just express my warmest thanks and hope that I have done justice to their thought. I have merely tried to do what many Americans are trying to do, to understand a little of the world, in Asia and in Europe, which we have only learned to know at all in recent years and still need to understand so much better.

E. J. H.

Paris
March 30, 1954

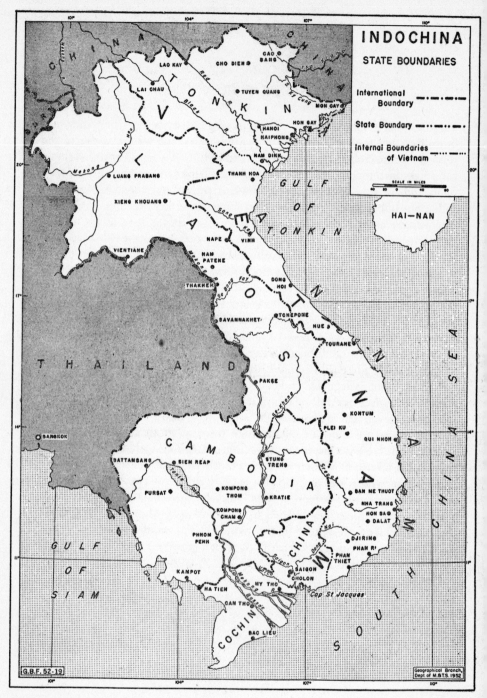

INDOCHINA
STATE BOUNDARIES

International Boundary
State Boundary
Internal Boundaries of Vietnam

SCALE IN MILES

HAI—NAN

CHINA

CHINA

LAO KAY
CHO DIEN
CAO BANG
LAI CHAU
TUYEN QUANG
MON CAY
TONKIN
HON GAY
HANOI
HAIPHONG
NAM DINH
Red R.
Black R.
Song Koi
THANH HOA

V I E T N A M

LUANG PRABANG
XIENG KHOUANG
Mekong R.
Nam Hou

GULF
OF
TONKIN

NAPE
VINH
VIENTIANE
NAM PATENE
DONG HOI
THAKHEK
Se Bang Fai
TCHEPONE
SAVANNAKHET
Se Kong
HUE
TOURANE

L A O S

T H A I L A N D

PAKSE
Mekong

KONTUM
PLEI KU
QUI NHON

BANGKOK

A N N A M

BATTAMBANG
SIEM REAP
STUNG TRENG
Tonle Sap
C A M B O D I A
KOMPONG THOM
KRATIE
BAN ME THUOT
PURSAT
Mekong
NHA TRANG
HON BA
DALAT
KOMPONG CHAM
Se Kong
PHNOM PENH
Song Nai
CHINA
DJIRING
PHAN RI
KAMPOT
Song Nai
PHAN THIET
SAIGON
CHOLON
MY THO
Saigon
Bassac
HA TIEN
Cap St Jacques

GULF
OF
SIAM

CAN THO
BAC LIEU
COCHIN

S O U T H   C H I N A   S E A

G.B.F. 52-19

Geographical Branch,
Dept. of M.&T.S. 1952

By courtesy of Canadian Dept. of Mines and Technical Surveys

Introduction

INDOCHINA – A WORLD PROBLEM

Since 1949, when Mao Tse-tung's victory in China raised the specter of Communist control over the whole of Asia, Indochina has been one of the critical points in the democracies' line of defense. It is the strategic gateway to Siam, Malaya, and Burma as well as to Indonesia, the Philippines, and even India. Since 1949, therefore, the affairs of Indochina have become a matter of increasingly urgent concern to the government and people of the United States, as well as to their European and Asian partners in the non-Communist world. This concern was strikingly expressed in August 1953, shortly after the Korean truce, when President Eisenhower in a major speech publicly called attention to the strategic, economic, and political importance of holding Indochina.

Even before the Korean armistice the situation in Indochina was grave. A Franco-Vietnamese war had dragged on nearly seven years, and there was still no end in sight. France, a pillar of the NATO organization in Europe, was slowly being bled white, despite substantial American aid. Notwithstanding their strong reluctance to relinquish any part of the French Empire, French politicians not only of the Left but of the Right were beginning to talk of a "negotiated settlement" in Indochina. A large segment of French opinion was demanding that France cut her losses and pull out of an unprofitable war. To such a retreat the United States was firmly opposed; but neither did it wish to send its own troops to Indochina.

Some saw a possible way out of the impasse by building up indigenous armies, with American equipment, to take over the major military load. But it still remained doubtful whether such a policy could bring victory unless the anti-Communist governments of Indochina were given the real independence which they never ceased to demand—and whether France would make the needed concessions in time. Even if she did, could non-Communist nationalists seize the psychological initiative from the Communists at this late date?

The signature of an armistice in Korea raised a new danger in Indochina but, at the same time, offered a new opportunity. Would Chinese Communist forces, released from Korea, strike again in a southward direction? Or did the ending of hostilities in one major battle area give hope that they might be ended in another?

Indochina had become a major international problem in which not only the United States and France, but also the countries of Asia were deeply interested; and many of them—Indonesia, Burma, and India in particular—saw the war primarily as the struggle of an Asian people to throw off the yoke of

3

Western imperialism, already liquidated in most of Asia. From their stand-point this was the main issue and Communist leadership of the Vietnamese struggle was only incidental. And what made the situation so desperately serious was that the majority of Vietnamese agreed with them.

When the Vietnamese started to fight, the cold war had not yet begun; their war then was just one phase of the revolt against colonial rule which swept through Asia after the defeat of Japan. India, Pakistan, Burma, Indonesia, and the Philippines have all since achieved their independence, all but one by peaceful means. Only in Indochina has the fighting persisted.

It has persisted because of the blunders of both sides. The French for a long time closed their eyes to the fact that this was in great measure a nationalist and popular war in Viet Nam and refused to deal with it as such. The Vietnamese, for their part, allowed the leadership in their national struggle to be taken over by the Communists, and thereby lost the friendship of a large segment of world opinion which might otherwise have supported them.

Many Vietnamese are still fighting against the French on the side of the Communist leader Ho Chi Minh and the Viet Minh. Many others, following Emperor Bao Dai, have joined the French against the Viet Minh. Neither man is wholly independent: Bao Dai still has to rely, to a certain extent, on France, as does Ho Chi Minh on Communist China, which has given him substantial aid. The Vietnamese people are fighting on both sides, however, because they want independence. Many of them now feel trapped in the struggle between the Communist world and the West. Tens of thousands of Frenchmen and Vietnamese have already died in what has become a war of attrition.

In 1945, when the French launched what they called "mopping up operations" to re-establish their rule over Viet Nam after the Japanese occupation, they said that the country would be pacified in a few months. Instead, they soon found themselves spending more than a billion dollars a year on the Indochina war. A French Cabinet Minister once said that any French government which wanted to withdraw from Indochina would be overthrown. And yet the demand for evacuation has swelled in France. It is not only the Left which would like to get out of Indochina; voices have been raised in favor of evacuation by important members of the Radical Socialist Party. Former Premiers and Cabinet Ministers have urged withdrawal before France's economic and military position in Europe is wrecked. They are worried that the French may not be able to maintain their hold over other parts of their empire, and that they may not be able to fulfill their commitments under the North Atlantic Treaty. They are disturbed about the ability of France to compete with the reviving army and industry of Western Germany. They are seriously concerned about the economic health of France itself. Directly after the second World War many Frenchmen blamed the United States for not helping France in Viet Nam. Today a number of Frenchmen are saying that France is fighting in Viet Nam only because the United States wants it to.

Since the end of 1949 there has been a common frontier between Communist China and Viet Nam; and the possibility of large-scale Chinese intervention in the Vietnamese war increasingly has haunted American policy makers. The Chinese, of course, know that while their military and economic aid is very welcome to the Viet Minh, their presence en masse probably would not be. The Vietnamese have behind them a thousand-year-old tradition of opposition to invasions from China. One of the highlights of that tradition dates back to the thirteenth century, when Vietnamese troops defeated the Mongol armies of Kublai Khan. And as recently as 1946 the Vietnamese had unpleasant experiences with Chinese occupation troops in North Viet Nam. Even were the Chinese to come, as friends, to "liberate" the country, the Vietnamese have no assurance that they would ever willingly leave.

Further, the Chinese are aware that intervention in Indochina might lead to action by the United Nations. The United States already has major commitments in the country. And British Foreign Secretary Anthony Eden specifically stated that a Chinese invasion of Indochina would be regarded as aggression and so dealt with. Chinese intervention would also increase the strain on an already strained Chinese economic and military organization.

But the best argument against Chinese large-scale intervention is still another. As long as the war goes on, French troops and American money and equipment will continue to be drained off into Indochina. The position of France has already been seriously affected by the Indochinese war, and this situation could only worsen as the war continued. At the same time, the Viet Minh, in need of continuing and greater aid, would be forced still further into the Chinese camp. Without sending any Chinese troops into Viet Nam, without awakening any dormant anti-Chinese sentiment among the Vietnamese, the Chinese could dominate the Viet Minh and keep the war going indefinitely. Neither side would win in that case, and only the Vietnamese people would lose.

On the other hand, the Chinese might decide to intervene before the French Union army and the troops which Bao Dai is raising become any stronger. If they do, they have already been warned of the consequences. On September 2, 1953, American Secretary of State John Foster Dulles spoke very clearly. He said:

Big wars usually come about by mistake, not by design. . . . It is . . . probable that the Korean war would not have occurred if the aggressor had known what the United States would do. . . . There is a risk that, as in Korea, Red China might send its own army into Indochina. The Chinese Communist regime should realize that such a second aggression could not occur without grave consequences, which might not be confined to Indochina. I say this soberly in the interest of peace and in the hope of preventing another aggressor miscalculation.[1]

1 *Department of State Bulletin,* September 14, 1953, p. 342.

A small colonial sore has been dangerously inflamed by the blunders of the Vietnamese and of the French in Indochina, where the Communist issue, injected into the Vietnamese struggle for independence, poses a grim dilemma. Although it has become a cliché to say that the United States must be prepared to offer a positive answer to Communism which cannot be simply a military one, the Indochina problem constitutes a specific and immediate test of the American ability to do so.

For the United States, the war in Indochina presents a grave challenge: to defend itself against the most serious threat it has ever known to its own independence, namely international Communism, and at the same time to defend, as it traditionally has done, the liberty of others.

The danger in dealing with the menace of international Communism in these tense times is that problems tend to be oversimplified; whenever the Communist threat is invoked, virtually all other considerations are obscured. To the extent that this occurs, it constitutes an abdication of America's initiative in making its own foreign policy; it plays into Russian hands and gives the initiative, by default, to the Soviet bloc.

A few years ago the most serious colonial problem in the world seemed to be India, and it was solved, as a colonial problem, mainly by two conservatives, a British Governor General, Lord Mountbatten, and an Indian pacifist, Mahatma Gandhi. The problem in regard to Viet Nam now, as to India then, is to get beyond a few political labels and to try to understand the complexity of the issue.

This is a war of a whole population, with guerrillas based upon the countryside, with families divided among themselves and fighting on opposite sides, with mass casualties. Yet it is a war which few people want, either in France or in Viet Nam.

It is a war which springs from the total political and economic experience of the Vietnamese people, going back many centuries. But it has been shaped by the specific experience of the recent past.

This book is an attempt to indicate something of that past. It is a story of a number of people, of what they said and how they acted. Sometime perhaps, in the future, these events will be presented as logical and inevitable, stemming from the imperatives of the political and economic situation in which they occurred. But that will be only when the writers are far removed from the actual scene. For, in fact, they were neither logical nor inevitable. The history of the last eight years in Viet Nam was conditioned by many factors, some obviously significant, some apparently trivial. The fact of the second World War and the Japanese occupation was of first importance, not only in breaking the continuity of French rule, but also in reshaping the form of that rule during the war years. And if Ho Chi Minh had not been a Communist, how different would the Vietnamese revolution have been; and how different its reception by the non-Communist world?

History, despite all that the West has had to learn about the nature of group political action and, more recently, about the international Communist conspiracy, is still a story of individuals as well as of organized political and economic groups. This is true of France and the making of its Vietnamese policy. In Asia, it is the more true because political life there has seldom been organized in parties as they are known in the West; and only a small ineffectual native middle class has stood between the peasant masses and their rulers. Vietnamese political life has tended to coalesce around certain men, brought forward by the needs of the moment, and because of the state of war and political transition, the role of individual leaders has assumed a special importance in Vietnamese affairs. Their story and that of the men around them, as of the Frenchmen they dealt with, their actions and their errors, their successes and their failures, have shaped the history of Viet Nam since the second World War.

Chapter One

BEHIND THE JAPANESE LINES

ON A NIGHT in August 1945, several days after the capitulation of Japan, two planes circled over opposite ends of French Indochina. One was in the south, over the rich region of Cochin China, beyond which lies the South China Sea. Colonel Henri Cédile, the new French Commissioner for Cochin China, parachuted from an American C-47 with two companions, to land in a ricefield. Far to the north, at the other end of the country in the region of Tonkin that borders on China, three other Frenchmen jumped at nearly the same hour from the other plane. They were a lieutenant, a captain, and the new Commissioner for northern Indochina, Major Pierre Mesmer.

The French had come back to Indochina.

Japanese troops had been in the country since 1940, although the French government of Indochina, which had sworn allegiance to Marshal Pétain and to Vichy, had been overthrown by the Japanese only in March 1945. Cédile and Mesmer arrived to bring back the rule of the French Republic to its richest colony. They came as had no French government representative ever before them, virtually alone, without troops or ceremony. With them they carried the authority of liberated France and a promise of a new freedom for Indochina. But in the gray revealing dawn of August 23 this had little meaning. They were a handful of Europeans bringing to an Asian country, which for five years had been cut off from the West, only words and the reminder of a past supremacy.

Cédile almost immediately met some of the Vietnamese he had come to liberate. They were uncordial, even hostile, and turned him over to the Japanese, who stripped him and his two companions of most of their clothes and of their possessions. Cédile was forced to lower his head before a Japanese soldier wielding a sabre. After waiting what seemed interminably for the blow that did not come, he looked up to find the assembled Japanese regarding him impassively, and then they began to laugh. Only then did he realize there was to be no execution that day. But the three men remained in Japanese custody. It was as a prisoner, huddled seminude with his companions in a Japanese military truck, that the man appointed by France to be its highest official in Cochin China arrived in Saigon, the Cochin Chinese capital.

Mesmer, meanwhile, was having his own difficulties. His goal was the city of Hanoi, the capital not only of Tonkin but of all Indochina. He did not reach it. No sooner had he landed than he was surrounded by Vietnamese who made him and his companions their prisoners. The three Frenchmen were able to keep their radio for a while and told their headquarters in Cal-

8

cutta they were being well treated. Then they were fed poison, and the oldest of them died. He was Captain Brancourt, a pharmacist who had lived in Indochina before the war and loved its people. His one concern at the end was that Mesmer, who had not known Indochina in prewar days, would have the wrong idea of these people who had gathered around, enjoying his agony. "Do not forget," he told Mesmer earnestly in his last moments, "they are not like that." Mesmer and Lieutenant Marmont, the other survivor, remained in prison for weeks until they were finally able to escape to the Chinese lines. By that time another man had been appointed Commissioner in Mesmer's place.[1]

But if, as Brancourt insisted, they were not like that, what had happened to the people of Indochina? The French came back slowly to the country in the summer and fall of 1945. Some Americans had parachuted in, months before the Japanese surrender, to work with Vietnamese guerrillas against the Japanese; others arrived immediately after the war ended. News of something stirring in the country, something strange and new, began to filter out of Indochina. Japanese soldiers wandered about freely, for in the first weeks of September there was no Allied force strong enough to intern them. The Japanese had given up trying to run the country and yet, remarkably, there was little anarchy. In Vietnamese towns and villages people formed committees and began to govern. They ran the public services. They maintained order. By and large they acted independently of one another and, since ordinary difficulties of communication had been increased by war damage, that was not surprising. Yet one committee after the other insisted it was part of a national Vietnamese government. In the city of Saigon in Cochin China sat a Southern Committee of that government and in Hué, the capital of Annam,[2] a Central Committee.

The palace of the Governor General and the public buildings in the capital city of Hanoi had already changed hands once within the year when the Japanese had taken over administration of the country from the French. Now the Japanese in turn had capitulated, but the buildings were not empty. Throughout the city new flags waved, bearing a gold star on a red field. Flags of the Allied nations seemed everywhere—American, Russian, Chinese, British—but nowhere in all of Hanoi was a French flag flown. Banners proclaimed slogans which were scrawled large on the walls of buildings, some in English: "Down with Imperialism! Independence or Death!" A Japanese general was still in command of the city where a French admiral had ruled a few months before.

1 These events have been described in Paul Mus, *Le Viet Nam Chez Lui* (Paris, 1946), pp. 11–12; and Jean-Michel Hertrich, *Doc Lap!* (Paris, 1946), pp. 7–16.

2 Although "Annam" was used under the French to designate only the central part of the country, the people of Tonkin and Cochin China as well as those of Annam were all known as "Annamese" or "Annamites" under the French regime.

But in the *Résidence Supérieure* sat a slight, bearded Vietnamese in a plain khaki uniform. His name was Ho Chi Minh and he claimed to be president of the Democratic Republic of Viet Nam.

This was a year of name-changing, as the French Empire turned into the French Union and the French Colonial Ministry into the Ministry of Overseas France; the French Governor General in Indochina became the High Commissioner and the Third Republic was on the verge of becoming the Fourth. And in Indochina the Annamese decided to call themselves Vietnamese.

The new republic claimed to represent the people who lived in the three Vietnamese regions, and traced its roots far back into the past. Centuries ago, when the Chinese conquered the Vietnamese, they called the country Annam, which was Chinese for "pacified south." It was once nominally united under the Lê dynasty at Hanoi in Tonkin, although in Annam and Cochin China another family wielded effective power. Rebellion toward the end of the eighteenth century swept the Lê emperor from his throne into exile in China. It was a member of the Nguyen family, with the help of a French bishop and French troops, who brought peace to the Vietnamese lands and united Tonkin, Annam, and Cochin China.[3] He took the name of Gia Long and founded the Nguyen dynasty which is still ruling the country. He set up his capital at Hué in Annam. And he called the country Viet Nam, land of the south.[4] During the years of French rule, when the French did all they could to keep separate Tonkin, Annam, and Cochin China, the name Viet Nam came to symbolize national unity and independence. Not surprisingly, it was as Vietnamese that the founders of the new republic assumed office.

First reports reaching France labeled the new government collaborationist. For years Japan had been spreading "Asia for the Asiatics" propaganda over Southeast Asia and it seemed to have fallen on fertile ground. French spokesmen called the Ho Chi Minh government a last-ditch attempt by the Japanese to leave chaos in Indochina. Neutral observers said that Japanese deserters were joining the Vietnamese, despite Vietnamese denials.

Pointing to the years of Vichy rule in Indochina, Vietnamese flung back upon the French with interest the charge of collaboration. The Vietnamese retorted that France and Japan had worked together hand in glove since 1940. As to the charge that they were creatures of the Japanese, members of the new Vietnamese government looked to the Allied missions in China (particularly the American Office of Strategic Services) to disprove it.

[3] "Nguyen" is, by far, the most common surname in Viet Nam. "Nguyen Phuoc" is the surname of the royal family. Ton That, however, is the surname of descendants of the princes who preceded Minh Mang.

[4] "Viet" is the Chinese "Yueh," the name of people who lived in Southeast China before the Ch'in and Han unification. The area occupied by the ancestors of the present day Vietnamese was south of them, in Tonkin, and perhaps also south and southeast Kwangtung.

One thing was certain: events in the country since the end of the second World War would have been very different if the Japanese had not come to Indochina.

INDOCHINA ON THE EVE OF WORLD WAR TWO

When the war in Europe broke out in 1939, Indochina in French eyes stood pre-eminent among France's overseas territories. (North Africa, neither colony nor metropolitan territory, was in a class apart.) "Indochina is, from all points of view, the most important, the most developed and the most prosperous of our colonies," said Albert Sarraut, Colonial Minister and onetime Governor General of Indochina, as early as 1923.[5] It was not really a colony at all, Alexandre Varenne, another former Governor General, remarked before the second World War. It was an empire.[6]

Indochina extended over some 287,000 square miles, an area a third larger than France, and was inhabited, according to official prewar estimates, by some 23 million people. Three-quarters of these were Vietnamese, in appearance and civilization closely related to the Chinese. The greater part of the Vietnamese country was mountainous, the plateaus of south Annam linked by the Annamese Chain to the high rugged mountains of northern Tonkin and China. But the Vietnamese were fearful of the malaria and evil spirits of the highlands and discouraged by the seeming poverty of its soils; they planted their rice only in the flat coastal areas along the length of the peninsula. They were crowded into the fertile delta regions of two great rivers —the Red River delta in Tonkin and the Mekong delta in Cochin China— and the plains of Annam which lay between them. The Tonkinese delta is one of the most densely populated areas in the world.

For a thousand years the Vietnamese had been governed by the Chinese and their social and governmental system bore the deep imprint of their neighbor to the north. Most of the Vietnamese were Buddhists of the Mahayana or Great Vehicle variety which came from China; but their Buddhism was diluted by animism and intermingled with Confucianism and Taoism. There were also some two million Catholics among them.

The French had moved into Indochina gradually during the latter half of the nineteenth century, and this was reflected in the administrative patchwork they created in the country. Captain Gosselin, a Frenchman who served in Indochina at the turn of the century, found the Vietnamese "the most homogeneous people imaginable, from the mountains of upper Tonkin to the frontiers of Cambodia, from the ethnic point of view as well as from the

5 Albert Sarraut, *La Mise en Valeur des Colonies Françaises* (Paris, 1923), p. 463.
6 Alexandre Varenne, "Les évènements d'Extrême-Orient et notre avenir en Indochine," *Politique Etrangère*, February 1938, p. 16.

political and social viewpoint."[7] It was the French who divided the Vietnamese country into Tonkin, Annam, and Cochin China. They wrested control of the three eastern provinces of Cochin China from the Emperor of Viet Nam as far back as 1862 and later made Cochin China a French colony under direct French rule, with a French representative in the Chamber of Deputies in Paris. Tonkin and Annam were not taken over until 1884, when other ideas of colonization prevailed; they became protectorates.

The Emperor of Viet Nam, whose capital was at Hué, traditionally appointed a viceroy to rule over Tonkin in his name. The French persuaded him to give up this vestige of control over the northern part of his domain and instituted direct French rule over Tonkin, even though they called it a protectorate. The Tonkinese cities of Haiphong and Hanoi, and Tourane in Annam, they took over as French enclaves, owning them as they owned Cochin China; and the frontier regions of Tonkin were administered by the French military.

More of the old pre-French forms survived in Annam, although French officials had scarcely less practical authority there than in Tonkin and all public works and services were under the control of French administrators. The Emperor continued to live in Hué, which lay somnolent behind the protective mountain called the Emperor's Screen, an old city of gardens and pagodas crowded with memories of the Vietnamese past. He lived in the Purple Forbidden City within the Citadel, on the northern side of the Perfumed River. From 1884 to the pre-World War II years, by a series of more or less diplomatic encroachments, the French authorities had gradually stripped the Emperor and his court of ministers of all traces of real political power. There were left to him only such duties as conferring honorary titles on a variety of celebrities ranging from Governors General to sacred elephants.[8] Visitors from the West generally were baffled by the highly intricate ceremonies still practiced at the Court of Hué, which contrasted with the total impotence of the Emperor and his ministers in regard to more earthly questions.

North of Cochin China and west of Annam, sharing a common frontier with Siam, were the two other divisions of Indochina—Cambodia and Laos—both of them sparsely settled countries. These too were regions of Indochina but the three million Khmers of Cambodia and the one million Laotians, with their Indian-like civilizations, were a world apart from the Vietnamese. They were devout Buddhists; and their yellow-clad, shaven-headed monks practiced the Hinayana (Little Vehicle) Buddhism, which they shared with Ceylon, Burma, and Siam.

Few bonds held the Laotians and Cambodians to the Vietnamese other

[7] Ch. Gosselin, L'Empire d'Annam (Paris, 1904), p. 7.

[8] In 1933, when the Ministry of War was suppressed by the French, this right to honor sacred elephants, which were used in making war, was also suppressed.

than those constituted by their French rulers. They had far more in common with the people of Siam although, in their time, they had fought off invaders from Siam; and longstanding boundary disputes divided them from their Siamese neighbors. The Cambodians and Laotians feared and distrusted the Vietnamese because of their history of aggressive expansion—in past centuries they had lost considerable territory to the Vietnamese—and also because of their greater enterprise. Already in Cambodia and Laos there were thriving Vietnamese communities doing business among the more indolent indigenous peoples; and the rapidly increasing Vietnamese threatened to engulf them by sheer weight of numbers as well.

Even their attitude toward France differed from that of the Vietnamese. Only by the threat and the use of force had the French been able to impose their rule on the Vietnamese Emperor at Hué. This was not the case with the Cambodians and the Laotians, whose kings had turned voluntarily to France, seeking protection against Viet Nam and Siam.[9] Cambodia too became a protectorate with a native king in 1863, as did the kingdom of Luang Prabang in Laos in 1893, the rest of that country being ruled directly by France.[10]

The Indochinese Union was thus five states and three peoples, as well as different ethnic minority groups—notably the Thai who lived in the Tonkinese mountains and the Moi who were mostly in the plateaus of South Annam.[11] Frenchmen pointed to them all with pride as loyal subjects of the empire when the second World War began.

Rice dominated the agriculture, the diet, and the exports of Indochina. Indochina was the third most important exporter of rice in the world, and it also exported large quantities of rubber and corn. Its wealth was not only in agriculture but also in minerals and timber; it had anthracite coal (most of which it exported), as well as iron ore, tin, zinc, phosphates, manganese, and wolfram. And it was one of the few colonies in the French Empire to export more than it imported.

On the eve of the second World War there were only some 40,000 Euro-

---

[9] The Cambodian King Norodom, however, who had welcomed the French twenty years earlier, objected when a restrictive convention providing for French control over the country was imposed on him in 1884. He launched an unsuccessful revolt against the French the following year, when the convention was supposed to go into effect.

[10] 1893 was the year of the signing of the treaty between France and Siam which enabled the French to set up their protectorate over Laos. The French did not sign a parallel treaty with the King of Luang Prabang, although they had signed treaties with the Emperor of Viet Nam and the King of Cambodia. This oversight has been explained by the tendency of the French Government to consider Laos as simply composed of principalities over which Viet Nam and Siam had fought for centuries. French officials at the time apparently did not realize that the King of Luang Prabang was "the chief of a real state, the legitimate descendant of a long line of kings." Paul Le Boulanger, *Histoire du Laos Français* (Paris, 1930), p. 316.

[11] The Indochinese Union was officially established in 1887 and Laos was made a part of it six years later. In 1898 the leased territory of Kwangchowwan, on the southeastern coast of China, was also included in the Indochinese Union.

pean residents in all Indochina, the great majority of them Frenchmen, but they dominated the country. Frenchmen ran the Indochinese administration, army, and police. Rubber plantations and mining were almost entirely in French hands. In 1938 there were US$384,200,000 worth of foreign investments in Indochina. More than 95 percent of them were owned by Frenchmen.[12]

THE JAPANESE MOVE IN

When the Japanese drew up their plans for Asian conquest, they put Indochina high on their list of objectives. It was a rich country which every year sent abroad quantities of rice and raw materials, and the Japanese knew they would need it if they were going to extend their lines beyond their own frontiers. Nor was it solely a potential supply base, for Indochina was strategically located; geography alone made it a key to the invasion of Southeast Asia. Whoever commanded its shores was within striking distance of the Philippines, the Dutch East Indies, Malaya, and Burma. Indochina touched the Burmese Shan States, shared an extended common frontier with Siam, and, most important, was on the southern boundary of China.

In 1939 Japan was already knee-deep in a war which it fobbed off on the fear-ridden West as the China Incident. The Japanese protested as military supplies moved into China across Tonkin, over the railroad which linked the Tonkinese port of Haiphong to the Chinese province of Yunnan. To appease them, the French stopped hauling armaments ordered after the fighting began in 1937; but they continued to transport gasoline and trucks bought in the United States for the Nationalist armies of Chiang Kai-shek. Neither the Japanese nor the Chinese were satisfied. The Chinese bitterly accused the French of stopping or delaying much-needed supplies. The Japanese, as indignantly, complained that the French were helping the Chinese war effort.

Legally, the Japanese did not have much of a case, for Japan should have been a prisoner of its own fiction; it had never admitted that a state of war existed with China, which alone would have justified cutting off military supplies. But the legal system of the interwar years was wearing thin, laying bare the realities of power which underlay it. France was weak in Asia and the Japanese knew it (although as yet they, like everyone else, had no inkling of how very weak France was). Early in 1939 they took over the Chinese island of Hainan in the Gulf of Tonkin and then the Spratley Islands, some distance from the Indochinese coast. As they succeeded in closing other land

---

[12] Helmut G. Callis, *Foreign Capital in Southeast Asia* (New York, 1942), p. 85. The Chinese, according to Callis, "are not foreigners in the same sense as Westerners are. A great many of the Chinese families have lived in the colony for several generations and feel completely 'at home.' We find the Chinese in different stages of assimilation . . ." Callis estimated Chinese business investments in Indochina at an additional $80,000,000.

and sea routes to Free China, the materiel arriving over the railway from Indo-china assumed a heightened importance in Japanese eyes;[13] the Japanese be-gan to blame this traffic for their reverses in China. They launched a violent press and radio campaign against the French. Sabres were rattled by the Japa-nese generals, already in South China near the Indochinese frontier. In April the Japanese attacked the railway from the air.

When in the spring of 1940 the news came that the French armies were crumbling on their own soil before the invading Nazis, the Japanese press and radio broke out in renewed vituperation. In Europe the beaten French, their impotence laid bare to the world, asked Berlin for an armistice. Half way across the world, Indochina was cut off from France; for the time, at least, it was completely dependent on its own resources. It was up to General Georges Catroux, Governor General of the colony, to decide what the next move would be.

Catroux played for the highest stakes. The future of Indochina hung in the balance and he had few trump cards in his hands to save the country from the Japanese. He had, in fact, few cards of any kind. The policy of the Third Republic had been to keep Indochina weak, economically and militarily de-pendent on France, and Catroux had reaped the unpalatable fruits of that policy.

The Colonial Minister of France in 1938 and 1939 was Georges Mandel, who was known among people from the empire for his attempts to bring humanity into the colonial administration. A farsighted man, Mandel had joined with Alexandre Varenne and a few others in urging that Indochina be encouraged to increase its manufactures, for the country had the raw ma-terials and the labor necessary for industry. Mandel accomplished something, but not enough. Some meager gestures in the direction of industrialization were made, but opposition to it remained strong in influential French circles. They insisted that Indochinese industry be kept down so that it would not compete with French manufactures. The country was to be only a source of raw materials and a market for French manufactured goods. This was a policy of dubious merit in peacetime. In war, it proved a grave error, for Indochina was left a satellite nation dependent on others for industrial prod-ucts and munitions.

This was the more true because Mandel's military plans for Indochina had fared little better than his economic ones. He wanted to build up a na-tional army, drawing on Indochinese manpower to a far greater degree than the French ever had before, but this plan won only qualified acceptance in France. Sixty-two-year-old General Catroux was called from retirement to become Governor General, the first military man to hold that post in half a

---

[13] See République française. Direction de la Documentation, *Notes Documentaires et Etudes*, No. 316, *Le Chemin de Fer du Yunnan*.

century. Some of Mandel's proposals were put into effect in the colony. In 1940 the French were building a naval base at Cam Ranh Bay, one of the best natural harbors in the Far East. They had started work on airfields and barracks, as well as on a few factories, but these were pathetically inadequate to Indochinese needs.

To defend its long and vulnerable coastline Indochina could muster only one cruiser and four cutters, along with some lesser vessels. French occupation forces policed the country from garrisons and frontier posts and stood guard in Tonkin near the Chinese frontier, where banditry festered. This was not an army capable of defending Indochina against an invader. Its air forces were virtually nonexistent, its modern planes numbering perhaps twenty-five. Some 50,000 men were under arms. They had with them limited supplies and munitions that Catroux estimated would not have lasted more than a month of fighting.[14] General Martin, who commanded the army in Indochina in 1940, testified during Marshal Pétain's trial that in his opinion the country would have been incapable of holding out for more than two or three months.[15] If it was to make a stand against the Japanese, Indochina desperately needed help from abroad. Catroux was playing for time when, on July 16, he announced the railway would stop carrying gasoline to China. This, he hoped, would momentarily appease the Japanese, giving him a chance to appeal to London and Washington for aid.

These were difficult days and Catroux moved as cautiously as he could. But in a cable to France, to Rivière, Pétain's Colonial Minister, he spoke his mind. Whatever France did about making a separate peace, Indochina would stand by the Franco-British alliance. Catroux's natural sympathies and Indochina's best interests, as he saw them, added up to the need for close co-operation with Britain. He looked forward to an arrangement by which both would profit, the British getting raw materials which they needed from Indochina, notably metals for India. Indochina was in urgent need of ships to carry the exports abroad, and these and other things the British could supply.

To Lord Halifax, the Foreign Minister of Great Britain, Catroux sent warm assurances of friendship, all at the moment that he could offer. Halifax, it seemed, could offer no more. The war, with the Japanese attack on Pearl Harbor still six months in the future, was still a European war, and the British were determined to keep it that way. They would do what they could on the diplomatic front to maintain the integrity of Indochinese territory. But what Indochina needed was military help, and that Britain was not prepared to give. Was it only in 1939 that the British and French had held an important

---

[14] *Notes Documentaires et Etudes,* No. 120. Rapport présenté par le général Catroux. *La crise franco-japonaise de juin 1940.* This report is the source of quotations and actions attributed to Catroux in the following pages, unless otherwise noted.

[15] République française. Haute Cour de Justice. *Procès du Maréchal Pétain* (Paris, 1945), p. 278.

conference to plan for the joint defense of Hongkong, Malaya, and Indochina? That meeting at Singapore had had few concrete results and the military situation had altered radically since then. Britain was staggering under the pounding of German bombs and the British Government was convinced that the future of the British Empire, like that of the French Empire, would be decided in Europe. Lord Halifax's message to Catroux was that Germany was the only real enemy of both countries. The main thing was to avoid a Far Eastern war; probably the Japanese would be glad to co-operate, limiting their demands on Indochina to what seemed necessary to win the war in China.

Toward the end of April Sir Percy Noble, Commander of the British Far Eastern Fleet, came to Saigon to see Catroux. When he left, all hope of British aid went with him. Like Lord Halifax, he warned against any action that might risk war with Japan. His argument was stronger than the Foreign Minister's because it was more unanswerable. He told Catroux that the British could not give him military support because they did not have it to give.[16]

The United States was Catroux's only other hope and by this time it too had become a forlorn one. French Ambassador de Saint-Quentin had put two questions to Undersecretary of State Sumner Welles. What would the United States do if Indochina was attacked? And would the United States supply Indochina with 120 planes and antiaircraft guns? On June 19 the Japanese presented an ultimatum to Catroux and gave him twenty-four hours in which to reply. Welles, however, had to tell the anxious Ambassador in Washington that the United States, which also hoped to localize the war in Europe, could not go to war with Japan. In that case, asked de Saint-Quentin, what choice did Indochina have but to capitulate to the Japanese demands? "I cannot answer you officially," Welles said, "but it is what I would do in your place." If the French still wished to send a purchasing mission to the United States to buy military supplies, it would be as welcome as that of any other friendly government.[17] Catroux replied by dispatching a mission under Colonel Jacomy which, as it turned out, arrived in the United States too late to do any good.

The last hours of the Japanese deadline were ticking out. Abandoned by the West, weak and ill-equipped at home, Catroux had no choice. He accepted the Japanese terms, closing the frontier to exports of gasoline, trucks, and other war materiel, and agreeing to permit a Japanese control mission

[16] The British later appear to have reconsidered this position, although they did not change it. Secretary of State Cordell Hull, recalling a conference he had with the British and Australian Ambassadors in September 1940, wrote: "Lothian [Lord Lothian, the British Ambassador] stressed the need for some steps that would deter Japan from occupying Indo-China, and indicated that the British Government was undertaking to render some substantial military aid to the Indochinese Government." *Memoirs of Cordell Hull* (New York, 1948), p. 906.

[17] *Notes Documentaires et Etudes*, No. 120.

on Indochinese territory to make certain that the French kept their word. In this he was following the advice of French representatives in Japan, notably the French Ambassador to Tokyo, Charles Arsène-Henry. He hoped once again to gain time by his concessions, to use the imminent rainy season as a respite in which to arm his forces with materiel to be purchased in the United States. And he looked to Rivière, Pétain's Colonial Minister, for pilots, planes, and arms. If all went well, he thought, he would be strong enough by October to speak firmly to Japan. In the meantime he maneuvered. "But be assured," he cabled Rivière, "that if I must fight I will do it totally."

When Rivière protested against Catroux's acceptance of the Japanese ultimatum on June 20, the Governor General bluntly disregarded his objections. The Pétain government, he said, was too far away to be able to judge the Indochinese situation. "Circumstances have placed me outside your effective sphere of action and I must be able to act freely. My aim is to preserve Indochina without arms if I can, with arms in the contrary case." Rivière reported this to the French Cabinet. He was very upset. He objected to the fact that the Japanese control mission had not been stationed in China and kept out of Indochina, and he did not like Catroux's independent attitude. He urged that the General be replaced. Admiral Darlan suggested as a likely candidate for the post Vice Admiral Jean Decoux, the Commander-in-Chief of the French naval forces in the Far East, a subordinate of his "who had the advantage of being on the spot and whose obedience he guaranteed."[18] Decoux was the man for the job, the Cabinet agreed; they dismissed Catroux.

Years later, when Catroux was Ambassador of the Fourth Republic to Moscow, he recalled that the Japanese radio in June 1940 had quoted Ambassador Arsène-Henry as saying that the appointment of Decoux meant no change in policy. "In other words," Catroux commented, "my behavior in the Japanese affair was not disavowed, but my rude sincerity and my independence and, without doubt also, my faithfulness to the British alliance had displeased and were penalized." These facts certainly influenced the decision of Pétain's government, but it came also from their lack of understanding of the Indochinese situation. They disliked the Japanese more than they did the Germans; more to the point, they feared them less. Appeasement was all right in Europe, but they did not, for the moment at least, see why they should export it to Asia.

Catroux did not share this view. He would not agree to a defensive treaty with Japan, but in the matter of the railway and the control mission he had to give way. He had wanted to declare openly for General Charles de Gaulle, and in this he was not alone. As General Martin reconstructed the scene before the tribunal trying Pétain in 1945, Indochina had learned of the request for an armistice with Germany on June 18, after four days without a word

---

[18] Paul Baudouin, *Neuf mois au Gouvernement* (*Avril–Décembre 1940*) (Paris, 1948), p. 216.

from the French Government.[19] The news had been received with stupor and consternation, and people's first reaction was to refuse to accept an armistice. Relations with British officials in Asia had been close since the Singapore conference, and there seemed no reason why the French and British Empires together could not fight the war in partnership. On the morning of June 26 a delegation of officials formally called on Catroux and requested him to carry on the fight.

Isolated from France, Catroux looked to Frenchmen in other parts of the empire to see what they would do. General Mittelhauser, who commanded the French troops in Syria, and General Noguès, Resident General of Morocco, both of whom had said that they wanted to fight, changed their minds. The French navy, instead of joining the British, put up an active resistance to their recent ally and to the Gaullists at Mers-el-Kebir. Even this did not convince all the French in Indochina that their future lay with Pétain. A number of people spoke up for de Gaulle, some in the army and others in the French administration. Businessmen who depended for their livelihood on trade with the outside world were not keen on cutting their ties with it. Most of the French people who lived in Hanoi, the capital of Indochina, were connected in some way with the French administration and being dependent on it for their livelihood, were generally content to follow wherever the government in France would lead. The French plantation owners and merchants of Saigon were not so compliant. They debated the question of allegiance among themselves, and even when the die had been cast for Pétain, some of the Saigonese remained Gaullists.

Catroux was fighting his own personal battle as well as that of France. No one knew better than he the tightrope he walked in Indochina. The Japanese had promised to preserve the status quo, but a shift of political allegiance might disrupt the uneasy equilibrium in Indochinese-Japanese relations and give Japan a convenient pretext for taking over the country. Decoux seems to have encouraged Catroux in his reluctance to turn over his authority until the order to do so was definitely confirmed from France.[20] Catroux delayed until July 20. Then, with Decoux's assurance that "my acceptance of power in no way means that I disavow your actions as Governor General,"[21] Catroux left to join General de Gaulle without any need to worry about the consequences of his action for Indochina.

Pétain's Foreign Minister, Paul Baudouin, was doing his best, meanwhile, to make sure that Catroux's experience with the Japanese would not be re-

[19] Haute Cour de Justice, *op. cit.*, p. 276.

[20] Decoux, in his apologia, *A la Barre de l'Indochine* (Paris, 1949), is critical of Catroux's delay and takes no resoponsibility for it. See, however, General Catroux's documented reply to his account in *Le Monde*, September 8, 1949.

[21] *Le Monde*, September 8, 1949.

peated.[21a] He called on Sawada, the Japanese Ambassador, and told him that France, not Indochina, was the place to discuss Franco-Japanese problems, and the Ambassador agreed. But on August 2, Tokyo sent another ultimatum to Indochina, this time to Decoux, demanding the right to cross Tonkin and occupy Indochinese airfields.

Again the French looked abroad for help. The American Government told Ambassador de Saint-Quentin that it firmly supported the Far Eastern status quo, but did not plan to do anything about translating its support into action. But what about the Germans? Firmly established in Paris by now, they might also have an interest in the French Empire. And unlike the United States, they might have some influence with the Japanese, with whom they were linked in the anti-Comintern pact. The French appealed to General von Stulpnagel of the German Armistice Commission in France. They suggested that Germany try to persuade its Axis partner to moderate its demands. Cynically appealing to Nazi racialism, French officials argued that supporting the French in Indochina would mean keeping an Asian foothold for the white race.[22]

The Chinese also took a hand in the discussions. Ambassador Wellington Koo came to Baudouin with a warning from his government against allowing Japanese troops to cross Indochinese territory on their way to fight in China. He told the Foreign Minister that the Chinese Ambassador in Berlin reported that Germany did not want France to lose its empire. (The Germans at this time may have expected to inherit some of it themselves.) Baudouin suggested that the Chinese also try to convince the Germans they should check Japan.[23]

To Ambassador Sawada, Baudouin explained that it was not so much the nature of the Japanese demands to which his government objected; it was their form. France insisted on formal recognition of French sovereignty over Indochina, and it could not accept any terms that were couched as an ultimatum. On August 30 the two governments found a face-saving formula. Japan recognized French sovereignty over Indochina and the territorial integrity of the country. France, in turn, in language similar to that the British had used in the Craigie-Arita formula the previous year, recognized Japan's special interest in the Far East and agreed to discuss economic conventions and to grant military facilities to Japan in Indochina, which the Japanese

---

[21a] Paul Baudouin had been governor general of the Bank of Indochina, which Indochinese identified with the worst aspects of the colonial administration (and he returned to the Bank after he left the Foreign Ministry). To the Indochinese, it was unfortunate that he was in a position to deal with their fate.

[22] La Délégation Française auprès de la Commission Allemande d'Armistice. Recueil de Documents publié par le Gouvernement Français, Tome Premier, 29 Juin 1940–29 Septembre 1940, pp. 107–8.

[23] Baudouin, *op. cit.,* p. 298.

promised to evacuate as soon as they had defeated China. The next step was for the soldiers to draw up their conventions.

The French Cabinet was still not reconciled to this policy of concessions. It split on whether Indochina at this point could risk a break with Japan, but Foreign Minister Baudouin, who was convinced that the country could not be defended, carried the day. There was still Decoux to deal with. He agreed that his army was not strong, but "if we must run the risk of losing Indochina, it is better to lose it in defending it rather than by betraying it." When he protested against the agreement with Tokyo,[24] Marshal Pétain wired Decoux that he counted on him "to give an example of discipline to all Frenchmen."[25]

Admiral Decoux however, did not prove as co-operative as the Japanese would have liked, and in September the Japanese Government issued a third ultimatum. In Tokyo, the Japanese Foreign Minister explained to American Ambassador Joseph C. Grew that Decoux was not willing to implement the recent agreement, "and since the Governor General was evidently not acting in good faith and since the Japanese authorities were aware that to foreign consuls stationed in Indochina the Governor had boasted that he was using obstructive tactics, the Japanese felt it necessary to present their ultimatum."[26] Again Vichy had to explain that it was not unalterably opposed to Japanese demands but it could not accept them in so arbitrary a form. Tokyo took the hint and resumed negotiations.

The French tried to persuade the Germans to let them send some of their military equipment to Indochina. Although for a while the German Armistice Commission seemed not unwilling, on orders from Berlin it refused. Baudouin approached German Ambassador Otto Abetz in the hope that Foreign Minister von Ribbentrop would restrain the Japanese. His argument for saving Indochina for the whites was stronger now. The Chinese had grown menacing on the Indochinese frontier at the prospect of more concessions to the Japanese. And the Siamese had revived old territorial claims against France in Indochina. Abetz agreed to pass on the message, saying that Germany could do no more than advise Tokyo.

In Vichy, Ambassador Wellington Koo proposed that Chinese troops move into Indochina from Kwangsi province to defend it against the Japanese. He made this proposal on several occasions, but the French were fearful of an open break with Japan; nor did they want to antagonize Japan's ally, Germany, who might possibly aid Vichy in dealing with the Japanese; and they were afraid of seeing Chinese troops set foot on Indochinese soil, which China once had ruled. Vichy rejected the Chinese offer.[27]

[24] Ibid., p. 328.
[25] Decoux, op. cit., p. 102.
[26] Joseph C. Grew, Ten Years in Japan (New York, 1944), p. 331.
[27] F. Charles-Roux, Cinq Mois Tragiques aux Affaires Etrangères (21 Mai–1er Novembre 1940) (Paris, 1949), pp. 70, 257.

Decoux was a loyal adherent of Pétain but he did not like the idea of giving way to Japan any more than had Catroux. He also appealed to Britain and the United States and succeeded in evoking a statement of American disapproval of Japan's course. But this had little practical value, particularly when it followed closely upon a British surrender to Japanese threats, for August 18 had seen the closing of the Burma Road (for three months), which left the Haiphong railroad Free China's sole outlet to the sea. Decoux hedged as long as he could, and officials around him talked of making a fight.

The Japanese became impatient as the negotiations dragged on. Once again they went through the byplay of offering an ultimatum and then withdrawing it, and even pretended to evacuate their nationals from Indochina. But they did not withdraw their army from the Indochinese frontier. It was clearly only a matter of time before they would have their way. The Japanese ultimatum was scheduled to expire on September 22, and Baudouin, in France, went to bed thinking that war might break out that night. But in Indochina, that day, Decoux yielded and signed an agreement with Japan. A limited number of Japanese troops were to land immediately at Haiphong, which was to be a port of transit for the Japanese army. Three Japanese air bases were to be established in Tonkin, where 6,000 Japanese troops were to be garrisoned.

These were the terms that Decoux arranged with the Japanese. However, the same day, the Japanese army in southern China took more drastic action. It moved across the Tonkinese border and on September 22 launched an attack on the cities of Lang Son and Dong Dang. French and Vietnamese troops resisted but Dong Dang fell that night to tank-supported Japanese. On the 24th Lang Son hoisted a white flag. The Japanese concentrated on the key axis from Dong Dang on the Chinese border through Lang Son and Dong Mo to Hanoi. Japanese sailors made surprise landings at unprotected coastal areas. Three bombs were dropped on Haiphong and Japanese planes flew over Hanoi. By the 25th, all French resistance had crumbled.

The French fought Japanese troops on two separate occasions in the five years between the fall of France and the surrender of Japan. This was the first. An official French source called it "the first of a series of glorious episodes in which the French army of Indochina showed that it knew how to fight against all hope, just for honor."[28] Foreign observers were more impressed with the brevity of the action and its ineffectualness.

When Baudouin heard of these events, he recalled how he had insisted Indochina could not defend itself, and wrote in his diary, "How right I was not to follow the advice of the soldiers."[29] The French had been overwhelmed by well-equipped Japanese veterans, and a number of untried Indochinese

[28] Direction Fédérale de l'Information, *La Situation en Indochine* (*Mars 1945–Juin 1946*) (Saigon, 1946), p. 2.
[29] Baudouin, *op. cit.*, p. 360.

soldiers had broken ranks and fled under fire. The French High Command had blundered miserably. Decoux reported to the French Foreign Office:

These last factors produced consternation, but they clearly revealed to the greater part of [French] opinion in Indochina, even in military circles, that only the conclusion of an agreement with the Japanese had prevented these latter from achieving decisive results. Practical unanimity has been reached on the need for the agreement and for collaboration with the Japanese.[30]

This brief taste of warfare brought down to earth many military people in Indochina, blinded by the legend of white supremacy, who had talked of strong action against the Japanese. They realized that they could not expect to get anywhere by force; at least, not yet. If they were to hold their own, it would have to be by more indirect methods. To start with, they held a promissory note from Japan to respect French sovereignty and to limit strictly the number of Japanese troops in the country; when they presented this note, as they promptly did, the Japanese declared their willingness to honor it. On October 5 the Japanese commander at Lang Son ordered the captured French and Indochinese troops to assemble before him. He got on his knees to receive an imperial rescript which he brought ceremoniously to his lips, and genuflected again before he read it aloud. The Emperor called the Lang Son incident an error which was unfortunate but not important. The invading troops would leave Tonkin quickly and the prisoners they had taken would be released. Lest there be any doubt, the Emperor himself said that Japan recognized French sovereignty over Indochina.[31]

In Washington, Secretary of State Cordell Hull told a press conference after the September 22 agreement: "It seems obvious that the status quo is being upset and that this is being achieved under duress."[32]

ENEMIES AT HOME AND ABROAD

An oppressive atmosphere hung over the French in Indochina in 1940. Alarmed and uncertain, they were afraid of attack from all sides. They feared the British might attempt a landing, and they worried about the Chinese. Indochina's record of appeasement of Japan at the expense of the Chinese had

---

30 Ibid., p. 361.

31 Decoux, op. cit., p. 120; André Gaudel, L'Indochine Française en face du Japon (Paris, 1947), p. 92.

"The Japanese government pledged itself, in the agreements which it forced upon Indochina, to respect its sovereignty and independence. But the Japanese records show that it had no intention of doing so. Certainly it would have retained permanent control of strategic points and a decisive voice in its political and economic affairs." Herbert Feis, The Road to Pearl Harbor (Princeton, 1950), p. 104.

32 Department of State, Papers Relating to the Foreign Relations of the United States: Japan 1931–1941 (Washington, 1943), Volume II, p. 297.

not endeared the French to Chungking. There were sporadic Chinese forays against the northern frontier and clashes between frontier posts; there was also Chinese banditry in the mountains of upper Tonkin. The Decoux government made up its mind that if the Chinese invaded in force, it would fight; and it would have to fight not only for itself, but also because the Japanese would expect it to. As things turned out, it was never called upon to make good on these plans because both the British and the Chinese waited until after the war was over to enter Indochina.

Decoux had other, more real enemies to worry about. The Siamese were demanding back the Laotian and Cambodian territory they had been forced to cede to France at the turn of the century. And within Indochina, Vietnamese nationalists tried to take advantage of the Japanese attack. They stirred up the mountain people from around Cao Bang and Lang Son, a number of them infantrymen who had deserted from the French army after the clash with the Japanese. When the French came back to the Lang Son area in the fall of 1940, they were confronted with open rebellion.

Several French battalions went into action against the rebels and tracked the veteran Vietnamese revolutionary Tran Tung Lap into the mountains. His army, which may have numbered some 3,000 at its height in October 1940, shrank rapidly under French blows. Against the ill-trained, ill-equipped Indochinese, the French used the weapons of modern war, including planes. It was a great French victory. They lay in wait for Lap with machine guns and captured him, after killing fifty of his companions.

Tran Tung Lap blamed his defeat on the undisciplined youths who fought with him. "If I die it is their fault," he said. "Ah! If I had my old companions you would never have taken me."[33] The French executed him at Lang Son at the end of December.

His surviving followers escaped to China to join other nationalists or went into hiding in the Tonkinese mountains. Throughout the war years Vietnamese nationalists infiltrated into this troubled frontier region. Northern Tonkin seemed fairly quiet by the beginning of 1941, but it never really was pacified.

The French put down another uprising at Do Luong in northern Annam. In Cochin China, near My Tho, the rebels got wholly out of control. Large-scale insurrection spread throughout the region late in November 1940 and there were few French troops to stop it. The Siamese were already becoming threatening and the French had to send most of their troops to the eastern frontier. The French police asked for help from Foreign Legion and Tonkinese battalions which were passing through Saigon on their way to Cambodia. The latter sent in three small units but after much shooting and cannon-fire they found they had underestimated the enemy.

[33] R. Bauchar, *Rafales sur l'Indochine* (Paris, 1946), p. 61.

By this time the danger from Siam had also grown acute. Confronted with the threat of war on two fronts, the French called in reinforcements. They rounded up the Foreign Legion battalion and also the battalion of Tonkinese, as well as two artillery units, one mechanized unit, and a naval unit, and sent them all converging on the My Tho area. They brought in planes to bomb the insurgents. Anyone who seemed suspicious, they arrested. Anyone who tried to fight or flee, they shot.

"We were cruel," commented a member of the French forces in Indochina. "The threat of Siam haunted us, but above all we had to show our strength to those who remained loyal to us and to those who thought they could profit from our reverses."[34] It was the way France had habitually dealt with rebellions, in Indochina and elsewhere in the empire, and the results were much as usual. The French won a breathing spell, while the nationalists who survived went underground, their grievances inflamed and multiplied, until the day when they, or others like them, could take up where they had been forced to leave off.

The Siamese, meanwhile, had progressed from threats and demands for Laotian and Cambodian territories, to frontier clashes. The militarist, pro-Japanese government of Marshal Pibul Songgram which was ruling in Bangkok had renamed the country Thailand and embarked upon an ambitious program of uniting with Siam all the Thai peoples in Burma and Indochina. The Siamese had signed a nonaggression pact with the French on June 12, 1940 but when France fell the Siamese lost interest in ratifying it. Instead, they demanded the "lost provinces," the Laotian lands on the right bank of the Mekong River which they had ceded to French Laos in 1904, and the provinces of Battambang, Siemreap, and Sisophon, which they recognized three years later as belonging to French Cambodia. If the Laotians were indeed a Thai people, the Khmers of Cambodia were not; but the leaders of the new Thailand were not interested in technicalities. The opportunity for expansion was ripe, the French were weak, and the Japanese far from disapproving.[35]

By the first week in January 1941, the French and Siamese were involved in an undeclared war. They fought a series of indecisive engagements. Then the French were beaten roundly in Cambodia; their plans were known and anticipated, the morale of their Indochinese battalions was bad, and their armament and equipment were shown up as inadequate. The next day, however, on January 17, the French fleet steamed into the Gulf of Siam, engaged the much stronger Siamese navy at Koh Chang and put 40 percent of it out of commission in two hours. It was a short-lived triumph. Before the French could follow

---

[34] *Ibid.*, p. 71.

[35] The French Government had hoped that the Japanese would act as a moderating influence on the Siamese. "But it did not take us long to see that in fact Tokyo was in league with Bangkok." Charles-Roux, *op. cit.*, p. 265.

up their victory, the Japanese stepped in with a plan of mediation and, with German help, persuaded Vichy to accept it in March.[36] The Japanese were counting on this acceptance. They wanted to move south toward Singapore across the Malacca peninsula, passing through Siam and Indochina, with air bases, port facilities and permission to station troops in Indochina. The right to do this was to be the price of their mediation.[37]

Treaty negotiations were held in Japan, where the French put up a stubborn but losing battle, gaining only a few meager concessions. By Japanese edict the three rich rice-growing Cambodian provinces—Battambang, Siemreap, and Sisophon—went to Siam, as did parts of Laos on the right bank of the Mekong. On May 9, 1941 the French and the Siamese signed their treaty of peace in Tokyo.

Defeated in Europe in 1940, France was defeated in Asia in 1941. One day the Vietnamese would cite their failure as proof that France had forfeited its right to "protect" Indochina.

THE JAPANESE TIGHTEN THEIR GRIP

The Japanese seemed quite content to leave a framework of French control in Indochina.[38] Decoux and the officials under him bore the burdens of government and kept order in the country, leaving the Japanese free to use Indochina more or less as they wished—to plug up a gap in the blockade of China, and to serve as a military base and a source of supply in the conquest of China and Southeast Asia. It was a profitable arrangement for both French officialdom and the Japanese military, and it opened the door to Japanese domination of the country.

On July 28, 1941, Japanese troops landed in force in Saigon to occupy strategic areas in the south, in accordance with an agreement signed in Vichy with Japan, which had been placed before Decoux with orders to implement it. On three separate occasions the Japanese had asked the Germans to join them in persuading Pétain to acquiesce in the occupation of Indochina. The Germans

---

[36] Feis, *op. cit.*, p. 152.

[37] *Ibid.*, pp. 151–52.

[38] There seem to have been sharp differences between Japanese military men and Japanese diplomats in Indochina, according to on-the-spot observers, who say that the military would not have been adverse to giving independence to Viet Nam earlier and more completely than was actually done. Japanese diplomats, however, are reported to have preferred to appease the French as long as possible in the hope that one day, when the war ended, France might act as an intermediary between Japan and the Western Allies; and this was the policy that the Japanese followed.

Admiral Decoux also had something to say on this subject: "Our country, given the privileged situation that it would thus have safeguarded in the Far East [had there been no coup of March 9, 1945], would have been able to play and should have played the important role of intermediary between the two parties and thereby would have contributed actively to the rapid re-establishment of order and calm in this part of the world. The Japanese diplomats living in Indochina did not hide from us, beginning in 1943, that such was their secret hope." Decoux, *op. cit.*, pp. 196–97.

may have been cautious at first, awaiting the outcome of Japanese–American talks then in progress, but in July 1941 Admiral Toyoda, the Japanese Foreign Minister, thanked the German Government for its co-operation in persuading Vichy to sign this accord for the "common defense" of Indochina.[39]

Who was defending whom, and against what, were the questions asked in Tokyo and Washington. Admiral Toyoda told American Ambassador Grew that the Japanese would withdraw from Indochina as soon as they ended the "China Incident." This was the same answer that they gave to President Roosevelt when he proposed a pact among the great powers to neutralize Indochina. To Acting Secretary of State Sumner Welles, the Japanese Ambassador in Washington explained that Japan needed an uninterrupted supply of rice and other foodstuffs and raw materials, the flow of which to Japan might be obstructed by the Chinese and the Gaullists. The Japanese were also trying to protect themselves against encirclement by other powers, by which, presumably, they meant the British who were on the defensive in Singapore and Malaya.

Or was it the Americans they were afraid of, or the hard-pressed Chinese, or the handful of Dutch in the East Indies? Roosevelt nailed the move for what it was: It "was being undertaken by Japan for the purpose of further offense."[40] It was an important step in the Japanese program for the conquest of Southeast Asia.

The chink in Indochina's defense against the Japanese had grown from the small hole that Catroux had permitted to be opened in June 1940, when he had hopes of plugging it soon afterward, to the larger one which Decoux had agreed to that September. The "common defense" accord breached the wall completely, and Indochina fell to Japan without a move of protest from Decoux. From Vichy came a tragicomic echo of the Japanese line. The French in Indochina, it was explained, needed Japan to protect them from the British and the Gaullists.

The Japanese brought more troops into Indochina during the remaining months of 1941. On December 6, on the eve of the Japanese attack on Pearl Harbor, President Roosevelt dispatched an appeal to Emperor Hirohito to withdraw Japanese forces from Indochina and so assure "peace throughout the whole of the South Pacific area."[41] That night (December 7, Asian time) Japanese troops infiltrated Hanoi and took up key positions throughout the city; the next day the Japanese issued a new ultimatum to the French. At 9 o'clock in the morning a Japanese general presented himself before Decoux and his staff to read a message from the Mikado, announcing that Japan was

[39] Feis, *op. cit.*, p. 231.
[40] *Papers Relating to the Foreign Relations of the United States: Japan 1931–1941, op. cit.*, p. 528.
[41] *Ibid.*, p. 786.

at war with the Allies. He asked for assurances that Indochina would do nothing to hinder the activities of the Japanese forces. Let Decoux supply these assurances, and his government would remain as before. If he refused, the Japanese army would take over Indochina.

Throughout the day the French debated these terms. In the evening the Japanese envoy returned to the office of the Governor General, and the Japanese and Frenchmen thrashed out the matter during the night. By dawn, December 9, they had reached an agreement. French sovereignty, for what it was worth, was confirmed once again. The French were still to control their own army and the administration of the country. And Japanese soldiers were to be free to fight their war against the United Nations from Indochinese soil.

Admiral Decoux tried to preserve the French economic position in Indochina against the Japanese, but economically as well as militarily he had to operate within serious limits. The country's economic life had been geared to heavy exports—it sent abroad each year some 1,600,000 tons of coal, 1,400,000 tons of rice, 500,000 tons of corn, 140,000 tons of cement, and 60,000 tons of rubber.[41a] In exchange, Indochina imported much-needed gasoline, oils, chemicals, metallurgical products, machinery, and textiles. The colony continued to trade with the Far East, Australia, and the United States in the first year after France fell. With French monopoly control gone, the Anglo-Saxon countries took a much larger percentage of the trade, as did Japan. But then the English-speaking countries, concerned with problems of self-defense, stopped their trade with Indochina. Japan was left master of the situation. It needed Indochinese products, it produced goods the Indochinese needed, and it was in a position to force its terms upon Indochina.

"We refused every Japanese demand at first, then began to bargain, which permitted us finally to give the minimum," recalled Major René Jouan, the French officer who was Decoux's liaison with the Japanese High Command.[42]

The French delayed their answers to Japanese demands, sometimes referring them back to Vichy to play for time. They set up syndicates of French foreign traders and merchants so that Japanese attempts to infiltrate into the economic life of the country were rigidly controlled. (Decoux's concern, characteristically, was for the French, not for the Indochinese; the syndicates confirmed already existing French firms in a monopoly of the country, permitting no Indochinese to supplant them.) Decoux could also claim credit for paring down Japanese demands for rice and other commodities in the negotiation of their various economic agreements.

On May 6, 1941, after long negotiations, Decoux signed the first of a series of annual economic agreements with the Japanese, by which they were to take

---

[41a] These figures refer to the annual overage for the period 1937–39. See Gouvernement Générale de l'Indochine. *Annuaire Statistique de l'Indochine* 1939–1940; *ibid.*, 1937–1938.

[42] Hertrich, *op. cit.*, p. 139.

Indochina's surplus in rubber, rice, and minerals in exchange for manufactured and industrial products. The Japanese paid for their imports in blocked yen. They paid their money, in other words, into French accounts in Tokyo and there, in the coffers of the Tokyo banks, it remained. In 1941 and 1942 the Japanese took all that was allowed them under the economic agreements, but increasingly few goods made the return trip from Japan to Indochina. Prices in Indochina rose sharply because of the shortage of supplies.

In 1943, even the one-way flow of goods to Japan began to slow down as American and British planes pounded away at Japanese shipping. They attacked Japanese installations in Indochina, destroying Indochinese industrial and commercial centers in the process, and severely damaging the north-south railway and coastwise shipping. This prevented the transport of desperately needed Cochin Chinese rice to Tonkin and northern Annam, bringing famine in the north late in 1944. Rubber piled up high at the Saigon quays but the Japanese were unable to ship it away, and stock accumulated in Saigon warehouses.

The Japanese army lived off the land in Indochina on piastres advanced to it by the Bank of Indochina, for the French had agreed to pay the costs of the occupation army. Tokyo soon began to default on its commitments under the economic and financial agreements, but the Bank of Indochina continued dutifully to fulfill its side of the bargain. Each year Japanese demands grew for rice and other Indochinese products, and for Indochinese piastres.

THE FRENCH IN CONTROL

Only in Indochina did a European people remain masters of a part of Asia during the second World War. Armed French troops moved freely throughout the country. The Japanese did not have much to do with the Indochinese population, rarely venturing into the hinterland where the French administrator ruled as he had before the war. Seeing him there on the job, most people did not stop to inquire who wielded the actual power in Paris or even in Hanoi. All that mattered was that a French government was still functioning in Indochina and they continued to look to it for direction.

Until Admiral Decoux was convinced that the Allies were going to win the war, he modeled his administration on Marshal Pétain's fascist National Revolution. He came naturally by this policy for he shared the prejudices of the men who had appointed him. Like Darlan and so many other men in the French navy, he disliked the British, was critical of democracy, and was predisposed to authoritarianism. This was an attitude familiar to Frenchmen in the colonies, whose very way of life bred reaction; they were ruling a subject people, and were cut off from the normal political currents of life at home. And in no part of the French Empire was this more true than in Indochina during the war years. Some shiploads of French soldiers arrived from Europe early in 1941, a welcome infusion of new blood into the ingrown French society and of new strength into the French army. When no more came after that, the last tie with France was cut; even the news they had of Europe was invariably an Axis version, either Japanese or Nazi.

Having no responsibility for the conduct of the war, and scant hope, at least at first, of influencing its outcome, isolated from homes and families in France, the French in Indochina created for themselves an unreal world. It had existed beyond its time. Paris was occupied by the Germans; the French Empire was split between Gaullists and Vichyites. French power had disappeared in Europe, leaving only a feeble vestige of its influence in the Far East. Yet Frenchmen, who in Europe had to bow before the "master race," were still nominally the masters in Indochina.

They had their problems, too, but these were mostly difficulties of daily living which loomed disproportionately large because they had no others. They experienced shortages of European food when the transports stopped coming. They had few vegetables, no sugar. They lacked machine parts and tools, oils and gasoline, and textiles. Cars and machines began to run down, factories were destroyed by bombs, medicines were used up and could not be replaced.

This was not a heroic atmosphere in which to live. Pétainism thrived and Admiral Decoux sounded its keynote. He ruthlessly applied the laws of Vichy against Gaullists, against liberals, against Freemasons, against Jews. And to Vietnamese, whether nationalists or communists, he applied the same policy. Some eight to ten thousand Indochinese political prisoners, most of them Vietnamese, were in French jails in Indochina in March 1945.[43]

Decoux himself was arrested by the French Republic in the fall of 1945, charged with collaboration, and jailed for more than two years before he was freed provisionally for reasons of health. He was cleared finally in March 1949. When this action of the High Court was criticized in the columns of the newspaper Le Monde, Decoux wrote an angry letter to justify himself. "During those five dramatic years," he said, "cut off from the Métropole, deprived of any armaments worthy of the name, I was able to preserve the sovereignty of France over the entire [Indochinese] Federation and to make its flag respected. My successors cannot say as much."[44]

But even while Admiral Decoux maintained intact the formal structure of French imperial control, his regime presided over its liquidation.

STIMULATING VIETNAMESE NATIONALISM

The Japanese units in Indochina did not number many more than 35,000 and were stationed only at strategic points. Many Frenchmen have preferred

[43] Mus, op. cit., p. 14.
[44] Le Monde, March 10, 1949.

to regard this as no Japanese occupation at all but only a *stationnement*. The presence of those Japanese, however, and the always implicit threat that more could be summoned, conditioned and reoriented the life of the country between 1940 and 1945.

The French had to accept the presence of the Japanese, and yet they did not want to collaborate blindly; every small concession wrung from the Japanese in the course of interminable bargaining and negotiation assumed an undue importance in French eyes. At the same time they tried to conserve the rule of France over the different peoples of Indochina.

But these years had a very different meaning for the Europeans and for the Asians who lived in Indochina. De Gaulle or Vichy? The Indochinese were not much interested in domestic French politics. As to collaborating or not with the Japanese, this could have even less meaning to an Asian people some of whose influential leaders had long been friendly toward Japan. Much more important to them was the policy that Admiral Decoux formulated to deal with the difficult problem of maintaining authority in a country cut off from France and ruled no longer by a single administration but by two competing powers.

Throughout the occupation, the French and the Japanese carried on a war in which the stakes were the Indochinese people. To counter the Japanese appeal of a "Greater East Asia," the French put forward the concept of an Indochinese Federation—a mutually beneficial organization of different peoples, each with their separate traditions, held together and directed by France. Within this federal framework the Decoux regime encouraged the development of the different states. It tried to strengthen the prestige, although it did not increase the functions, of Bao Dai, Emperor of Annam (who made Decoux "Prince Protector of the Empire of Annam"), and of the Kings of Cambodia and Luang Prabang in Laos. It urged closer and more egalitarian relations between the French and the Indochinese "élite." It encouraged the teaching of the Vietnamese language. At the same time it furthered French prestige by a large-scale program of public works.

When the Japanese forced the teaching of their own language in the schools, sponsored Vietnamese-language newspapers to serve as vehicles for Japanese propaganda and brought into Indochina Japanese movies, cultural missions, and exhibitions, the French countered with an educational offensive of their own. They opened new schools, and the number of Indochinese students attending French schools increased substantially under the Japanese occupation. Nationalists had long been critical of the lack of technical and vocational training in the country. Now, for the first time, the French began to slant their teaching in that direction.

The French also felt compelled to organize a youth movement for sports and physical education as well as paramilitary training. This was both "necessary and urgent," according to Decoux. "To tell the truth," he wrote, "I did not have any choice: this movement had already been launched in France—and the Indochinese knew about it. If we had refused to organize similar activities in the Federation, these would have been launched without us, that is to say, against us and with the more or less camouflaged support of the Japanese."[45]

Over a million strong, the movement was revolutionary even under French control. In a country where age had always been venerated, large numbers of young people proved to themselves and to others that youth too could make a positive contribution to society. They learned to think of national service and of the national interest. The youth organizations became hotbeds of nationalism.

In administration, Decoux moved to end what he called the "flagrant disproportion" between salaries earned by Europeans and Indochinese for the same work.[46] He operated on the principle of "the same rank for the same job; and for the same job the same salaries."[47] He opened to the Indochinese more and higher posts in the civil service, posts which until then only Frenchmen could hold. The number of Vietnamese in the middle and upper ranks of the administration doubled between 1940 and 1944.[48] Many of them later placed their experience at the service of the Democratic Republic of Viet Nam.

Vietnamese had new and valuable opportunities under Decoux in other fields as well. Isolated from the West, Indochina was forced to rely almost entirely on its own resources; and Frenchmen and Vietnamese worked together in an attempt to deal with some of the more serious economic and industrial shortages which resulted. They developed a metallurgical industry and built the first smelting furnace in Indochina. They transformed what had been a virtually nonexistent chemical industry into productive use. They made great strides in pharmacy and by 1943 were able to fill Indochina's essential needs in quinine. They learned to use rice alcohol in place of gasoline and to make lubricating oils out of native products so that at least some trains, cars, and machines could continue to run. In agriculture they succeeded in varying the traditional rice monoculture—to grow oil-producing crops for lubricants and jute to help relieve the textile shortage. And in the process they proved that Indochina, economically, could stand far more on its own feet when put to the test than had generally been supposed; and that Indochina could accomplish this largely by the efforts of its own people.

Thus the Decoux regime encouraged the Vietnamese in their conviction of

[45] Maurice Ducoroy, *Ma Trahison en Indochine* (Paris, 1949), p. 14. Ducoroy was Commissioner General of Sports and Youth under Decoux, who wrote the preface to this account of the *mouvement sports-jeunesse.*

[46] Decoux, *op. cit.,* p. 399.

[47] *Ibid.,* p. 402.

[48] Philippe Devillers, *Histoire du Viêt-Nam de 1940 à 1952* (Paris, 1952), p. 85.

their separate identity and of their own ability and importance. At the same time, however, Decoux's policies made very clear the limits within which he intended to confine the Vietnamese. Admiral Decoux himself wrote: "If I thus recognized, even encouraged particular 'patriotisms,' I formally condemned 'nationalism' of all kinds because it had a xenophobic and anti-French tendency and received its instructions from abroad."[49] He carried on a strict military and police repression of nationalist elements.

Decoux pursued a deliberate policy of paternalism which made concessions only to a small group of conservative and traditionalist natives—the so-called "élite"—and made those concessions not to lessen French authority in the country, but to consolidate it. The idea was to give the native élites more participation at the "levels of direction and of execution, even of authority," but "we, on the other hand, found ourselves at the same time obliged to reinforce and improve the organs of control, of command and of security which more than ever had to be held firmly in French hands."[50] The political police played a key role in the Decoux government.

Even as the Admiral opened more posts in the administration to the Indochinese, he carefully excluded them from any real voice in the government of their country. All electoral bodies in Indochina, except for the municipal councils, were dissolved in November 1940. In 1941 Decoux created a Federal Council of Indochina with twenty-five native members "chosen just for their merit and their feeling of loyalty to France."[51] This gave way in 1943 to a joint Franco-Vietnamese Grand Federal Council in which Vietnamese outnumbered Frenchmen, 30 to 23. But the new council did not have even the limited budgetary powers or the restricted elective basis of the prewar Grand Council of Economic and Financial Interests. It had no power to do anything except advise the administration; and none of its members were elected, they were all appointed by Admiral Decoux.[52]

The French administration was clearly not prepared to give up any of its control to the people of Indochina. Far from appeasing nationalists, it merely whetted their appetites. The French radio drew comforting parallels between Pétain and Confucius, and sometimes compared the Marshal to Joan of Arc because both had saved France, but not many Vietnamese cared. Although some entered into direct relations with the Japanese occupation authorities, most Vietnamese had little contact with the Japanese; but French policies stimulated Vietnamese nationalism, which in the end proved as potent a threat to French rule over Indochina as the Japanese could have wished.

[49] Decoux, *op. cit.*, p. 389.
[50] *Ibid.*, p. 390.
[51] *Ibid.*, p. 393.
[52] These and other shadow reforms instituted by Decoux were analyzed by Roger Pinto, *Aspects de l'Evolution Gouvernementale de l'Indochine française* (Paris, 1946).

THE FRENCH RESISTANCE

Even the resistance movement which the French tried to establish against the Japanese played into the hands of Vietnamese nationalists.

After the fall of France, a few Frenchmen in Indochina risked their lives to send out radio intelligence to the Allies. At the Free French Mission in Calcutta other Frenchmen tried to build up this resistance from outside the country. Prominent among them was Paul Mus, a scholar who, having spent his life in Indochina and studied its civilizations, had come in close contact with Vietnamese circles. General de Gaulle sent Major de Langlade to work with the resistance in the country in 1944, and later that year Mus also returned secretly by parachute. The Free French Military Mission in Kunming, which in 1945 was headed by Jean Sainteny, had been established in 1943 with "its first task that of maintaining a discreet contact between our French comrades who remained in Indochina and Free France."[53]

As the tide turned against the Axis, many Frenchmen in Indochina became Gaullists out of opportunism if not conviction. Even Decoux entered into relations with the Free French, and in November 1944, after the Liberation of France, he received instructions from General de Gaulle to remain in power, in order to hide from the Japanese the French plans for military action against them. Admiral Decoux was perhaps better placed than any other high official in Indochina to direct a resistance movement, but in 1944 de Gaulle was distrustful of Vichyites and unwilling to work with them. He appointed General Mordant to lead the resistance, and Decoux made Mordant Vice President of a new Council of Indochina which he established after consulting with the de Gaulle government.[54]

Some of the civilians in the early resistance were inexperienced and sometimes even foolish men. But others among them were farsighted enough to understand the problems of building up an undercover network of resistance, where guns could be less important than radios and where secrecy was vital. There were even a few civilians like Paul Mus who thought that the Indochinese peoples should be brought into the resistance. The army, which by 1944 had taken over the resistance, did not. It had no patience with civilians. Who, it argued, was better qualified than the military to lead a resistance? They had arms already. They were trained to fight. They had to move about the country in any case, so it would not be difficult for them to pick up equipment dropped by parachute. A number of the younger officers, who hoarded the supplies parachuted to them against the day when they could be used,

[53] Jean Sainteny, *Histoire d'une Paix Manquée* (Paris, 1953), p. 21.

[54] For General Mordant's account of his activities before and after September 1944, when he was named General de Gaulle's representative in Indochina, see his book *Au Service de la France en Indochine* (Saigon, 1950).

grasped the complexity of the problem and moved cautiously; but others in the army, particularly in the higher ranks, were more unrealistic. The idea of resistance caught on rapidly among the French of Indochina. It became an outdoor parlor game, played with a lack of caution which would have been ludicrous if the people who were playing it had not been grown men and the stakes had not been their lives.

All of the French in Indochina talked resistance. Soldiers went into the country at night to pick up military supplies dropped by parachute, and in the morning these supplies turned up systematically arranged in the regimental arsenals. The French drilled and maneuvered, and in between times they talked. They had got hold of a myth and they repeated it so often that they believed it. The Americans were coming. They were going to launch a landing operation on the Indochinese coast, just as they had in North Africa. The French army would open a surprise attack and as the Americans fought their way up the beaches, they would fight their way down to meet them. Together they would liberate Indochina.[55]

It was a dream, but normally responsible people had made up their minds it would happen. Perhaps they had reason to be optimistic. For all these years they had managed to keep their hold on Indochina. They were, indeed, the only Europeans who still ruled in Asia. They had had to make certain concessions to the Japanese which they did not particularly relish, but they still had their arms and, more important, French sovereignty over Indochina was still unchallenged. They had accomplished that by being patient and biding their time. Soon the Americans would come and the French army would show it also could fight for France. For that time they would continue to plan, to organize, and to wait. It was, by then, March 1945. They forgot only one thing, that no resistance movement was feasible without the active support of the native population.

[55] See, e.g., Mus, *op. cit.;* Bauchar, *op. cit.;* General G. Sabattier, *Le Destin de l'Indochine* (Paris, 1952).

Chapter Two

END OF AN ERA

THE FRENCH POLICE sent out a warning that the Japanese were planning large-scale action against French troops on March 9, 1945. Such warnings had come before. But the French had been in a constant state of alert for so long that they had become inured to alarms.

French and Japanese soldiers, having confronted each other for several years on Indochinese soil, seemed to be getting on rather well. On the afternoon of March 9, at Ha Coi in the Mon Cay region, members of the Japanese garrison were playing basketball with some of the local Chinese, and the commander of a nearby French military post came over to umpire the game. And at Ha Giang, Japanese officers arrived at French headquarters, where they had been invited to cocktails. A ceremony had evolved over the years that when a French or Japanese commander arrived in a sector, the other side would invite him to drinks. The Japanese commander had a social engagement with the French because he had just come to Ha Giang. At Lang Son, where the French officer was the newcomer, the same little ceremony was occurring in reverse.

The French official resistance found such formalities a convenient way of masking its sympathies. The resistance was growing stronger every day. By the beginning of 1945 an Allied ferry service was dropping men and equipment into Indochina on an average of twice a week. The French administration was a honeycomb of resistance, its center in the office of statistical services, and a picture of General de Gaulle hung openly in the offices of the French High Command. Admiral Decoux was still governing, but General Mordant and his resistance seemed to hold the reins of power. They were dispersing French troops as widely as they could in the mountains and the countryside. The strategy was to get them out of the cities so that they could not be bottled up by the Japanese when the time came to strike.

The Japanese brought in new troops in January and February, occupying the plateau of Tran Ninh in Laos, which until then had been free of Japanese. Reinforcements arrived in Upper Laos, enabling the Japanese already there to move south and reinforce garrisons on the Annamese coast, and other detachments moved toward Thakhek in Laos. When the French established themselves outside the cities, the Japanese went too, setting up their garrisons conspicuously close by. They held maneuvers near resort towns in the hills, where French women and children were staying. But beyond this, they did not go. The Allies were already in Burma and the Philippines, and liaison with them was very close. Having hung on so long to their positions, most of the French saw no particular reason to begin worrying now, with victory so close.

A few people took the reports of pending Japanese action more seriously. General Sabattier, who was in command of the French forces in Tonkin and head of the official resistance in the north, alerted his troops and on March 8 secretly left the capital for his headquarters in the mountains. Various officials heard that a Japanese action was imminent, and the telegraph carried their warnings throughout the country. But still people went about their everyday activities. In Hanoi, on the 9th, the High Command even partially lifted the state of alert imposed on the French garrison.

Admiral Decoux was in Saigon on March 9, in the midst of complicated negotiations with Japanese officials. The Japanese had been rather more difficult than usual; their demands had seemed exorbitant, and they had been threatening. They wanted large piastre advances for their troops. They were displeased by the refusal of the French to surrender captured American fliers or to agree to the arrival of more Japanese troops, and it would have been like them to order menacing troop movements just to put pressure on the Governor General. On the 9th, however, the worst seemed over. The agreement was about to be signed.

That afternoon Decoux met again with the Japanese Ambassador, Matsumoto, Consul General Kono, and other Japanese diplomats. They discussed the rice that Indochina would supply Japan under the Tokyo treaty of May 6, 1941, and finally they signed an agreement. Eye-witnesses commented later that the Japanese seemed unusually slow in completing the final formalities. At 6 o'clock Matsumoto asked if he could have an audience with Decoux later that evening. He arrived promptly at eight o'clock and presented the Admiral with an ultimatum; it was the last Japanese ultimatum that the French were to receive in Indochina. The Japanese Government had decided to take certain precautions in view of the development of events. It announced plans to place the French army, navy, police, and administration under Japanese command and to take over control of French banks. Decoux was given two hours in which to reply.

He hastily called a meeting of all the high French civil and military officials who happened to be in Saigon. They agreed that they could not accept the ultimatum and drafted an answer asking for more time so that Decoux could notify the members of the government in Hanoi of the new demands and draw up counterproposals. This was the kind of reply the French had given to other Japanese ultimatums in the past, but this time it did not work. The Japanese were no longer in the mood to play Decoux's bargaining game.

At 10:50, ten minutes before the deadline, Decoux sent his answer to the

Japanese. Matsumoto looked at it briefly, called it a rejection, and ordered the machinery of the Japanese army into motion.[1]

The Japanese moved immediately on the palace of the Governor General in Saigon and seized Decoux. Throughout Indochina, Japanese troops seized administrative buildings and public utilities, took over radio stations, telegraph centers, banks, and industries. They attacked the police and the military garrisons, and arrested French civilian and military authorities.

The next day the Japanese radio offered Japan's explanation of its action to the world. The accusation against Decoux was, specifically, that he had refused to comply with Japanese demands for co-operation in "the joint defense of the country."

They had little difficulty in justifying their coup. They blamed it on the change in the attitude of the French authorities in recent months and on the existence of a French information service working with the Allies; on the arrival by parachute of enemy agents; on the accumulation of munitions stocks and the dispersing movements of French troops; on the disappearance of a spirit of collaboration between the French and the Japanese. They blamed it, in short, on the resistance, which had been secret, it appeared, from no one, least of all the Japanese.

Actually, it was fear of an Allied invasion that precipitated the Japanese action. American troops were only seven hundred miles away in the Philippines. In Tokyo, Premier Kuniaki Koiso told the Japanese Imperial Diet that the military situation had "become so intensified that a full-scale invasion of the region may be expected at any moment."[2] In Indochina Decoux had adequately served the purposes of the Japanese for some four years, supplying an experienced administration and a body of trained technicians to run the country. Much the same thing had happened in France. The Germans had permitted Pétain to keep his shadow independence only so long as it did not hinder the Nazi war effort; then they took over themselves. Decoux had survived the Pétain regime, becoming virtually independent of France, if not of Japan. But when the scales of power shifted in Europe in favor of the Allies, Decoux had shifted with them. He made overtures to General de Gaulle, became increasingly unco-operative toward the Japanese and allowed the resistance to organize.

Admiral Decoux later said that the break would never have come if his more cautious policy had been maintained until V-J Day. But Decoux himself seems to have been more than a little responsible for the lack of caution. He ordered pictures of Pétain removed from public roads and buildings; and he publicly

1 This account of Indochinese conditions and events in March 1945 is based primarily on Decoux, *op. cit.*, Bauchar, *op. cit.*, and Gaudel, *op. cit.*
2 *New York Times*, March 12, 1945.

expressed himself as friendly to liberated France. A Frenchman who lived in Indochina during the occupation wrote:

> The Governor General suggested the constitution of a 'Council of Indochina,' which seemed to everyone, including the Japanese, a governmental body preceding the Liberation. He took a series of measures which prepared the return to 'republican legality,' abrogating the laws of the Vichy government. He . . . openly expressed his desire for the liberation of Indochina.
>
> This new and public attitude of the Governor General, contrary to the directives and practices followed until then, did not fail to attract the attention of the occupation authorities. The ex-Governor believes today that the organization of the official resistance 'was one of the determining factors, doubtless the essential cause, of the seizure of Indochina by the Japanese.' His governmental volte-face during the last quarter of 1944, as much as the imprudence of certain military leaders, provoked the coup of March 9, 1945.[3]

Decoux's indiscretion made it clear that French sovereignty over Indochina was no longer compatible with Japanese security. Like Pétain before him, Decoux, by March 1945, had outlived his value to the Axis. All that remained of the Mikado's guaranty that the French would continue to rule over Indochina was a French admiral, sitting in a palace he no longer controlled, and telling a Japanese officer, who did not care, that the Emperor had broken his promise.

Decoux began several years of confinement, first under Japanese guards and then under the French. The stage in Indochina was taken up by others, by the handful of French soldiers who were not prepared to give up to the Japanese without a fight, by the Vietnamese, the Cambodians, and the Laotians to whom the Japanese appealed for support.

Off on the sidelines, where there was little publicity and scant interest in its activities, a resurgent nationalist movement prepared for the time when it would take over.

REACTIONS TO THE JAPANESE COUP

Most of the French troops in the country were taken off guard on March 9. That French captain in Mon Cay, who had left his post to referee a game of basketball at a Japanese garrison, was told by his hosts to give orders in writing to his soldiers to lay down their arms. When he refused, he was tortured, and he died that night.

Some garrisons, although encircled, refused to surrender. At Lang Son and Dong Dang, those same frontier towns which the Japanese had invaded four and a half years before, French troops fought the Japanese. Lang Son fell after

[3] Roger Pinto, "A Propos des 'Mémoires' de l'Amiral Decoux," *Politique Etrangère*, December 1949, p. 584.

two days of savage fighting in which hundreds of Frenchmen and Indochinese died; and the Japanese, furious at the stubbornness of its defenders, massacred most of the survivors. Dong Dang, too, had its brief time of heroism. It withstood repeated assaults and did not surrender until March 12, when Japanese reinforcements arrived from captured Lang Son; the survivors were killed. Toward other garrisons, like that at Hanoi, the Japanese were not so vindictive, and they were permitted to surrender with all the honors of war.[4]

The French troops in Cochin China and Annam did not offer an effective resistance, although the garrison at Hué and several others fought back, and some of the troops managed to escape to the mountains. The little fighting that occurred was mostly in the north. Resisting troops made for the mountains of northern Tonkin and Upper Laos where they could take refuge in the brush. They found friends among the mountain people, the Moi, the Meo (Miao), the Man, the Thai, and others of the aboriginal tribes. The Laotians rallied to the retreating French, and the propaganda services of the Free French gave wide publicity to the gathering in a forest, in the presence of Laotian royalty, where hundreds of Laotian guerrillas came for weapons to fight the Japanese. French officers formed many of them into detachments; but they had to turn many away for lack of arms.

But all the publicity, all the anxiety to make much of the fighting, to present the world with the spectacle of the French army militant and united against the invader, could not hide the fact that this was, at best, a scattered and feeble resistance. The over-all record of the French in these critical days was neither stirring nor heroic. There were, however, a number of examples of personal bravery, notably among the soldiers whom General Alessandri and other officers led through the mountains of Tonkin, fighting with dogged courage not only the Japanese but also disease, heat, and rain, in the long and difficult days before they made their way to the Chinese frontier and safety.

The army had been ordered not to risk destruction in the deltas, but to take to the mountains and organize guerrilla warfare. With the French troops came Vietnamese contingents of the Indochinese army. There was little food in the high regions, not enough to feed them all, and for this reason most of the Vietnamese troops were disbanded. Paul Mus, who was there, saw some of them leave with tears in their eyes. They went back to their villages, still in their French uniforms, and some were killed by Japanese whom they refused to salute. Vietnamese soldiers had long since been indoctrinated with nationalism and since the beginning of the century there had been nationalistic risings among them of which the mutiny at Yen Bay in 1930[5] was the most publicized. In 1940 certain Vietnamese elements in the Indochinese army had

4 See Bauchar, *op. cit.*; Sabattier, *op. cit.*
5 See below, p. 83.

hoped in vain for encouragement from the Japanese to turn against the colonial administration. When the Japanese failed to support them, many Vietnamese soldiers had remained with their French comrades only to learn in
March 1945, as Paul Mus did, all the differences which separate a colonial army
from a national army, and they did not forget.[6]

The Vichy administration having outlived its value, the Japanese tried for
more direct control of the colony. "The colonial status of French Indochina
has ended," announced the Japanese radio on March 10. The following day,
the Vietnamese Emperor Bao Dai declared the independence of the kingdom
of Annam, uniting Tonkin with Annam. On March 13, King Norodom
Sihanouk of Cambodia announced his country's independence, and in April
King Sisavong Vong of Luang Prabang in Laos followed suit.

These were crucial days for France in Indochina. For the first time the continuity of French sovereignty had been disrupted, and the French did not have
the strength to reassert it. Although they had offered little more than token
resistance to the Japanese in 1940, the Indochinese had an exaggerated idea of
French power; the Japanese may have been the actual masters of Indochina,
but French officials still governed in the countryside and the villages where the
Japanese rarely, if ever, set foot.

The events of March 9 changed all that. Individual Frenchmen demonstrated great bravery and suffered cruelly, but, for the Indochinese, French
rule had ended. They were not concerned with the various diplomatic defeats
of Catroux and Decoux, the international situation meant little to them. But
they saw French soldiers disarmed and interned, Decoux and his colleagues
jailed, French people herded together in restricted areas in the large cities.
Some Frenchmen were imprisoned by the Japanese. Only a few were permitted
to stay on in their old jobs, generally technical positions which neither the
Indochinese nor the Japanese could fill.

Yet in the spring of 1945 Frenchmen escaping from the cities uncovered a
reservoir of good will among the Indochinese. Many French people eluded
the Japanese only because of the aid they received from the Vietnamese, the
mountain people, or the Laotians. In some areas this aid was more organized.
Frenchmen came upon a whole network of escape—Vietnamese who lived in
camps in the mountain regions, helping Allied fliers and refugees to get out
of the country, and harrying the Japanese.

It was the first enounter of many Frenchmen with the Communist-led resistance which called itself the Viet Minh.

Many times in the preceding four years the Viet Minh had called upon the
French to work with it against the Japanese. But the French authorities had
chosen to regard its members as bandits, of which the Tonkinese countryside
had seen many, and had started a clean-up drive against them, bottling them

[6] Mus, *op. cit.*, p. 21.

up in the forests. Even as late as March 1945 the Viet Minh received no help from French officials. This was one of the grievances enumerated in the Viet Minh Declaration of Independence. "Before taking their flight they even killed a great number of our patriots who had been imprisoned at Yen Bay and Cao Bang."

Few Frenchmen joined forces with the Viet Minh after March 9. They were willing to lead Indochinese soldiers, as they did in Laos; they were glad to use the Indochinese as guides and to rely on them for help in making their escape, but that was all. It was rather late in the day to expect complete confidence from either side. French soldiers who did seek refuge with the Viet Minh guerrillas were not ill treated, but some complained that they were not permitted to move about freely in Viet Minh-controlled areas.

The Viet Minh was anti-imperialist, as much opposed to Vichy as to Tokyo; but it was not anti-French and, in fact, frowned upon any Francophobia among its rank and file. This moderation was very different from the hostility Mesmer and Cédile encountered when they arrived in Indochina by parachute a few months later. The Viet Minh helped French men, women, and children to escape to safety, caring for them until they could be picked up by Allied planes and evacuated to China. Two French teachers, Maurice Bernard and his wife, wrote a letter to their friends in Hanoi, describing with gratitude and in glowing terms their stay in a Viet Minh camp. When the Vietnamese Government published this letter in the fall of 1945,[7] it was already a testimonial to a vanished past.

After years of wartime isolation, Indochina was abruptly swept back into the vortex of international politics in March 1945. The Japanese coup came at a time when General de Gaulle was trying hard to reassert the authority and prestige of France among her allies. At that time, too, the United Nations Conference at San Francisco was in the offing. Gaullist groups, always fearful about what they claimed to be American designs on the French Empire, were obsessed by the worry that the United States might force some form of international trusteeship upon Indochina. President Roosevelt, they knew, blamed France for allowing the country to become the springboard for Japan's attack on the Philippines, Malaya, and the Dutch East Indies, and he did not make any secret of his contempt for the way the Third Republic had administered the country. As far back as January 1944, he had sent a memorandum to Secretary Hull, favoring an international trusteeship for Indochina. Roosevelt wrote:

France has had the country—thirty million inhabitants—for nearly one hundred years, and the people are worse off than they were at the beginning. . . . France has

[7] Bernard, Maurice and Yvonne, *Lettre aux Amis d'Hanoi* (Hanoi, 1945).

milked it for one hundred years. The people of Indochina are entitled to something better than that.[8]

Since the beginning of the war, the Free French had frequently reasserted their right to rule Indochina. They had declared war against the Japanese the day after Pearl Harbor. Throughout the war years, when words were virtually the only substitute they could offer for the power they did not have, they had taken the consistent line that they would continue fighting until Japan was defeated and Indochina liberated. It was difficult for the Free French to regard the French administration in Indochina very harshly, for through Admiral Decoux and his colleagues France could claim uninterrupted sovereignty over Indochina.

On March 14, 1945 General de Gaulle announced in Paris that the French National Committee had long been working secretly to organize resistance in Indochina. "Today the fight between the invader and our forces there follows a plan drawn up by the Government and orders given by leaders the Government has designated." He criticized the Allies for their slowness in coming to the aid of the French in the colony and for their failure to provide transports to bring French armies to the Far East. "It is not her [France's] fault if the forces she had long prepared to aid Indochina are not yet in line beside those of the Allies." He left no doubt that, in his mind at least, this was *French* Indochina that was struggling with the Japanese and that *French* Indochina it would remain. "By the trials of all and the blood of the soldiers at this moment a solemn pact is sealed between France and the peoples of the Indochinese Union."[9]

Later that month the French Cabinet offered a detailed plan of reform for Indochina and outlined a federal government for the country, implementing the promise made by the French Committee of National Liberation on December 8, 1943, that Indochina would have "a new political status within the French community." France, it was officially announced on March 24, 1945, had always thought that Indochina merited a special position within the "French community," an autonomy proportionate to its evolution and its attainments.

Today Indochina is fighting, and in its army, Indochinese and Frenchmen are striving together for victory, side by side. All the people, the leading classes as well as the masses who cannot let themselves be misled by the enemy's contrivances, are holding out with courage and gallantry for the triumph of the cause which is

---

[8] Hull, *op. cit.,* p. 1597. Mr. Roosevelt's estimate of Indochina's population is probably more correct than the results of the official census, because of the known reluctance of Vietnamese to submit to the census, which they linked to the compulsory use of a certain amount of alcohol and opium per capita. See below, pp. 68–69. This attitude toward the census dated back to the Vietnamese Empire, long before the French came, when taxation was based upon the census.

[9] *New York Times,* March 15, 1945.

that of the entire French community. Thus, Indochina is acquiring further rights to the special position that is its due.[10]

This was a partial explanation of the new plan; two other motives were also involved. For one thing, it was necessary to offer Indochina special inducements to return to the French community, if for no other reason than to counteract the effects of the Japanese offer of independence. And in the background was the recurrent fear of international trusteeship; if the French did not make some concrete gesture of liberalism, their allies might do it for them. Both Marshal Stalin and Generalissimo Chiang Kai-shek professed themselves as not unwilling to see Indochina under an international trusteeship. According to President Roosevelt, it was Prime Minister Winston Churchill who prevented the realization of this plan.[11]

By the spring of 1945, the American Government had apparently ruled out the possibility of any drastic interference with the French position in Indochina.[12] But the French themselves were in no position to implement their

[10] *Notes Documentaires et Etudes,* No. 548. *Documents Relatifs aux Problèmes Indochinois I Accords entre la France et le Viet-Nam.*

[11] At a press conference held aboard the U.S.S. *Quincy* on February 23, 1945, en route to Yalta, Roosevelt said: "For two whole years I have been terribly worried about Indochina. I talked to Chiang Kai-shek in Cairo [November, 1943], Stalin in Teheran [also in November, 1943]. They both agreed with me. . . . The first thing I asked Chiang was, 'Do you want Indochina?' He said, 'It's no help to us. We don't want it. They are not Chinese. They would not assimilate into the Chinese people.' I said, 'What are you going to advocate? It will take a long time to educate them for self-government.' He said they should not go back to France, that they have been there over a hundred years and have done nothing about educating them, that for every dollar they have put in, they have taken out ten, and that the situation is a good deal like the Philippines were in 1898. . . . I suggested at the time to Chiang, that Indochina be set up under a trusteeship—have a Frenchman, one or two Indochinese, and a Chinese and a Russian, because they are on the coast, and maybe a Filipino and an American, to educate them for self-government. . . . Stalin liked the idea. China liked the idea. The British didn't like it. It might bust up their empire, because if the Indochinese were to work together and eventually get their independence, the Burmese might do the same thing to England. The French have talked about how they expect to recapture Indochina, but they haven't got any shipping to do it with. It would only get the British mad. Chiang would go along. Stalin would go along. As for the British, it would only make the British mad. Better to keep quiet just now." *The Public Papers and Addresses of Franklin D. Roosevelt,* 1944–45 Volume, *Victory and the Threshold of Peace,* pp. 562–63.

[12] In a cable to General Patrick J. Hurley, American Ambassador to China, the State Department outlined American policy as approved by President Roosevelt: ". . . the trusteeship structure, it was felt, should be defined to permit the placing under it of such of the territories taken from the enemy in war as might be agreed upon at a later date, and also such other territories as might voluntarily be placed under it. . . ." This "would preclude the establishment of a trusteeship in Indochina, except under the French Government. The latter seems unlikely. Nevertheless, it is the President's intention [the reference is to President Truman] at some appropriate time to ask that the French Government give some positive indication of its intention in regard to the establishment of basic liberties and an increasing measure of self-government in Indochina. . . ." (Hearings before the Committee on Armed Services and the Committee on Foreign Relations, United States Senate, Eighty-Second Congress, First Session: *To conduct an inquiry into the military situation in the Far East and the facts surrounding the relief of General of the Army Douglas MacArthur from his assignments in that area,* p. 2892.)

declaration of March 24, which could only go into effect when Indochina was liberated.[13] French officials in China were highly critical of what they regarded as the "incomprehensible hostility" of the Americans and the Chinese who did not give the French troops the air support they requested in March and April 1945.[14]

The Indochinese peoples meanwhile were having their first taste of independence under Japan.

"INDEPENDENCE" UNDER JAPAN

When the Japanese had first come, a number of Indochinese were not sorry to see them. The Japanese, after all, were not alien whites like the French, but fellow Asians who might better understand the problems of Indochina. An English traveler told of crowds gathering in Saigon to gaze on three Japanese cruisers anchored in the harbor. "Why the curiosity?" he asked. "You often see cruisers here." But these, they told him, "are built by men like ourselves and they say these ships are as good as Europeans, and they belong here."[15]

Tokyo had proclaimed itself the leader of a new "Asia for the Asiatics." It appealed to the nationalists, to the dissatisfied, to the ambitious. The average man, the peasant or *nha que,* may have been indifferent at first, but he suffered from the economic deterioration which came in the wake of the Japanese—the shortage of textiles, the rising cost of living, Japanese requisitions, and the insistence of the Decoux regime under the Japanese that nonfood crops such as jute, oil crops, and opium be planted in some areas instead of rice.

Although the broad stream of Vietnamese nationalism had never been directly under the influence of Tokyo, some nationalists had looked to Japan for help ever since its victory over Russia in 1905. The Vietnamese patriot Phan Boi Chau, who encouraged a number of Vietnamese students to go to Japan, had taught early in the century that Japan would be the savior who would free Viet Nam from the yoke of French imperialism. In 1906 he fled to Japan with Prince Cuong De of the Royal Family of Viet Nam; from Japan they called upon their countrymen to rise against the French. Phan Boi Chau soon left Japan to become involved in various conspiracies; he became

[13] The Vietnamese did not wait for V-J Day to make known their opinion of the March 1945 declaration. There were over 25,000 Vietnamese in France, some intellectuals, the great majority workers. After the Liberation of France they established a Délégation Générale des Indochinois en France which issued a detailed criticism of the March declaration, finding it inadequate on the grounds that it offered far less than autonomy to Indochina.

[14] Sainteny, *op. cit.,* p. 30. According to Sainteny, General Chennault "was practically the only one to understand the interest that the Allies had in supporting the French army. . . . Soon, orders arrived from Washington. . . . Against their desire, despite their good will, General Chennault and his aides had to give way and refuse our troops almost all air support." *Ibid.*

[15] Alan Houghton Brodrick, *Little China* (London, New York; 1942), p. 49.

the leader of a nationalist movement which was monarchist in essence and recognized Cuong De as legal pretender to the throne. Many of the nationalistic demonstrations and attempted risings which occurred in Viet Nam, particularly in the years before the first World War, were inspired by Phan Boi Chau and Cuong De. Eventually captured by the French and condemned to death, then reprieved and set at liberty, Phan Boi Chau had retired from political activity by 1930. But Prince Cuong De stayed on in Japan. He was there when the second World War broke out, and there were recurrent reports in the years that followed that the Japanese had brought him to the island of Hainan. They were supposed to be keeping him in readiness for the day when he would replace the Vietnamese Emperor, Bao Dai.

The Japanese, however, contrary to what is generally believed, did not plan to establish an independent state of Viet Nam; in their Indochinese policy they sacrificed long-term political planning to expediency. After March 9, 1945 they did not make any move toward Cuong De. They approached Bao Dai instead.

Bao Dai, who was then thirty-one years old, had grown up in France and returned home with a number of Western ideas. He introduced some modern reforms into the government at Hué but, as the imperial government had only formal authority and no real power, these reforms had scant effect on the people of Viet Nam. Over Tonkin and Cochin China, the other parts of the Empire of Annam which his ancestor, Gia Long, had also ruled, he was allowed no authority at all. Bao Dai had complained that in twelve years he had been allowed to go to Tonkin just once, and he had never been to Cochin China, although he had married a Cochin Chinese. Only during the Japanese occupation was the Emperor invited to Cochin China, at a time when Admiral Decoux was trying to bolster his own position as protector of the Vietnamese people.

Back at Hué, surrounded by the tombs of his ancestors, Bao Dai was generally restricted to playing tennis and golf, to hunting and dashing about in his automobiles. At the proper intervals he conducted the traditional ceremonies honoring the royal dead, which constituted the most weighty of his royal duties.

On March 9, 1945 Bao Dai was not at Hué, but some twenty-five miles to the north near Quang Tri, where he was entertaining the French Résident Supérieur, who was his guest at a hunting party. When Bao Dai returned to Hué at three o'clock in the morning, he found that the doors of the Citadel, usually kept closed, were open, and he heard shooting. The Citadel was crowded with Japanese soldiers who at first would not let him proceed to the palace. He only learned of the Japanese coup when a Japanese captain came to tell him that his country was free. The Japanese Ambassador, who arrived to confirm this, informed the Emperor that Japan expected in return the friendship and co-operation of Viet Nam in the building of a Greater East Asia. Bao Dai immediately called a meeting of his Council of Ministers and on March 11, 1945 he announced to the people that Viet Nam was independent.

A year later when Bao Dai, then a member of the government of the Democratic Republic of Viet Nam, was recalling these events for the benefit of a correspondent of *Le Monde,* he said that the French by their own actions had ended their protectorate over Viet Nam when they defaulted on their obligation to defend the country. When he was asked why he had accepted independence from Japan, he said, "I could have accepted it or refused it. But in the latter case they [the Japanese] would have imposed their administration; also I chose what would save my people from the worst. And then they gave us our independence which was the first thing."[16] When Bao Dai told this story to the press again, in 1948, he was leading the opposition to the Viet Minh and was in close relations with the French. He said then that the Council of Ministers had had to accede to the Japanese because it could not possibly hold out against them.[17]

Bao Dai also said that he told the Japanese he would not object if they decided to replace him with Cuong De, but that they showed no interest in the refugee prince. Their one concern seemed to be in maintaining the continuity of the Vietnamese government and administration, and for this reason they had to support Bao Dai as Emperor.

Bao Dai adapted to the reality of Japanese control and went on record with statements as warmly pro-Japanese as any he had made in favor of the French when they were in power. At the same time he tried to win concessions for Vietnamese nationalism. He denounced the old treaties which established the protectorate under the French. And he tried to rally nationalist support behind him.

He was most anxious to get rid of Pham Quynh, his Minister of Interior, the equivalent of Prime Minister in the imperial Cabinet, to replace him with a man more representative of Vietnamese opinion. Pham Quynh was a Tonkinese scholar, the author of a number of books in French and Vietnamese, who for years had preached Vietnamese obedience to the French. During the first World War he had played an active part in recruiting Vietnamese soldiers to serve in France, which did not endear him to the younger generation of Vietnamese nationalists. His unpopularity had increased during the interwar years because of his identification with French policies. Pham Quynh was so widely disliked in 1945 that Bao Dai asked for his resignation. When the Viet Minh assumed power later that year, they condemned Pham Quynh to death, and executed him in November 1945.

16 *Le Monde,* February 23, 1946.
17 *Ibid.,* February 20, 1948.

After the Japanese coup in March 1945, Bao Dai's Cabinet split on what course it ought to follow. Bui Bang Doan and Prince Ung Uy, both of whom later joined the Viet Minh, insisted to the other ministers that it was the duty of them all to resign, now that the country was supposed to be independent, in favor of a new, more representative government; and their point of view, which reflected that of many Vietnamese, won out. The Cabinet was dissolved.

Popular demonstrations broke out in Hué in favor of Ngo Dinh Diem. Diem had been antagonized by Admiral Decoux; and with some other leading Vietnamese nationalists who were friendly to Prince Cuong De, he had turned to the Japanese for support. In March 1945, when Diem was living in Saigon under Japanese protection, Bao Dai sent him a telegram, inviting him to become Prime Minister.

The Japanese, however, were not anxious to have Ngo Dinh Diem lead the new government. He wanted a real independence and unity for the country which they were not prepared to give, but which they would have found politically awkward to refuse when requested by a man as popular among the Vietnamese and as friendly to Japan as Ngo Dinh Diem. It has been reliably reported that because of Japanese interference, Bao Dai's telegram to Diem was never delivered.

Ngo Dinh Diem, for his part, knowing that the Japanese were not prepared to make radical changes in the status of the country, did not put himself forward. After waiting in vain several weeks for some word from Diem, Bao Dai asked Tran Trong Kim to take office. A respected old scholar and a prominent Freemason, Kim had sought Japanese protection against what appears to have been a wholly illusory French menace to his safety. After the Japanese coup, he went immediately to Hué, and he accepted Bao Dai's invitation, becoming Prime Minister in April.

The men who joined his Cabinet had been trained in French schools and could hardly be called anti-French; nevertheless they were all nationalists. They realized that Japan might eventually be defeated but they had no idea that that defeat was so close: in the meantime they wanted to make the most of their new independence. Their hope was to leave the country with a working nationalist regime that could survive the Japanese and meet the French and their allies as an independent government.

Several nationalist groups supported the new regime, among them the *Dai Viet Quoc Dan Hoi* or Dai Viet (National Party of Greater Viet Nam), a wartime creation, and the *Viet Nam Phuc Quoc Dong Minh Hoi* or Phuc Quoc (Viet Nam Restoration League), founded before the first World War under the aegis of Phan Boi Chau and Cuong De. The Phuc Quoc had fomented numerous conspiracies and disorders against the French, and even after many of its members joined the Communists, emigrés in China, Japan, and Formosa kept the Phuc Quoc alive. It was responsible for the rising led by Tran Tung Lap in the Lang Son area in 1940, which was suppressed when the Japanese failed to support him against the French. Later, however, the Japanese political police, the *Kempeitai,* encouraged the reorganization of the Phuc Quoc and worked with several other pro-Japanese nationalist groups. (The French arrested a number of these nationalists and protested Japanese activities among them, but only with temporary effect.) The Japanese also made friends among Vietnamese mandarins and intellectuals. In 1945, as a result, a number of Vietnamese were ready to join Tran Trong Kim.

The first action of the new government was to rename the country, to return to the old designation used by Gia Long and to appeal to the nationalist sentiment of the people under the name of Viet Nam, rather than Annam, as the country had been known under the French. Bao Dai resumed the privilege his predecessors had abdicated and sent an imperial envoy, Phan Ke Toai, to Tonkin; and in both Annam and Tonkin the Japanese gradually turned over many of the functions of government to the new Viet Nam.

But the Tran Trong Kim Cabinet was made up of middle-class intellectuals with little experience of politics and no revolutionary background. Government, to these men, seemed a series of theoretical problems rather than a scheme of practical political action and organization. They discussed a new constitution for Viet Nam and a fiscal reform. The Minister of Education, Hoang Xuan Han, put through an educational reform, giving the Vietnamese language priority over French in the schools and for the first time emphasizing science and mathematics. But despite the proclamation of independence, real power throughout the country was still in the hands of the Japanese; and as the weeks passed, a sense of impotence grew among members of the government. Once in office, also, they came to realize, as they had not before, that when peace came they would be regarded as having collaborated with the Japanese; and this realization had the effect of further immobilizing them.

Perhaps the major achievement of the Tran Trong Kim government was the work of Phan Anh, Minister of Youth, who carried on the youth organizations begun under Decoux, working with young people of all classes, giving them military training and a sense of political purpose and political importance. At the same time, and to the same end, the scout leader Ta Quang Buu organized the Vietnamese boy scouts into a paramilitary force.

The Tran Trong Kim government never had much authority, even in Tonkin and Annam. Famine ravaged the north, where the shortage of rice was desperate. In the south there was plenty of rice and the granaries of the Japanese army were well stocked, but the government could not feed its own employees, much less the starving millions of Tonkin, hundreds of thousands of whom died.

Kim told a Vietnamese visitor in June:

I know that the people are suffering, that the Japanese are going to leave, and I myself, like Emperor Bao Dai, am suffering at the sight of the people starving. But there is nothing we can do. I have been told that there is a party called the Viet Minh. But where is this party? Let it come and I will give it power. The Emperor also asks that. If you know any leaders of the Viet Minh, let them come and I will give them my place.[18]

But the Viet Minh was waiting for Japan to capitulate before it would move from the sidelines.

Throughout the north and center of Viet Nam, where the famine raged, stories spread of rice stocks collected by the French for their own use in case of an Allied invasion; and of quantities of rice piled high at the Saigon quays which had been burnt by the French as fuel while Vietnamese were starving. Even at this time of desperate scarcity the Japanese army continued to requisition rice for its own purposes, but this fact did not appear in the Vietnamese-language press, which, under the Japanese, found a new freedom in giving vent to its nationalism. As the death toll in the north increased, press attacks on the French became more violent and xenophobic.

The structure of the established order had been disrupted, engendering a new ferment in the country. The idea of independence was itself a disruptive one: to some peasants it meant an end to all taxes; to some intellectuals, a Vietnamese cultural renaissance. No one seemed to know precisely what independence was or how it should, or could, be implemented. An administrative paralysis spread over Viet Nam, and rioting and lawlessness broke out. The Japanese opened French jails and freed prisoners from the notorious penal colony on the island of Poulo Condore. A number of veteran revolutionaries were set at liberty and they returned among the people, rebuilding their network of organization and capitalizing on the popular discontent.

COCHIN CHINA—LIMITATIONS OF JAPANESE POLICY

An independence celebration was held in Cochin China after the Japanese coup, but it was not joined to Bao Dai's other domains; Japanese officials simply succeeded to positions that Frenchmen had previously held. It was more difficult than in Tonkin and Annam to find experienced Vietnamese officials; the colony of Cochin China had been ruled directly by the French for a long time with relatively few Vietnamese intermediaries. The Japanese, in any case, may have intended to exploit the rice and rubber riches of Cochin China for themselves. On March 30, 1945 the Japanese Governor told a group of Vietnamese officials:

This is a great misunderstanding on the subject of the independence of Indochina. It is entirely under the military control of Japan. The independence of the

[18] Un Nationaliste Vietnamien, *Du Viet Minh au Gouvernement Ho Chi Minh.*

Empire of Annam and that of Cambodia have been proclaimed. Cochin China not only is under military control, but is still under Japanese military control. Thus no independence for Cochin China.[19]

The fact that the Japanese kept direct control over Cochin China helped to discredit the Bao Dai regime.

Over a period of time, however, the Japanese had to bring an increasing number of Vietnamese into the administration of Cochin China. It was not difficult to find people willing to work with Japan. A number were supporters of Cuong De. A branch of the Phuc Quoc had been organized under Japanese auspices in Cochin China during the Decoux regime and it was joined by two political-religious sects in the south—the Cao Dai and the Hoa Hao. Some Trotskyites also were friendly to the new regime; the Vietnamese police in Cochin China was heavily infiltrated by Trotskyites.

The Cao Dai traced its origins back to 1919 and to an island in the Gulf of Siam, where a Vietnamese official named Ngo Van Chieu began to hold seances to talk with voices from the spirit world. One of the spirits revealed itself to him as Cao Dai, the Supreme Being. This, at least, is the story as Caodaists tell it. When Chieu was recalled to Saigon to assume new duties there, he brought this revelation with him. A group of Vietnamese officials took up table-tapping in 1925, and Cao Dai again made himself known. The new religion was formally established in November 1926 after three days of solemn ceremony.

The seat of the Cao Dai was Tay Ninh, except for several dissident sects that broke away in 1933. Their religion was an amalgam of many faiths, ranging from the spirits, so important in the belief of the Vietnamese village, through Christianity, to the three great religions of the east, Taoism, Buddhism, and Confucianism. The Caodaists worshipped their god in the form of an eye. Their revelations came from famous writers like Victor Hugo, from Western philosophers, and from Christian saints. The Cao Dai priesthood, which was organized in a hierarchy modeled on the Catholic, was headed by a pope.

When the first "Temporal Pope" of the Cao Dai, Le Van Trung, died, Pham Cong Tac took over in 1935 and led the movement into nationalistic channels. Caodaism spread rapidly among government officials, landowners, and students, and found many converts among the peasants. The authorities at first were tolerant, but the quick growth of the new religion, its close-knit organization and its secret meetings made them nervous. The protectorates of Annam and Cambodia outlawed it in their territory. Only in the colony of Cochin China was it allowed to continue, having hundreds of thousands of adherents. The nationalism of some of its leaders was oriented toward Japan and they talked of Cuong De as the man who would save Viet Nam.

[19] Quoted from the stenographic record in Gaudel, *op. cit.*, p. 17.

In 1941 the French instituted strict control over the Cao Dai, closing its chapels and forbidding its meetings. Some of its leaders were arrested and Pham Cong Tac was exiled to Madagascar, charged with pro-Japanese activities. After that the Caodaists were little heard of, but they were meeting secretly in hidden chapels and at isolated altars. Their relations with the Japanese grew increasingly close and they became restive under French rule. In 1945 they appeared openly as supporters of the new regime and helped the Japanese to police Cochin China. The members of the Cao Dai were not all easy to control, and even as their leaders professed friendship for the new regime, some of the rank and file were responsible for disorders in the Cochin Chinese countryside.

Less numerous than the Cao Dai was the Hoa Hao, a religious movement, which had been founded on the eve of the war by Huynh Phu So. This idealistic young leader was followed devotedly by many thousands of untutored peasants to whom he quoted ancient prophecies as he preached, somewhat vaguely, independence and social reform. When Huynh Phu So was interned by the Decoux administration, the Japanese took him under their protection. In 1945, however, he spoke privately against what he called "Japanese imperialism" and "pseudo independence."

With the approval of the Japanese, still another nationalist group took shape in Cochin China, a patriotic youth movement which called itself the "Advance Guard Youth" and was founded by Pham Ngoc Thach, a young doctor who later announced his membership in the Communist Party. Unlike Annam and Tonkin, where the Tran Trong Kim government was working among young people already steeped in nationalism, Cochin China did not have a recent history and tradition of revolt. However, Pham Ngoc Thach succeeded for the first time in indoctrinating large numbers of French-trained young Cochin Chinese in Vietnamese revolutionary nationalism.

Under nationalist attack for his failure to unite the country, Tran Trong Kim appealed to the Japanese to join Cochin China with the rest of Viet Nam; but they refused. Cochin China was permitted to become a part of Viet Nam only in the last days of the war. When they were on the verge of defeat, the Japanese agreed to give way, Cochin China was officially restored to Viet Nam on August 14 and Bao Dai dispatched an imperial envoy to Saigon.

A member of the Nguyen dynasty ruled once again from Hué over Gia Long's Empire of Viet Nam.

Two days after Japan had capitulated to the Allies on August 15, the Japanese radio announced a statement by Tran Trong Kim. "The people of the Vietnamese Empire refuse to be subjugated by France," he said. They were determined to defend their independence.

The Japanese might have left behind an effective nationalist government based on popular foundations, but they had waited too long before demolishing the structure of French control to rally many Vietnamese; by the time the Japanese did act, it did not serve their policy to make vital concessions to Vietnamese nationalism. The Tran Trong Kim regime, as a result, ceased to exist during the third week in August. Viet Nam was ready to defend its independence, but not at the behest of the powerless Kim. The leader it followed was Ho Chi Minh.

Chapter Three

"WE HAVE FOUGHT A THOUSAND YEARS"

HATRED of colonial rule was strong in the land long before the coming of the Japanese. In 1884 the French had signed a treaty giving them a protectorate over Tonkin and Annam (Cochin China they had had since 1867) and insurrection had swept through the country. The mandarins and scholars of Viet Nam bitterly resented the coming of the French. The young Emperor Ham Nghi, then fifteen years old, fled to the mountains with his Regent Ton That Thuyet and raised an army against the foreigners.[1] For more than three years they fought guerrilla war against the French and against the ineffectual brother of Ham Nghi whom the French had made Emperor in his stead. It was a broadly national movement. The rebels included, according to Captain Gosselin, who arrived in Indochina in 1887, "the partisans of the old regime represented by Thuyet and his young sovereign and all the enemies of the prince whom we installed on the throne, in other words, almost the whole of Annam."[2]

Then, in 1888, Ham Nghi was betrayed to the French. He was taken prisoner and later exiled to Algeria. The Regent Thuyet sought asylum in China. Thuyet's twenty-two-year-old son, the "Second Minister of War" and royal envoy in the northern provinces, wrote to Ham Nghi, "It will be the eternal regret of all the civil and military mandarins who, prostrate before the Emperor, implore him to pardon them [for allowing him to fall into French hands], assuring him of their faithfulness for ten thousand years."[3] Then he killed himself.

The resistance laid down its arms when the Emperor was captured and the French let the men who had gone to war against them return to their homes. But guerrilla fighting broke out again late in 1893 and the man who had betrayed Ham Nghi was killed by the insurgents. They were led by the scholar Phan Dinh Phung, who directed the struggle with unexpected brilliance for two years, until his death. The revolt collapsed soon afterward. Gosselin reported that "all the rebels who did not succeed in gaining Siam by crossing Laos were brought to Hué and put to death. The repression was terrible."[4]

In the turbulent upper reaches of Tonkin, however, the fighting and disorders went on. Hoang Hoa Tham (known as De Tham) and others also led guerrillas against the French. Banditry intermingled with xenophobic warfare

[1] The co-Regent, Nguyen Van Tuong, who did not join the Emperor in the mountains, was also involved in the rising.
[2] Gosselin, *op. cit.*, p. 247.
[3] *Ibid.*, p. 307.
[4] *Ibid.*, p. 314.

in the mountains of Tonkin until it was hard to tell where one ended and the other began.

These men who fought the French in the late nineteenth and early twentieth centuries had no particular wish for social or political reform. Their one desire was to drive out the French so that the Nguyen Emperors and the mandarinal bureaucracy could rule in independence once again and the old order could be secured. They fought for independence from France as their ancestors had fought to oust the Chinese from Viet Nam since the first century A.D.

"Evil, ambitious, grasping," the Chinese had been interested only "in satisfying their personal interests, in enriching themselves at the expense of the people," wrote Nguyen Van Huyen, a Vietnamese scholar. "History has recorded their exactions, their injustice and their cruelty."[5] From the day of the Trung sisters, the Joans of Arc of Viet Nam, throughout a thousand years of Chinese rule, the Vietnamese rose time and again against alien domination. They achieved independence in the tenth century but still the struggle against China was not over. Three centuries later they repulsed the armies of Kublai Khan. Internecine war disrupted Viet Nam but when the Chinese tried to take over the country again in the fifteenth century, they met with determined resistance. Even today Viet Nam is dotted with pagodas and temples honoring the men who led the war against the Chinese. They worked out an arrangement finally by which the Vietnamese Emperor recognized the Emperor of China as his suzerain lord and sent him tribute; and from the imperial court at Peking the ruler of Viet Nam received the tributary's seal.

With the years, the Vietnamese people moved southward from their homes in Tonkin. They defeated the Cham people and took over their kingdom of Champa in the region which came to be known as Annam. They moved still further south, warring with the Khmer people of Cambodia, pushing them back to the present frontiers of Cambodia. They colonized even as they fought, and through war and intermarriage they took over all of Cochin China by the middle of the eighteenth century.

There were already Frenchmen in Indochina by that time, Catholic missionaries who, despite sporadic persecutions, succeeded in making a number of converts among the Vietnamese. When the country was torn by civil war late in the eighteenth century, Prince Nguyen Anh, heir to the Vietnamese throne, called on one of these French missionaries, Monsignor Pigneau de Béhaine, Bishop of Adran, for help. The bishop responded warmly; he went back to France and in 1787 negotiated a treaty of mutual defense and alliance between the Vietnamese prince and King Louis XVI which would have given the French many rights and considerable influence in Viet Nam. But the French Revolution broke out soon afterward and the French Government lost interest in Asia; the treaty lapsed. In French India, however, the Bishop of

[5] Nguyen Van Huyen, *La civilisation annamite*, p. 10.

Adran succeeded in finding volunteers and military aid for Nguyen Anh. This French help enabled the prince to unify the country and, in 1802, to ascend the throne as the Emperor Gia Long. "A sage, the intimate confidant of all my secrets," Gia Long called the Bishop when he died, and spoke of "my sadness and tenderness for this illustrious foreigner."[6]

After years of fighting, the country was at last at peace. Gia Long reorganized the administration and finances of Viet Nam, and drew up a law code for the country. He sponsored many schools—education had been neglected during the wars and in Viet Nam education was traditionally held in high esteem. He encouraged agriculture and local industries, and built up the army and navy. Gia Long recognized something of the power of the Occident and in his attempts to deal with it by opening Viet Nam to Western trade and technical progress, he was far in advance of his contemporaries elsewhere in early nineteenth century Asia.

His successors, however, retreated behind a wall of antiforeignism. Raised in the traditions of Chinese culture and Confucianism and insulated from all contact with their people by the elaborate ritual of the court, they chose to follow China at a time when it was stagnating behind its own great wall. They cut off all trade with the West and bitterly persecuted foreign priests and Vietnamese Catholics.

This policy was inaugurated by Minh Mang, the fourth son of Gia Long.[7] Not all the Vietnamese had yet accepted the dynasty of Gia Long by the time Minh Mang became Emperor in 1820. And some of those who had were loyal to Prince Canh, Gia Long's eldest son and the pupil of the Bishop of Adran. Although Canh had died while his father was still alive, his supporters, who tended to be pro-French, thought that his son, rather than his younger brother, should be placed on the throne. Minh Mang felt the insecurity of his position and acted accordingly.[8] He succeeded in consolidating the empire which Gia

[6] Michel Duc Chaigneau, *Souvenirs de Hué* (Paris, 1856), p. 11.

[7] Although in theory the eldest son of the Emperor's first wife succeeded to the Vietnamese throne, in practice the Emperor had the right to designate which of his sons should succeed him. (On occasion this choice was overruled by high court officials after the Emperor's death.) Gia Long, after the death of his eldest son, had designated as his heir Prince Dam, who became the Emperor Minh Mang.

[8] Desirous that his line, rather than his brother's, should rule after him, Minh Mang was determined that his male descendants should be easily identified. To this end he wrote a poem and ordained that the first word in it be inserted between the surname and the given name of each of his sons, that the same be done with the second word for each of their sons, and so on, generation after generation.

His poem read:

Mien huong ung buu vinh,
Bao quy dinh long truong.
Hien nang kham ke thuat,
The thuy quoc gia xuong.

Each royal prince, on ascending the throne, took a new dynastic name but, in common with all male members of their family, up to the present they have all been named after the tradition laid down by Minh Mang. Bao Dai, Minh Mang's great-great-great grandson, is thus named Nguyen Phuoc *Vinh* Thuy and his eldest son is Nguyen Phuoc *Bao* Long.

Long had created, strengthening the administration like his father (although a scholar and poet, he was, like his father, an excellent administrator) and taking strong military action against men who rose against him in Cochin China and Tonkin. He also turned against the Catholics whom his father had befriended, and to whom he owed so much, on the ground that they threatened the traditional Chinese culture of Viet Nam in which religion and social structure were intimately aligned in support of each other and of the state. Minh Mang found himself in a position, a sympathetic French biographer pointed out, in which he had

... either to make his peace with Catholicism, in other words, to accept not only a decrease in his authority but also the rapid transformation of public opinion by the abolition of century-old traditions, or to go resolutely to war against this element of trouble and disorganization. The error made by the Emperor was to confuse the religious problem with the problem already posed for Annam by Western diplomacy. He was unaware of the historical fatality which did not permit him to remain aloof from the great currents of European civilization and his blindness was the principal cause of the chaos from which his successors struggled to extricate themselves.[9]

Minh Mang rebuffed all French overtures for closer relations with Viet Nam until, late in his reign, British military action in Asia shocked him into an awareness of the weakness and isolation to which he had condemned his country. He saw the British go to war when the Chinese attempted to cut off all trade with Britain and end the opium traffic. In the same period, the British moved closer and closer to the Vietnamese frontier as they took over Malaya and Burma.

Minh Mang tried to reverse a policy of twenty years. He sent an ambassador to Paris to negotiate a commercial treaty as a prelude to a treaty of alliance by which the French would protect Viet Nam against aggression by other powers. But he was too late; Gia Long was dead and there was no Bishop of Adran to intervene in his favor. The Society of Foreign Missions protested energetically to King Louis Philippe, complaining of Minh Mang's cruel treatment of Catholics and urging vigorous action in their defense. Minh Mang's ambassador, rebuffed in France and England, was on his way home when he heard of the Emperor's death.

Belatedly, Minh Mang had come to realize that terms had to be made with the French if his empire was to be preserved. But Thieu Tri, the new Emperor, turned his back on his father's attempts at a rapprochement with the West. He took refuge in a blind xenophobia, continuing the persecution of Catholics and keeping the door firmly closed to commercial intercourse with the West. His anti-French and anti-Catholic policies caused the French to sink his fleet in the Bay of Tourane in 1847.

Tu Duc, who succeeded to the throne that year, carried on his predecessor's

9 Marcel Gaultier, *Minh-Mang,* pp. 83–84.

policies. But a tide of imperialism was beginning to sweep through Asia and Africa from the West, opening these areas to radically new influences and dislocating the settled patterns of their society. Viet Nam, lost in the contemplation of its own past, was ill-equipped to withstand the impact of such a shock. The French came to Cochin China in 1858 and this time they came with force, as members of a joint Franco-Spanish expedition which arrived to punish the Vietnamese for their treatment of missionaries from the two countries. They compelled Tu Duc to cede the three eastern provinces of Cochin China to France in 1862.

The Spaniards left then, with the assurance that their missionaries would be able to operate in safety throughout Vietnamese territory. The French stayed on. Captain Gosselin wrote:

Our compatriots, not well informed on history, suppose that France came to intervene in Annam solely for the protection of missionaries, or to seek vengeance for acts of hostility committed against them and for persecutions against the Catholic religion. The missionaries, in reality, have only been the pretext for our action against Annam. The loss of India in the eighteenth century, the increasingly rapid extension in the Far East of our perpetual rival England imposed on us the obligation to set foot in the China seas, the only alternative being our falling into a state of contemptible inferiority. Annam gave us the opportunity, the massacre of Frenchmen who were there as missionaries gave us the pretext.[10]

When Tu Duc tried to get back his three lost provinces, the French moved on the rest of Cochin China. Vietnamese mandarins in the south took to the bush to fight them and the Vietnamese viceroy in Cochin China, in the time-honored tradition of Vietnamese generals and governors, committed suicide because he could not defend the territory assigned to him. In 1867 the French took over the remaining three provinces of Cochin China and Vietnamese officials and scholars withdrew to the north, unwilling to live under foreign occupation.

Unable to hold out against the French in the south, Tu Duc did his best to obstruct their activities in Tonkin and Annam. And so it came about that, to preserve their conquests in Cochin China and in the hope of opening the road to trade with China, the French moved on Annam and Tonkin. In 1882 Tu Duc raised Tonkin against them and called on China for help. But neither the Chinese nor the Vietnamese had the strength to expel the French. Tu Duc died in 1883 and the Treaty of Hué, signed the following year, established a French protectorate over all of Tonkin and Annam. China surrendered its rights over Viet Nam in 1885.

When young Ham Nghi went to war against the French, they deposed him. Five Emperors of Viet Nam have succeeded to the throne since then, but Ham Nghi, who died during the second World War, lived to see the end of

[10] Gosselin, op. cit., p. xix.

the French rule he had fought so bitterly when it first began. The revolt of Ham Nghi confronted the French with the problem of finding an emperor who would be willing to rule under their protection. They made one of Ham Nghi's brothers Emperor under the name of Dong Khanh, but he lived only until 1889.[11] His successor, Thanh Thai, became Emperor when only a child.[12] In his own way he apparently carried on the nationalist tradition and even had a gold seal delivered secretly to Prince Cuong De when his cousin left Viet Nam to lead the struggle for independence from abroad.[13] French officials took advantage of Thanh Thai's increasing eccentricities and personal excesses to depose him in 1907. His son, not yet in his teens, became the Emperor Duy Tan.

But Vietnamese scholars and mandarins were not reconciled to French rule; from the time the protectorate was imposed upon Viet Nam, they never ceased to struggle against it, sometimes by peaceful means, sometimes by force. In the early part of the twentieth century they were profoundly influenced by events in China and Japan. The Vietnamese had long been sensitive to political currents across the frontier, and China, so long a citadel of the past, yet crumbling with decadence, was in the midst of a new ferment as the rule of the Manchu Emperors neared its close. The Vietnamese learned of reform and then of revolution from China. At the same time, they read in Chinese books about revolutionary nationalism in nineteenth century Europe and studied with interest the Italian struggle for unification and the careers of men like Mazzini, Garibaldi, and Cavour.

While China was laboriously modernizing its political system, the emergence of Japan on the world scene stimulated the imagination of Vietnamese intellectuals. The myth of white invincibility suffered a resounding blow throughout Asia when the armies of imperial Russia were defeated by the Japanese in 1905, and a strong and free Viet Nam seemed to a number of Vietnamese to be more than just a dream; if the Japanese could reorient themselves so successfully to the modern world, as Gia Long had tried to do many years before, surely other Asians could do the same. Vietnamese nationalists began to talk of "modernizing" their country so that they would be powerful enough to oust the French.

From France itself they received a stimulus to revolution but this came later

11 Three emperors ruled briefly between Tu Duc's death in 1885 and Ham Nghi's accession to the throne the following year. Duc Duc, Tu Duc's nephew who was his adopted son and his chosen heir, ruled one day and was then jailed and later starved to death. He was followed by Hiep Hoa, Tu Duc's brother, who was killed late in 1883. Third came Kien Phuoc, another of Tu Duc's nephews and adopted sons, who died in 1884. Ham Nghi was his brother as was Dong Khanh.

12 Thanh Thai was the son of Duc Duc.

13 Cuong De was a descendant of Prince Canh, elder brother of Minh Mang and eldest son of Gia Long.

and was more indirect. Although the French brought with them the seeds of revolt, in their history and their political ideas, French history, as it was taught in Viet Nam, tended to concentrate on the glories of France, on the Ancien Régime and on the victories of Napoleon. Vietnamese students learned little of the French Revolution; they had to go to Chinese translations to read Montesquieu and Rousseau and discover French revolutionary democracy.

Discontent and conspiracy marked the unruly years in the Vietnamese lands before the First World War. Phan Boi Chau, who went to Japan with Prince Cuong De, studied the lessons of the Chinese and the Japanese and in Canton, in 1912, he organized the Phuc Quoc, which looked to Cuong De as its leader. At the same time, Phan Boi Chau inspired and directed the underground revolutionary movement in Viet Nam. The pre-World War One years were marked by considerable violence in Tonkin and Annam. Leading scholars organized and agitated against the French; Phan Chu Trinh, one of the most prominent, led demonstrations and preached reform and democracy.

Although nationalists were agreed on their desire to expel the French, not all of them believed that this would be accomplished merely by help from abroad and by violence; some favored educating the people in modern and Western ways. A move to establish free education in scientific and Western subjects resulted in the setting up of a special school in Hanoi. At the same time, a movement of "Hair-Cutters" sprang up, directed at modernizing the country by breaking with such traditional forms as wearing the hair long and bound at the back of the head in a chignon. Cutting the hair in defiance of the Confucianist practice was a revolutionary event in early twentieth-century Viet Nam. The Hair-Cutters demanded social reform, notably the lowering of taxes. Like the "Free School," they were regarded by the French as dangerous to their administration; in 1908 the school was closed and the Hair-Cutters were suppressed.

Political unrest was great in 1908, when an attempt was made to poison the French garrison at Hanoi, and again several years later. De Tham, the guerrilla leader, continued his activities in Tonkin until the eve of the war, when he was assassinated. In Cochin China the French uncovered the Gilbert Chieu conspiracy, which linked Vietnamese nationalism with Japanese espionage.

When the first World War broke out, Prince Cuong De and Phan Boi Chau were still secretly in touch with mandarins at Hué who were their fellow-conspirators. Indochina provided more than half the wartime loans and gifts made to France by her colonies, more raw materials than any other part of the Empire except West Africa; and more than 43,000 Indochinese soldiers and almost 49,000 workers were sent to Europe.[14] But the country they left behind was not quiet during the war.

[14] Sarraut, op. cit., pp. 44, 47, 50.

In 1916 a group of scholars and mandarins (generally from among the lower ranks of the mandarinate) organized a revolt aimed at expelling the French from Annam.[15] They were led by a scholar named Tran Cao Van, who had already served time on Poulo Condore for his revolutionary activities. At the center of the plot, unknown even to his Ministers, was the young Emperor Duy Tan, then eighteen years old and, despite his youth, by all accounts one of the most enterprising and intelligent of the Nguyen Emperors. The conspirators had an armed force at their disposal; and a number of Vietnamese troops, stationed temporarily in Hué on the way to the port of Tourane from where they were to be sent to France, were prepared on a given signal to take over the Citadel of Hué and disarm the French. The conspirators were also in touch with Vietnamese abroad in China and Japan. Nguyen Hai Than, who had left Viet Nam years before and, as it turned out, never returned until 1945, was expected to lead troops across the Chinese frontier. Phan Boi Chau was also involved.

The rising was thought out in such detail that its leaders had agreed on a plan of administration for all of liberated Annam. Duy Tan had already appointed men to govern the different administrative divisions and had sent them seals of office so that they could take over authority immediately. They had even debated whether to establish a monarchy or a republic and, in deference to Duy Tan, had decided in favor of a monarchy.

This plan for revolt was remarkably ambitious, with wide support among key elements in the population. It has gone almost unnoticed in the European accounts of the period because it did not succeed. The conspirators were impatient men, their communications were poorly organized, and they moved too soon, enabling the French authorities to thwart them at the start and to disarm the Vietnamese soldiers in Hué before they could take any action.

With the conspiracy uncovered, Duy Tan, like Ham Nghi before him, fled into the mountains. He resisted all efforts to bring him back, even when Tran Cao Van offered to take on himself the whole responsibility for the rising. The scholar-poet who had planned the revolt insisted that he alone should be blamed for it; but Duy Tan refused to disclaim his part in the plot and to return peaceably to the court at Hué.

Several hundreds of the conspirators were executed or sent to the forced-labor camps on Poulo Condore and Lao Bao. Duy Tan was deported to the island of Réunion in the Indian Ocean, where his father was also sent.

In Hué, French officials found a member of the royal family, a son of Dong Khanh, who appeared more amenable than his relatives, and he became

[15] The following account is based largely upon that in *Cu Tran Cao-Van*, written by Hanh Son.

the Emperor Khai Dinh. But Khai Dinh reigned only a few years; he died in
1925, leaving another boy king on the throne. His name was Vinh Thuy and
when he became Emperor he took the dynastic name of Bao Dai.

BEFORE THE FRENCH CAME

"We have fought a thousand years," was once the boast of Vietnamese nationalists. "And we will fight another thousand if need be." To war against
foreign domination is an ancient practice in the Vietnamese lands. It was one
of the traditions inherited by the Nguyen Emperors at a time when Viet Nam
in many things seemed closer to the institutions of ancient China than China
itself, where the arrival of foreign dynasties and alien peoples had served to
modify the old ways.

In the empire of the Nguyens, absolute power had been vested in the Emperor, as with the Chinese Emperor, the Son of Heaven. However, the Emperor, no less than the officials and the common people, was bound by certain
ethical norms, and the state was conceived of as founded on the people. The
Emperor governed through a bureaucracy of mandarins in whom, as in himself, both religious and civil powers were vested. The mandarins were recruited by examinations in the Chinese language and in Chinese literature,
for education in Viet Nam was exclusively literary: the Chinese training
seemed to produce a corps of administrators who were able enough but it also
helped to blanket Viet Nam with the past, imposing an immutable mold
upon its civilization and its society.

Only in religious and military matters did the central government exercise
a strong and continuing control over the peasantry, who constituted the mass
of the population. For this reason foreigners have tended to over-emphasize
the localism of Vietnamese society when, as a matter of fact, it was permeated
by the concept of a unified state of which the Emperor was the symbol.

The life of the people was regulated, according to custom, within the con-
fines of the village, the basic unit of Vietnamese society. A man's rights and
duties were determined by his place in the social system, and individual rights
did not exist. As Vietnamese moved southward along the length of the
peninsula, setting up new villages, each village in turn was formally recognized by the Emperor. The imperial government had no direct contact with
the individual but only with his village, which paid taxes and provided men
to labor on public works and to serve in the army. For the rest, the village directed its own affairs, supervised by a Council of Notables recruited from the
village oligarchy. But if the village had a genuine autonomy, as expressed in
the old Vietnamese saying, "The King's law bows before village custom,"
there was never any question of challenging the supreme and overriding au-

thority of the central government, and individuals who were honored for their services in the state received precedence in their native villages.

The average peasant raised enough food for himself and his family, generally little more. There were many rural artisans and a number of village industries, whole villages sometimes specializing in a single craft like carpentry or weaving; and there was a limited trade among them. But the villages, each surrounded by a thick stand of bamboo, were virtually self-sufficient units. It was a static, self-contained society. The peasant was rooted in his village and had little interest in what went on outside it.

Vietnamese society did not allow for extremes of poverty and riches; nor for cruel and arbitrary rule. Education was widespread throughout the country and the examinations by which the mandarins were chosen were open to everyone. Titles of nobility were not hereditary; no matter how high a man rose in the mandarinal hierarchy, he could not pass on his titles or his position to his sons, who had to make their own place for themselves. And very important was the fact that the ownership of land was widely dispersed.

A strong co-operative tradition existed in the villages. They maintained communal lands, most of which were regularly divided among taxpayers to supplement their own private land. A considerable portion of the communal land was set aside for the support of the old and poor. The village also maintained a granary in which it kept rice to provide against the time when the people might be in want.

The village had its tradition of self-rule, albeit under a select minority. The peasant had the right to appeal the decision of an official to the mandarin above him; in theory, even to the Emperor himself. And in the background, too grave a thing to invoke except in time of great need but always omnipresent, was the doctrine of "the mandate of heaven." The authority of the Emperor had a religious sanction which only the sacrilegious would question. But if the Emperor were to abuse his power, to prove himself unworthy to rule, he would forfeit the heavenly mandate and the people could rise against him and depose him, even at the cost of civil war.

This was the Empire of Viet Nam, built on an efficient system of checks and balances. Then the Europeans came.

THE IMPACT OF FRENCH RULE

Frenchmen came to Viet Nam for a variety of reasons. There were missionaries and explorers, soldiers and administrators, planters and businessmen. A few came as Catholics and humanitarians. Some came to assert the position of France in the world and to enable their country to hold its own, particularly against Great Britain, in the race for colonial empire. Others came in the hope of opening a large-scale trade with China and for other economic motives as well. Jules Ferry, Premier of France in 1883–85, during the war with the Vietnamese and the Chinese, and "the first French statesman whose foreign policy has been dominated by the concern for colonial expansion,"[16] was the prophet of a new economic imperialism. "Colonial policy is the daughter of industrial policy," he wrote.[17] He favored a policy of industrialization at home and, as its corollary, assured markets abroad for the export of manufactured goods and of capital. In a world of intense competition and growing protectionism, he argued, colonies were a necessity. The alternative was to descend to the level of a third- or fourth-rate power.

The population of Indochina more than doubled under the French, for they brought peace and security to the country. French scientists worked at the Pasteur Institutes, doing notable research in tropical diseases, distributing vaccines, and dealing with problems of sanitation and hygiene in the cities; and the French built hospitals and dispensaries. The French also strengthened and substantially extended the old dike system, particularly in the Red River delta in Tonkin, with which, over the centuries, the Vietnamese had tried to keep back the unpredictable waters. They irrigated hundreds of thousands of acres. And in the south they drained large areas, creating thousands of acres of new farmland.

They introduced new crops into the country and in Cochin China they accomplished what the well-known French writer Roland Dorgelès called "the miracle of rubber." In 1925 he wrote:

Less than forty years ago, there was not a rubber tree in the colony. . . . Today rubber trees can be counted by the millions on immense plantations. [This was accomplished] despite sickness, despite the flight of coolies, despite years of drought, despite plants which died, despite storms which ruined roads, despite fires which devastated the land, despite everything . . . and these miserable lands which were not worth a piastre bring fortunes: ships take on rubber at Saigon by the thousands of tons.[18]

The French extended and vastly improved the old Mandarin Road begun by the Chinese two thousand years ago and continued by the Vietnamese Emperors as they extended their domain southward. Under the French it became Colonial Highway No. 1, twisting along the coast from Saigon to the Chinese frontier in the north; and from this main highway they built a number of other roads. They also built the Trans-Indochinese Railway which parallels the Mandarin Road, and laid down some 2,908 kilometers of railroad track.

The French carried on a considerable cultural work in Indochina, which

[16] Robert Delavignette and Ch. André Julien, *Les Constructeurs de la France d'Outre-Mer*, (Paris, 1946), p. 264.
[17] Jules Ferry, *Discours et opinions*, Vol. V, p. 557. See *ibid*.
[18] Roland Dorgelès, *Sur la Route Mandarine*, pp. 184–86.

they regarded as their *mission civilisatrice,* the Gallic equivalent of the White Man's Burden. They succeeded in implanting French civilization among the small upper class, many of whom sent their sons to study in French schools in Indochina and even in France. It was from republican France that some of the most ardent opponents of French rule acquired many of their ideas of liberty and of the rights of man. Admiral Decoux, in fact, warned against sending students to France at all. He recommended that only a very small number, "selected with care," be allowed to go, and that over these there should be "vigilant control and surveillance during their entire stay in the mother country, so as to keep them away from bad company and from dangerous and subversive propaganda."[19]

Admiral Decoux was far removed in spirit from the men who came to Indochina in the nineteenth century believing in the possibility of assimilation—that is, subjecting Asians and Africans to the opportunities and influences of French civilization over a period of time—up to the point where they would be transformed into Frenchmen. This once was, and in limited degree still is, the professed aim of French colonization. It was actually realized in three colonies—Guadeloupe, Martinique, and Réunion—the first two in the Caribbean Sea, the third in the Indian Ocean. In 1946 the final stone in the edifice of assimilation was put into place when these three so-called "old colonies" became *départements* of France, as if they were not far-off islands at all, but parts of the French mainland.

These three islands, however, were first acquired in the seventeenth century; it took all this time for the process of assimilation to reach its logical conclusion. Presumably the same evolution might have occurred on a vaster scale and over a longer period in Indochina. But history did not stand still; there was simply not enough time.

Even so, the French made an indelible imprint on Viet Nam. They opened the country to the West. To people bogged down in their own past they brought a new science and technology, new patterns of living and thinking. An alien rule and an alien civilization were intruded into the closed and backward-looking society of Viet Nam. The effect, of course, was highly disruptive. The Vietnamese felt the shock of it in every part of their life—socially, economically, culturally, and politically.

Thus the pattern of land distribution changed, and the gap between rich and poor grew wider. This development was certainly not deliberate on the part of the French, but it was none the less real. Population increases in Tonkin and Annam, combined with the peasant's practice of dividing his land equally among his children, dwarfed the size of holdings. Sixty-two percent of the Tonkinese peasantry owned less than nine-tenths of an acre each, and 30 percent had less than four-tenths. The situation was only slightly better in An-

19 Decoux, *op. cit.,* p. 402.

nam. Yet at the same time, with the breakdown of the old closed economy and the greater availability of credit, a number of large estates grew up in the north with the French occupation. They were acquired generally by the practice of usury, through which a number of more fortunate landowners battened on the poverty of their countrymen until the estates of this privileged group, in turn, fell into the hands of the all-powerful Bank of Indochina.

The peasant labored under a grinding burden of debt. The French tried to alleviate his dependence on the usurer, but much of the credit which they made available went to line the pockets of the large landowners, who borrowed only to relend at exorbitant rates. Usury thrived, and the local Chinese and Indians joined wealthy Vietnamese in raking in the profits. Tonkin and Annam were only nominally lands of free peasants, for, however tiny their holdings, many of the farms were actually controlled by the moneylender. When in 1952 the French-sponsored Prime Minister Nguyen Van Tam promised a program of agrarian reform for the country, even he had to say:

In the past the [French] government encouraged rice cultivation by lending to the big landowners who, in turn, helped their farmers with state money at a usurious rate. . . . After one or two bad harvests the peasant became literally the slave of his master just because of usury.[20]

The Cochin Chinese landlord often collected more in usury than he did in rent. Cochin China was the center of French economic activity in Indochina. The abundant benefits of usury, combined with the French practice of granting extensive concessions in undeveloped land to French companies and rich Vietnamese, led to the development of many large estates owned by absentee landlords. These estates were worked by tenant farmers and landless agricultural laborers. The *ta dien* or sharecropper worked between 60 to 80 percent of the Cochin Chinese farmland. He generally had to give far more than half his annual harvest to his landlord, partly as rent, partly as usurious interest.

No longer could the peasant turn to his commune for help. Many of the communal lands were lost at a time when they were more desperately needed than ever—the result of population increases and of the breakdown of village authority. There was speculation in communal lands which was inadvertently encouraged by the French administration; and mandarins and village Notables were also involved. As a result, the communal lands shrank to one-fifth the total cultivated area in Tonkin, to one-quarter in Annam, and to 3 percent in Cochin China.

In Tonkin, Vietnamese were employed in French textile industries and in French-owned mines. Vietnamese laborers also worked the French rubber plantations in Cochin China. Many of these plantation workers were recruited

---

[20] *Le Monde*, August 15–16, 1952; *Viet-Nam* (Paris), September 15, 1952.

in the villages of Tonkin, which they were reluctant to leave, and sent south far from their homes to work under a semimilitary system. They were bound by three-year contracts which gave their employers the right to regulate their labor by force. They lived and worked under the most miserable conditions.[21]

The industrial working class never numbered more than 221,000 at any one time, according to official figures. But there was a large turnover. Wages were very low; and also, in this country where men were rooted in their natal villages, no man, if he could help it, left his village for good. These figures, in any case, cover only Vietnamese employed in European undertakings. Far more numerous were the small landowners in Tonkin and Annam, ruined by poverty and debt, who became tenants of others; the ta dien in Cochin China; and the landless workers who roamed the Cochin Chinese ricefields in gangs, hiring themselves out as seasonal labor "The Annamite working class undoubtedly exists," wrote a French official of the International Labor Office, "and its numerical importance may be assessed by multiplying the figures given in the statistics by four or five."[22] The emergence of a proletariat increased instability in the Vietnamese lands.

The French brought with them a Western economic and administrative system which disrupted the traditional framework within which the people had regulated their lives. They helped to break down the old localism by stripping the village of much of its autonomy. The large-scale public works system launched by the French also operated against localism.

The old Vietnamese legal and social structure disintegrated under French rule. In Annam they made use of the traditional monarchy but only to discredit it. They took away its power; they put their authority behind venal mandarins[23] and behind cais (native foremen on French-owned plantations and in French-owned mines and industries), giving an official sanction, in Vietnamese eyes, to frequent extortions and abuses. The mandarins became part of the machinery of French control over Indochina. And under the French, the people no longer had any right of appeal against them.

The French ended the Vietnamese Empire in fact, if not in form, and they

21 Vietnamese recruited from Tonkin and North Annam for service in the French Pacific Islands were bound by similar contracts for five-year periods.

22 Jean Goudal, *Labor Conditions in French Indo-China*, p. 274.

23 This venality, while perhaps not unrelated to the lowered prestige of the Vietnamese administration, was made much more certain by the low salaries paid to the mandarins. Captain Gosselin, who came to the country during the French conquest, wrote: "The salary of mandarins of all ranks is derisory and this results from the doctrine of Confucius; according to this philosopher, the official should remain poor. . . . In practice, these officials, obliged to live in a manner befitting their rank, enabled to do that only insufficiently by their income from the state, are constrained to have recourse to other, and illicit means." Gosselin, *op. cit.*, pp. 40–41. Fifty years of French rule apparently did not change this situation. Admiral Decoux wrote that when he arrived in Indochina as Governor General, the mandarins still received "derisory salaries which, it must be recognized, hardly were of the sort to keep them away from numerous attempts at *baksheesh*." Decoux, *op. cit.*, p. 399.

failed to set up a more equitable system in its place. Instead, they perpetuated some of its practices in harsher guise because they disregarded the customs and traditions which had softened their impact.

Peasant and laborer were subjected to a number of direct and indirect taxes, some of which, like the *corvée* and the *gabelle*—forced labor on public works and the salt tax—both dating back to the Vietnamese Empire, were reminiscent of those against which the French peasantry revolted in the eighteenth century.

Public works were paid for by Vietnamese taxes and built by Vietnamese labor but, according to Paul Bernard, a French authority, "the present interest of the network of roads and railroads is much more political or touristic than economic and, in any case, their extension does not correspond to the state of parallel development of the private economy."[24] Nationalists complained that the essential concern of the French was to make conditions safe for themselves rather than to pursue an active improvement program, whether in the field of medicine, where it was essential to stave off epidemics that might paralyze the economy of the country and also infect Europeans,[25] or in building roads over which Europeans might travel while Vietnamese lacked the vehicles, the money, and the passports.[26] Observers who were neither nationalists nor radicals remarked that the savings and profits of Frenchmen in Indochina contributed little to the welfare of the country because they were not invested in Indochina but were sent back to France.

A focal point of nationalist criticism was the threefold monopoly on salt, opium, and alcohol. The small salt worker had to sell what he produced to the French administration and then buy back what he needed for himself at higher prices; and salt was important to him, for he used it in preparing the fish which was a vital part of the Vietnamese diet. The French administration had a substantial interest in spreading the use of opium and alcohol because it profited directly from their sale. It assigned each village a quota of alcohol which it was required to consume. Thus, on August 28, 1934, an order was

[24] Paul Bernard, *Nouveaux aspects du problème économique indochinois* (Paris, 1937), p. 156.

[25] All the justly famous work of the Pasteur Institute in Indochina did not alter the fact that medical assistance remained poorly organized and insufficient, particularly in the countryside, where the mass of the people lived. In the Philippines there was one doctor for every 3,200 native inhabitants; in Indochina there was only one for every 38,000. See Lauriston Sharp, "Colonial Regimes in Southeast Asia." *Far Eastern Survey,* February 27, 1946, p. 49.

[26] A French scholar, Pierre Gourou, has written much the same thing: "It is to the amelioration of the lot of this peasant population that all efforts should be deliberately directed, for each piastre expended by the State has, directly or indirectly, been taken from the minute incomes of the peasants. If this thought had always been kept in mind, perhaps certain expenditures which were not beneficial to the mass of the population (expenses of urban improvement, certain roads and railways, etc.) would have been reduced, and researches would have been developed that would benefit the peasant (agronomic research, artisan development, etc.), customs policies would have been oriented exclusively toward a defense of peasant interests. . . ." Pierre Gourou, *Land Utilization in French Indochina,* pp. 224–25.

issued by a French prefect that in the canton of N., under his jurisdiction, 800 liters of alcohol had to be consumed each month. Each village was to report what it had sold or consumed. "The villages which have consumed much will be recompensed," the order provided, "and the villages which have consumed or sold little will be punished."[27]

In France, the smoking of opium was a criminal offense; in Indochina it was one of the financial props of the government. This was true of other European powers in their Southeast Asian territories, true also of the Siamese Government, which was independent, but that did not mollify nationalists. And although the French National Committee in Algiers announced in 1944 their intention of terminating the opium monopoly, the French Government did not in fact institute this reform after the war.

In Indochina, as elsewhere in colonial Asia, a money economy was grafted upon the traditional subsistence economy. Taxes estimated in terms of the new Western administration were imposed upon a population geared to another economic system, with the result that peasants paid as much as one-fifth of their meager annual income to the government. Concerning this, Paul Mus wrote:

Such a state of affairs, in which the people's livelihood is calculated in terms of one world and their taxes in those of quite another, cannot endure. . . . A modern-style monetary tax, based on the regular registration of births and deaths, induces the taxpayers to consider their rights and duties, strips them of their cloak of communal anonymity, and converts them into individuals who must be reckoned with in social and political as well as economic affairs. . . . The translation of the economy into monetary terms will in time create a need for ballot boxes.[28]

Few people were thinking in terms of ballot boxes for the peasants in the interwar period. The peasants had enough to do merely to feed themselves. They could not always do that.

The Vietnamese peasants worked tiny plots of land in the densely populated Red River delta and north Annam, and in somewhat larger areas in Cochin China. Some 6,500,000 people were crowded into the 5,790 square miles of the Tonkinese delta, or 1,123 per square mile. They tended each small rice plant with the intensive care of a gardener, using only the most primitive tools and few draft animals; and they were prodigal of human labor, since it was desperately cheap. There was "a real competition between man and beast. Animal labor is as expensive as human labor, as man does not earn much more than is strictly necessary to feed himself, and the feeding of an animal is as costly as the feeding of a man."[29]

27 Quoted in Andrée Viollis, *Indochine S.O.S.*, p. 29.
28 Paul Mus, "The Role of the Village in Vietnamese Politics," *Pacific Affairs*, September 1949, p. 269.
29 Gourou, *op. cit.*, p. 241.

Three-fifths of the population of the Tonkinese delta spent 80 percent of its income on food—mostly rice. Pierre Gourou found it "not surprising that the land can support so great a number of persons, as these do not ask from it much more than their food, do not require it to produce a large surplus for their clothing, pleasure and housing, and as they work their land almost frantically."[30] They planted two rice crops a year in Tonkin and north Annam, Yet famine was still endemic in the region, which depended on rice imports from Cochin China in time of poor harvests.

The tremendous increase in population which occurred under French rule was of little benefit to the Vietnamese; the peasants were 90 percent of the population and their standard of living remained appallingly low.[31] The population had been unequally distributed when the French came, most of them crowded into the north, the ancient home of the Vietnamese people, with fewer in the south, which the Vietnamese had only begun to settle in the seventeenth century. The situation continued under the French, and the overcrowding in the north was intensified. The number of people living in the Tonkinese delta swelled by 100,000 a year. Frenchmen profited at first, for they were able to build large public works swiftly, and to develop mines and plantations. "But today," wrote Charles Robequain, a leading French authority, in 1939, "it appears to be a heavy obligation and an increasingly painful responsibility."[32]

The majority of Tonkinese could afford only two meals a day during most of the year. They managed three around harvest time, when they had to work harder than usual, but this came after a period of privation. Almost every year there was a time before the harvest when the peasant could not afford to eat more than once a day. He did not even have enough rice for that, unless he boiled it so long that it became a soup which looked and tasted like a gluey paste.

"These peasants are not serfs brutalized by a crushing poverty," Gourou wrote in 1939, "they are free men who are ready to seize the first opportunity to better their position."[33] And this, in time, was what they did. Finding all

---

[30] *Ibid.*, p. 550. For a remarkable study of the area, see Gourou, *Les Paysans du Delta Tonkinois.*

[31] The various agricultural hydraulic works built by the French in the north "have resulted only in putting at the disposal of the perpetually increasing population a nearly constant food ration, without any sensible change in the material conditions of the life of individuals." Bernard, *op. cit.*

[32] Charles Robequain, *The Economic Development of French Indochina*, p. 59. Professor Robequain took issue with the assertion of Pierre Gourou that, because the entire population is employed in Tonkin during the time of heaviest agricultural demands, there is no overpopulation. Robequain pointed out that "the answer to this is that the native techniques had unconsciously adapted themselves to the very abundance of manpower and the number of mouths to be fed, with the result of an unprecedented waste of manpower" (p. 74).

[33] Gourou, *op. cit.*, p. 551.

other channels closed to them except that of force, they followed the leaders who urged them to revolt.

SECOND-CLASS CITIZENS

A new middle class developed in the predominantly peasant Vietnamese society as a result of the activities introduced by the French. It was made up of officials and intellectuals as well as landowners and, in Tonkin particularly, people active in industry and commerce who, however, generally had close links with landed property. But it was a small and fairly ineffectual middle class, for it was strong only to the degree that the French permitted it to be strong; and it was French policy to exclude it from all positions of political and economic power.

Vietnamese landowners who tried to get a foothold in industry and big business were generally kept out by the French colonial monopolies. By and large, Vietnamese were excluded from both the control and the profits of the modern economic enterprises which the French brought to Indochina and grafted onto the native economy. Rice cultivation remained the province of the Vietnamese; the rice trade was in the hands of the Chinese. But the great rubber plantations in the south and the mines and factories in the north were French-owned. The Indochinese economy was dominated by French banks, chief among them the powerful Bank of Indochina. The country was dominated by an alien minority—and, almost inevitably, in an alien interest.

Roland Dorgelès demanded to know, in 1925:

Who owns these mines, these factories, these banks, these warehouses, these ships, these plantations?

In the old days, colonists came, struggled, got rich. That was good. It was necessary that the fleece be golden to attract Jason. And some of these men shared their riches with the colony, since they established new enterprises there, cultivated lands, built factories. But the invasion of capital came to overwhelm all that: the people who profit are in Europe; in the colony are the people who exhaust themselves with difficult work.[34]

Was this good or bad? Dorgelès asked. And he answered:

A good, doubtless, since the uncultivated brush is going to produce, the mountain is going to deliver up its riches, canals and roads are going to be opened up. A good, because the entire world needs raw materials and the sole excuse for colonization is to go to look for them wherever they are. A good, because if this capital were not invested there it would flee abroad. A good, because without this money nothing could be undertaken and the Chettyar [Indian] and the Chinese moneylender would reign more harshly.

But it was an evil also, a mortal evil, because these monopolies are going to in-

[34] Dorgelès, op. cit., pp. 204-5.

crease hate all around us; an evil because France did not go to conquer these far-off lands for the sole profit of a hundred large stockholders; an evil because many of these businesses, swollen by speculators, will fail; an evil because the native, freed by France from the tyranny of the mandarins, is now falling into the power of these new tyrants; an evil because small miseries produce big revolts; an evil, finally, because on the other side of the Great Wall of China there are four hundred million yellow people who are awakening.[35]

Indochina was subordinated in every way to metropolitan France. Industrialization eventually might have helped to raise living standards but it was not far advanced beyond such processing and light industries as sugar refineries, rice mills and distilleries, and paper, cotton, and cement factories. The French treated Indochina pre-eminently as a source of raw materials for France and as a market for French manufactures. They kept the country inside the walls of the French tariff system, forcing the Indochinese to pay more to import from France the goods which they might have bought elsewhere at lower prices; and each year since 1930 they bought more goods from France and her colonies than from any other country.[36] In Indochina, as in many other colonial countries, there was an overemphasis on producing raw materials and foodstuffs for export. "Dry" secondary crops were encouraged to vary the rice monoculture, but they went largely for export. In the 1930's, at a time when the Vietnamese people did not have enough to eat, Cochin China exported rice in considerable quantities; even Tonkin managed to export some.

Neither in the government nor in the administration of their country could the Indochinese play an effective role. The five areas of Indochina were represented in the Grand Council of Economic and Financial Interests, of which half the members were French; there was also a Colonial Council in Cochin China, partly French and partly Vietnamese; and in Annam and Cambodia there were separate councils for Frenchmen and for natives. All of these bodies were concerned generally just with local economic affairs, and had advisory powers only. Vietnamese members were either appointed by the government or elected under a system of very restricted suffrage.

Regardless of labels, authority was entirely in the hands of the highly centralized French administration. Policy was laid down in France, sometimes by Parliament, more often by ministerial decree. It was implemented in Indochina by the French bureaucracy, which extended downward from the Governor General, the Résident Supérieur of the protectorates, and the Governor of Cochin China, to a network of lesser officials.

[35] *Ibid.*, pp. 206–7

[36] "On the one hand, this bilateral trend in trade is the result of the French drive for imperial self-sufficiency. . . . On the other hand, it gives an instructive illustration of the close relationship between trade and investments: the bulk of Indo-Chinese international trade is with France and China, and the principal investors in the country are the French and the Chinese." Callis, *op. cit.*, p. 82.

What future could the educated Vietnamese find in colonial Indochina? During his student days, if he were one of the fortunate few who were permitted to study in France, he encountered Western democracy in action (although by the 1930's he found it under serious attack elsewhere in Europe and in France itself); but back in Indochina it was rapidly borne in upon him that he belonged to a subject race. He was a second-class citizen. Socially, he was treated as an inferior by the French; he found important jobs in the colony closed to him; and he received a much lower salary for those he did get than Frenchmen in similar positions.

A French official who visited the Philippines in 1925–26 was struck by the fact that all the services with which travelers came in contact—health, police, customs—were staffed by Filipinos. In Indochina they were all French, not only in 1925 but also in 1940.[37] They held jobs which white men in other colonies considered below them, with the result that the proportion of French officials to Indochinese was higher than that of European officials to the people of any other Southeast Asian dependent area. This "white proletariat" meant an increased tax burden on the Indochinese. It meant also that the Vietnamese had contact with a poorer and less qualified type of French official, often incompetent and ill-trained to deal with them. And it increased discontent among Vietnamese kept out of jobs in the government service which they might well have filled.

Nationalists were embittered by arbitrary police methods and the absence of personal liberties in the colony. They complained of political arrests, of brutality and torture; they saw the judicial system as a tool of the police. There was little freedom of press or assembly. The Vietnamese were not permitted to form political parties or trade unions, and could not travel among the three Vietnamese regions without permission; to go to France, they needed a police visa. The French Government, in its March 1945 declaration, listed democratic liberties as one of the reforms to be introduced into Indochina after the war.

Only a handful of Vietnamese acquired either French citizenship or French civilization; few met the qualifications for French citizenship, and most of those who were qualified did not request it.[38] The mass of the population thus had no representatives in the government either of France or of Indochina.

At the same time, the widely diffused Chinese educational system, teaching history and morality as well as language, which linked Viet Nam with its past, was abolished. Although Quoc Ngu (a romanized script developed by European missionaries for writing the Vietnamese language) achieved a limited

[37] Paul Delamarre, "La situation en Indochine," *Le Monde Français,* March 1946, p. 425.
[38] "These 'naturalizations' were never numerous. In 1937, 29, in 1938, 58. Altogether, in 1937 there were just 2,555 'naturalized Frenchmen' in the three Annamese countries; 3/5 of them were in Cochinchina." Devillers, *op. cit.,* p. 33.

currency, most of the people were not literate in their own or any other language.

Vietnamese society stagnated under the layer of Western economy and Western culture introduced by the French. Many of the old forms and traditions remained, but the center of power in Viet Nam had shifted to an alien state and an alien civilization. Under its French rulers, Viet Nam was a politically static country offering little future to its young people, and this killed initiative among them. A corroding irresponsibility afflicted all levels of Vietnamese life. Corruption and decadence were rampant. There was no Vietnamese science[38a] and little art or literature.

Most Vietnamese withdrew entirely from political life, silently if unmistakably indicating their passive resistance to foreign rule Some turned to violence and revolution. Before the first World War, it had been chiefly the scholars, who were closest to the ancient traditions of Viet Nam, who had been prepared to fight to the death against foreign domination. After the war, elements which had previously been willing to collaborate with the French felt the economic pressure of the protectorate for the first time and they too began to chafe under it. A number of the small Westernized élite participated in the economic and administrative superstructure with which the French overlaid Indochina, but many of them also became active nationalists. Beneath the apparent tranquillity of daily life, revolutionaries were organizing and planning, and in this atmosphere the Communists thrived.

COMMUNIST BEGINNINGS—HO CHI MINH

The old generation of nationalists had asked only to return to the Empire of Viet Nam, but the generation which grew up in the period between the two wars had learned its history and politics from Europe. It was by modern Western standards as well as those of nineteenth century Viet Nam that nationalists judged French rule and found it wanting.

Many of the soldiers and workers who had been sent to Europe to help in the French war effort during the first World War returned home with news of France and of Europe, of Western technological progress, of democracy and its contradictions. They had seen white men slaughtering one another. From members of the French Left-Wing, a number of them had learned for the first time of socialism, and then of Communism.

Revolutionary ideas came not only from France, but also from Russia. The Revolution of 1917 had set off a chain reaction throughout Asia, helped along by the dynamic methods by which the Russians injected anti-imperialist propaganda into Southeast Asia, and by the more than thirty Vietnamese who were

[38a] See Ng. Ph. Buu Hoi, "The Contribution of the Far East to Contemporary World Science," *Asian Horizon*, 1948.

educated in the Soviet Union and returned to Viet Nam during the 1920's. But the fundamental appeal of Communism in the Vietnamese lands, after the first World War as after the second, was that the Communist system seemed to offer racial equality to subject peoples. President Woodrow Wilson's Fourteen Points, which epitomized the ideals of the liberal West toward colonies, seemed to them to be only that—ideals worth little more than the paper on which they were written when the time came to translate them into practice. Ho Chi Minh liked to point out that liberty, equality, and fraternity, although real enough in France, apparently were not for export. A Vietnamese nationalist arrested by the French police in 1931, told them, "I love the Soviet Union because it does not want slave people."[39]

From the beginning, Communism found a following among Vietnamese only because it opposed French domination over their country.

The Indochinese Communist Party owed its existence to the efforts of one man—Ho Chi Minh.[40] Born in 1892, in the revolutionary province of Nghe An, in North Annam, he had, on the eve of the first World War, shipped out on a merchant vessel bound for the West. He visited England and went on to France. Like many revolutionaries, he was known by different names throughout his career. As Ho Chi Minh, a name he assumed late in life, he was to become President of the Democratic Republic of Viet Nam. But the name by which he was known in the 1920's was the one which appeared in the police records of half a dozen countries and in the columns of the French Left-Wing press. It was Nguyen Ai Quoc, which means Nguyen the Patriot.

Attracted by the promise of Woodrow Wilson's Fourteen Points, spokesmen of the various peoples who wanted independence followed the leaders of the victorious Allies to Paris in 1919. Along with the Indians, the Koreans, the Irish, and the Arabs, Ho Chi Minh came with a list of Vietnamese grievances and a plea for Vietnamese autonomy. He arrived at Versailles in rented evening clothes to deliver his appeal. But the statesmen assembled in Paris had no time for the problems of the subject peoples of the French Empire, and nothing came of it.

The next few years he spent in Paris, where he earned a meager living as a photographer's assistant, retouching photographs; but his consuming interest was politics, and he spent much of his time writing articles and attending political meetings. He came to know Socialist leaders like Léon Blum and Marcel Cachin, who was to become one of the chiefs of the French Communist Party; the Socialist newspaper *Le Populaire* published some of his articles.

[39] Viollis, *op. cit.*, p. 8.

[40] Ho Chi Minh himself has not publicly admitted to being the same man who founded the Indochinese Communist Party under the name of Nguyen Ai Quoc. Although they are generally believed to be one and the same person, there are still those who insist that Nguyen Ai Quoc died years ago and that Ho Chi Minh simply exploited his reputation.

Slowly the character of the man who was to be one of the leaders of revolutionary Southeast Asia was forged. Little is known about his years abroad. He spent much time in jail, but where and when? Ho himself deliberately kept the story vague, telling questioners only, "Time in prison is long," and "Prisons are much alike." It is possible only to list the various events in his career, although even such a listing cannot be complete.

He became a member of the French Socialist Party just at the time the party was divided over whether it should remain with the Second International or join the Third. When in May 1920 the Socialists met in congress at Tours to decide on a course of action, Ho Chi Minh was there; he voted with the majority to break with the Socialists and found the French Communist Party. In 1921, at the first congress of the Communist Party, held in Marseille, he stood up to ask for greater consideration of colonial questions. The following year, he and a delegate from North Africa complained that the party was neglecting the colonies. He wrote a small book in Paris called *French Colonization on Trial,* an attack on French colonial policy, which, smuggled into Indochina, became the bible of nationalists. It was studied secretly and discussed with heat among young students, and the name of Nguyen Ai Quoc became a rallying cry among them.

In Paris he came to know people from French North Africa and French Madagascar, with whom he set up an Intercolonial Union which issued propaganda aimed at the freedom of colonial peoples, and held meetings to which came Frenchmen as well as people from the colonies. In 1925 the Comintern chose from its ranks the first Vietnamese to be trained in revolution at the Stalin School in Moscow.

Ho Chi Minh became the guiding spirit behind a newspaper, *Le Paria,* which spearheaded the Intercolonial Union's attack on imperialism. A number of Vietnamese nationalists wrote in its columns under his name, signing their articles Nguyen the Patriot, Nguyen Ai Quoc. When the authorities refused to permit *Le Paria* into the colonies, and made its possession a criminal offense, nationalists smuggled it in, relying in part on sympathizers in the crews of ships that dropped anchor in Indochinese ports.

Ho Chi Minh stayed on in France until 1923, when the French Communist Party chose him as its delegate to the Congress of the Peasant International (the Krestintern) which met in Moscow that October. He made his first trip to the Soviet Union then, but what he did there and how deep was its influence upon his later life is cloaked in obscurity. It is known only that he did not leave the Soviet Union after the meeting, but remained there for more than a year, studying Communism, its techniques, and its organization, firsthand. He came to know many of Communism's great and near-great during this period, as before he had come to know the leaders of the Left-Wing movement in Paris.

China was next on his itinerary. Vietnamese nationalism was part of an Asia-wide movement. "With India afire and China afire," wrote Louis Roubaud, a French journalist, Indochina "cannot remain a block of ice between two conflagrations."[41] There were interchanges between nationalists in India and Indochina. Between Indochina and China there was constant intercourse; Canton was the Mecca of the Vietnamese nationalist movement. Young intellectuals arrived from Tonkin, Annam, and Cochin China, many to become students at the Military Institute at Whampoa. In Republican China during the 1920's they learned not only the techniques of modern war, but also Western arts and science and the revolutionary three-point doctrine of Sun Yat-sen. To Canton also came young men and women from the Vietnamese provinces to honor the tomb of Pham Hong Thai, a Tonkinese student who had killed five Frenchmen in 1924 while trying to assassinate Governor General Merlin.

Ho Chi Minh arrived at the Soviet consulate in Canton in 1925, during the period of Soviet-Chinese friendship; the Chinese Communists were allied with moderates and Rightists within the Kuomintang and the Russian, Borodin, was advising the government. Ho Chi Minh was supposed to be a Chinese translator at the consulate but his major job, as always, was politics. All that he had done and learned before, in France and in Russia, was preparation for this moment. He was back in the Far East, skilled now in the methods of revolution as he had not been when he left his homeland, and Indochina was just across the border.

He studied the work of Sun Yat-sen and it has been said that he regarded Sun's Three Principles as adaptable to Viet Nam—nationalism which was independence, democracy, and livelihood or well-being for the people.[42] Indochina was not yet ready for Communism, he decided. He explained in 1927 that a Communist Party could not be created in Indochina "because no one yet understood the meaning of the word Communism.—However, it has been possible to constitute an Annamese national-socialist revolutionary party whose leaders have been charged with gradually leading all the members to Marxist orthodoxy."[43]

His idea in 1925 was to bring the revolution to Indochina in two stages; Viet Nam would have to win independence under a bourgeois democratic regime before the proletarian revolution could come. The first step was to create a revolutionary cell. It took him some six months to pick out several of the Vietnamese living in Canton, indoctrinate them, and form with them an Association of Vietnamese Revolutionary Youth. He also tried to establish a

[41] Louis Roubaud, *Viet Nam,* p. 26.
[42] These statements of Ho Chi Minh's attitude are derived from *Biographie du Président Ho Chi Minh,* issued by the Viet Minh Information Service.
[43] Gouvernement Général de l'Indochine. Direction des Affaires Politiques et de la Sûreté Générale. *Contribution à l'histoire des mouvements politiques de l'Indochine française.* Vol. IV. *Le Dong-Duong Cong-San Dang (Parti communiste Indochinois) 1925–33,* p. 15.

League for Oppressed Peoples in Canton, along the lines of his Intercolonial Union in Paris. This League did not last very long, but the Revolutionary Youth Association thrived and Ho Chi Minh began editing a newspaper which he called *Youth*.

The first of the Vietnamese he had trained in Canton secretly made their way back to Indochina before the end of 1925. Ho Chi Minh's agents received them at the frontiers and the ports, and kept in touch with them while helping new recruits to slip off into China. The reins of power remained abroad, in the hands of the central committee at Canton, which saw to the printing of the party newspaper, to propaganda, and to the training of the emigrés. Inside Indochina the returning people had their own job to do, setting up revolutionary cells.

THE FRUSTRATION OF THE MODERATES

There was an upsurge of nationalist activity in Indochina during the 1920's. Albert Sarraut, a liberal Radical Socialist, brought important reforms to the country when he became Governor General in 1911, and promised more; but Sarraut left Indochina soon after the World War, and Vietnamese waited impatiently for reforms that did not come, for democratic liberties and self-government. Some were willing to fight for independence; others talked of more limited reforms achieved in collaboration with the French.

Cochin China, as a French colony, allowed wider latitude to Vietnamese political activity than the protectorates of Tonkin and Annam. There was greater freedom of the press in Cochin China and there was also a Colonial Council of twenty-four members, ten elected by Vietnamese under a system of restricted suffrage, ten by Frenchmen, and two each by the chambers of commerce and agriculture. In 1923 a Constitutionalist Party was organized in Saigon. Directed by Bui Quang Chieu and Nguyen Phan Long, it was made up of officials, intellectuals, and wealthy landowners. It was the first legal political organization to be formed by Vietnamese in French Indochina.

When a Socialist Governor General, Alexandre Varenne, arrived in the country in 1925, moderate reform groups were active among the Vietnamese, and the outlook for change and reform seemed good. In Annam, Pham Quynh, the Tonkinese intellectual and mandarin, urged the formation of another party which could function legally and co-operate with the French. He was never again to be as popular as he was then; some twenty years later he met death at the hands of his own people in the early days of the Viet Nam Republic. But in 1926, Pham Quynh's scheme for a Viet Nam People's Progressive Party, to which Vietnamese could belong openly and without fear, attracted a number of moderate nationalists. The old revolutionary, Phan Boi Chau, who had been arrested and condemned to death, then freed, declared himself in favor of collaboration with the French.

However, the Governor General refused to recognize the new party as a legal organization and the movement collapsed. Only the revolutionary nationalist movement profited from its failure. Some members of the Constitutionalist Party, finding their attempts at reform blocked by the French administration, joined the underground nationalist movement in the 1920's, as did many of the Vietnamese who had been prepared to work with Pham Quynh's Progressive Party. The old Phuc Quoc of Cuong De and Phan Boi Chau was revived in Annam.

In this same period a number of members of the Constitutionalist Party turned to the Cao Dai religious movement, which was launched in 1926 and rapidly took on political significance. By 1930 it had over a million members organized in various sections. Its leaders were critical of French rule and strongly nationalistic; and from 1934 they were in secret relations with the Japanese. Many of them supported Prince Cuong De as pretender to the throne of an independent Viet Nam.

Regrettably for the future of both the French and the Vietnamese, the structure of the French administration in Indochina offered no channels through which popular discontent could be translated into constructive political activity. Political parties, under strict control in Cochin China, were not permitted to exist at all in Tonkin and Annam; and Vietnamese appointed to government posts were not expected to have any popular following or to make radical innovations or demands. By declaring political opposition illegal and subject to police reprisals, the administration left nationalists who desired action no alternative but to operate clandestinely, as revolutionaries. They formed a series of movements aimed at freeing Viet Nam from the French which, by and large, looked for support abroad. These were not political parties in the Western sense of the word, because their program was practically confined to the liberation of the country. The only party with Western mechanics of action to develop in Viet Nam was the Communist Party. It developed out of the Revolutionary Youth Association founded by Ho Chi Minh in Canton.

THE INDOCHINESE COMMUNIST PARTY

In 1927, when Chiang Kai-shek turned abruptly against the Communists in his Kuomintang coalition and led the Right-Wing in an attack upon them, Borodin, the Russian Communist, no longer found it safe in China and left for home; Ho Chi Minh had to flee Canton, too. He took refuge in Hankow and later went back to Moscow.

Although the Chinese welcomed any movement which threatened their French neighbors across the frontier, they arrested several members of the directing committee of the Revolutionary Youth Association which Ho had left behind. These men were soon released, but the committee did not feel secure in Canton. They decided to move their headquarters, locating them finally in Hongkong.

At least 250 Vietnamese had their revolutionary education in China under the auspices of the Revolutionary Youth Association and some 200 had returned to Indochina by the time the party held its first and only congress in 1929 (according to the estimate of the French police, who put the total number of party members and sympathizers at 1,000). The Revolutionary Youth Association had a committee in each of the three Vietnamese countries, although it was supported by a number of cells only in Tonkin. Most of its Tonkinese members were from the working class. They were more mixed in Annam and Cochin China, including workers, teachers, students, and peasants. Young men who had learned their work at Canton held the key positions.

The plan of the party was to organize a hierarchy of committees pyramiding upward from village sections through sections representing larger administrative units up to a central directing committee. This hierarchical structure, with authority concentrated at the top like that of the Chinese Kuomintang, resembled that which the Soviets had set up in Russia. After the second World War they brought it to the northern part of Korea. By that time Ho Chi Minh had become President of the Democratic Republic of Viet Nam, and had begun to organize the government of Tonkin, Annam, and Cochin China in much the same way as the Revolutionary Youth Association had envisaged it years before.

"We want to hand over factories to the workers, ricefields to the peasants, the sources of revenue to the people, and power to assemblies of representatives of all the working classes of the nation." So ran a manifesto issued by the party at its Hongkong congress in 1929.[44] It called for a dictatorship of the proletariat and direct elections by the country's workers, peasants, and soldiers. They planned to take over ricefields and landholdings of more than 200 hectares and distribute them among the peasants. Alluvial land and abandoned ricefields were also to be divided among the peasants. Arable land was to be nationalized and its sale forbidden.

The Hongkong congress of the Revolutionary Youth Association appealed to workers, peasants, soldiers, merchants, young people, and "all oppressed Vietnamese" to unite against French imperialism, against the mandarins and the capitalists. They envisaged a large-scale program of nationalization. And alongside this went calls for social reforms. It was an ambitious and a comprehensive program, ranging from co-operation with all social revolutions and recognition of the rights of all people—Cambodians, Laotians, and the ethnic minorities in the Vietnamese lands—to self-government and suppression of the court of Hué.

[44] Quoted in Gouvernement Général de l'Indochine, Direction des Affaires Politiques et de la Sûreté Générale, Vol. IV, op. cit., p. 54.

Of the seventeen delegates who came to the Hongkong congress, four represented the central committee in China and two came from Siam; the others came directly from Tonkin, Annam, and Cochin China. The congress had hardly opened when three delegates just arrived from Indochina proposed changing the name of the party to the Indochinese Communist Party. The central committee, supported by the majority of the delegates, refused, for this ran counter to Ho Chi Minh's original scheme to set up a revolutionary nationalist party with socialist tendencies. The three dissidents walked out of the congress. They went back to Indochina and established their own Indochinese Communist Party, shocking the central committee of the Revolutionary Youth Association into the awareness that it had lost much of its authority over party members inside the country. Fearful of losing more, they set up their own Vietnamese Communist Party. It did not do very well. The Association lost influence in Tonkin and Annam, and in Cochin China it competed with the Indochinese Communist Party and had to give way to it.

It failed also in an attempt to gain recognition from the Third International. When the Revolutionary Youth Association had asked for recognition, the Comintern had replied with a searching critique of the party's statutes and rules. It accused the leaders of being too petit-bourgeois. The whole idea of acquiring power by steps it attacked as reformism, not Communism. Calling for a union of the different Indochinese revolutionary groups, it criticized them for the small proportion of workers and peasants among their members. The creation of the Vietnamese Communist Party did not mollify the Comintern; it would not support any movement which was divided against itself.

The Vietnamese countries had three Communist parties in 1929, for an offshoot of the Phuc Quoc—in a last minute and, as it turned out, hopeless bid for survival against competition from the Revolutionary Youth Association and against pressure from the French police—had created its own small Communist Party. In Cochin China, a small group of radicals had been not unsuccessful in the rural regions; when their leader, Nguyen An Ninh, was arrested, most of his followers joined one or another of the Communist parties.

The central committee of the Revolutionary Youth Association watched these developments helplessly from Hongkong; the revolutionary movement was disintegrating into splinter groups and there was nothing they could do about it. But then the committee learned that the elusive Ho Chi Minh was not far away. He was in Siam, working secretly to organize the 30,000 Vietnamese living there into a nationalist association.

The Hongkong committee sent an urgent message to Siam, asking Ho Chi Minh to save the party before it was too late.

It took him until January 1930 to arrive in Hongkong, where he talked with delegates from the different Communist parties and persuaded them to join forces in what they called the Viet Nam Communist Party. In October 1930, at a Communist congress in Hongkong, they changed their name to the Indo-chinese Communist Party, to substantiate their claim to embrace the entire Indochinese Union and so qualify as a national section of the Third International. The foundations were also laid for a network of organizations affiliated with the Communists—associations of women, peasants, and workers, an anti-imperialist league, and a branch of the international Red Aid Organization.

A number of intellectuals and officials became Communists because they saw in that party an instrument for action against the French. If they behaved like fanatics, remarked one Frenchman, it was not so much because of their new political faith as because of their nationalism. The man who made this observation was a member of the French police, one of whose major tasks was tracking down Vietnamese Communists.[45]

The Communists succeeded in extending the roots of the party into the peasantry; the Indochinese Communist Party was said to be some fifteen hundred strong in 1931, and to have a hundred thousand peasants affiliated with it through peasant organizations controlled by the party. It had links with the Comintern Far Eastern Bureau at Shanghai, with Communist movements in Siam, Indonesia, and Malaya which Ho Chi Minh directed in 1930 and 1931 as chief of the Southern Bureau of the Comintern, and with the French Communist Party. In April 1931 the Indochinese Communist Party was welcomed officially into the Comintern.

The headquarters of the central committee were transferred from Hongkong back to Indochina, first to Haiphong and then to Saigon. Although party members abroad were used to transmit instructions and link the Indochinese Communists with the outside world, Ho Chi Minh was the only Vietnamese to wield authority over the party from outside the country. He was its liaison with the different Comintern bodies. This was excellent for security but dangerous, for a great deal depended on one man.

THE VNQDD

While leaders of the Revolutionary Youth Association were still in Hongkong, new violence was brewing in Tonkin. The *Viet Nam Quoc Dan Dang* (VNQDD), the Viet Nam Nationalist Party, had been founded in 1927 by young men who ran a publishing company in Hanoi specializing in political books. It was headed by a former teacher, like them under thirty, named Nguyen Thai Hoc.

The VNQDD was the most important non-Communist revolutionary nationalist organization in Indochina in the period between the two wars. It had links with the Chinese Kuomintang, on which it modeled itself, and it looked to the Chinese for aid in expelling the French.

[45] *Ibid.*, p. 6.

The VNQDD was supported by several wealthy Tonkinese and its gospel of force drew recruits to it. It had some fifteen hundred members by the beginning of 1929. The French police learned of its existence for the first time that year when some of its members, after failing in an attempt to kill Governor General Pasquier, murdered a Frenchman named Bazin who was in charge of recruiting workers for the plantations of Cochin China and New Caledonia. The VNQDD included teachers, students, and soldiers. At least half of its members, the French discovered, were on the payroll of the French administration.

The French police replied to the attack on Bazin with a series of arrests in which a number of local sections of the VNQDD were destroyed and its leadership seriously weakened. Nguyen Thai Hoc, however, remained at large. The VNQDD tried to eliminate the traitors in its midst; it marked the bodies of its victims with the indictment, "for not having kept the blood oath." But it had been careless in admitting members and some informers remained undetected. The police uncovered some VNQDD arsenals and they were on the trail of a number of members.

Desperate but not despairing, the VNQDD decided not to go underground, but to risk everything on one grand uprising. Some members favored holding off until they could be more certain of success, but Nguyen Thai Hoc persuaded the majority to gamble on the dissatisfaction among the masses of the people. The party infiltrated among the soldiers in the Vietnamese garrison at Yen Bay, which was on the Chinese frontier and controlled the Red River valley. On the night of February 9-10, 1930, the soldiers rose against the French officers, massacring them and taking over the post. Bombs were thrown in Hanoi and there were disturbances in other cities. But the mutiny at Yen Bay was short-lived. It was supposed to be just one of a series of similar uprisings, but it proved to be virtually the only one, for the police got wind of their plans.

In the bloody days of 1930, the VNQDD reaped the fruit of its failure. French troops ranged through the countryside, bombing, shooting, and arresting. Nguyen Thai Hoc and a number of his companions were captured.

Hoc spent his last days in prison writing a letter in which he took full responsibility for the uprising and said that his party had aimed at expelling the French and setting up a democratic republic. He wrote in this last testament that if the French wanted to occupy Indochina peacefully and without revolution, they would have to call a halt to all brutal and inhumane methods, to behave not as cruel masters of the people but as friends. They would have to respect such rights of the individual as liberty of travel, education, association, and press. They would have to end the corruption in official places, educate the people, and develop trade and native industries.[46]

46 Roubaud, *op. cit.*, pp. 147-8.

With twelve of his comrades, Nguyen Thai Hoc died on the guillotine at Yen Bay in June 1930, crying "Viet Nam!"

The VNQDD was finished, for the time, as an effective force in Vietnamese affairs; a number of the survivors joined émigrés who had been active in China, in Canton, and in Yunnan, under the influence of Phan Boi Chau and Prince Cuong De and the Phuc Quoc. In Canton, the VNQDD had been organized as far back as 1925, in opposition to the Communist tendencies of Ho Chi Minh's Revolutionary Youth Association. With Chinese aid it had tried, like Ho Chi Minh, to establish a League of Oppressed Oriental Peoples and, like Ho's League, the attempt had failed. The Kuomintang paid a regular subsidy to the VNQDD of Canton, which went so far as to set up a "Provisional Indochinese Government" at Canton in 1932, a move frowned on by the Chinese Government, which was not prepared to endanger its diplomatic relations with France.

The VNQDD of Yunnan was actually a section of the Chinese Kuomintang which protected VNQDD members for some time against the Chinese Government while they illegally raised funds by robbery and extortion in Yunnan and Tonkin. Their marauding became so serious that the Chinese Government finally clamped down on that branch of their activities, but the VNQDD continued active. Its members were trained in the Yunnan Military School; some were enrolled in the Chinese army; others learned to make weapons and explosives in the Yunnan arsenal.

During the late 1930's some members of the VNQDD launched a modernist literary movement in Indochina. In China, where the VNQDD did not give up the practice of looting border settlements, the Yunnan and Canton groups had joined forces in 1933, and ambitious Vietnamese intrigued for control of the émigré organization. They waited in China until the second World War offered them an unexpected opportunity to recoup the fortunes of the VNQDD.

1930-31: THE YEARS OF TERROR

The year 1930 ended in Indochina, as it had begun, in terror. It was a year of famine in many parts of the country. In some regions, starving villagers turned, in their need, to French administrators. They marched along the roads in processions, without arms, seeking help in their misery. They were dispersed by force.

The town of Vinh in the province of Nghe An, the birthplace of many patriots, suffered terribly. It had been afflicted by drought, flood, typhoons, and locusts. It had three bad harvests, one after the other. All the same, the French levied 525,000 piastres worth of taxes on Vinh; the starving people managed to pay all but 15,000.[47]

[47] Viollis, *op. cit.*, p. 62.

Louis Roubaud wrote in 1931:

Many Frenchmen of Indochina shrug their shoulders and repeat: 'All this agitation is due to a handful of discontented intellectuals: the peasant doesn't care.'

But I note that four companies of soldiers revolt at Yen Bay; that a thousand peasants march in arms on the citadel of Thanh Hoa and two thousand without arms on the factories of Ben Thuy....

The revolutionary movement of Annam [Viet Nam] has a head and a body![48]

The new Indochinese Communist Party brought leadership to this popular unrest. Scarcely had the VNQDD rising been frustrated, than the Communists, on May Day, launched an offensive of their own. They led the peasantry in a series of mass demonstrations. They organized illegal labor unions; strikes broke out among the workers. The police intervened and there was fighting in which hundreds were killed.

In the way of peasant revolts everywhere, in Asia or in the West, in twelfth-century England, eighteenth-century France, or twentieth-century Indochina, the peasants attacked the most visible symbols of control, destroying village archives and tax rolls, hoping thus to regain the free use of their land. "The troubles which occurred in Indochina between May 1930 and June 1931 . . . would seem to indicate the existence of a real social class all suffering from the same abuses and making a collective demand for improvements. There was a definite peasants' revolt—a real *jacquerie*."[49] The Communists managed to set up their own "soviets" in two provinces of Annam, Ha Tinh and Nghe An. They attacked unpopular landlords and tried to break up large estates, but they were quickly repressed. There was great damage and brutality; and French retribution was swift and cruel.

If to many Frenchmen 1930 was the year of the Red Terror, nationalists and Communists knew 1931 as the White Terror. The French threw all the machinery of their police and administration into action against the rebels. Suspects were dragged before criminal commissions and condemned en masse, often without real trials or evidence. The Communist Party suffered greatly. In vain did the Comintern warn against isolated acts of terrorism which did not have mass support and led to wholesale arrests, threatening the foundations of the party. In vain also did it urge upon party members the need for secrecy. It ranged from injunctions urging the use of aliases at all times and keeping the addresses of comrades secret from each other, to such outspoken indignation as this: "We have just learned of a Communist meeting that lasted fifteen days. For the love of God! We have never heard of such a thing! How could you, faced with the White Terror, expose our best comrades to

[48] Roubaud, *op. cit.*, pp. 126-7.
[49] Goudal, *op. cit.*, p. 187.

danger during a two week period and just so that they could attend a meeting?"[50]

The French police did not find the task of suppression as simple as they might have wished. It was one thing to put down demonstrations, quite another to track down their leaders, particularly when many officials were helping the rebels to cover their tracks and Communist cells just across the Chinese frontier were offering them refuge. But still the police and the army, replying to Vietnamese violence with violence of their own, bringing into play the weapons of the West against the rebels, were brutally effective. The Foreign Legion terrorized north and central Annam. The prisons were filled and thousands were killed. The year 1931 was a time of terror in which perished not only many Communists, but nationalists and liberals, and many others, innocent victims of French action.

The French extended their network of control even outside the borders of Indochina. In Hongkong, the British arrested Ho Chi Minh in 1931; two other key Comintern officials in Asia were also arrested. The Far Eastern Bureau of the Comintern was temporarily thrown out of commission and the Indochinese Communist Party was isolated. Although Ho Chi Minh was soon released, he disappeared from the political limelight, and after a while the word came that he was dead.

REFORMERS WITHOUT REFORMS

The repression which opened the 1930's dealt the revolutionary movement heavy body blows and many of the Communist cells in the Vietnamese lands were extirpated. Tonkin and Annam quieted down after that.

A number of Vietnamese still thought they could achieve moderate nationalist goals by peaceful means. In 1933, the year after the young Emperor Bao Dai returned to Viet Nam following his education in France, he appointed as his chief minister Ngo Dinh Diem, then a young mandarin of thirty-two, already widely respected for his honesty and ability. But Diem soon found himself at odds with French officials who chose this time to restrict still further the functions of the nominally autonomous Vietnamese government. They had already abolished the post of Prime Minister, leaving the Minister of the Interior the most important member of the Cabinet, and they assigned the Prime Minister's functions to the French Resident, who was authorized to preside over and participate in Cabinet meetings. When Diem proposed reform measures, notably the establishment of a deliberative assembly, the French administration refused to discuss the matter. At the same

[50] Letter from the Far Eastern Bureau to Nguyen Ai Quoc [Ho Chi Minh], head of the Bureau of the South at Hongkong, May 12, 1931. Quoted in Gouvernement Générale de l'Indochine, Vol. IV, op. cit., p. 108.

time, it took measures which had the effect of further separating Tonkin from Annam. Finding his protest hopeless, Diem resigned rather than accept subservience to France.

Pham Quynh became more influential in the Vietnamese Government after the resignation of Ngo Dinh Diem. Although he was much more conciliatory toward the French, even Pham Quynh hoped for a liberal grant of autonomy for the Vietnamese, perhaps Dominion status, as in the British Empire To Paul Reynaud, the French Colonial Minister, who was visiting Indochina to investigate the recent troubles, he said "We are a people who are looking for a country and have not yet found it. . . . For us, Mr. Minister, that country cannot be France."[51]

Andrée Viollis, the French newspaperwoman who accompanied Reynaud on this trip, reported an interview with a moderate nationalist who belonged to the Colonial Council of Cochin China and the Grand Council of Economic and Financial Interests. Her use of initials does not hide the fact that she was talking with Nguyen Phan Long, the journalist who in 1950 became Bao Dai's first Prime Minister in the state of Viet Nam. "All that our efforts bring us," he told her, "[is] the distrust of the nationalists, who reproach us for our lack of courage, and that of the Governor General who believes that we are betraying him."[52]

"I hoped to collaborate with the French," another journalist, Huynh Thuc Khang, told Andrée Viollis, explaining why he resigned from the native council in Annam. "But every time I began to speak and expressed a wish, the Résident Supérieur complained that I was sabotaging French sovereignty . . . I preferred to devote myself entirely to my paper."

Men like Huynh Thuc Khang made no great demands:

I recognize that we are not yet mature enough to direct ourselves. We only ask of the French a loyal, if limited, collaboration, that they keep seven-tenths of the power, but leave us three-tenths; that they accord us the elementary liberties which French citizens and certain natives of their colonies enjoy so completely: liberty of movement, freedom of speech, freedom of the press. . . .

When Huynh Thuc Khang talked with Madame Viollis in 1931, he discounted the influence of Communism among his people.

The Vietnamese masses are totally ignorant of the doctrines of Lenin. Several young people who have lived abroad have imported them, but the people hardly understand them and have adopted them like any theory which would promise them help in their terrible misfortunes. . . . We must remedy these misfortunes. It is still necessary to exercise a severe control over Vietnamese officials, to

51 Viollis, *op. cit.*, p. 62.
52 *Ibid.*, p. 90.

purge the mandarinate, to punish severely those who have betrayed their trust, those who oppress and cynically trample on the poor peasants of the villages. . . .

He was silent for a moment, and then he said:

It is high time to repair these political errors, yes, high time. The same causes, by perpetuating themselves, will bring the same effects, and the time will come when repression will be futile.[53]

Huynh Thuc Khang concentrated on his newspaper in the following years, as he said he would. But this did not prevent him from antagonizing the French authorities and he spent a number of years in the penal colony at Poulo Condore. After the second World War, he became Minister of the Interior in the government of Ho Chi Minh. When he died in 1947, at the age of seventy-two, Huynh Thuc Khang was one of the national heroes in the new Democratic Republic of Viet Nam.

In the course of her trip through Indochina in 1931, Andrée Viollis saw one man whose great years were already past. She talked at length with Phan Boi Chau. He told her:

I do not know the French people, but only French books, French ideas; and I have not found these principles in the hearts of Frenchmen of Indochina. They do not treat us as brothers, as equals, as it is written in your Declaration of the Rights of Man that you have taught us to admire; they treat us as slaves and sometimes as dogs. . . .

I cannot deny it, I keenly desire the independence of my country; it is for that that I have fought twenty years, that I have been exiled in China, in Japan, that I have suffered, risked death; but since my return I have noted, like others, that we have not arrived at the stage of independence. We are a gentle and peaceful people: if we were administered according to principles of justice and humanity, if they had offered us a frank and loyal collaboration, we would have forgotten the word independence and the tricolor flag would be our flag. . . .

Tell the French people that the old revolutionary Phan Boi Chau sincerely desires a loyal collaboration with France. But have them hurry or it will be too late! Too late![54]

This plea went unanswered. Little attempt was made to remedy any of the conditions which led to misery and discontent among the people. Paul Reynaud declared that Dominion status was out of the question, that it would be dangerous to give so much liberty to a population which had no middle class but only an immense mass of unlettered peasants behind a thin layer of intellectuals. Reynaud's reluctance to initiate any bold reforms was shared by influential Frenchmen. Public opinion in France was uninterested in the colonies and as a rule left imperial affairs to the small group of men

[53] Ibid., pp. 90–92.
[54] Ibid., pp. 95–98.

who were associated with business and financial interests in the empire and with the colonial administration.

Even when reforms were proposed in France, they were rarely implemented in Indochina, for Frenchmen in the colonies tended usually to be highly conservative, cut off from the free interplay of party politics at home, a minority bent upon maintaining its domination over an alien majority. The French Socialists and Communists, as well as a minority in the Radical Socialist Party, took a stand in favor of colonial reform, but few of their plans and promises were translated into action.

Roland Dorgelès wrote in 1925:

If our statesmen, our governors, giving way to pressure from the people who are profiting from the colony, apply a policy of force in Indochina, if they refuse to give more extended rights to the native, if they do nothing to increase his well-being and consider him much longer as a tool living solely to enrich them, then, before thirty years are past, France will lose its most beautiful empire.[55]

REVOLUTIONARIES IN THE SOUTH

The new center of political activity among Vietnamese revolutionaries during the 1930's was in the south. In the city of Saigon, capital of the French colony of Cochin China, where the people were closest to the interplay of French politics and where the French-language press, at least, had a certain freedom, the Communists were still active. Tran Van Giau, who had studied at the Stalin School in Moscow, arrived to inject a new vigor into the party.

Another group of Communists, who looked to Leon Trotsky and the Fourth International for leadership, was organized in Cochin China in 1932 by Ta Thu Thau, who had been a student in France. Like other groups, they had to reorganize after the 1932 repressions, but early in 1933 some Trotskyites worked out an arrangement with Giau and the Stalinists to set up a joint legal political movement.

This marked the beginning of a schism in the Trotskyite ranks; small though the movement was, it was divided within itself almost from the start. The International Communist League, which was bitterly opposed to collaborating with the Stalinists, was known as the "October" group, after their illegal publication, and was centered in Hanoi. Other Trotskyites, not unwilling to experiment with a common front, were mostly in Saigon, where they joined the Stalinists in publishing a newspaper called *The Struggle* (*La Lutte*).

The new "Struggle" coalition elected two of its candidates, a Stalinist and a Trotskyite, to the Saigon municipal council in 1932. *The Struggle* hailed

[55] Dorgelès, *op. cit.*, p. 207.

their election as demonstrating the wish of the Saigon workers "to affirm their will to fight for life in the class struggle against exploitation of the laboring masses. The small merchants, the lesser officials, in voting for the workers' list wanted to mark their will to unite their forces with those of the proletariat to defend themselves against the yellow and white sharks of industry and finance."[56]

Elsewhere in Indochina the Communist Party revived slowly. It followed a more cautious policy now, discouraging violence on the grounds that it could only lead to terror and to new repression. In Tonkin, the first cells to be reformed were along the Chinese frontier, closest to the party's centers of strength across the border. A number of political prisoners were free by 1933, having either served their time or been pardoned. Most of the people arrested in the 1930 troubles were out of jail, more revolutionary-minded than ever after the intensive propaganda which had been secretly passed around inside their prisons. The world depression, which had already begun to cause unemployment in Indochina, helped to make the soil fertile for Communism.

The fact that its links with the Comintern were in abeyance in this period did not hurt the Communist Party. It was saved from the difficulties which afflicted the Indonesian Communists, for example, who found by bitter experience that the directives laid down in Moscow did not always suit the Asian scene.[57] Thrown on their own, the Vietnamese Communists worked out their policy and their program in terms of the actual situation in Indochina. They re-established the League Against Imperialism as an organization of labor unions, peasant organizations, and nationalist parties; within this coalition the Communist Party maintained its independent line. Its membership rolls grew, its influence over the peasantry increased, and a network of Communist cells again began to cover the Vietnamese lands.

Even in the early 1930's the Communists kept up their outside contacts, through Vietnamese sailors whose ships stopped in at the ports of Shanghai, Nanking, and Hongkong, and through Chinese Communists in Siam. Remnants of the party appeared at a meeting in Laos in 1933. Then, in 1935, the party sent delegates to a conference in Portuguese Macao, where it formally reaffirmed its adherence to the Comintern. It tightened the organization of the party, and the central committee, which had been transferred to Siam, returned to Saigon-Cholon.

The Macao conference was a turning point in the history of the Indochinese Communist Party. The order came from Moscow, as laid down at the Sev-

---

[56] Quoted in Anh-Van and Jacqueline Roussel, *Mouvements Nationaux et Lutte de Classes au Vietnam*, p. 55.

[57] See in this connection, J. T. P. Blumberger, *Le Communisme aux Indes Néerlandaises* (Paris, 1929), and Virginia Thompson and Richard Adloff, *Leftwing Movements in Southeast Asia.*

enth World Congress of the Communist International, for all Communist parties to join forces with non-Communists in the war against fascism. This required a *volte-face* in the policies of European Communists and in Asia it called for political gymnastics of a high order. It meant that the Communists had to lay aside their opposition to their European rulers and campaign for democratic rights so that they could work together with the colonialists against the Axis threat from abroad.

In France the year 1936 was the beginning of the Popular Front interlude when the Communists joined parties of the Left and Center in an antifascist coalition. The new government announced a policy of reform for the colonies and the Socialist Colonial Minister Marius Moutet was encouraging:

The black peasants of millet and ground nuts and the yellow cultivators of rice and hevea [rubber] are akin to our workingmen and to the men who cultivate French soil. We place them all on a plane of moral equality, social justice and human brotherhood. . . . We, without sectarianism or partisan attitude, deny none of our republican or socialist convictions, and after thirty years of political and social action in favor of the working masses, especially colonial, will take our role of civilizer and emancipator seriously.[58]

The new government replaced the repressive, unpopular Governor General René Robin and declared an amnesty for political prisoners. Encouraged by this, and in the hope of further concessions, nationalists staged strikes in the colony. The French set up a Commission of Inquiry to recommend improvements in their colonial system and in Indochina the Communists joined with moderate and conservative parties in a legal front movement, the "Indochinese Congress," to draw up a bill of grievances to present to the Commission. They also set up "action committees" of labor and peasant unions and fraternal organizations. When the Commission of Inquiry, headed by Justin Godart, arrived in Indochina, it was greeted by demonstrations and strikes. [59]

But the French Leftists in power were no longer the anti-imperialists they had professed to be while members of the opposition. They were up against a growing desire among Frenchmen to make greater use of their colonies, a desire which had been heightened by the restrictions on international trade caused by the depression. From the colonies the French Leftist parties received word that their members there feared what the natives might do to them if France gave up its colonies. And who, actually, could be sure that the colo-

[58] As quoted in Jean-Yves Le Branchu, "The French Colonial Empire and the Popular Front Government," *Pacific Affairs*, June 1937, pp. 129–30.

[59] In the latter months of 1936 "a certain want of unity became evident in the ranks of the Indochinese working classes. It seems that the committees originally appointed to draw up the 'lists of demands' had been undermined by Communist influences and as a result the more moderate elements rebelled. Personal and party squabbles, and the fact that the social movement was contaminated by politics, led to a real cleavage, and finally three Communist leaders were arrested." Goudal, *op. cit.*, p. 131.

nies would remain independent if France were to leave them? In Indochina, for example, Japan might be only too willing to take over.

All these considerations added up to a colonial policy very little different from that of other French governments. The Vietnamese gained certain limited advantages in regard to labor legislation. But they had asked particularly for the legal rights of freedom of assembly and of the organization of trade unions, and they received neither. In September 1936 Moutet telegraphed to officials in Saigon: "You will maintain public order by all legitimate and legal means, even by the prosecution of those who attempt to make trouble, if this should prove necessary. . . . The improvement of the political and economic situation is our preoccupation but . . . French order must reign in Indochina as elsewhere."[60] This abortive experiment in colonial liberalism by a Popular Front government was the harbinger of another experiment by a second Popular Front government that was to result in similar though more violent failure a decade later.

The "action committees" meanwhile led strikes to improve working conditions, raise wages, and permit the establishment of a legal trade union movement. Stalinists and Trotskyites were both active in these committees. The "Struggle" coalition held together long enough to elect three members to the Saigon municipal council in 1937—Thau, the Trotskyite, and two Stalinists, Nguyen Van Tao, who was re-elected, and Duong Bach Mai. After that the coalition fell apart. The Trotskyites refused to join the Popular Front and accused the Indochinese Communist Party of betraying the Indochinese in the interests of the French Communist Party and the Soviet Government. On July 14, 1937, the Trotskyites and the Stalinists met together for the last time.

The Trotskyites succeeded in taking over *The Struggle* in 1937, and Ta Thu Thau launched the new line with an article on "The Popular Front of Treason," which brought him two years in jail. In 1939 the Trotskyites won a resounding victory in the elections to the Cochin Chinese Colonial Council, with 80 percent of the votes going to their candidates. After this the Stalinists split; Duong Bach Mai remained head of the official party while Nguyen Van Tao led a group of dissidents.

When the Popular Front fell in France in 1938, its Indochinese counterpart, the Democratic Front, went underground. The Paris government outlawed the Communist Party in September 1939 and the party was also outlawed in Indochina; Duong Bach Mai and Nguyen Van Tao, as well as other prominent Stalinists, were jailed by General Catroux's administration.[61] A number of Trotskyites were also thrown into French jails. But this time the Commu-

---

[60] As quoted in Roger Lévy et al, *French Interests and Policies in the Far East*, p. 125.

[61] Among those arrested was Le Hong Phong, who, along with Ho Chi Minh, had been active in the founding of the Indochinese Communist Party. He and his wife were executed in 1940.

nists did not suffer the same defeats as in 1930. Turtle-like, they simply with-drew the head of the movement, which was its legal activity. It did lose some of its leaders temporarily, but the organization of the party was intact, its se-cret cells undisturbed, its network of sympathizers and party workers still loyal.

To the outsider, Indochina seemed unusually prosperous and quiet in 1939 when the war began, a docile outpost of empire ready to lend its full support to the French war effort. But the nationalists, regardless of their politics, were neither dead nor disinterested. They were waiting for an opportunity to act.

Chapter Four

THE VIET MINH

THE YEAR 1940 marked the beginning of the end of French rule over Indochina. It was the year that France fell in Europe and that the Japanese moved into Tonkin. It was perhaps France's last chance to win over the Vietnamese with a bold offer of postwar reform. But the France of Vichy and Decoux would not move in where the Popular Front had feared to tread.

From the Communists, reorganized in a United Front of Anti-Imperialist Indochinese Peoples, came urgent appeals to expel the French and oppose the Japanese. They called on the people to rise; and not only the workers and peasants, but also government officials, landowners, intellectuals, and soldiers. They attacked Prince Cuong De, accusing him of being a Japanese puppet, and claimed that pro-Japanese Cao Dai elements would be the first to suffer if the Japanese were victorious. The Communists directed pamphlets at the French also, criticizing the Governor General's policy of making concessions to the Japanese and urging Franco-Indochinese solidarity against reaction and against Japan.

But should the party move from propaganda and demonstrations to outright insurrection? Some Communists thought they should. Others urged caution, but they were overruled in the south. Although the central committee of the Indochinese Communist Party, which had fled to China, disavowed their action, Cochin Chinese Communists led by Left-Wing elements in the party prepared for revolt. Also in Cochin China, a number of conservative nationalists planned a rising of their own.

The time seemed right for violence. The Japanese were pressing down on the northern frontier while the Siamese were growing threatening in the west. Conservative nationalists greeted the Japanese hopefully; but Tokyo was prepared to give only limited, backhanded aid to Vietnamese nationalism in 1940. When revolts broke out in north, central, and south Viet Nam the Japanese stood aside and allowed the French a free hand to put them down. This happened in the Lang Son area of Tonkin, at Do Luong in Annam, and at My Tho in Cochin China.

The plans of the non-Communists in the south were frustrated by the French police before they had a chance to carry them out. It was the Communists who organized the abortive rising near My Tho in November 1940.[1] In their attempts to capitalize on peasant unrest in Cochin China they were joined by Trotskyites and pro-Japanese nationalists. Rumor had it that some of these were Caodaists, for opposition to the French administration seemed to level political differences.

[1] See above, pp. 24–25.

The reply of the French was swift and harsh, proving that those among the Communists who had urged postponing the uprising had, after all, been right. When the revolt failed, the wrath of the Communist Party against those who had favored the rising, if more controlled than that of the administration, was no less pitiless. It ordered the execution of two of its members and expelled others.

All plans for insurrection in Indochina in 1940 and 1941 came to nothing. Faced by the alliance of Vichy and Tokyo, the revolutionaries were helpless. Many conservative nationalists still did not despair that ultimately the Japanese would come to their aid. Others, however, along with the Communists, looked elsewhere for support. They turned to China.

UNDER CHINESE AUSPICES

By 1941 Left-Wing Vietnamese revolutionaries had shifted their headquarters once again to China. The Chinese had an old interest in Viet Nam, having tried for many centuries to reassert their rule over Tonkin. They also had a score to settle with the French for their prewar economic penetration of Yunnan province and their closing of the Haiphong railway; and to this was added a new urgency, for Indochina had become a Japanese base. The Chinese thus had good reasons for not wanting Japan to control the Vietnamese nationalist movement. If the Japanese were not ready to take advantage of the opportunity to exploit Vietnamese nationalism for their own ends, the Chinese were not going to make the same mistake.

In south China, close to the Tonkinese border, the Vietnamese Communists reorganized. They held a congress there in the spring of 1941, to which came men who had only recently escaped across the border, and others who had behind them years of exile in China. There were people from the "national salvation associations" of peasants, workers, soldiers, and women, all of which had been founded by the Communists. Individuals associated with other groups were also present. But the key figures were members of the Indochinese Communist Party, and among them was the frail bearded man who was supposed to have died in Hongkong years before, the founder of the party. Ho Chi Minh or, translated, Ho the Enlightened, had emerged from almost a decade of political obscurity.

Aware that independence was the only issue on which they could rally Vietnamese of all social classes, Ho Chi Minh and the Communists made no declaration of Communist orthodoxy during the congress. Instead, they set up a united front organization which both individuals and parties could join. They called it the *Viet Nam Doc Lap Dong Minh Hoi* (League for the Independence of Viet Nam), which came to be known popularly as the Viet Minh, and Ho Chi Minh was named General Secretary. They pledged themselves to fight both Japan and Vichy for the victory of the Allied forces and the independence of a "democratic Viet Nam."

But the new Viet Minh soon ran into difficulties with the Chinese, who arrested Ho Chi Minh. The Chiang Kai-shek government regarded the Communist leaders of the Viet Minh with deep distrust, and was anxious to counteract their influence and restore more of a balance among the leadership of the Vietnamese nationalist movement; when the Chinese looked about for other Vietnamese who could be more easily persuaded that the fortunes of their country were linked indissolubly to China, they were not hard to find.

In October 1942, while Ho Chi Minh was still in a Chinese prison, the city of Liuchow in south China was the scene of another gathering of Vietnamese émigrés under the sponsorship of the military governor of Kwangsi province. Members of various nationalist groups were present. Many belonged to the VNQDD; others came from groups friendly to the Japanese, notably the Phuc Quoc, a number of whose adherents had taken refuge in China after their unsuccessful rising at Lang Son in 1940. (These so-called pro-Japanese were nationalists first of all, maintaining links with each of the two camps that might bring independence to Viet Nam.) People from the Viet Minh were also there. The Chinese directed the welding of these diverse elements into what they intended as a more docile nationalist coalition, the *Viet Nam Cach Menh Dong Minh Hoi* (Viet Nam Revolutionary League) or Dong Minh Hoi. At the head of the new coalition, they placed Nguyen Hai Than, an old nationalist who had been in China since before the first World War, working closely with the Kuomintang.

Although the Allies had looked to the Dong Minh Hoi to do espionage in Indochina, to keep them informed on Japanese troop movements, they soon found that they could learn little of these from any Vietnamese group except the Viet Minh; only the Viet Minh had a network of cells throughout the Vietnamese lands, which it had inherited from the Communist Party and its affiliates. This was the reason that Ho Chi Minh was finally released from jail in 1943 and appointed chief of the Dong Minh Hoi, replacing Than.

Until 1944 the Vietnamese revolutionaries in China continued in an uneasy coalition. The Dong Minh Hoi received a subsidy from the Chinese Government, as did the Viet Minh because it was a section of the league. The Chinese also gave them military training and supplied them with arms. But despite all the talk of co-operation at Liuchow, the Viet Minh never merged its organization with the others; the Dong Minh Hoi never really existed as an all-inclusive league of revolutionaries (as distinct from the pro-Chinese political party it was to become after the war), except in name.

This was not at all what the Chinese had planned, and in March 1944 they made another effort to redistribute the balance of power in the nationalist movement by convoking another nationalist congress at Liuchow which appointed a republican government for a future liberated Viet Nam. Ho Chi Minh was supposed to be only one of several ministers in the government, but the Viet Minh, which was by far the most active member of the Dong Minh Hoi inside Viet Nam, profited most from this move, as it had profited most from the formation of the Dong Minh Hoi. It intensified its propaganda in the country, claiming to act in the name of the united revolutionary parties and of the new republican government.

When the Viet Minh's relations with the Chinese became strained, as they soon did, it tried for American support. It offered the Allies co-operation in the war and asked in return that the great powers, particularly the United States, give the Vietnamese military support and recognize their eventual independence under the Atlantic Charter. Although no such recognition was forthcoming, the Viet Minh established friendly relations with the Americans in Kunming, who began to supply it with arms.

Viet Minh placards turned up on Vietnamese walls and on Vietnamese streets, as they had since early in the war, calling on the French to make common cause with them against the Japanese. But the French administration had no desire to collaborate with the Vietnamese, and the Gaullists for a long while preferred to play a lone hand.[2] By 1944 the Viet Minh had begun operations against the Japanese near the Chinese border in northern Tonkin. Men of the Viet Minh helped American pilots out of the country and several Americans joined them to organize the work of bringing Allied pilots to safety. A number of Vietnamese slipped across the frontier from China to work with the Viet Minh, as did Ho Chi Minh himself late in 1944.

The Viet Minh did not waste its men on any major actions against the Japanese but concentrated on organizing and extending its strength in the Vietnamese countries. By 1945 it had ready and waiting an army of some ten thousand men led by a young teacher and Doctor of Law, Vo Nguyen Giap, who revealed an unexpected genius for military organization. Born in Annam in 1912, a veteran of French jails whose wife and sister-in-law had been killed by the French police, Giap was a professed Communist. He had spent some time at Yenan, the capital of Communist China, and returned home well versed in the tactics of guerrilla warfare.

Vo Nguyen Giap worked in the northern regions of Tonkin, where, protected by the mountains and forests and close to the Chinese frontier, the first Communist cells to be re-established in the 1930's after the White Terror were still strong. Giap not only recruited Vietnamese; he also organized the

2 Both the Decoux administration and the Free French mission which was stationed in south China were disturbed by the threat which Sino-Vietnamese collaboration constituted to the future of French sovereignty over Indochina. Beginning in 1943 they maintained a certain liaison and this enabled "an extremely precious exchange of information on the activities of Annamese [Vietnamese] revolutionaries and the Chinese, on the one hand, and the Japanese on the other." Devillers, *op. cit.*, pp. 106–7.

Tho and the other minority peoples who lived in the Tonkinese mountains. By a combination of propaganda and force, the Viet Minh apparently won over many members of the minorities in the north—an important factor in the future relations between the mountain peoples and the Vietnamese.[3] This was one of the major accomplishments of the Viet Minh during the war years. At the same time, Giap and his colleagues built up the guerrilla units that were to become the first contingents of the army of the Democratic Republic of Viet Nam.

A POSTWAR PROGRAM

Even while it organized on the military front, the Viet Minh planned for the more distant future. It was the only Vietnamese group to draw up a comprehensive postwar program.

The Viet Minh called for a popular representative assembly to draw up a republican constitution guaranteeing democratic rights and privileges. It promised an end to French taxes, which were to be replaced by others based on "democratic principles." The aim of the Viet Minh was a national, not a colonial economy, with industry developed and agriculture modernized and improved. With this was to come a program of social legislation, not unlike that which the Popular Front had brought to France, but revolutionary for Indochina—the eight-hour day, unemployment insurance, a minimum wage, aid to large families. Education was to be developed at all levels, as was intellectual life generally. Medical facilities were to be increased.

The Viet Minh announced its belief

in the sacredness of those principles for which the world has already shed and is shedding so much blood and which are defended by the great democratic world-powers—the United States, Great Britain, Russia and China. In the name of those principles, during more than half a century, the Annamese [Vietnamese] people have fought practically unknown and unaided. But history marched on and now they have with them the whole civilized world.

All this, however, was only words so long as Admiral Decoux continued to govern in Indochina. The problem for the Viet Minh was to overthrow the French administration, and that they could not do by themselves. They had to wait until the Japanese did it for them.

THE AUGUST REVOLUTION

With the French out of the way after March 9, 1945, the Viet Minh became more active. The Japanese did not bother to send their troops into the north-

[3] According to French sources, the minorities had always needed protection against Vietnamese encroachments. Philippe Devillers, however, wrote: "The population [in the Cao Bang region], the majority of which was Tho, had always had a rebellious attitude, which had been strengthened by the often brutal policy of the administration." *Op. cit.*, p. 102.

ern provinces of Tonkin and the Viet Minh took over the region for itself. It issued a proclamation calling on the people to rise up against the Japanese "and make of Viet Nam a powerful country, free and independent." Attacking the Tran Trong Kim government as a Japanese puppet regime, it warned:

In overthrowing the French yoke, the Japs plan to occupy our country and turn it into a Japanese colony where they will reserve to themselves the monopoly of plundering our people, abusing our women, slaying our patriots. They are not here to liberate our people. They are here to seize our rice stocks, our cotton, our oil; they will arrest all our young men and turn them into Japanese cannon-fodder . . .

The Viet Minh laid down a program of action:

Organize demonstrations, processions and strikes; close down all the markets and hinder, through boycott and other means, the enemy's last desperate effort. Destroy all communication and transport facilities; tear down all telegraph wires and destroy their ammunition dumps and foodstores; launch surprise attacks on their isolated outposts and ambush their patrol units in order to prevent them from turning against our population.[4]

Former political prisoners, members of the professions and intellectuals, mandarins and village Notables were exhorted to lead the people in a campaign of non-co-operation, to hold back rice and taxes demanded by the Japanese.

The Viet Minh invited the French to join them against the common enemy. Only a few accepted but the Viet Minh contacted the Gaullist mission in Kunming, asking arms and instructors; and in July a six-man Franco-American mission arrived by parachute at Viet Minh headquarters. The Viet Minh also asked for a guaranty of Vietnamese independence; but that the French officials in China were not in a position to give.[5]

Ho Chi Minh established his headquarters in a village not far from Thai Nguyen, on the way to Cao Bang in northern Tonkin. Northern Tonkin was a troubled place between March and August 1945. French columns were making their way to China fighting against illness as well as the Japanese. Women and children escorted by French soldiers came through, trying to elude the Japanese, and some of them died there. It was the headquarters of Chinese bandits, and the home of various mountain tribes. American and French parachutists traveled about, in touch with both the retreating French and the Viet Minh. And from their hidden camps in the Tonkinese mountains, Viet Minh guerrillas sallied out to harry the Japanese.

In April a Viet Minh military conference at Bac Ninh mapped out a strategy for the coming national revolt and appointed a general staff for the army

[4] Appeal to the population to fight the Japanese, March 15, 1945. Viet Nam Cultural Association for National Liberation, *Factual Records of the Viet Nam August Revolution*, p. 20.
[5] See below, p. 129.

headed by Vo Nguyen Giap. They created what they called a Liberated Zone the following month in the seven northern provinces of Cao Bang, Lang Son, Ha Giang, Bac Kan, Tuyen Quang, Thai Nguyen, and Bac Giang.

An appeal to the people dated July 1 set forth Viet Minh goals:

The properties of the population of the Liberated Zones are being effectively protected. Properties belonging to the invaders have been seized. They have become public property or have been distributed to the poor. Democratic rights and liberties are being translated into actual deeds. All citizens are equal in status. All men and women have equal rights before the law. The sick and the poor are given assistance, robbery and banditry are completely stamped out. All taxes and impositions have been abolished, and land taxes reduced. The working hours are shortened. Boys and girls are either pursuing their studies or fighting on the battlefields. Rich and poor, young and old, are working day and night to supply our armies. Over one million of our compatriots already enjoy revolutionary liberties and happiness. A 'New Viet Nam' has come into being.

Later the Viet Minh talked of liberated zones when it meant areas which were taken over from the French rather than from the Japanese. It exhorted the people against the French as, in July 1945, it did against the Japanese: "No sacrifice is unworthy of you. Our combatants in the rear must increase production, help our soldiers and support our guerrillas.[6]

While the Viet Minh organized the northern mountain regions, occasionally clashing with small Japanese detachments, a number of Viet Minh agents were active in the delta area, exploiting the widespread misery caused by the famine and Japanese requisitions, to make many converts among the peasantry. The Japanese political police tried to track them down, but the Japanese could not prevent the following of the Viet Minh from growing. The Viet Minh even infiltrated the pro-Japanese parties and the Vietnamese Government at Hué. And everywhere the Viet Minh demonstrated the remarkable organizational ability it had inherited from the Communist Party; it set up a number of revolutionary committees with provincial organizations above them and, at the top, a national central committee. It identified itself in the popular mind with the cause of the Allies; as an Allied victory approached, Viet Minh leaders prepared to share in it.

However, they did not expect it so soon, and the sudden news of the Japanese surrender changed the Viet Minh timetable. Even in the northern part of the country, the Viet Minh had not had the time to organize its following among the broad masses of the people; in the south it had much less strength, being almost entirely dependent upon the old Communist Party organization there. But the end of the war forced it into action.

"The hour has struck for a general offensive on all fronts," proclaimed Military Order Number 1 issued at Viet Minh headquarters. To the guerrilla

[6] Viet Nam Cultural Association for National Liberation, *op. cit.,* p. 22.

troops, now called the Viet Nam Liberation Army, it announced that a Central Military Committee had been created, and directed them, under its command, to "exert all your efforts and immediately launch attacks on towns, cities and strategic posts now held by the enemy; you must cut off their retreat routes and disarm them. In all circumstances you should do your duty toward the country with an iron courage and an inflexible determination."[7]

The Japanese, as it turned out, had little intention of fighting the Viet Minh, even though they would have preferred to leave Viet Nam in the hands of pro-Japanese nationalists; if they had chosen to fight, the Viet Minh would have had neither the men nor the equipment to withstand them. One of the results of this order, however, was that a number of Viet Minh militants who had arrived in the Liberated Zones for a meeting called by the central committee had to leave hurriedly for their posts while others, still on their way, turned back. The remainder, some sixty out of the original hundred (according to Viet Minh sources), constituted a congress which met on August 16 at Tran Tao in Thai Nguyen province and appointed a People's National Liberation Committee to lead the revolution; they unanimously elected Ho Chi Minh as its president.

The revolution took different forms in different sections of Viet Nam. Some areas did not receive the order for the general rising. Some turned against Vietnamese who had held high office or much property under the French, and there was sporadic violence in the countryside. In Quang Tri province, Annam, an abortive attempt by the French to make contact with Pham Quynh, Bao Dai's former Minister of Interior, was the immediate cause of Pham Quynh's death at Viet Minh hands. Ngo Dinh Khoi, an influential mandarin who had been governor of Quang Ngai province and was a brother of the Catholic leader Ngo Dinh Diem, was also killed by the Viet Minh in Annam because of his past anti-Communist record. He had been dismissed by the French as a dangerous nationalist in 1942.

In Annam the Viet Minh clashed with some Japanese troops. The Japanese had given arms and military equipment to the Tran Trong Kim government but they took them back after this encounter. As the anti-Japanese propaganda of the Viet Minh continued, the Japanese burned some military supplies at Hué rather than have them fall into Viet Minh hands. Elsewhere, however, the Japanese gave over material directly to the Viet Minh. By their reluctance to encourage and concede Vietnamese independence, the Japanese had helped to discredit the nationalist groups which they would have preferred to leave in control in Viet Nam; but in the end, even a Vietnamese government led by Communists who had been generally anti-Japanese seemed to them preferable to returning the country to the French. The Viet Minh could never have come to power so easily without the benevolent neutrality of the Japanese.

[7] *Ibid.*, pp. 23–24.

In China the Dong Minh Hoi was still preparing for the time when it would take over power in Indochina, but the time to take over power had already come, and the Viet Minh was on the scene to do it. "Minh," in the Vietnamese language, means "allies," and when Vietnamese heard of the Viet Minh, which came to them with the promise of independence, they believed it had the power of the victorious Allies behind it. Revolutionary "people's committees" sprang up throughout the country, throwing out the old Councils of Notables, and the people rallied to them.

There was no effective government in existence in Viet Nam to forestall the Viet Minh, and no organized independent group to compete with it. In August 1945, as a result, the Viet Minh became a broad national movement, uniting large numbers of Vietnamese regardless of their politics, and reaching down into the masses. As military support it had not only Giap's small army, but also the young people who had been trained under Phan Anh and Ta Quang Buu. Both men were to become members of the new revolutionary government and the young people they organized became its vanguard; impregnated with nationalist ideals, they were in the forefront of the revolution.

As Vo Nguyen Giap and his soldiers moved on Hanoi, there were demonstrations in the city celebrating independence. Bao Dai's viceroy, Phan Ke Toai, surrendered his authority to the revolutionaries; and the Viet Minh youth groups and militia took over the city, while the Japanese stood by.

In Hué, the old imperial capital, Bao Dai watched these developments uncertainly. There was no longer a government at Hué, for Tran Trong Kim had resigned and Hué too now had its revolutionary committee. Bao Dai sent one of his ministers to Hanoi to invite the Viet Minh to replace the Kim Cabinet with one of its own. He also sent an appeal to the Allies to recognize the independence of Viet Nam.

Bao Dai addressed a special message to General de Gaulle. The Emperor wrote:

You would understand better if you could see what is happening here, if you could feel this desire for independence which is in everyone's heart and which no human force can any longer restrain. Even if you come to re-establish a French administration here, it will no longer be obeyed: each village will be a nest of resistance; each former collaborator an enemy, and your officials and colonists will themselves ask to leave this atmosphere which they will be unable to breathe.[8]

Ho Chi Minh later implied that he had been prepared to operate within the framework of the monarchy with Bao Dai as a constitutional ruler, thus establishing the new regime on the firm foundations of the past and making it more likely to be acceptable to the Allies. In August 1945, however, when such reasoning might have changed the course of events, Ho Chi Minh said noth-

[8] Quoted in André Blanchet, *Au Pays des Ballila Jaunes*, p. 187.

ing. Instead, messages came from Hanoi urging Bao Dai to abdicate, and pro-Viet Minh people around the Emperor argued in favor of abdication. The officials and intellectuals gathered in Hué knew that they were in no position to fight the Viet Minh. At the same time, the story spread throughout the country that the Viet Minh had actually achieved independence guaranteed by the Allies. Its prestige was enormous. Bao Dai decided that he had no alternative; he telegraphed Hanoi, telling the new government that he was ready to abdicate.

This was welcome news to the Viet Minh; with the Emperor ready to resign of his own free will, the continuity between the old regime and the new seemed assured. It would make the transition much easier and it would look well abroad because it would strengthen the claim of the Viet Minh to be the leader of a truly national revolution. The National Liberation Committee in Hanoi sent a delegation to Hué to receive the Emperor's abdication. It was headed by Tran Huy Lieu, a Communist with a long background of revolutionary activity, who became Minister of Propaganda in the Ho Chi Minh government.

The delegation made a triumphal progress from Hanoi to Hué, according to Lieu,[9] passing through cheering crowds and stopping at villages to explain to the people the meaning and promise of the revolution. Along the way they saw flags with the yellow star on the red background, and the people shouted, "Long live the Democratic Republic of Viet Nam!"

In Annam, south of the city of Quang Tri, on the borderline between the provinces of Quang Tri and Thua Thien, the delegation was met by the chairman of the Hué People's Committee. The time was particularly propitious, for that day American planes, with their star insignia, had flown over Hué and the members of the People's Committee had told the citizens of Hué that they were Viet Minh planes. The people were in a state of mind to believe almost anything they were told about the power of the Viet Minh and their new freedom, and they lined the road to the imperial capital to welcome the envoys from Hanoi.

In the offices of the People's Committee in Hué, the delegation talked with Bao Dai's secretary. They agreed that the government would care for the temples and tombs of the Royal Family, which were to remain national monuments; the Royal Family was to have free access to them and the right to carry on the cult of their ancestors. Everything in the royal palace with the exception of the Emperor's personal property was to be taken over by the state, but the Emperor was to remain owner of the estates which bore his name.

Bao Dai received the delegates in private audience, and for the first time in

[9] Tran Huy Lieu, "The Emperor's Golden Sword," Viet Nam Cultural Association for National Liberation, *op. cit.* The following account is based upon this report, except for the incident of the American planes, which was described to the writer by an eyewitness.

the history of Viet Nam an Emperor shook hands with one of his subjects. On the following day, August 26, a ceremony took place at the imperial palace. The red flag with the yellow star, which had already been put up, was taken down and the old yellow flag of the Vietnamese Emperors was hoisted once again. At 6 o'clock Bao Dai appeared in a brocaded tunic and yellow turban, and read to the assembled crowd his abdication speech.

He was acting, he said, in the interests of peace and unity.

In view of the mighty democratic forces in the north of Our Realm, We were at first apprehensive lest conflict between the North and South should be inevitable, if We were to await the opening of a National Congress before taking a decision; and We were aware that this conflict, should it occur, would entail much suffering for Our peoples besides giving a golden opportunity to the invader to despoil Our territory.

His reign had not been a very satisfactory one, for "Our position has been such that it was well-nigh impossible for Us to render any appreciable service to Our country."

He concluded, calling upon

all parties and groups, all classes of society as well as the Royal Family to strengthen and support unreservedly the Democratic Republic of Viet Nam in order to consolidate our national independence. As for Us, We have known great bitterness during the twenty years of Our rule. Henceforth, We are happy to assume the status of a free citizen in an independent country. We shall allow no one to abuse Our name or that of the Royal Family to sow discord among Our compatriots. Long live the independence of Viet Nam! Long live Our democratic Republic!

Tran Huy Lieu accepted the two symbols of royalty, the gold seal and the gold sword with the ruby-encrusted handle. The imperial flag was hauled down and the yellow star on the red field put up in its place, while the people applauded. Lieu announced that the era of the monarchy was over, and he pinned to the tunic of the former Emperor, now plain Citizen Vinh Thuy, a red insignia with a yellow star. On the left bank of the Perfumed River, crowds paraded, shouting, "Hail the democratic spirit of Citizen Vinh Thuy! Hail the delegates of the Provisional Government!" And they echoed the Emperor's last words, "Long live the democratic republic!"

Never before had Viet Nam seemed so united. Emperor and people, Catholics and Confucianists, conservatives and Communists, they all seemed to support the new republic. In Hanoi, now the capital of Viet Nam, Ho Chi Minh reorganized the National Liberation Committee, bringing in a Catholic and several more moderate nationalists to form the Provisional Government of the new republic. Eight of its fifteen members belonged to the Viet Minh and of those, five were Communists. Citizen Vinh Thuy, the ex-Emperor, was given the title of Supreme Political Advisor.

On September 2, Ho Chi Minh addressed the people of Hanoi for the first time. Millions of words and many thousands of documents had been penned by Vietnamese in the course of the long struggle against the French. Books, pamphlets, newspapers, leaflets, legal and illegal, they all contributed to the statement Ho made before packed crowds. It was the declaration of independence of Viet Nam.

It took its first paragraph from the stirring words of the American Declaration of Independence: "We hold these truths to be self-evident. That all men are created equal, that they are endowed by their Creator with certain inalienable rights, and that among these are Life, Liberty, and the Pursuit of Happiness." It indicted the French for "deeds counter to the ideals of humanity and justice."

It did not even admit that it was from France that independence had been won, for "since the autumn of 1940, our country ceased to be a French colony and became a Japanese possession. . . . The truth is that we have won back our independence from Japanese hands and not from the French." The declaration concluded: "Viet Nam has the right to be free and independent and, in fact, has become free and independent. The people of Viet Nam have decided to mobilize all their spiritual and material forces and to sacrifice their lives and property in order to safeguard their right to liberty and independence."

September 2 was Independence Day for Viet Nam. The people of Hanoi cheered wildly. It looked to them as if the war were over and Viet Nam were free.

Chapter Five

SOUTH OF THE SIXTEENTH PARALLEL

THE VIET MINH seizure of power in Hanoi found Cochin China disunited and ill-prepared for independence. After eighty years as a French colony, closer to the unsettling effects of French political and economic activity than the protectorates to the north, and with little experience of political power which might have taught responsibility and moderation, Cochin China was afflicted with a multiplicity of rival political and religious groups. Members of the Cao Dai and the Hoa Hao, other nationalists who had worked with the Japanese, Trotskyites, and Communists, they were each determined to maintain independence, but only in their own way and in their own image. At the same time, the small number of Vietnamese in the south who had profiteered in the period of French rule hoped and planned for the return of the French.

Superimposed upon this background of Vietnamese rivalries, some of them highly personal, were Indian occupation troops, French soldiers and administrators, and the surrendered Japanese army, all of them under the orders of a British general who followed a policy in Cochin China which differed markedly from the policy of the British Labor Government in its own empire. The situation in the south after V-J Day was thus both confusing and confused.

The Vietnamese struggle for political control in Cochin China began directly after the Japanese collapse, before any new foreign troops had arrived in the country. The Japanese permitted Cochin China to unite with Tonkin and Annam just before V-J Day and Bao Dai sent an imperial delegate to Cochin China. The Emperor abdicated soon after, before Ho Chi Minh could extend the authority of his government to the south, but the Cochin Chinese did not wait for that. "People's Committees" mushroomed in Saigon, and armed groups of young people demonstrated in the streets, celebrating independence. Violence broke out in the Cochin Chinese countryside. The peasants turned on the village Notables in some areas and killed a number of wealthy landlords and unpopular officials. Some Caodaists set up a state of their own in the section of the Cochin Chinese hinterland around Tay Ninh, the Cao Dai capital. The Hoa Hao established their own state at Can Tho.

The Viet Minh, meanwhile, was organizing behind the scenes. In Cochin China, even more than elsewhere, it relied almost entirely on the old Communist Party; the handbills that began to appear on Saigon walls were signed jointly by the Viet Minh and the Indochinese Communist Party. They proclaimed their disapproval of "all acts of provocation and violence against Indochinese regardless of their origin and race." They would "endeavor with all the means at their disposal to protect the people and repress disorder from any source."[1]

The means at their disposal were, at first, very limited. The Communists themselves were few in number. They gained a certain strength from the Advance Guard Youth organized by Pham Ngoc Thach, which ardently supported the Viet Minh and supplied it with the nucleus of a military force in the south. Against them, however, were aligned the groups which had come to the fore under the Japanese. The Cao Dai, the Hoa Hao, and a number of intellectuals and middle-class nationalists, many of whom had belonged to the Phuc Quoc, together with Trotskyites from the "Struggle" group, formed what they called a United National Front to take over power in Saigon. Some Japanese, more interested in furthering Vietnamese independence from France than in obeying the terms of the armistice between Japan and the Allies, gave arms to members of the new front, notably to the Cao Dai, which already had a number of troops of its own. Disturbed by the Communist aspect of the Viet Minh, Japanese were reliably reported to have also made offers of support to Ta Thu Thau, the Trotskyite leader, who was reputed to be a moderate. There is no evidence, however, that he accepted them.

Members of the United National Front sponsored an independence celebration in Saigon on August 21, when thousands of men and women gathered in the Place Norodom and marched along the war-devastated boulevard. Caodaists marched with Hoa Hao peasant columns behind the imperial flag. Trotskyites participated also, with an enormous flag of the Fourth International, carrying banners with revolutionary slogans: "Long live the world revolution! People's committees everywhere! Toward a popular assembly! Land for the peasants!" Although well organized and possessed of some militant and competent party stalwarts who gave the Trotskyites an influence greater than their numbers, the Trotskyites could not claim many members. However, they set up a printing press and began issuing communiqués to the people. They planned to step up their political activity and train groups for military action.[2]

But on August 22 the Viet Minh came into the open and called on the United National Front to accept the leadership of the Viet Minh, which already was on good terms with the Allies. The alternative, Viet Minh spokesmen argued, was to have the Allies dismiss the entire Vietnamese nationalist movement as a creature of the Japanese. With the United National Front apparently ready to defer to this argument, at least for the time being, the Viet Minh held its own demonstration on August 25 and the large turnout indicated that its prestige and organization had won for it wide popular support.

[1] Quoted in Andrée Viollis et al, *La Vérité sur le Viet-Nam*, p. 42.
[2] For a Trotskyite account of these events, see Lucien, "Quelques Etapes de la Révolution du Nam-Bo du Viet Nam," *Quatrième Internationale*, September–October 1947.

That same day the Viet Minh set up a Committee of the South to rule Cochin China. Headed by Tran Van Giau, it was dominated by Communists, among them such well-known party members as Nguyen Van Tao and Duong Bach Mai. It also included Pham Ngoc Thach, not yet known to be a member of the Communist Party. The Committee of the South took over power in Saigon swiftly and peaceably. It occupied the public buildings and ran the public services. Although the Committee recognized the authority of the Hanoi government, of which it regarded itself as the southern representative, in practice it functioned quite independently. It concentrated on maintaining order.

With the country already independent in fact, the Committee of the South believed that the Vietnamese had only to convince the United Nations of their ability to rule themselves, and their independence would be recognized by the world. Coupled with this optimistic estimate of the international situation, however, went a very realistic approach to domestic politics. The first problem to which Viet Minh leaders addressed themselves was asserting Viet Minh dominance over the nationalist movement in the south, despite strong opposition from other Cochin Chinese nationalists and revolutionaries.

The Trotskyites organized in the International Communist League, unlike the "Struggle" group, would not even consider the idea of joining a Viet Minh-led coalition. Primarily interested in social revolution, they went among the peasants stirring them up against the large landowners. Nguyen Van Tao, speaking for the Committee of the South, warned that anyone who provoked the peasants to seize private property would be punished severely. This was no Communist revolution which could solve the agrarian problem, he said. It could not be expected to solve it. "Our government, I repeat, is a democratic and middle-class government, even though the Communists are now in power."[3]

But the groups which had formed the United National Front were not satisfied to see the Communists in power. They heard that the Committee of the South was in touch with Colonel Cédile, the new French Commissioner of Cochin China, who, having parachuted into a ricefield after the Japanese defeat, was already in Saigon. They began to feel that the Communists were using the nationalist movement for their own ends, and their uneasiness grew with the impending arrival of British troops to take over the Japanese surrender.

Viet Minh leaders, however, proclaimed their faith in the Allies, declaring that anyone inciting the people to arm themselves would be treated as a saboteur or a provocateur. On the eve of September 2, Independence Day, which was to be the scene of another mass demonstration, government spokesmen drove through the streets of Saigon, appealing for order. Allied repre-

[3] Quoted by Lucien, *op. cit.*, p. 45.

sentatives were due to arrive in Saigon on September 2, they told the people. It was important to the future of Viet Nam that the Allies receive a favorable impression of peace and security in the city.

Crowds milled about the streets on September 2, and in the afternoon men and women marched in orderly columns along the broad Rue Catinat toward the cathedral. Before its portals appeared Father Tricoire, who was known as a friend of the Vietnamese. Shots rang out suddenly as he stood at the threshold of the cathedral. He was hit, and died there. More shots were fired. Four other Frenchmen were killed and others hurt. Several of the Vietnamese demonstrators were killed. Who actually began the shooting was never established, although Vietnamese extremists, Frenchmen, and Japanese provocateurs were variously blamed.

With the shooting, the crowd broke ranks. Some of them forced their way into French houses, pillaging and looting. A number of French people, among them women and children, were rounded up by the Viet Minh; and their houses were ransacked while they were gone. What had started off as a day of celebration and a demonstration of the power and stability of the Committee of the South degenerated into mass disorders.

Tran Van Giau deplored the excesses in his newspaper and the head of the Viet Minh police, Duong Bach Mai, took the lead in freeing French prisoners, all of whom were released within two days. But the French residents of Saigon had been afraid that the Vietnamese intended to turn on them and now they believed they had proof of it. To the "infamy" of March 9 was added the shock of September 2. In fear of their lives, they counted the days until a French army would come to protect them.

The Japanese forces in Indochina, still intact, were under Allied orders to keep the peace until an Allied army of occupation arrived, and Tran Van Giau appealed to the Vietnamese population, supporting a directive from Japanese headquarters which ordered the general disarmament of the people and banned political movements threatening order and security. The Japanese and Allied authorities, he said, were afraid of new and more bloody outbreaks. "In the interests of our country, we call on everyone to have confidence in us and not let themselves be led astray by people who betray our country. It is only in this spirit that we can facilitate our relations with the Allied representatives."[4]

But the rumor spread among Vietnamese that the British planned to bring back French colonial rule. The Cao Dai, the Trotskyites, the Hoa Hao, and other nationalists did not agree with the Viet Minh that by negotiation alone they would be able to maintain independence. They did not trust the Viet Minh; they refused to give up what weapons they had.

The Trotskyite International Communist League held meetings demanding

[4] Leaflet issued September 7, 1945.

arms for the people, and when the first British troops arrived in Saigon during the second week in September, it issued a manifesto denouncing as treason and capitulation the decision of the Committee of the South to welcome the British. The Committee's response was quick and drastic. Duong Bach Mai sent an armed detachment of police to surround the meeting place of the league central committee. Taken by surprise, outnumbered and inadequately armed, the Trotskyites surrendered without a fight.

The Viet Minh tried to appease other nationalist groups by transforming the Committee of the South into a more representative nationalist body. Tran Van Giau stepped down from the chairmanship in favor of an independent, Pham Van Bach. The Committee membership was broadened and, instead of being mostly Communist, independents and representatives of the United National Front were also brought into it. But within the framework of the newly enlarged Committee of the South, the battle for leadership went on.

The Viet Minh closed in on Trotskyites who belonged to the "Struggle" group as well as to the International Communist League, and a number were killed. Ta Thu Thau, on the way back from a trip to Hanoi, drove into Annam with a member of the Japanese Cultural Mission, then decided to travel alone. On orders from Hanoi, he was arrested on the way. He was tried three times by local People's Committees and acquitted each time. But Tran Van Giau, ruthless in the pursuit of power, reportedly felt that his position in the south was threatened by Ta Thu Thau's popularity. He seems to have served a sort of ultimatum on the Viet Minh central committee in Hanoi—either himself or Thau—and Hanoi gave way. Ta Thu Thau was killed in Quang Ngai, Annam, on orders from Tran Van Giau.

When the Cao Dai and the Hoa Hao, in their turn, challenged the Viet Minh's conduct of affairs, the Viet Minh replied by directing military and police action against them. The Hoa Hao leader Huynh Phu So, who had just been made a member of the Committee of the South, barely escaped arrest. Viet Minh troops clashed with elements of the Cao Dai and the Hoa Hao in many sections of the Cochin Chinese countryside.

As early as August and September 1945, there were thus serious divisions in the nationalist movement in the south, and the Viet Minh had already come to blows with otoher nationalists. However, despite these internal differences, the main objective, Viet Minh leaders agreed with their opponents, was still Vietnamese independence. Operating through the Committee of the South, the Viet Minh did its best to maintain a façade of unity as it prepared for negotiations with the British.

THE FRENCH PREPARE TO RETURN

The French people of Saigon anxiously awaited the British and the French soldiers they would bring with them. Although the Committee of the South urged moderation on the Vietnamese population and spoke firmly against xenophobia, with the two peoples, the former masters and the resurgent subjects, juxtaposed, the atmosphere was charged with tension.

Saigon in September 1945 was becoming an alien city for Frenchmen. The Vietnamese tore down statues the French had erected to commemorate the glories of their empire. In the manner of so many revolutionaries newly come to power, the Vietnamese changed the names of public buildings, of streets, even of stores, to extirpate all traces of French colonial rule—but not of France. The Rue Pasteur remained unchanged and the Rue Catinat, the main avenue of Saigon, became the Street of the Paris Commune.

The French troops interned by the Japanese after March 9 were still confined to barracks but some 20,000 French people were living in Saigon, a handful in friendly relations with the Committee of the South, the great majority pinning their hopes on the time when an army would come from Europe to restore the privileges previously enjoyed by Frenchmen in Indochina. For these people, by and large, the war had begun in earnest on March 9, 1945. It had meant privation, living in restricted quarters, and daily uncertainty, worse since September 2. For some, it had meant Japanese jails. At a time when Indochina, as never before, was in need of far-sighted men willing and able to strike out along new and untried paths, this group of frightened, angry people had their eyes fixed firmly on the past. "For us," wrote the former director of Radio Saigon, "the cessation of hostilities meant the immediate arrival of large numbers of troops and, if not a return to French administration as we knew it, at least the end of all Annamese agitation."[5]

The position of the French Government was not so very different. While awaiting the arrival of the British, Commissioner Cédile told members of the Committee of the South about the new regime France planned to institute in Indochina. In 1943 the Free French had talked of federalism for Indochina and they had debated their colonial policy at length when the de Gaulle government was still located in Algiers. At a conference in Brazzaville, the capital of Free French Equatorial Africa, in 1944, they had formulated a set of principles to govern their empire which seemed to presage a special concern for the development of their colonies in their own interests and not simply as appendages of metropolitan France. Then, on March 24, 1945, before the Ho Chi Minh government existed, the French Provisional Government had issued a declaration on Indochina.

It provided for a federal Indochina within a French Union that would include France and other members of the "French community." Nationals of the Indochinese Federation were to have a double citizenship, entitling them to all federal offices in Indochina and in the Union "on the sole ground of merit and without discrimination because of race, religion, or national ori-

[5] Jacques Le Bourgeois, *Saigon sans la France* (*Des Français au Viet-Minh*), pp. 182–83.

gin."[6] Foreign affairs and defense were to be in French hands, but the Federation would have its own armed forces and these would be open equally to Indochinese and to nationals of other parts of the Union. Social and cultural growth, as well as economic development, were to be promoted. The country was to be enabled to industrialize and to develop closer ties with non-French countries, notably China. Freedom of thought, religion, press, and association were to be the basis of all Indochinese law.

But there was another side to the reforms Cédile outlined to the Committee of the South; although a considerable advance over past French policy, they were cast in a traditional mold. The Governor General, renamed "High Commissioner," was to continue in control, flanked by ministers appointed by and responsible to him. There would be a federal representative assembly, "chosen in accordance with the mode of election best suited to each of the states of the Federation," in which French interests as well as each of the states would be represented. It would vote on taxes, approve the federal budget, examine commercial treaties, and discuss bills. It would have no other powers.

This added up to some kind of autonomy but, as Paul Mus once remarked, it was autonomy for the Governor General, not autonomy for the Indochinese. And finally, "the five states which form the Indochinese Federation and which differ in civilization, race and tradition, will keep their own character within the federation." Cochin China, Tonkin, and Annam were to continue separate.

What help could such proposals offer for reaching an understanding with a government that described itself as the Democratic Republic of Viet Nam and considered Tonkin, Annam, and Cochin China as integral parts of its territory? Tran Van Giau and his colleagues had already proclaimed their independence.

But only the Vietnamese thought in terms of independence at this time. In August, Admiral Georges Thierry d'Argenlieu had been named High Commissioner for Indochina. A Carmelite monk on leave from his monastery with high rank in the Free French navy, he shared General de Gaulle's uncompromising ideas about maintaining the French Empire for the glory of France, whatever the cost. His orders were to re-establish French sovereignty in the country, and he intended to carry them out to the letter.

Members of a French mission waiting in Calcutta for the word to return to Indochina were shocked to hear the Saigon radio declare that Viet Nam had become free and independent. The barriers between Cochin China, Annam, and Tonkin had been broken down, the radio proclaimed. It accused the French of having imposed their rule against the will of the Indochinese people. "We will continue to respect your possessions. You can continue to work in

[6] *Notes Documentaires et Etudes*, No. 548.

our country, but on condition that you submit to our laws. Put aside your arms. We want to live in liberty."[7]

The returning French were totally unprepared for this kind of talk. Military and civilians alike, they neither expected it nor understood it.

TENSION RISES

With the French and the Vietnamese so far apart—with the Vietnamese in control of the administration and the French unprepared to recognize that control—the immediate future depended on whatever military force arrived in the country to upset the tenuous equilibrium between the two. In Cochin China that force happened to be British.

On September 12 British and Indian troops arrived in Saigon by plane from Rangoon, and with them the first elements of the army which the French had trained in Africa when they still hoped to participate in the Pacific war; British General Douglas D. Gracey arrived the following day. Along the road from the airport the troops passed through empty streets, under banners and past walls bearing messages welcoming the Allies and attacking the French. They passed British, American, Chinese, and Russian flags and the gold star on the red field of the Viet Minh.

It was a strange occupation; the Indian division which the British had assigned to Cochin China did not provide sufficient manpower for this task, and the Allies continued to rely on the Japanese to keep order. Although the British were in command, Japanese patrols were active throughout Saigon.

The ten days after General Gracey's arrival were crucial days in Saigon. Everyone was waiting—the British for more troops and the French for reinforcements which had already set sail from Marseille. At the City Hall, Allied flags were flying on both sides of the Viet Minh flag, and Viet Minh soldiers were on duty at the door. Inside sat the Committee of the South, its job daily becoming more difficult as tension heightened between the French and the Vietnamese. Vietnamese, Frenchmen, Japanese, Indians, Englishmen, Chinese, and Americans all rubbed shoulders on the streets of Saigon; and none of the French civilians were armed.

The British and Indians were in the city for certain specific reasons. They had been ordered to Indochina by the Allied High Command, which had decided to divide the country at the sixteenth parallel, sending in Chinese troops to the north and British to the south, in order to disarm the Japanese and evacuate Allied prisoners of war. These were jobs that had to be done; there were not enough French troops on hand or nearby to do them, and the French had neither the ships to transport more men nor the weapons to arm them. Bringing in foreigners, however, underlined to the native population the

7 Hertrich, *op. cit.*, p. 21.

weakness of France at a time when the French wanted, above all, to appear strong, if they were to reassert their prewar authority. It persuaded the Vietnamese that the Allies, following Roosevelt's lead, were opposed to the return of the French.

This impression was heightened by the fact that neither the British nor the Chinese arrived in Indochina immediately after V-J Day. "My responsibilities were immediate and urgent," Vice Admiral Mountbatten, Supreme Allied Commander in Southeast Asia, wrote, "but neither the troops, the shipping, nor the Intelligence I had asked for were available to me."[8] By the time Allied troops arrived in the country, the Democratic Republic of Viet Nam had proclaimed its independence and French authority had been replaced by a new authority.

Along the Rue Catinat, Frenchmen told each other and the British how easy it would be to end the existing uncertainty, now that the Allies had finally come. All that they had to do was to rearm the French soldiers whom the Japanese had interned and throw the Vietnamese out of the public buildings, and it would be over, because the revolutionaries, as everyone knew, were cowards at heart. Commissioner Cédile was under attack both from the Right and the Left. The French colonialists wondered why he did not demand strong action against the Vietnamese; they were irritated at his insistence on talking things over with the members of the Committee of the South. Left-Wingers among the French colony, of whom there were some, criticized Cédile for not more readily understanding the position of the Committee and making concessions to it.

This was a time when a man of prestige and authority might have had the foresight and the power to break with the past and make a gift to the Vietnamese of the independence they expected. It was a time to be generous while a grant of independence would still have constituted generosity, and not simply a concession wrung from France when the French had no other alternative. Cédile, however, was in no position to be generous. He was a good man, competent and honest, but a colonial official without the authority to go beyond the March 24, 1945 declaration, which was totally inadequate to the situation. He could temporize and negotiate, but he could not go against his instructions.

"We have our independence," members of the Committee of the South told French reporters. "We demand that it be recognized." Let that be done and Frenchmen would be welcomed into the country as planters, engineers, and teachers. But there would be no place for arrogant minor French functionaries. And, of course, there would be no place for the French army.[9] The Committee

---

[8] Vice Admiral the Earl Mountbatten of Burma, Report of the Combined Chiefs of Staff by the Supreme Allied Commander, *South East Asia 1943–1945,* p. 183.

[9] Hertrich, *op. cit.,* pp. 68–69.

of the South appealed for help to André Malraux and Andrée Viollis, French writers who in past years had been outspoken friends of Vietnamese nationalism, and to all French Left-Wing intellectuals. They asked that Vietnamese independence be recognized and, above all, that the French bring no more troops to Indochina.

The French soldiers already at large in Saigon, not yet having any military equipment of their own, had come in British uniforms, speaking English because they were working with Englishmen; to the Vietnamese this appeared evidence of a deeply laid plot. The French had done nothing to defend the country, the Vietnamese argued, and nothing to win it back. Unable to return openly, they seemed to be coming in clandestinely through the back door. It did not give the Committee of the South much confidence in the future.

The Vietnamese press took on an inflammatory and increasingly anti-French tone. Few Vietnamese appeared in the streets and Vietnamese bands pillaged isolated French houses and attacked French and Allied military convoys. Vietnamese *boys,* the servants on whom the French women depended, left their employers' houses and did not return. Vietnamese merchants refused to sell to Frenchmen, while the local Chinese merchants who continued to deal with Frenchmen did so secretly so as not to antagonize the Vietnamese. Although a small group of Left-Wing Frenchmen kept in touch with the Viet Minh, they could do nothing to further an agreement with the French authorities, and relations between the French and the Vietnamese in the streets of Saigon worsened daily.

Commissioner Cédile held out for a while against demands by elements of the French population for strong action; but finally he gave way to their pressure and went to urge General Gracey to protect the French population against the Vietnamese. To newspapermen he said that the Committee of the South did not represent popular opinion and could not maintain order. The next step was up to General Gracey.

THE FRENCH TAKE OVER

The British commander was confronted with a political problem for which he had neither the background nor the advisors to deal with. He had been sent to Indochina on a military assignment and his instructions were strict: "Sole mission: disarm the Japanese. Do not get involved in keeping order."[10] He disregarded those instructions, however, with serious political consequences. At a time when the British Labor Government was already committed to freeing India and Burma, General Gracey took it upon himself to restore Indochina south of the sixteenth parallel to the French and thereby engaged the British Government in a responsibility for the war which followed.

[10] Devillers, *op. cit.*, p. 158.

General Gracey apparently started off with certain prejudices. While still in India, before coming to Cochin China, he had said: "The question of the government of Indochina is exclusively French. . . . Civil and military control of Indochina by the French is only a question of weeks."[11] General Gracey was willing to see members of the Committee of the South, but when Commissioner Cédile appealed to him for help, Gracey responded with all-out support of the French position. He forbade the Vietnamese press to appear, proclaimed martial law, and imposed a strict curfew. He banned all demonstrations and public meetings and made illegal the carrying of arms of any description, including sticks, staves, and bamboo spears, except by Allied soldiers. Crimes against public order became military offenses and the penalty for sabotage and looting was death. Although in a proclamation dated September 21, 1945, General Gracey announced his "firm intention to ensure with strict impartiality that the period of transition from war to peace conditions is carried out peaceably," the measures he took were aimed directly at the Committee of the South.

Early in the morning of September 22, the British took over Saigon jail from the Vietnamese. That same day, Frenchmen went quietly to the barracks of the French 11th Colonial Infantry Regiment where Decoux's army had lived under guard since March 9, ill-clothed and increasingly restless, spoiling for a fight. They selected over a thousand men, gave them arms, and alerted them for immediate action. Before dawn the next morning, ragged soldiers and paratroopers recently arrived from France, some 1,500 in all, moved swiftly and silently down the streets of Saigon. They took over the public buildings before the Vietnamese were aware of what was happening.

For some four weeks Vietnamese had sat in the very seats from which the French had once ruled Cochin China. On September 23 the French threw them out. The Vietnamese offered only a scattered and disorganized resistance which was without casualties and wholly ineffectual.

A few hours later it was daylight and the French people began to come out of their houses. Where Vietnamese had stood guard the night before, they saw men of the 11th Infantry. The French rounded up a number of Vietnamese in a house-to-house search but all except one of the members of the Committee of the South, warned in time, escaped into the countryside.

On the Rue Catinat, no longer the street of the Paris Commune, the French population went wild; they insulted and attacked any Vietnamese who dared appear on the streets, while French and British soldiers looked on. Correspondents, both French and foreign, who happened to be on the scene, were shocked by the outrages. The official British account did not mince words. It stated:

11 Hertrich, *op cit.,* p. 49.

It was indeed unfortunate that the manner in which this coup d'état was executed together with the behavior of the French citizens during the morning of Sunday, 23 September, absolutely ensured that countermeasures would be taken by the Annamites [Vietnamese]. The more emotional of the French citizens, who, after all, had suffered considerably at the hands of the Annamites during the past few months, unfortunately took this opportunity of taking what reprisals they could. Annamites were arrested for no other reason than that they were Annamites; their treatment after arrest, though not actively brutal, was unnecessarily violent.[12]

Cédile drove through the city on September 23, urging peace and moderation on the French population. He ordered that there should be no arbitrary arrests and that only criminals be jailed. The French of Saigon were not happy about this policy of conciliation, but Cédile and Gracey were not interested in vengeance; they wanted only to re-establish conditions in which negotiations could be resumed, this time without question on the basis of the declaration of March 24, 1945. The coup d'etat of September 23, they believed, had made that possible.

They reckoned without the Vietnamese. Some Vietnamese had hoped for support from the French Communists, then the largest party in France, but they did not receive it. An American newspaperman later was permitted to read a document prepared by the few French Communists in Saigon for the Indochinese Communist Party. Dated September 25, two days after the French had taken over the city, the document

. . . advised the Annamite [Vietnamese] Communists to be sure, before they acted too rashly, that their struggle 'meets the requirements of Soviet policy.' It warned that any 'premature adventures' in Annamite independence might 'not be in line with Soviet perspectives.' These perspectives might well include France as a firm ally of the USSR in Europe, in which case the Annamite independence movement would be an embarrassment. Therefore it urged upon the Annamite comrades a policy of 'patience.' It advised them in particular to wait upon the results of the French elections, coming up the following month, in October, when additional Communist strength might assure the Annamites a better settlement. In the meantime it baldly proposed that an emissary be sent not only to contact the French Communist Party but also the Russians 'in order to acquaint yourselves with the perspectives of coming events.'[13]

The Vietnamese, whether Communists or not, were not prepared to wait. France had declared war on them and they fought back. With the Committee of the South taken unawares, disorganized and in flight, the center of nationalist resistance shifted to Hanoi; but the fighting in Cochin China was not over.

[12] Supreme Allied Command, Southeast Asia, Commission No. 1, Saigon, *Political History of French Indochina South of 16°, 13 September–11 October 1945*. Quoted by George Sheldon in an unpublished manuscript.
[13] Harold Isaacs, *No Peace for Asia*, pp. 173–74.

A CITY WITHOUT LAWS

If September 24 was a day of uncertainty in Saigon, September 25 was a day of terror. The lights in the Cochin Chinese capital were off because the Vietnamese had cut the power supply, and there was no water; shooting was heard in the outskirts and large fires were set. French women and children hurried in panic to the sentry-guarded refuge of the Hotel Continental, which was so crowded that hundreds had to sleep in the corridors. A fire began in the big central market and was only stopped by the desperate efforts of Chinese and Indians to put it out before it reached their shops and houses.

The city was divided into sectors, one part held by French troops and another by Indians. In the Tan Dinh area, which included the district called the Cité Héraud where a number of French officials lived, the Japanese were in charge. They were there on September 25 when a wild band of Vietnamese descended on the Cité Héraud, inflicting appalling atrocities. Men, women, and children were tortured and massacred and others were carried off, while the Japanese stood by, doing nothing to prevent it.[13a]

Gracey severely reprimanded the Japanese commander, telling him in no uncertain terms that his troops were expected to do their part in maintaining order. But Saigon was a city without laws. The French people had no arms, and were barricaded in their houses with no one to tell them what to do. The Vietnamese set up a blockade of Saigon and in the city itself armed Vietnamese made it unsafe for Frenchmen to go out alone. At the end of important streets there was fighting, and the suburbs were afire.

The small group of Americans working for the Office of Strategic Services who had their headquarters in two outlying villas had no thought of taking military precautions. With their American uniforms and the Stars and Stripes painted on their jeeps, they thought that no one could confuse them with either Frenchmen or Britons, and the United States was known to be a friend of the Vietnamese. But Saigon was in the grip of an indiscriminate xenophobia and snipers did not stop to look at the cut of the uniforms or the markings on the equipment of the white men at whom they shot.

On September 26 Colonel A. Peter Dewey, chief of the OSS in Saigon, was driving in his jeep when he was attacked, and only had time to cry, "Je suis américain," before he fell under Vietnamese shots. Frightened by approaching Allied reinforcements, the Vietnamese ran off with Dewey's body. For a time it seemed that the murder might have serious political consequences: the Vietnamese blamed it on the French who, they said, were trying to win over the Americans; and the French, with more reason, blamed it on the Vietnamese. But the American Government, which had the last word, de-

---

[13a] This terroristic attack was subsequently attributed to members of the Binh Xuyen. See below, pp. 229–30.

cided it was simply a deplorable incident; the OSS moved its headquarters into the city and the matter was dropped.

Slowly the French took over authority in Saigon. There was no leadership at all in the days immediately following September 23. Then, on the 26th, an order written by hand was posted on a wall at the Hotel Continental telling the refugees to return home, assuring them that they would be safe and that they would not starve. Two printed appeals appeared the following day, announcing that a police force was being recruited and asking for volunteers to maintain the different services. Finally, at the end of the month, a British warship arrived in the harbor, the first to come to Saigon since Admiral Sir Percy Noble sailed away after his interview with General Catroux in 1940. The ship was the first of an Anglo-French convoy. The French ship *Richelieu* dropped anchor at Cap St. Jacques and the *Triomphant* appeared in Saigon harbor. French reinforcements had arrived at last.

But the Japanese, ordered to join the French and the Indians in disarming the Vietnamese, still seemed reluctant to do so. When General Gracey threatened to regard them as war criminals, Japanese General Numata replied that his men were afraid of reprisals if they fired at Vietnamese; he even offered to act as an intermediary between the French and the British on the one hand and the Vietnamese on the other.[14] After this interview, however, the Japanese began to attend to the job of enforcing order with more enthusiasm. An Allied spokesman described their clashes with the Vietnamese as resulting from "a more marked inclination" on the part of the Japanese to obey Allied instructions to maintain law and order.[15]

ANGLO-FRENCH CO-OPERATION

In Ceylon, Admiral Mountbatten watched these developments with concern, uncertain as to how the British Labor Government might react to General Gracey's intervention in Franco-Vietnamese affairs. When General Leclerc, the new commander of the French forces in the Far East, came to see Mountbatten, the Supreme Allied Commander told him that Gracey had overstepped his orders and that he was going to disavow him. General Leclerc, however, persuaded Mountbatten to leave the British general in authority.[16]

In London, British liberals recoiled from reports of Royal Air Force attacks on Vietnamese in support of French troops, and the Liberal *News Chronicle* talked of Lidice. In India, Pandit Nehru said:

We have watched British intervention there [in Indonesia and Indochina] with growing anger, shame and helplessness that Indian troops should thus be used for

[14] Devillers, *op. cit.*, p. 161.
[15] *New York Times*, October 11, 1945.
[16] Adrien Dansette, *Leclerc*, p. 187.

doing Britain's dirty work against our friends who are fighting the same fight as we.[17]

General Gracey did make one attempt to stop the fighting. When General Leclerc made a triumphal entry in Saigon on October 5, he found the city in the midst of a temporary truce which Gracey had just helped to negotiate. But although Cédile and Gracey met several times with members of the Committee of the South, it was no use. Some hundred French hostages had been taken after September 23 by the Vietnamese, who now appeared unable to surrender them. This, however, although the occasion for bitter recrimination by the French public, was hardly the fundamental issue. The Vietnamese, blaming all the disorders on the presence of Allied troops, particularly the Indians, demanded that their government and their police be returned to them, that French troops be disarmed and concentrated in a limited area. An independent government might well have imposed such conditions on an alien army; they were not conditions even remotely acceptable to the French, who had not the slightest inclination to regard themselves as alien to the country or the Vietnamese as independent.

The truce, in which virtually no one believed, lasted only ten days; on October 11 it was over and the killings began again. Saigon had become a beleaguered city. Though it was once the largest city in all Viet Nam, few Vietnamese still lived there, most of them having fled to the countryside. The shops along the Rue Catinat were closed, cafés were deserted, and there were no rickshaws in the streets.

The only agreement achieved by the French in the fall of 1945 in Indochina was with the British. By an accord which the French Ambassador René Massigli signed in London on October 9, Foreign Minister Ernest Bevin recognized the French civil administration as the only one entitled to direct nonmilitary affairs south of the sixteenth parallel. Bevin told the House of Commons of continued Vietnamese looting and attacks, of clashes between Frenchmen under Gracey's command and the Vietnamese. British policy, he said, was one of "close and friendly co-operation between the British and French Commanders." Its aim was to bring enough French troops to Saigon to enable them to take over.[18]

On October 25 General Leclerc began the reconquest of Indochina for France. He said that it would take about a month before what he called his "mopping-up operations" were concluded. An armed column moved toward My Tho slowly because of the roadblocks left by the Vietnamese, along a deserted road.

Victorious at My Tho, temporary headquarters of the Committee of the South, which fled at their coming, the French moved next on Tay Ninh, the

17 *New York Times,* January 1, 1946.
18 Parliamentary Debates, House of Commons, October 24, 1945, 2149-50.

Cao Dai capital, and the main Cao Dai sects surrendered early in November. Together, the British and the French took over strategic areas throughout Cochin China, while the Vietnamese, unable to meet them in open battle, resorted to guerrilla warfare and sabotage.

The French were critical of the British as the fighting continued. In Europe, they complained, their allies failed to supply them with adequate shipping to bring their men to the Far East and with weapons to arm them, and in Indochina they did not seem as anxious as were the French to re-establish French authority.

Of one facet of British policy, however, the French had no reason to complain at all. That was their behavior in Cambodia.

RETURN TO CAMBODIA

After the Japanese took over Indochina in March 1945 and declared the independence of Cambodia as well as of Viet Nam, a Cambodian nationalist, Son Ngoc Thanh, had returned home from Japan to become first Foreign Minister and then Prime Minister of Cambodia. He held a plebiscite after V-J Day in which the Cambodian people voted to support him and favored ending the French protectorate. But Thanh did not remain Prime Minister very long after the British arrived in Indochina. On October 10, French, British, and Indian troops took over Pnom Penh, the Cambodian capital, and the British permitted General Leclerc to seize the Prime Minister, explaining that his activities "threatened the security of Allied forces and he was working against Cambodian interests."[19] He was brought to Saigon, and then sent to France to await trial as a collaborator.

King Norodom Sihanouk selected as Thanh's successor Kim Tit, Minister of Defense, who had gone to Saigon to ask Lerclerc to send French troops to Cambodia. The atmosphere in Pnom Penh became more friendly to the French. Vietnamese living in the capital who had actively supported the ex-Prime Minister fled or went into hiding. The French, for their part, promised to get back for Cambodia the provinces that Siam had wrested from it during the war. They also made it clear that they were not opposed to changing Cambodia's prewar legal status. It was not only the deposed Prime Minister Thanh who favored such a change. Kim Tit himself told French newspapermen, "We want our complete independence, but guaranteed by France. As England, for example, guarantees that of Siam."[20]

Kim Tit was soon replaced as Prime Minister by Prince Monireth, and General Alessandri arrived to be the new French Commissioner. In November they worked out the bases of an accord between their two countries. The young King, then in his early twenties, announced:

[19] *New York Times,* October 22, 1945.
[20] Blanchet, *op. cit.,* p. 35.

... that the new France has understood us perfectly and that this comprehension can only lead to a durable and real entente between our two nations ... The protectorate regime presented inconveniences of which one of the principal was that it did not permit the Cambodian people to take a real part in the administration of the country. The nation and the King are happy now to obtain a larger autonomy ... that will permit us to work for our country ourselves. However, the French will become the great technical advisers of our administration.[21]

The agreement formally concluded between the French and the Cambodians on January 7, 1946 revealed that the French protectorate had ended only in name. There was talk of full internal autonomy for Cambodia, of a new era and a new independence, but effective power was still in the hands of Frenchmen. Only now they were called "advisers." In Cambodia, at least, the declaration of March 24, 1945 was being applied much as the French had intended to apply it before the Democratic Republic of Viet Nam appeared on the scene. The transition had been a peaceful one and the French seemed once again ensconced firmly in the country.[22]

THE ADMIRAL AND THE ADMINISTRATORS

General Gracey had done his job in Indochina by the beginning of 1946. He had attended to the Japanese and to the Allied prisoners of war, as he had been directed. He had also, on his own initiative, helped the French to regain a foothold in the country. On January 1 the British Navy withdrew from Saigon and when Gracey left at the end of the month, the bulk of the British forces had also gone.

In a series of statements Admiral d'Argenlieu, the new High Commissioner, laid down the objectives of French policy:

"It is the sacred duty of France to re-establish order, respect for law, freedom to work, and security for all wherever she extends her authority," he said. French soldiers were coming to liberate the Vietnamese, who, according to the Admiral, were "persecuted and sometimes martyrized by men of force."[23] He reminded the Vietnamese of the culture and the disinterested sympathy and understanding they had received from France and which they would need in the future. Alongside this went his assertion, which he was reported as pronouncing with particular emphasis: "We will never give up."[24]

Admiral d'Argenlieu had talked of conciliation and the benefits of French rule to the Vietnamese, but to his soldiers General Leclerc sounded a much

21 Ministère des Colonies, *Bulletin d'Information*, November 15, 1946.

22 At midnight March 4, 1946, the Southeast Asia Command formally surrendered to Leclerc's authority over Indochina south of the sixteenth parallel.

23 French Press and Information Service (New York), Document Série II, 3339E, December 14, 1945.

24 *Le Monde*, January 20–21, 1946.

more martial note. He told them that they were "fighting for the re-establish-ment of French greatness."[25] Yet two weeks later d'Argenlieu could say, "France has not come guided by material or financial interests, but by human-ity."[26] In the early days of 1946 it was difficult to determine from official state-ments just where France stood.

Saigon, where for a short time the intrigues and clashes of Vietnamese po-litical groups had held the center of the stage, had become a French city once again. With the British gone and Vietnamese nationalist leaders with the guerrillas or underground, it was the French who made policy. The differ-ence between Gaullists and Vichyites, although sometimes sharp on the per-sonal level, were obscured politically by their common desire to reassert French sovereignty over Indochina. After the Japanese capitulation, Admiral Decoux had actually asked the British for permission to re-establish his own French government in Saigon, superseding Cédile.[27] His request was in vain; Cédile remained High Commissioner and, in time, Admiral Decoux and some of the men who had been most important in his administration were arrested and sent to France to stand trial for collaboration. It was not only the under-standable reluctance of representatives of liberated France to deal with men of Vichy which led to their removal. The Decoux administration had lost prestige among the Indochinese population because of its defeat by the Japa-nese and the imprisonment of French officials. And their close identification with the old colonialism would have made impossible any hope of achieving a peaceful settlement with the Vietnamese. However, these objections to Ad-miral Decoux and his associates, which were put forward by representatives of the de Gaulle government, were not extended by them to men who had served in subordinate positions under Decoux. On August 23 General de Gaulle had stated that most of the French officials in Indochina were accept-able to the new government in Paris. "All the services of Cochin China, all the provinces," Cédile wrote subsequently, "were put under the control of former officials of the country. For me, there never was a gap between the oldtimers and the newcomers."[28] Jean Sainteny followed much the same pol-icy when he became French Commissioner in Northern Indochina.[29]

Gradually Admiral d'Argenlieu, the High Commissioner for Indochina and Cédile, Commissioner for Cochin China, both of them stationed in Saigon, fell under the influence of some of the Frenchmen in the Cochin Chinese capi-tal—administrators, planters, military and professional men—who were most

[25] Ibid., December 27, 1945.
[26] Ibid., January 13–14, 1946.
[27] See the letter from Commissioner Cédile, Le Monde, October 16–17, 1949.
[28] Ibid.
[29] In the services of the French administration for Tonkin and North Annam, re-established under Sainteny, the proportion of "new Frenchmen" or "Frenchmen of 1945" was never more than 15 to 20 percent of the total personnel. Sainteny, op. cit., p. 123.

interested in restoring the prewar status quo, or as close an approximation of it as possible. Philippe Devillers, who arrived in Cochin China himself in October 1945 with General Leclerc's soldiers, wrote:

The Admiral arrived in Indochina full of generous intentions. He had prepared speeches which probably would have created a real psychological shock. For reasons still unknown, they were not delivered. . . . From the beginning the Admiral was surrounded by officials and military men. His ideas seemed dangerous to the administrators. . . .[30]

Commissioner Cédile, in his turn, particularly because of his desire to create an advisory Vietnamese assembly as a step toward bringing the March 24, 1945 declaration into effect, "by his liberal and 'progressive' tendencies, disturbed colonists, planters and his administrator colleagues in Indochina."[31]

The professional administrators had little difficulty in taking over. By their familiarity with the country, the long continuity of their positions, and their sure knowledge of what they wanted, they came increasingly to make French policy in Saigon both under Admiral d'Argenlieu and the men who followed him. At first they were influential only in Cochin China, but later, as Saigon became the French capital of Indochina, they left their stamp on French policy for the entire country.

They recognized that they could not deal directly with the disturbed political situation; they had to work through Vietnamese. There was some talk at this time of sponsoring the return to power of ex-Emperor Duy Tan, exiled to Réunion in 1916, who had fought for the Free French during the second World War; but Duy Tan was interested in Vietnamese independence, which was not to the taste of the French administration. French officials found their answer to the Viet Minh nearer at hand among a group of Vietnamese in Saigon itself, where because of the peculiar nature of French rule over Cochin China since the 1860's, men willing to collaborate with the French administration were easily available.

The French conquest in the mid-nineteenth century had destroyed the mandarinal administrative framework in Cochin China, leaving its people without any responsible native authorities. Cochin China became a French colony, the only one of the five prewar divisions of Indochina with the right to a representative (in practice, always a Frenchman) in the Chamber of Deputies in Paris. The French had set up a system of direct administration which had the effect of cutting off Cochin China from its indigenous roots, breaking down its social and cultural system, and imposing in its stead an inapplicable and inadequate French veneer and an overlarge French officialdom. There was little to stand in the way of this development; the Vietnamese had come later to Cochin China than to Tonkin and Annam and had not accumulated as

[30] Devillers, op. cit., pp. 169–70.
[31] Ibid., p. 172.

resistant a tradition in the south. There were no mandarins left in Cochin China to uphold the nationalist tradition. The new bourgeoisie was largely identified with the French, whose activities had brought it into existence. Vietnamese nationalism remained strongest among the Cochin Chinese peasantry.

Under the Japanese, Cochin China had been kept separate from Tonkin and Annam almost until the very end. Then the British came, again cutting off the region from the north, and on their heels the soldiers of General Leclerc.

Although the French claimed to have reasserted their rule over Cochin China, their control did not extend much beyond the city of Saigon; but this did not faze Admiral d'Argenlieu and his advisors, who set about strengthening the French "federal" machinery in the colony. At the same time they encouraged, among the small Gallicized bourgeoisie of big landowners, officials, and business and professional men, a Cochin Chinese separatist movement aimed at keeping Cochin China separate from the rest of Viet Nam and outside the authority of the Viet Minh government in Hanoi. Some of the political adventurers among these separatists later carved out substantial careers for themselves in French-controlled Viet Nam.

On February 12, 1946 an Advisory Council was established in Saigon with four French members and eight Vietnamese. This Council, the successor to the prewar Colonial Council, was charged with advising Commissioner Cédile and keeping him informed on popular opinion. But its Vietnamese members were French citizens wholly identified with the social and economic system that the French had created in Cochin China; all of them were French appointees; and seven of the eight were French citizens.

The French press in Saigon launched a campaign against alleged Tonkinese imperialism, contrasting the poverty of the crowded northern provinces with the prosperity of Cochin China, and branding the Tonkinese as potential exploiters. It tried to stir up Cochin Chinese public opinion against the skilled laborers in the shops and on the plantations who came from Tonkin and northern Annam.

Demonstrations in Saigon demanded "Cochin China for the Cochin Chinese," all of them reported in the French press. Americans in Saigon noted that these demonstrations were not only small, but were directed from the sidelines by men with megaphones. Nationalists insisted that they were inspired by French capitalists and planters interested in Cochin Chinese rubber and rice, and by groups allied with the Bank of Indochina, all of them anxious to protect the privileged status which the French administration had given them and which the Viet Minh threatened.

Not all the French people of Saigon, however, believed that separatism was the answer to Vietnamese demands. In February 1946 the Socialist newspaper *Justice* began a series of attacks on General Leclerc's troops, criticizing their lack of discipline, and urging that hostilities cease and more moderate terms be offered to the Viet Minh. A group of anticolonialist Frenchmen drew up a motion asking the French government to grant independence to Viet Nam. It was not for publication, but a Vietnamese newspaper got hold of the text and published it. Added to this, d'Argenlieu, who had gone to France, was soon due back in Indochina and it was expected that he would bring with him directives for a more moderate policy towards the Vietnamese. All of this was too much for Leclerc's soldiers. They rioted in the streets of Saigon, demonstrating against the Socialists.

Frenchmen who were not very pleased at the behavior of the troops were still not sorry to see the Socialists under attack. They had little patience with any talk of compromise, nor did they like the fact that *Justice* took it for granted that during the war French civilians in Indochina had collaborated with the Japanese. The atmosphere among the French people of Saigon was sullen and self-righteous. It was not an atmosphere conducive to clear thinking or to moderation.

In the Cochin Chinese hinterland, meanwhile, Leclerc pushed his mopping-up operations, and each day made clear that the job would be neither as short nor as effective as he had prophesied. When French troops moved through the countryside during the day, they rarely saw an enemy soldier—only peaceful peasants working in the fields, or roads and fields from which all the Vietnamese had fled. Vietnamese guerrillas crouched low in the waters of the ricefields, breathing through hollow bamboo sticks until isolated Frenchmen were close by, when they attacked without warning; and the harmless *nha que* laboring in his ricefield sometimes turned suddenly into a Vietnamese soldier; but generally the countryside seemed deserted by day.

At night, darkness and surprise made up for the lack of arms and equipment. Vietnamese guerrillas attacked French outposts, and even infiltrated into Saigon itself; and French soldiers who walked out alone of an evening, sometimes with a Vietnamese girl who seemed friendly and into whose politics they did not inquire, did not always return. In the daytime French troops came upon the bodies of their comrades lying massacred and sometimes horribly mutilated, and their feeling for the unseen enemy, whom they had regarded at first with the relative impersonality of men doing a job under orders, was transformed into a real and personal hate.

By the early part of 1946 French troops held the cities of Cochin China, and the rich rubber plantations were again in French hands. The number of French civil servants in Indochina reached 14,000, four times as many as there had been in 1939. Some arrived to replace Frenchmen still in Indochina, others to replace Vietnamese who had joined the Viet Minh.[32] Vietnamese Notables, who had fled when the fighting began, returned to their homes in the shelter

[32] James Baeyens, "Indo-China," *The Asiatic Review,* October 1950, pp. 1170–71.

of the French-controlled zones. The French planters went back, too, although few Vietnamese remained to work their lands for them.

Outside the areas they controlled in the Cochin Chinese countryside, the French could move only in convoys, and even those were not always safe from attack. But the Vietnamese guerrillas were not well prepared to fight; and they were not united. By February 1946 most of their leaders had fled, either to Hanoi or to Siam.

Chapter Six

THE CHINESE IN THE NORTH

In TONKIN there still was peace. The sixteenth parallel, where the British zone of occupation in the south ended and the Chinese zone began, was a boundary between two different worlds. In the paddy fields of Cochin China, French soldiers and Vietnamese guerrillas fought and died day after day; the Vietnamese Committee of the South was in hiding, while the French officials sat in the government buildings of Saigon and the French High Commissioner laid down the directives by which they ruled. In Tonkin no Frenchman was in any position to give orders to Vietnamese. This was Vietnamese territory in which Frenchmen moved cautiously and with fear. Once a city of French functionaries, the headquarters of the French administration of Indochina, Hanoi had become the capital of the Democratic Republic of Viet Nam. Ho Chi Minh presided over the new government, while Vietnamese police patrolled the streets and Vietnamese officials ran the administration and the public services.

The new republic was strongest in Hanoi, the seat of its authority, weaker in the rest of Tonkin and Annam. Its official policy, where it was in control, was to frown upon violence, against Frenchmen and against Vietnamese; and for a revolution, it was a relatively peaceful one, at least in August and September of 1945.

But Ho Chi Minh and his government could not prevent some disorders. The Tonkinese delta had been ravaged by famine soon after the Japanese coup in March, and then, in August, by flood. In the wake of these disasters, which disrupted the established order, bandits roamed through the provinces, raiding French properties. The French soldiers in Hanoi, some four to five thousand, were still in the Hanoi Citadel, where the Japanese had confined them months before, and were still without arms. French doctors were thrown out of the Pasteur Institute and much of their equipment destroyed or dispersed, and the doors of the French School of the Far East were closed to French scholars. French civilians in Hanoi, outside the Citadel and nominally free, lived in fear of Vietnamese pillaging and attacks.

In Kunming a group of Frenchmen waited for the time when they could go to Indochina. Several of them were to play an important role in Indochinese affairs. One was Jean Sainteny, chief of the French Military Mission; a gallant figure in the French resistance, he was to become Commissioner of the Republic in North Indochina and do yeoman duty in the service of Franco-Vietnamese relations. Another was Jean de Raymond, who represented the Ministry of Overseas France and later was Commissioner in Laos and then in Cambodia (where he was assassinated in 1951). A third French official in Kunming, like de Raymond a veteran of the Colonial service, was Léon Pignon, who three years later was to be appointed High Commissioner of Indochina. General Alessandri, who became the official representative of General de Gaulle, was also in Kunming.

When the first feelers toward negotiations were put out by the Vietnamese, these were the men they reached. It was July 1945 and the war was still going on. Admiral d'Argenlieu had not yet been appointed High Commissioner when a message came to Kunming over an American radio from the camp in Tonkin where Ho Chi Minh had his headquarters, proposing an agreement with France which would guarantee independence to Viet Nam in five to ten years. No one in Kunming had the authority to accept these or any other terms. All that they could reply was that they were prepared to negotiate.

V-J Day came soon afterward. Pierre Mesmer was appointed Commissioner of the Republic and made his audacious descent into Tonkin, only to be captured and imprisoned by the Vietnamese. Sainteny, who had directed parachute and commando operations in northern Indochina from Kunming, wanted to go to Hanoi also, but when he looked for a plane to take him there, he found himself up against a wall of Chinese and American indifference; neither government was keen on helping the French to return to Indochina.

The Chinese placed a French plane under seal to prevent its taking off, but just about the time that Mesmer was leaving on his mission, Sainteny also left for Indochina as a member of a joint Franco-American mission. His plane, even then, was delayed in its departure from China, and the word came to turn back when they were already on their way, but they disregarded it and continued to Hanoi.

They were received by Japanese soldiers and escorted to the Hotel Métropole through a silent and watching crowd, under banners denouncing French imperialism. They barely had been taken to their rooms when a Japanese officer appeared to tell them that the Japanese could not be responsible for Sainteny's safety if he remained at the hotel. The Americans were permitted to stay; the Frenchmen succeeded in establishing themselves in the palace of the Government General, where they lived under guard, virtual prisoners of the Japanese, although in radio contact with Kunming.

The Japanese seemed intent on keeping the Vietnamese and the French apart, and in this they were not alone; the Americans in Hanoi, who tended to be critical of French colonialism, did not appear much more anxious to bring them together. Three groups of Americans came to Hanoi in August and September 1945. A mission under Colonel Nordlinger was there to look after the needs of prisoners of war. General Gallagher arrived in September to head an American military mission. Also in Hanoi was a contingent of the Office of Strategic Services under Major Patti which seemed to the French to be the most pro-Vietnamese and anti-French of them all. Many Frenchmen were obsessed by the bogey of American business infiltration into Indochina and of American strategic designs on the country; to them the OSS was the vanguard of a new imperialism.[1]

The French were not happy about American actions in these critical days. A number of them felt, and freely admitted, that only the presence of the Americans had saved the French population from wholesale massacre toward the end of August. But having given the Americans their due for saving French lives, the French found them seriously at fault for failing to save French sovereignty.

The Americans were the only Allied group which could move freely in Hanoi; they were the liaison between the French and the Japanese. They were the only people who might conceivably have convinced the Japanese that they ought to recognize French authority over Tonkin. That, at least, was the way the French reasoned; the Americans did not. There was among them a strong feeling of anticolonialism which derived both from sympathy for a subject people and from disapproval of the backward policies that the Third Republic had sometimes adopted in Indochina.[2] They were also critical of the spinelessness and collaborationism of the Decoux regime. Major Patti, the head of the American mission with which Sainteny had arrived, was sympathetic to the Vietnamese and did not hide it. It was he who first presented Vo Nguyen Giap, then Ho Chi Minh's Minister of Interior, to Sainteny. After that, although he continued to visit the palace of the Government General, he did not bring any more Vietnamese emissaries with him. "We seemed to the Americans," wrote Sainteny, "incorrigibly obstinate in reviving a colonial past to which they were opposed in the name of an infantile anticolonialism which blinded them to almost everything."[3]

Sainteny's position was particularly difficult because the Japanese refused to deal with him, and Patti saw no reason to intervene on his behalf. The French authorities in Calcutta and Kunming would do nothing to help him when Sainteny appealed to them to still Japanese doubts by confirming his right to speak for France. He and the earnest young men in his entourage were keenly aware that these were crucial days for France in Indochina. Firm and quick action might impress upon the Japanese that they could not disregard French

[1] According to a French report, OSS agents went so far as to propose to Ho Chi Minh that economic interests with which General William Donovan, OSS chief, was associated would help reconstruct Vietnamese railroads, roads, and airfields in exchange for economic privileges in the region. Ho, says this French account, rejected the offer. Le Monde, April 13-14, 1947.

[2] These policies were personified, for Vietnamese and for many outside observers, by Governor General Merlin, who in the 1920's had made explicit the "horizontal" scheme of education which prevailed in the country under France. It permitted Vietnamese just enough instruction to make them auxiliaries of the French but did not give them the technical training which would have enabled them to operate the economic and administrative machinery of the country.

[3] Sainteny, op. cit., p. 125.

claims, but if Sainteny were not given every support by his government, the opportunity might slip through his hands and never come again. He asked for official French recognition of his mission. If it were simply a matter of personalities which stood in the way, he offered to resign in favor of some other man in whom his government would have more confidence. But his superiors did not seem to understand the situation. They would not withdraw Sainteny and neither would they give him any power.

On September 2, the members of the French mission in Hanoi stood at their windows and watched a large and peaceful crowd march past the palace of the Government General, celebrating Vietnamese independence. The French were powerless to do anything but watch. Two American planes, with their star insignia, flew low over the demonstrators, giving the appearance, as they had on other occasions, of the American support which Viet Minh leaders claimed so insistently.

Vo Nguyen Giap made an important speech that day. "As regards foreign relations," he said, "our public opinion pays very much attention to the Allied missions . . . at Hanoi, because everyone is anxious to know the result of the foreign negotiations of the government." He spoke of "particularly intimate relations" with China and the United States "which it is a pleasant duty to dwell upon . . ." And then he spoke of less pleasant things.

They [the French] are making preparations to land their forces in Indochina. In a word, and according to latest intelligence, France is preparing herself to reconquer our country. . . . The Vietnamese people will fight for independence, liberty and equality of status. If our negotiations are unsuccessful, we shall resort to arms.[4]

Had the French been able to arrive in force in August, they might have succeeded in re-establishing themselves in Tonkin, but there were no ships to bring their troops to Indochina. General Alessandri did have some soldiers waiting in China, but the Chinese would not permit them to cross the frontier.

Had Sainteny been given more authority in his dealings with the Vietnamese, he might have succeeded in hammering out an understanding with them. That, however, is more questionable, for the Vietnamese wanted at least the forms of independence, and there is no evidence that Sainteny was prepared to offer them that.

The moment in which the scales might have been tipped in favor of a quick settlement, in any case, soon passed. The Japanese permitted the Vietnamese to take over. The Americans did not prevent them, and the French could not. Then the Chinese came.

The French were fearful of Chinese designs on Indochina. Convinced that the northern part of the country had been given to the Chinese to compensate "for the dangerous concessions made to the U.S.S.R. at the expense of China

---

4 Democratic Republic of Viet-Nam, *Documents*.

by President Roosevelt during the course of the Yalta Conference," Sainteny had warned his government that the Chinese, "supported by certain important American leaders," were determined to expel the French from Indochina.[5] The French Government protested against the division of the country in appeals to the American Government and to Admiral Mountbatten, chief of the Southeast Asia Command. Mountbatten was not unsympathetic but the veto lay in Washington; and the United States would not go back on its decision that Generalissimo Chiang Kai-shek and his soldiers would oversee the Japanese surrender in Indochina north of the sixteenth parallel.[6]

The arrival of the Chinese was preceded by gestures of friendship between Paris and Chungking. On August 18 the French returned to China the leased territory of Kwangchowwan, a part of the Indochinese Union which had been in their possession since 1898. Six days later Chiang Kai-shek disavowed any territorial ambitions in Indochina. China, he said, was sympathetic to the freedom of "weak" nations and hoped that Indochina would achieve independence; but in northern Indochina he would remain neutral, he declared, neither encouraging the independence movement nor helping the French to put it down.[7]

But it was impossible to be neutral in Indochina, even if the Chinese had wanted to be, which was open to doubt. In Cochin China the British talked about neutrality, but General Gracey ended up fighting France's battles for her. The Chinese did not come to Tonkin until the Viet Minh had established itself in power; and, arrived in a country they once had ruled, whose people and civilization were very like their own, the Chinese regarded it with different eyes than the British in the south. China had no identity of interests either with France or Great Britain as a white, a European, or a colonial power. The Chinese had not nurtured Vietnamese nationalist movements on Chinese soil for so long in order to oust the first independent regime which had ruled Viet Nam in sixty years. Although the Vietnamese suffered from the behavior of the Chinese army of occupation and the Viet Minh, throughout its stay, was under continuing Chinese pressure to share power with pro-Chinese nationalist groups, the cause of Vietnamese independence profited enormously from the presence of the Chinese.

THE CHINESE ARRIVE

The Chinese arrived in mid-September 1945, with some well-trained troops with American arms and equipment and many ragged, ill-disciplined local units. Black marketeering and looting swelled with their arrival, although not

[5] Sainteny, op. cit., p. 50.

[6] R. de L., "L'intervention des troupes chinoises en Indochine à la suite de la capitulation japonaise," Politique Etrangère, June–July 1950, pp. 343–45. See also Mountbatten, Report to the Combined Chiefs of Staff, op. cit.

[7] New York Times, August 25, 1945; October 14, 1945.

as much as both Viet Minh and official French sources have since alleged. General Lu Han, the Chinese commander, took over the lavishly appointed palace of the Government General, leaving Jean Sainteny, who had just been appointed French Commissioner in North Indochina, to find quarters elsewhere.

No sooner had they arrived, than the Chinese set about dismantling French military fortifications from Lao Kay to Mon Cay on the Sino-Vietnamese frontier. At the same time, they began the operation which they had been delegated to perform by the Allies; they disarmed the Japanese in the north and concentrated them near the coast until repatriation ships could arrive to take them home to Japan. Japanese still mingled with Vietnamese, Chinese, and Americans in the teeming Hanoi streets, but far fewer Japanese were at large in Hanoi than in Saigon. The southern capital was a deserted city after September 23 while Hanoi, still at peace, was crowded with Vietnamese as well as Chinese. The cafés and pastry shops were open, and loudspeakers on the streets broadcast Vietnamese government propaganda to the crowds.

The French found General Lu Han stubbornly un-co-operative. Speculation in Paris wavered between assertions that the General (whose relatives in Yunnan province were having their own difficulties with the Chinese Government) had broken away from the control of Chungking to pursue his own anarchic anti-French way, and suspicions that anarchy and hostility to the French were Chinese policy in Indochina and that he was just following orders. General Alessandri, the French representative, withdrew in anger from the Japanese surrender ceremonies at Hanoi when he found that the French flag was not displayed with those of the other Allies. Alessandri's relations with the Chinese were not good, and it took some time for the French to understand why. The fact was that the Chinese were not willing to emulate the political amnesia of the French in regard to the General's activities in Indochina before March 9, 1945. So far as the de Gaulle government was concerned, Alessandri had purged himself of the Vichy taint by his heroic odyssey after March 9 when he led 6,000 Frenchmen to China and to safety; but this feat did not seem to the Chinese to warrant returning to Tonkin a man who was so closely identified with the Decoux regime and its capitulation to Japan.

France's difficulties with the Chinese, however, were far more serious than merely a matter of personalities; all signs pointed to the fact that whatever the Chinese Government chose to say at this time, Chungking did not want the French to come back to Indochina. From the Chinese point of view, there was after all no reason to restore French authority unconditionally in the country. The Chinese turned a deaf ear to repeated French requests to bring in French soldiers and civil administrators. The Vietnamese were permitted to keep their weapons, whereas Frenchmen in Hanoi were disarmed and every Frenchman arriving in Tonkin was liable to search and the confiscation of any arms that he might be carrying. Government buildings, communications, and virtually the whole of the civil administration remained in Vietnamese hands.

The French were bitter as the Chinese occupation continued and the unruly Chinese army spread over the countryside as though it were there to stay. It lived off the land and afflicted Tonkin like an invasion of locusts, looting Hanoi and surrounding regions. Chinese civilians suffered at least as much as Vietnamese. "The Chinese army is worse than the atomic bomb," a Chinese merchant in Hanoi told a journalist.[8]

LAOTIAN INDEPENDENCE

Following their instructions to take over Indochina north of the sixteenth parallel, the Chinese also moved into Laos, even though the French insisted that they had the situation there well in hand.

The arrival of the Chinese postponed for many months the return of the French to Laos. Like the Cambodians, the Laotians had achieved a new freedom during the war years—under the Siamese (a Thai people, like themselves), who took over territory on the right bank of the Mekong River, and under the Japanese, who left the Laotians considerable independence of action. After the experience of having been governed by people of the same race, and even having been permitted to govern themselves, Laotian leaders, no less than the Cambodians, regarded French rule as discredited and hastened to reassert their independence after the Japanese surrender.

On September 1, 1945, Prince Petsarath, who had become Prime Minister under Sisavang Vong, King of Luang Prabang, read a proclamation at Vientiane, stating:

In consequence of the failure of the French rulers the kingdom had to proclaim itself independent.

The juridical bonds tying us to France by treaties and agreements have been broken off in fact, because France has not met her engagement to defend us against external forces.

The division of Laos—with the south under direct administration by the French, whose capital was at Vientiane, and the north ruled by the King of Luang Prabang as a French protectorate[8a]—had continued under the Japanese, but on September 15 Petsarath declared the unification of the country as the Kingdom of Laos under the crown of Luang Prabang.

French officials, who had been interned by the Japanese and freed late in August by a small group of French soldiers who arrived in the country by

---

[8] Blanchet, op. cit., p. 227.

[8a] Under Admiral Decoux three northern provinces, until then under French administration, had been added to the Kingdom of Luang Prabang in order to compensate for the territory it had lost to Siam.

parachute, tried to reassert French authority over Laos after V-J Day; there were armed clashes between French soldiers and Laotians in September 1945. In Vientiane, Laotian nationalists, the so-called Free Laotians or Issarak, elected what they called a People's Committee which on October 12 promulgated a provisional constitution and appointed a provisional government under Phaya Khammao. Supported by members of the royal family and of the nobility, by officials and by intellectuals, they forced the resignation of King Sisavang Vong.

Unlike the situation in Cambodia, where the Anglo-Indian troops of General Gracey rapidly put an end to the independence proclaimed by Prime Minister Son Ngoc Thanh, opening the country to French troops, the Chinese occupation sheltered the Laotians from the French; and like the Tonkinese, the Laotians paid a price for this protection in the form of much Chinese looting. "The Japanese soldiers were far better disciplined than the Chinese," Prince Petsarath said later.

THE CHINESE OCCUPATION

The Chinese occupation of one half of Indochina cost the country several times more than the Japanese occupation of the whole, mourned a *Le Monde* correspondent late in 1945;[9] and if simply the cost of material depredations were counted, this may well have been true. But there is more to the life of a country than that; the behavior of the Chinese troops did not compare badly with the terrible burden of thought control imposed on other countries under foreign occupation and, more important, the presence of the Chinese enabled the Vietnamese to consolidate their own independent regime.

The Chinese, however, had their own reasons for coming to Indochina and while it was their policy to encourage Vietnamese independence, they were immediately more interested in winning certain specific concessions from the French for themselves.

During the war the Chinese had learned the importance of the Tonkinese port of Haiphong. They had learned it the hard way, by having the port and the railway closed off to them, and for that they blamed the French. In peace the railway was the indispensable outlet over which the trade of southwest China passed to reach the sea. It had served in earlier days as the opening wedge of French economic influence in southern China, but now it was the Chinese who were in a position to bargain, and they had no intention of leaving the railway and the port under exclusive French control.

By the same token, the Chinese were now in a position to force the surrender of the various special rights which France, like other European countries, had acquired in China after it was opened to the West.

[9] *Le Monde,* November 3, 1945.

Also at issue between the two countries was the status of the well over 400,-
000 Chinese in Indochina who played a prominent part in economic life. The
largest Chinese community was in Cochin China, in Cholon, the all-Chinese
city adjoining Saigon. Cambodia too had a considerable Chinese population:
one-third of the population of Pnom Penh, its capital, was Chinese, one-third
Vietnamese, and one-third Cambodian. The Chinese lived even in over-
crowded Tonkin; there was a powerful and prosperous Chinese colony in the
busy port city of Haiphong.

Intermediate between the French plantation, mining, and financial interests
and the Indochinese peasant, the Chinese covered Indochina with a network
of economic control. They were closer to the Indochinese than were the
French; they lived more intimately among them and knew them better. As the
businessmen, the merchants, and the moneylenders of Indochina, the Chinese
controlled most of the internal trade of the country and owned most of the rice
mills, the sugar refineries, and the sawmills. They held much property in the
cities; only French law prevented them from owning mines and the best
rubber and rice-growing lands.

The Chinese were generally supposed to be unpopular with the Vietnamese,
as with most Southeast Asians. The most active and often the only middle
class in Southeast Asia, they sent much of their earnings home to China; they
did not create wealth from which the people among whom they lived could
benefit. They were usually too rich and too successful, too linked emotionally
with China even if they worked as coolies, and too concerned with their own
safety and that of their holdings in the countries where they settled, to make
friends among the indigenous population. In Viet Nam, however, where they
lived in communities or "congregations" (each under a head who was responsible to the French for maintaining law and order among his compatriots and
paying their taxes), much of their lack of popularity stemmed from the special
privileges granted to them by the French administration. Even so, the anti-
Chinese riots in Haiphong long before the second World War are alleged by
well-informed Vietnamese not to have broken out spontaneously, but to have
been stirred up by the French police in order to discourage Vietnamese public
opinion in its hope for Chinese support of the various Vietnamese nationalist
movements.

Although the status of the Chinese was far superior to that of the Vietnamese, the native inhabitants of the country, it was not as good as that of other
foreign residents. Even after the Treaty of Nanking in 1935, which declared
them "foreigners with privileged status" in Indochina, the Chinese chafed
under close French supervision, under taxes heavier than those levied on other
foreign groups, and under administrative restrictions which discriminated
against them. When the Chinese army arrived in Tonkin in 1945, it regarded

the congregation system as humiliating to its compatriots, and temporarily abolished it.

But despite their grievances against the French, the Chinese of Indochina, like the Chinese elsewhere in Southeast Asia, had little sympathy for nationalist movements which threatened to upset the status quo; they tended to identify themselves with the established order which allowed them to go about their business as usual. In 1945, however, when Anglo-Indian and French troops presumably represented the established order in Cochin China, lawless elements among them plundered a number of Chinese establishments in Cholon and their actions turned the resident Chinese against the French. The Chinese population in the south, as a result, tended to be pro-Vietnamese in the fall and winter of 1945; and when news of the difficulties of the Saigon-Cholon Chinese with the occupation troops reached the north, the Chinese military was infuriated. The position of Frenchmen in Hanoi, who were already not safe from attack, became even more precarious.

Relations between the Chinese and the French worsened because of the financial situation in the north, where inflation, already begun under the Japanese, increased sharply during the Chinese occupation. One of the most effective of the different techniques which the Chinese used to loot the country was to overvalue grossly the Chinese dollar at the expense of the Indochinese piastre. The Chinese also gained control of a large number of 500-piastre notes, many of which had been issued by the Japanese authorities the previous August. When High Commissioner d'Argenlieu's advisers in Saigon chose this time to call in all 500-piastre notes issued between March 9 and September 23 and to announce that they would no longer be valid, the Chinese, particularly, were hard hit; they threatened the French with trouble, which was soon forthcoming. It broke out at the Bank of Indochina, the citadel of French finance imperialism which until then had withstood all the years of collaboration, occupation, and attack. A Vietnamese crowd gathered outside the Bank, demanding compensation for 500-piastre notes, when shots rang out. The Vietnamese panicked and the Chinese sentries at the Bank fired wildly into the crowd. It was all over quickly, and the Vietnamese carried off their dead, but it was on French heads that the Vietnamese placed the blame.

This episode effectively served the purposes of the Chinese, who met with Sainteny and French functionaries and bank officials, under the chairmanship of the American General Gallagher, and worked out a formula which satisfied the Chinese. But that was not the end of the affair at the Bank of Indochina. Early in January, when one of the Bank officials was leaving his office, he was shot to death by unknown assassins.

Hanoi, so far as the French population was concerned, was in the grip of terror in January 1946 as pro-Chinese nationalist elements launched a campaign of violence against the Viet Minh and the French indiscriminately. The

Chinese apparently expected to benefit from this situation, to discredit the Viet Minh in French eyes so as to prevent any Franco-Vietnamese agreement which might lead to the loss of Viet Nam by China; and to put forward their own candidates for power through whom they hoped to gain control of the country. At the same time, the Chinese seemed to regard the insecurity of the French residents as strengthening the bargaining position of China in the negotiations with France which had just begun in Chungking.

An official British representative in Hanoi during the winter of 1945–46 gave it as his opinion that Commissioner Sainteny's single-handed efforts saved the entire white population of the city from attack. He blamed the semi-anarchy upon the Chinese policy of "absolute neutrality," combined with the lack of an effective police force.[10] Whatever the cause, he reported, murders and assaults had become so common by the end of January that Sainteny sent a cable to Paris asking that the United Nations be requested to investigate the Chinese occupation; and the British and American representatives in Hanoi sent telegrams to their own governments to support him.[11] The British were rather awkwardly situated to be critical of the Chinese; if British police action in the south was considerably more effective, it was also considerably bloodier, and it resulted in a war which has not yet ended. The question of the Chinese occupation, however, never came before the United Nations. The French finally persuaded the Chinese to leave Indochina in the only way they could be persuaded—by accepting their terms. And when the Chinese went, the last buffer between the French and the Vietnamese went too.

But the goal of a Viet Nam independent of France—but not of China—was one that the Chinese abandoned reluctantly; and as long as they were in the country, they maneuvered toward that end.

OPPONENTS OF THE VIET MINH

When the Chinese arrived in Tonkin in September 1945, they brought along men active in the pro-Chinese Vietnamese groups which had worked closely with the Kuomintang during the war. A red flag with a blue square crossed with three white horizontal bands appeared in Hanoi; it was the flag of the Dong Minh Hoi, to which Ho Chi Minh had promised allegiance not so long before. But the wartime alliance was dead. Ho Chi Minh and the Viet Minh had broken away from the Dong Minh Hoi during the war years. This had left the VNQDD the most powerful group in the Dong Minh Hoi and it too had preferred to go its own way, leaving the Dong Minh Hoi just one

[10] According to Sainteny himself, "despite the very special conception [held by the Chinese] of cooperation between allies, the presence of the Chinese armies certainly contributed to avoiding a massacre of the 30,000 Frenchmen confined north of the sixteenth parallel." Sainteny, op. cit., p. 159.

[11] P.T.S.J., "Franco-Vietnamese Relations," Asiatic Review, October 1946, p. 376.

of several nationalist parties. Still chief of the Dong Minh Hoi was the old revolutionary and longtime political exile, Nguyen Hai Than. Nguyen Tuong Tam, who had been active for a time in the pro-Japanese nationalist movement, led the VNQDD.

Neither the Dong Minh Hoi nor the VNQDD had any concrete program, although they were considerably more conservative ideologically than the Viet Minh. Immediately, pressure was put on Ho Chi Minh to include them in the Vietnamese government and re-establish the league of revolutionaries founded in Liuchow.

The pressure came from two sides: from the Chinese, who sought control of the new republic through control of its leaders; and from the Dong Minh Hoi and the VNQDD themselves, joined by elements of the Dai Viet and some young intellectuals. Aware of the advantages of enlarging the political base of his government, Ho Chi Minh tried to close the nationalist ranks under Viet Minh leadership, so that neither the Chinese then nor the French later could capitalize on Vietnamese disunity. In October the Viet Minh succeeded in reaching an agreement with some Dong Minh Hoi members to unite in the "common struggle against the aggressive attempts of the colonial French in order to defend the liberty and independence of the Democratic Republic of Viet Nam."[12]

But this did not heal the breach between the Viet Minh and the other nationalist groups. The Viet Minh was powerful in Tonkin in the cities and among officials and intellectuals generally in the fall of 1945, but even in the north it had not yet penetrated deeply among the peasantry. Its main strength then, as in the years to come, was that it was leading the war against the French, at this time still limited to the south; and people rallied to it as the symbol of national independence and resistance.

Yet when the Dong Minh Hoi and the VNQDD arrived on the scene with arms and supplies from the Chinese, they had little difficulty in finding supporters. The Dong Minh Hoi was handicapped by the fact that it seemed to many to be a creature of the Chinese. But the VNQDD was an old movement which had played a proud part in the nationalist history of Viet Nam. It still had some prestige, particularly among middle-class intellectuals, although it had never fully recovered from the losses inflicted on its leadership by the French after Yen Bay.

By the end of 1945, the traditional supply lines between Tonkin and China were out of Viet Minh hands. The VNQDD controlled the Lao Kay region and, together with the Dong Minh Hoi, it dominated the area around Lang Son; their strength was in the provinces which bordered the Chinese frontier. Elements of the Dong Minh Hoi and the VNQDD lived off the countryside

12 *La République*, October 25, 1945.

and on the tribute which they levied on the people. To add to the general uncertainty, each group had its own small army with its own sources of supply,
and there were bloody clashes among them.

THE VIET MINH IN POWER

By force alone the Viet Minh, at best a small minority in the country, could
never have remained in power: the strength of the Viet Minh in the fall of
1945 lay in the wide popular following it commanded among non-Communist
Vietnamese. Even while it struggled to assert its authority over the VNQDD
and the Dong Minh Hoi, the new national government claimed support from
diverse elements in the population of Tonkin and north Annam, from conservatives and radicals, from men who had worked for the prewar French
administration and others who had been members of Bao Dai's court, from
moderate nationalists, from men much further to the Left, and from many
with no political affiliations at all.[13]

The thirst for independence was so great that the majority of the two million Catholics made common cause with the Viet Minh government, and the
four Vietnamese bishops appealed to the Pope to support Vietnamese independence. However, the widely dispersed Catholic community resisted Viet
Minh attempts to organize it into a "national salvation association" under
Viet Minh control. In the fall of 1945, on the occasion of the ceremonies attending the consecration of Le Huu Tu as Bishop of Phat Diem, prominent
churchmen discussed the formation of a federation through which Catholics
might defend their interests now that the country was independent; but they
were unable to establish this federation on a national scale. It could only have
been founded with the consent of the bishop of each diocese, and most of the
bishops of Viet Nam were French, and some were Spanish, with no interest
in creating any such organization. Not even all the Vietnamese bishops were
present at the Phat Diem discussions; Ngo Dinh Thuc had been unable to
leave Cochin China to attend. As a result, important branches of a Catholic
Federation developed only in Hué and Vinh in Annam.

As individuals, Catholics were as nationalistic as anyone else. A missionary
wrote:

In the struggle for independence the pastors of Annam [Viet Nam] have not
hesitated to affirm that Catholics, far from showing themselves luke-warm or indifferent, should on the contrary display an ardent patriotism. They have reminded
their flocks that they have not only the right but the duty to be in the front lines in

13 "All information indicated that the majority of the population supported it [the Ho Chi
Minh government], that in any case it represented a powerful national movement which was
both irreversible and uncoercible. The desire for independence which animated the Vietnamese
people (Leclerc and his associates were convinced of it) . . . was the logical culmination of a
long and heavy history." Devillers, *op. cit.*, p. 207.

the struggle, that in that way they will remain faithful to Christ and to their country . . . The Annamese Catholic community, with its one thousand five hundred
priests and its two million faithful, has not hesitated to follow the lesson of its
bishops. It has shouldered its responsibilities. No other proof of this is needed than
the spontaneous attitude of the Catholic youth of Hanoi, who themselves provided
the government troops with several 'shock' battalions.[14]

The Ho Chi Minh government, for its part, preached tolerance of all religions. However, the Catholic villages were virtually the only organized
groups to exist outside the Viet Minh coalition; and over a period of time the
dioceses of Phat Diem and Bui Chu in Central Tonkin, where Catholics were
especially numerous, gradually assumed a semi-autonomous status and began
to train and arm their own militia.

National unity was the watchword of the Viet Minh as it strove to consolidate its control over the north, and to this end it spared no weapon: force, propaganda, political manipulation, and political organization were all brought
into play.

One Viet Minh tactic at this time was to minimize the role of the Communist Party in the revolution; and on November 11, 1945, the Indochinese Communist Party, founded by Ho Chi Minh fifteen years before, formally dissolved itself. The rank and file, many of whom had joined the party because
of its nationalist resistance record rather than its ideology, either joined other
groups or lost interest in politics. The nucleus of the party, however, remained
intact: its key members, militant and unswerving Communists like Tran Van
Giau and Vo Nguyen Giap, reorganized in what they called a Marxist Study
Group.

Aware that if national power could be seized in Hanoi, it could be consolidated only in the countryside, Viet Minh leaders directed drastic changes in
the administrative structure of Viet Nam. The mandarinate and the Councils
of village Notables were abolished and replaced by new administrative organs, so-called People's Committees, set up at all levels—the region, the province, the city, the prefecture, the village. The most conservative elements of
the country were concentrated behind the bamboo hedges which surrounded
each village, where custom ruled and French penetration had been relatively
slight, and most conservative of all was the old village oligarchy, the Council
of Notables. The People's Committees which the Viet Minh ordered substituted for them were theoretically chosen by the inhabitants of the village; actually they were controlled by the Viet Minh. Given powers unknown in the
old Vietnamese villages but not unknown in Communist countries which
were based on "soviets," they were expected to function politically, culturally,
and socially—to rally support to the Ho Chi Minh government, to fight illiteracy, to wipe out what were regarded as bad habits: smoking, drinking, and

[14] "Le Chrétien annamite et l'indépendance du Vietnam," Le Bulletin des Missions, 1946.

gambling. Three or four villages were sometimes combined into one, further demolishing the old administration and neutralizing opposition elements. The traditional social and self-help organizations of the villages went the way of the Councils of Notables; and in their stead the Viet Minh sponsored and controlled mass "national salvation" organizations of peasants, workers, youth, and women which functioned throughout the country.

The new government did not hesitate to use force in order to consolidate its control and it took strong action against the Notables, as it did also against the mandarins, arresting some, executing others. But it did not countenance sporadic violence, which tended to divide rather than unite the population; and for this reason it frowned upon attempts at social revolution in the countryside. When local People's Committees made their own revolutionary policy, seizing land and property, the Viet Minh central committee intervened, doing its best to temper them.

To strengthen its position, the Viet Minh carried on an intensive propaganda campaign in favor of national unity and independence under Ho Chi Minh. It trained a popular militia and continued the organization and indoctrination of the young people of the country which had been begun during the Japanese occupation.

The Viet Minh banned prostitution and gambling, and the use of opium and alcohol. It passed legislation to protect workers, women, and children, decreed allowances for the poor. It abolished the more onerous taxes which had flourished under the French, like the head tax and the revenues from alcohol, salt, and opium. At the same time, however, it instituted government loans and encouraged what it called voluntary contributions and public subscriptions. In the end, these turned out to be at least as heavy as the tax load imposed by the colonial regime.

Even while the Viet Minh talked revolution, it made every effort to give the new regime a legitimate basis. Bringing Bao Dai into the government was only one aspect of this policy. Ho Chi Minh had barely assumed office when he decreed universal suffrage and announced that there would be general elections in all Viet Nam.

Despite worsening political and economic conditions throughout the country, the Viet Minh kept to this resolve. In the north, it was confronted by the levies of the Chinese occupation army and the open opposition of the pro-Chinese parties as well as of some nationalists who had worked with the Japanese. In Cochin China there was disorder, and then war. Nature joined with man to complicate the situation as floods and famine ravaged Tonkin and northern Annam. Yet popular interest in the elections grew as the weeks passed and Viet Minh propaganda intensified throughout Viet Nam.

The elections were scheduled for December 23, and some localities did actually hold them at that time; but in most of the country the elections were postponed. Ho Chi Minh reached a last-minute agreement with the major opposition groups: he promised that regardless of the outcome of the elections, 50 of the seats in the new national assembly would go to the VNQDD and 20 to the Dong Minh Hoi.

The press in French-controlled Saigon greeted this announcement with mockery. Clearly this election could only be a farce. And what else could one expect of a people who had never voted before? The Vietnamese answer to that, as to most French comments on their inexperience, was to place the blame for their lack of experience upon France; although the people had long had the habit of elections at the village level, they had never before been given an opportunity to vote in national elections.

It was, in fact, impossible to talk of real fairness and accuracy in a country-wide election held in conditions of quasi war and among people who had no knowledge of the techniques of democracy. This was the first general election Viet Nam had ever known and enthusiasm was such that candidates appeared even in warring Cochin China. On January 6, men and women of 18 and over voted, not only in Tonkin and Annam, but also, in clandestine elections, throughout Cochin China.

Many things were irregular about the elections. They were dominated by the Viet Minh; and often there was only one candidate running in a district. A number of people who were illiterate came to the polls with the names of their candidates written down by friends on scraps of paper, or with advisers to tell them how to vote. Voting officials asked publicly for whom they wanted to vote so that they could write down the names for them; there was little secrecy in the casting of ballots. Even the figures issued by the Viet Minh on the election results were open to serious question.

In the light of the nationalist sentiment which swept the country, however, even had the elections been conducted according to the strictest of Western forms, a few more conservatives might have been chosen, but the general sentiment in favor of independence—and independence under the men who had already proclaimed it—would almost certainly have been just as marked.[15]

The men and women of the new assembly were, on the whole, well qualified to represent the Vietnamese people. Among them, elected from his ancestral province of Thanh Hoa, was Vinh Thuy, the former Bao Dai, who

[15] "Can one speak of free elections? Yes and no. The choice of the voters among the various candidates appeared to have been free on the whole, but this choice was limited. There were hardly any other candidates than those agreed to by the Viet Minh Front. 'Collaborators,' 'corrupt' and suspect elements were eliminated. But wasn't this the common lot of all the liberated countries? In France itself, at this time, was the choice before the voters so wide, could one then conceive of the candidatures of a Maurras, a Flandin, a Georges Bonnet or a Paul Faure? The Ho Chi Minh government created a democratic base by the same methods and the same means as that of General de Gaulle and M. Bidault, methods, it must be said, which were more liberal than those which have since prevailed behind the iron curtain or in Algeria." Devillers, *op. cit.,* p. 201.

had come to live in Hanoi after his abdication. Most of the members were intellectuals; some were peasants; a few were women. The successful candidates ranged from conservative mandarins to Communists; almost half of the total did not belong to any political party. Most of all, the elections were a victory for Ho Chi Minh, running in the Hanoi district, who was said to have received 98 percent of the vote. If the specific figure could be questioned, the sentiment of the people could not: large numbers in Cochin China had felt themselves to be a part of Viet Nam and had acted accordingly; and the great majority everywhere looked upon Ho Chi Minh as their leader.

A number of men active in the Dong Minh Hoi and the VNQDD, however, did not include themselves in that majority. The agreement on seats had appeased them only temporarily, and their campaign against the Viet Minh rapidly regained its virulence. Along with certain other nationalists, they even demonstrated in favor of expelling the Viet Minh regime and placing Bao Dai at the head of the government.

Ho Chi Minh, by this time, had his own reasons for desiring representatives of the opposition groups in his Cabinet; an agreement might soon be reached with the French and it was by far the better part of wisdom to have the anti-Viet Minh groups share the responsibility for any agreement with France by joining the government which signed it. It was only with difficulty that they were persuaded to do so. The Chinese General Siao Wan, who was in charge of Chinese relations with the Vietnamese nationalists, had consistently supported and even inspired the hostile activities of the VNQDD and the Dong Minh Hoi directed against the Viet Minh; after the January elections, however, apparently impressed with the patent political superiority of Ho Chi Minh and his associates, he placed his support behind Ho, hoping to bring him under Chinese influence and prevent him from reaching an understanding with France. Siao Wan brought strong pressure to bear on the VNQDD and the Dong Minh Hoi before they would accept Ho Chi Minh's overtures. In February Nguyen Hai Than, the Dong Minh Hoi chief, agreed to become Vice President in the Ho government; the Ministry of Foreign Affairs went to Nguyen Tuong Tam of the VNQDD; and other VNQDD members took over the Ministries of Economy and Social Welfare.

To placate the Chinese, Ho Chi Minh dropped from his Cabinet two leading Communists, Vo Nguyen Giap, Minister of Interior, and Tran Huy Lieu, Minister of Propaganda. Giap still held a key position in regard to the army he had built up; he was named head of a new Committee of National Resistance. Vinh Thuy, the former Bao Dai, still nominally political adviser to the government, was appointed head of a new National Committee of Advisers. This seemed to be what the Chinese wanted and, as long as they remained in control, Ho had no choice but to defer to them.

The Viet Minh, in any case, was in no position to concentrate all its energies on this three-cornered struggle for power among the French, the Chinese, and the Vietnamese. It was forced to grapple immediately with urgent economic and social problems.

FAMINE AND ILLITERACY

The north country had been laid low by economic disaster. It had been decimated by famine early in 1945, resulting at least in part from the requisition policies of the Japanese and the Vichy French, and from their insistence that nonfood crops like jute, oil seeds, and opium be grown in certain areas instead of rice. There was rice to be had in the south, but Allied bombs destroyed the railroads and ships that could have brought it to north Annam and Tonkin. The starving Vietnamese died by the thousands and corpses rotted in the streets of Hanoi. Estimates of the dead ran from the Vietnamese claim of 2,000,000 to a French figure of 600,000.

Most of the Frenchmen who had built up the intricate Indochinese dike system that was needed for the ricefields had been thrown out of their jobs after March 9. The Vietnamese who took their places had not been taught how to keep up the dikes; and it was a time of abnormally heavy rainfall. Floods swept through the Tonkinese delta at the time of the founding of the Republic. When Ho Chi Minh travelled along the road from Thai Nguyen on the way to Hanoi in August 1945, he passed through ravaged lands. Roads were under water and the ricefields had become lakes which seemed to have no shores. Much of the food that remained was destroyed, as were cattle and agricultural machinery. The transport system, already damaged, was still further disrupted.

Drought followed, devastating the higher lands which had escaped the flood. In north Annam there was another flood. The people who had survived the famine were on the verge of starvation.

The new Vietnamese Government met the challenge of the famine with a nationwide production campaign. "Not an uncultivated square foot of land, not an unemployed man," was the slogan throughout Viet Nam. All land that was lying fallow was requisitioned by law and turned over to whoever would cultivate it; after the harvest it reverted to its owners. They planted dry crops like sweet potatoes, corn, and soy beans, which could be harvested before the rice was grown. Men and women of all ages and from many different walks of life, soldiers as well as civilians, worked together in the fields and on the dikes.

The Viet Minh asserted later that it had succeeded in increasing the area of paddy fields by 150 percent, in increasing fivefold the potato output, in producing four times more corn than ever before. It is impossible to check on these figures; but for the Vietnamese claim that the revolution had triumphed over famine, there is proof: when the spring of 1946 came, the people did not starve. Conditions were still not good, but the Viet Minh had succeeded in doing what the French had not always been able to do: they had saved the country from famine by the unaided efforts of their citizens.

The Viet Minh was active at the same time in another field—education. Here there was no threat of immediate devastation to unite the country in an all-out effort, but there were other things. There was the fact that some 80 percent of the country was illiterate. In nationalist movements everywhere there seems to be the strong urge to invigorate and unify the people by making them literate in their own language; and literacy in the hands of the Viet Minh could be a powerful weapon, making it possible to indoctrinate and rally the peasantry. There was the added impetus that education had always been held in high regard since the days when it had been the means to position and advancement in the governing mandarinal bureaucracy of the Vietnamese Empire.

At a time of crisis on all fronts, the Ho Chi Minh government announced compulsory instruction in Quoc Ngu, the romanized script originated by European missionaries in which the Vietnamese language is written. Using as a model the work of an Association for the Diffusion of Quoc Ngu, founded by a group of Vietnamese intellectuals in 1938, the government set about the intensive training of teachers of Quoc Ngu, who in turn were to train others to follow in their footsteps. Some four months were sufficient to learn this written language. A government decree of September 4, 1945 provided: "Within one year all Vietnamese over eight years of age should know how to read and write Quoc Ngu. After this period any Vietnamese over eight not knowing how to read or write will be fined."[16]

The government organized a vast network of committees to carry on the work of popular education. They issued all manner of penalties against the illiterate. The order went out that no one could enter a marketplace without proof that he could read and write. If he could not, he was supposed to be ordered home to learn the first letters of the alphabet, and it was supposed to be the same at bridges and ferry crossings. Illiterates, it was said, were forbidden even to marry.

THE CHINESE COME TO TERMS

The Viet Minh did remarkable work in the fall and winter of 1945 and in the beginning of 1946: the campaign against famine was successful; and the campaign against illiteracy, if necessarily slower, was moving along well.

---

[16] Délégation de la République démocratique du Viet-Nam en France, *Deux Victoires de la Révolution vietnamienne.*

All this occurred while the Chinese were still in the country and with their tacit approval; but the period of Chinese occupation was nearing an end.

Discussions with the Chinese Government initiated by the French late in 1945 had been going on intermittently in Chungking and Hanoi. On February 28, General Raoul Salan, the French representative, signed a series of agreements in Chungking in which China promised to withdraw her troops by March 31, 1946.

To gain this promise, France renounced her extraterritorial rights and concessions in China. She guaranteed exemption from customs and transit duties to Chinese merchandise shipped over the Haiphong-Kunming Railway, and promised a free zone for Chinese goods at Haiphong. She agreed also to deliver to China ownership and management of portions of the railway lying in China, which the Chinese Government had requisitioned during the war. The existing position of Chinese nationals within Indochina was confirmed and stabilized. They were assured the legal rights of French nationals (which included the right to be tried under French law) and they were to pay taxes no greater than those paid by Indochinese nationals.

In a later agreement of March 15 the French and Chinese military authorities worked out in more detail the aspects of the agreement most important to France—the conditions under which the Chinese would be relieved by French troops. The French were to begin to take over by March 15, and the transfer of authority was to be completed by the end of the month.

But the operation fell behind schedule. The Chinese provoked incidents and clashes with the French to delay their departure; they would not have been sorry to see a breach between the French and the Viet Minh serious enough to justify Chinese intervention. To French proddings, the Chinese replied with new promises of evacuation, and again denied having any territorial designs on Indochina.

It was difficult for the French to pry the Chinese loose. Only by the summer of 1946 had the bulk of the Chinese army left Indochina. The question in Viet Nam then was whether another army, the French, would be able to replace it.

Chapter Seven

"A FREE STATE"

THE VIETNAMESE in Hanoi were outraged at the news of the French coup of September 1945 in Saigon. Vietnamese propaganda took on a new violence and the Hanoi radio appealed for help to President Truman, Marshal Stalin, Prime Minister Attlee, Generalissimo Chiang Kai-shek, and the United Nations. The British flag vanished from Hanoi, as had the French flag several months before. Slogans on walls and rickshaws proclaimed support for the national independence struggle and "our heroic fighters of the South"; and Hanoi celebrated a Resistance Day in October.

Ho Chi Minh was in Hanoi, but d'Argenlieu and the members of his staff were in Saigon, out of touch with Vietnamese politics and with the Republic. There was only Jean Sainteny, the French Commissioner in Tonkin, to keep them informed.

The negotiations that Sainteny had begun with the Vietnamese early in September did not stop. They became less official for a time, at least on the Vietnamese side, but Sainteny and Léon Pignon continued to see such men as Vo Nguyen Giap, the Minister of the Interior, and Hoang Minh Giam, the Socialist who later became Minister of Foreign Affairs, as well as Ho Chi Minh himself. In December 1945 plans were discussed for d'Argenlieu and Ho Chi Minh to meet and talk over the difficulties between their two countries, but the meeting did not take place, largely because of opposition from the Chinese.

Another Frenchman who had a hand in the negotiations was a schoolteacher from Hanoi named Louis Caput who had been in touch with the Viet Minh even before the Japanese surrender, and wanted to make a personal contribution to smoothing the course of Franco-Vietnamese relations. Although he had no official status, he talked often with Vietnamese leaders, trying to explain the French position to them, and he tried to do the same with the French for the Vietnamese. He was a member of the Socialist Party, a fact which aided him in his dealings with the Vietnamese, among whom he had friends.

Franco-Vietnamese negotiations were in full swing by January, when a fourth French spokesman appeared on the scene. Sainteny and Pignon had been away from France for some time, and Caput for much longer; they were out of touch with political currents in France, where the old Radical Socialist Party, the ruling party in the Third Republic, had shrunk into temporary insignificance and a new political party, the MRP (Popular Republican Movement), joined the Socialists and Communists in the government coalition. It

148

was Max André, a member of the MRP and a former director of the Franco-Chinese Bank who had fought in the French resistance, who left for Indochina to join in the talks with the Vietnamese.

When André arrived in the country early in 1946, the French population of Hanoi was living in a state of insecurity and fear. They had to barricade themselves in their homes at night against terrorist attacks. Having no guns, they had to defend themselves with sharpened bamboo sticks. Killings and kidnapings of Frenchmen were commonplace in the streets of Hanoi.

André's mission, although he came without written instructions—responsible only to his party and not to the French Government—was to discuss the terms of an agreement with Ho Chi Minh. He was surprised at Ho's moderation.[1] The Vietnamese President accepted the idea of a division of power between France and Viet Nam in security matters, with national defense the joint concern of the two (which seemed to imply French bases in Viet Nam); the Vietnamese alone were to control their internal policing. He admitted that independence (which no French representative was authorized to offer) was not only impossible if Viet Nam were to remain within the French Union, but also impracticable.

There were times, early in 1946, when the negotiations seemed to be on the verge of breaking down. With Bao Dai now become Citizen Vinh Thuy and a republican, Admiral d'Argenlieu and his advisers in Saigon toyed with the idea of setting up as Emperor his young son Bao Long and appointing as regent the boy's mother, Nam Phuong, a Catholic Cochin Chinese. D'Argenlieu went so far as to send emissaries to the ex-Empress, who only agreed to see them on the insistence of the Apostolic Delegate. But the royal family was not yet ready to make its peace with France. The story goes in Vietnamese circles that she did not bother to answer, but went over to the piano and played the new national anthem.

In Hanoi, even if Frenchmen might have preferred other Vietnamese to the Viet Minh, they could find no alternative to Ho Chi Minh at this time. Nguyen Hai Than, the Dong Minh Hoi chief, seemed to French officials to have no power; and the VNQDD would have nothing to do with the French representatives. Since Bao Dai also refused to see them, this left the Viet Minh the only organized group which was both willing and able to negotiate with France.

Having convinced the French representatives that he was the logical man with whom to deal, Ho Chi Minh was confronted with the problem of persuading other nationalist leaders to support him in his negotiations with the French. With men such as Ngo Dinh Diem, he had no success at all: Diem was seized by members of the Viet Minh early in 1946 and exposed to the perils of illness and hunger in the Tonkinese mountains, then taken to see

[1] This statement is based on the writer's interview with Max André.

Ho, who invited him to join his government. When Diem, whose brother had been killed by the Viet Minh, refused to do so without far more information on Viet Minh activities and plans than he had yet been given, Ho Chi Minh said, "Well, I see it is useless to discuss matters with you while you are so irritable, but stay around a little while." But when Diem remained intransigent, he permitted him to go home.[2]

If Diem's refusal to end his abstention from politics was a disappointment to Ho, the behavior of the pro-Chinese groups and of extremist elements within the Viet Minh constituted a dangerous threat to his position. He had adopted a policy of moderation in his dealings with the French; he was prepared to compromise for the time being if that was the only way he could ultimately achieve independence. Communist extremists, however, opposed any and all concessions to the French. And a similar intransigence was manifested by the pro-Chinese groups who, in their efforts to outbid the Viet Minh for popular support, demanded total and immediate independence for Viet Nam as a prerequisite to any negotiations with France. They became so vociferous in their demands that, as late as February 1946, Ho Chi Minh seems actually to have considered giving up the presidency. He is said to have proposed to Bao Dai, his "supreme political advisor," that he take over the government, to quiet Chinese and American suspicions of Vietnamese Communism and to facilitate an agreement with France. But no sooner had Ho Chi Minh made this offer, than he withdrew it, presumably because he had received assurances from the Chinese authorities that they would put pressure on the pro-Chinese nationalists to join his governing coalition.

AGREEMENT ON MARCH 6

Franco-Vietnamese negotiations were still going on when the new Vietnamese Assembly held its first session on March 2, 1946, in the Municipal Theatre of Hanoi. Nguyen Hai Than, the Dong Minh Hoi leader who had been named Vice-President in the new government, had left the country suddenly on the eve of the Assembly meeting, but other members of the pro-Chinese parties were still working with Ho. Nguyen Tuong Tam, the Foreign Minister, who belonged to the VNQDD, even joined in the talks with the French.

It was a time of extreme gravity for Viet Nam. France had just signed the treaty with China, lifting the protective screen in the north behind which the Republic had dug in. French troops were increasing their pressure on the Vietnamese in Cochin China and were preparing to invade Tonkin. The Assembly met to give its approval to the "national union government," the coalition Cabinet into which Ho had brought members of the VNQDD and the Dong Minh Hoi. At the same time, however, a Permanent Committee was

2 This account is based on an interview with Ngo Dinh Diem.

set up to function while the Assembly was not in session, and it was composed entirely of Viet Minh members. Another committee was appointed to begin drafting a constitution.

The Assembly issued a proclamation in which it called on the Vietnamese people to "devote all their forces to the defense and reconstruction of the Motherland in order to make rapid progress toward their happiness." Then it adjourned so that its members could return to their homes to prepare for the forthcoming struggle against France.

But the situation had altered radically since the time, six months before, when Viet Nam had proclaimed its independence and Vietnamese leaders had believed that France had finally left Indochina, and that the United States would watch over their new republic. American political stock had been high in Hanoi in August and September of 1945, when the name of the United States evoked associations with the Declaration of Independence, George Washington, Abraham Lincoln, and the Atlantic Charter; and American OSS agents had not hidden their sympathy for Vietnamese aspirations. But the United States, it was soon clear, would do nothing to aid the Viet Minh. The Chinese, so helpful to the Republic in its early days, seemed to be losing interest in preserving it. And the French, far from having given up, were fighting stubbornly in Cochin China.

The Vietnamese had to try to safeguard their republic without foreign help. They might have tried to hold off the French by force of arms, but they decided against it. They had several apparently sound reasons for this decision. For one thing, the French political situation was not unfavorable to Viet Nam at this time and many Vietnamese believed in the myth of a new France, risen from the ashes of defeat, which was ready to break with the colonial policies of the past. The Socialists and Communists, who sympathized with Vietnamese nationalism, were already prominent in the French governing coalition. Even the MRP, then the third largest party in France, was Left of Center in many ways and, unlike the Radical Socialist Party, it had few vested interests in the empire; neither economically nor politically was it committed to the defense of old colonial policies. In Viet Nam Ho Chi Minh, who had only secondhand information about French politics, seems to have been convinced that Leftists might take over the French Government in the next elections.

It was also quite possible, particularly in view of Leftist strength in France, that international Communist strategy dictated a policy of Franco-Vietnamese co-operation in 1946.

At home, Viet Nam was beset with serious economic difficulties. The dike system was in serious disrepair; industry and transport had broken down in many places; the finances of the government were not good. "Since we do not yet have solid economic foundations," Vo Nguyen Giap admitted in March 1946, "a long drawn-out resistance would have made the economic danger greater every day." The Viet Minh was not even sure of its hold on the people. Giap said:

At certain points where the revolutionary movement is not very deep, many people have not taken it very seriously and if we had continued to resist, there would have been a collapse in certain sections or a loss of fighting spirit. In continuing the military struggle, we would have weakened ourselves and gradually lost our land. We would have only been able to hold several regions.[3]

And to these pressures toward agreement was added another—the Chinese. When the Chinese decided to sacrifice Vietnamese independence for French economic and political concessions, as they did in February 1946, the Vietnamese had to make their own terms with France. It was in their interest to reach a preliminary agreement with the French as soon as possible so that further negotiations could proceed while the Chinese were still in the country, increasing the bargaining power of the Viet Minh in its dealings with the French.

General Leclerc, for his part, was also prepared to compromise if, by so doing, French troops could return to Tonkin peaceably. Leclerc was convinced that the Viet Minh represented a national movement which France did not have the military power to subdue; and when in mid-February Admiral d'Argenlieu went on a visit to France, he left the General in authority. "We never intended to launch an armed conquest of North Indochina," Leclerc wrote. "The Cochin Chinese experience demonstrated that to accomplish that, we would need forces much stronger than those which we now have."[4]

The French were in no position to fight, Marius Moutet, Minister of Overseas France, explained to the French Assembly a year later when he was justifying the agreement his government finally signed with Ho Chi Minh. In March 1946 there were some 185,000 Chinese soldiers north of the sixteenth parallel and some 30,000 Japanese, many of them still in possession of their arms. All the French troops in the north were disarmed and held prisoner in the Hanoi Citadel, where the Japanese had left them; there were also some 25,000 Frenchmen living in Hanoi. Only 15,000 French troops were in Saigon and they had to travel several days to get to Haiphong before they could go to Hanoi. Without a prior accord with the Viet Minh, Moutet did not believe that they would have found many Frenchmen alive when they did arrive.[5]

How to land French troops in Haiphong without fighting constituted a serious problem with the complexity of the political situation compounded by problems of navigation: the French troops could enter Haiphong only during

---

[3] Quoted in Devillers, op. cit., p. 229.
[4] Dansette, op. cit., p. 199.
[5] Journal Officiel, Assemblée Nationale, Session of March 18, 1947, p. 876. (All dates cited below for the Journal Officiel refer to the specific session rather than to the publication date.)

high tides, which came infrequently in the spring. They could count on having high tides early in March, but after that would come the rainy season and they would be able to do nothing more until October. The sixth of March, accordingly, was the deadline for the negotiations with the Vietnamese.

First, however, it was necessary to appease the Chinese in order to eliminate the danger of an armed clash when the French arrived in the north. As soon as the Franco-Chinese treaty was signed on February 28, one of Leclerc's officers wired to Saigon from Chungking, "Agreement obtained. The fleet can leave."[6] The following day the French ships left Saigon bound for the north.

But the Chinese army in Tonkin still had to be persuaded to allow them to land, and the Chinese procrastinated until they were sure that an agreement had been reached with Ho Chi Minh.

On March 6, this was finally accomplished. Sainteny signed an agreement in Hanoi with Ho Chi Minh and Vu Hong Khanh (representing the VNQDD) by which France recognized the Democratic Republic of Viet Nam as "a free state with its own government, parliament, army and finances, forming part of the Indochinese Federation and the French Union."[7] The French Government pledged itself to a referendum to determine whether the three Ky—Tonkin, Annam, and Cochin China—should be united. In return, the Vietnamese agreed not to oppose the French army when it arrived in Tonkin and northern Annam to relieve the Chinese.

"I am not happy about it, for basically it is you who have won," Ho Chi Minh said to Sainteny after the agreement was signed. "You know very well that I wanted more than that. But I understand that you cannot have everything in a day."[8]

A military annex to the March 6 Agreement fixed the number of troops to occupy Viet Nam at 25,000—15,000 Frenchmen and 10,000 Vietnamese—under over-all French command.[9] The French soldiers in charge of the Japanese were to leave as soon as their job was completed, with a deadline of ten months. Units guarding naval and air bases were to have the length of their stay determined later. As to the rest—the units which would join the Vietnamese in keeping order north of the sixteenth parallel—they were to be withdrawn in five equal annual installments. In 1952 no French troops would be left in Viet Nam, with the possible exception of those guarding bases. This assurance that

---

6 Devillers, op. cit., p. 219.

7 Notes Documentaires et Etudes, No. 548.

8 Sainteny, op. cit., p. 167. "Ho Chi Minh declared that he understood that he could not have everything immediately and that he would be contented with a relative independence, relying on the word of France that, in a certain period of time, total independence would be accorded to his country. In this," according to Sainteny, "he was certainly sincere. This had been his plan for thirty-five years, he knew how to wait a little longer. . . . With independence acquired or promised on installments, he was ready to envisage a particularly advantageous understanding with France which, in Viet Nam, would benefit from a special and broadly preferential status."

9 This military annex was supplemented by a more detailed agreement on April 3.

the French would evacuate the country was one of the key provisions of the agreement which made it possible for the Vietnamese to agree to the return of French troops to Tonkin.

The Chinese, however, remained reluctant to see the French return to Tonkin at all. Despite the careful preliminaries on the part of French officials directed at avoiding any possible clash with the Chinese, when French troops tried to land at Haiphong harbor on March 6, they were fired on by Chinese shore batteries; not until the following day did the Chinese permit the first French contingents to disembark. The Vietnamese population of Haiphong, not yet aware of the Hanoi accord, celebrated the encounter as a joint victory for China and Viet Nam.

Dictated on both sides by opportunism, the March 6 Agreement enabled the French and the Vietnamese each to achieve their limited aims. The French came back to northern Indochina and not a Vietnamese gun was fired against them. They kept most of their troops south of the sixteenth parallel, but from that time on elements of the French army were to be found in Hanoi, Haiphong, and other sections of Tonkin and northern Annam. Vietnamese strength remained concentrated in the north, but the Ho Chi Minh government also had military as well as political representatives in the south. The Viet Minh had won recognition from France and counted on the promise of the military annex that in five years all French troops would be out of Viet Nam. If by some chance that promise were not carried out, the Vietnamese had at least won a breathing space in which to consolidate their forces and prepare for the future.

The Viet Nam radio announced the arrival of General Leclerc's troops in Hanoi on March 18 and asked the people of Hanoi to show them the greatest courtesy. It hailed the troops, fresh from the Liberation of Paris, as the incarnation of Free France. But it was not an easy thing to sell the March 6 accord to the Vietnamese They found it difficult to understand why they were to welcome the French after the many months in which they had known them as enemies, more difficult to understand why, having declared their independence, they should have to accept something less than that.

The government had to justify its action to the people. "Once we have liberty, we will go on to independence, to complete independence," Giap told a cheering crowd gathered at the Hanoi Municipal Theatre on March 7. The Vietnamese, he said, had chosen to negotiate because they did not have the military strength to fight the French. He said frankly, "We have negotiated above all to protect and reinforce our political, military and economic position." Vu Hong Khanh also promised that this was just a step on the road to full independence. But only because Ho Chi Minh placed his great personal prestige behind the agreement would the majority of the nationalist movement accept it. "You know that I would rather die than sell our country," Ho told the crowd. "I swear to you that I have not sold you out."[10] Independence was not abandoned, he insisted, it was deferred. It would come in five years when the French army completed its evacuation of Viet Nam.

Several Vietnamese political groups, however, were unwilling to gamble on such an uncertain future. The fact that both the VNQDD and the Dong Minh Hoi belonged to the government which had signed the agreement, and that Vu Hong Khanh of the VNQDD had joined Ho in signing it, did not prevent important elements of both parties from attacking the accord bitterly, calling it capitulation to the French. The Trotskyites, who had not joined the government, also would have no part of any treaty which fell short of unqualified independence.

Although it is clear now that the March 6 accord was a major diplomatic victory for the French, Frenchmen at the time were also divided on the terms of that agreement. In Paris, although official optimism was tempered by the misgivings of informed observers, the tendency was to regard the accord as evidence of a new and enlightened policy. But it was all very well for people in France to approve the accord; they were not on the spot to apply it. Most of the Frenchmen in Saigon, who had known Indochina under the prewar regime when their privileges were secure and French control was unchallenged, saw no reason for change and regarded the March 6 Agreement as evidence of weakness and blundering. This sentiment was prevalent in administrative circles around d'Argenlieu, and when the Admiral returned to Indochina from France, he declared his amazement—"yes, that is the word, my amazement that France has such a fine expeditionary corps in Indochina and yet its leaders prefer to negotiate rather than to fight."[11] Elements of the French military in Indochina were also strongly opposed to the agreement because it called for a military evacuation of the country. They expressed their opposition in good faith but it followed from all of this that the agreement would be applied neither wholeheartedly nor even in good faith by the men upon whom depended whether or not it would be translated from words to action.

However, General Leclerc, who called upon Ho Chi Minh as soon as he arrived in Hanoi, had every intention of honoring the March 6 Agreement. He regarded military action in Indochina as necessary, but only within strict limitations. A French military conquest of the country he considered impossible. "At the present time," he said, "there is no question of imposing ourselves by force on masses who desire evolution and innovation." The very best the French could do, he believed, was use their military successes as bargaining

10 Devillers, op. cit., pp. 228–31.
11 Ibid., p. 242.

points and prevail upon the Vietnamese to sign agreements confining Franco-Vietnamese collaboration to economic, cultural, and military matters.[12]

General Leclerc had accomplished some remarkable successes since V-J Day. He had arrived at a firm understanding with the British, which had preserved France's position in the south; and under his authority the complicated parallel negotiations with the Chinese and the Vietnamese had been brought to a successful conclusion. But General Leclerc's political role in Indochina was about over. With Admiral d'Argenlieu back in the country to assume political control, relegating Leclerc to strictly military functions, and with the colonial administration and the High Commissioner openly antagonistic to the March 6 Agreement, there was little left for Leclerc to do. On July 14, 1946, General Leclerc, at his own request, was removed from his post and named Inspector of Land Forces in North Africa.

The following month, he revealed that by March 6, some 1,200 Frenchmen had been killed in Indochina, and 3,500 wounded. Japanese casualties were considerably higher.[13] Losses among the Vietnamese were the highest of all. But in March 1946 the main thing seemed to be that the fighting was over. This "preliminary accord" provided for the immediate cessation of hostilities. And at a conference soon to be held, "friendly and open negotiations" were to begin.

THE FREE LAOTIANS

One effect of the French treaties with China and Viet Nam was to reopen Laos to the French in the spring of 1946; with peace assured in Tonkin, the French were free to move on Laos. General Alessandri, whose troops had escaped to China with Laotian help after the Japanese coup in 1945, headed the French units which arrived in Laos in March 1946 to replace the Chinese.

They encountered resistance from Laotian nationalists. The Chinese, although still in the country, did not help the Laotians. "They would have fought for us if we had been able to pay them," a member of the Free Laotian government said later. The Free Laotians received no help from the Vietnamese either, except from longtime Vietnamese residents of Laos.

The Free Laotians fought for, and lost, city after city. They fought along the Mekong River at Luang Prabang, Vientiane, Savannakhet, and Thakhek. In April they restored King Sisavang Vong as the constitutional ruler of an independent country, and the King recognized them as representing the legitimate government of Laos. But the Free Laotians were defeated on all sides. Thousands of them fled into Thailand across the Mekong River, including Prince Petsarath, his brothers Souphanouvong and Souvanna Phouma, and the entire Free Laotian government.

Under King Sisavang Vong an administration favorable to France took

---

[12] Dansette, op. cit., pp. 209–10.
[13] Ministère de la France d'Outre-Mer, Bulletin d'Information, August 26, 1946.

over the country and, on August 27, signed a *modus vivendi* with France (recognizing the King's authority over the southern provinces as well as Luang Prabang) along the lines of the agreement signed with Cambodia the previous January. Peace seemed to have returned to Laos as to Cambodia.

CLASHES IN THE SOUTH

In Viet Nam, the March 6 accord did not bring peace. Marius Moutet described it as an "accord of good faith," and that description was the key to its failure. It was simply an armistice that provided a transient illusion of agreement where actually no agreement existed. The months that followed indicated that without some agreement on fundamentals, the French and the Vietnamese would not keep good faith.

Even after the March 6 Agreement, guerrilla fighting continued in the south. The French wanted Cochin China to remain walled off from the other Vietnamese lands, as they had kept it since their arrival in the south during their piecemeal conquest of Indochina. The Vietnamese, on the other hand, were determined to regain Cochin China, even if they had to compromise on their independence to do it. They thought that they had won their point in the March 6 Agreement, which they read as admitting the unity of the Vietnamese countries, leaving a referendum to settle only the forms of administrative reorganization within their union. However, when the separatist Cochin Chinese Advisory Council, which d'Argenlieu had established in February, protested against the accord, complaining that it infringed on Cochin Chinese sovereignty, Commissioner Cédile was reassuring. He said at a meeting of the Council on March 12 that the accord "did not imply any recognition by the French Government of a single government for the three Annamese countries." At this session of the Advisory Council Dr. Tran Tan Phat, a separatist leader, declared: "As Annamese we think like Indochinese, but we act like Cochinchinese."[14] He was murdered by nationalists at the end of the month.

Outside Saigon the various nationalist resistance groups, weakened though they were by the months of warfare with the British and French, still controlled large sections of the Cochin Chinese countryside. Ho Chi Minh proposed to General Leclerc the sending of mixed Franco-Vietnamese commissions to establish peace in Cochin China after the signing of the March 6 accord, but the General saw no reason for this in what was supposed to be French territory; he suggested instead that Ho Chi Minh order his followers by radio to cease fighting. When Ho sent his own emissaries to the south, they were arrested by the French who continued to regard Cochin China as a French colony, claiming a free hand there until the referendum could be held. This led to difficult local problems, as in the case of the Vietnamese emissary sent by one Vietnamese zone commander to discuss a cease-fire with the local

14 *Le Monde*, March 14, 1946.

French commanding officer. The emissary was unceremoniously informed that the French expected complete capitulation—the surrender of arms and prisoners—and that this was an ultimatum. They had until the 31st of March to comply; if they failed to do so, the fighting would begin again. Before the Vietnamese left French headquarters, the French officer took his name and it was soon public knowledge that the French had put a price on his head as well as on that of his commander, Nguyen Ngoc Bich. In this particular region of Cochin China fighting resumed by the end of the month.

The March 6 Agreement was never applied to Cochin China. When the disorganized resistance in the south refused to lay down their arms (as most of them did), the French attacked them in the name of mopping up and police operations. The bombing and burning of villages, arbitrary arrests, and executions were frequently reported during this period.

Even in this time of emergency, when the very future of the Cochin Chinese resistance was at stake, the bitter struggle for power among its members, begun in Saigon the previous summer, went on. The uneasy alliance between the Cao Dai, the Hoa Hao, and the Viet Minh, which had already been strained to the breaking point, was never completely mended; as they vied for power outside the French zones, they sometimes clashed among themselves. The fact that many of the guerrillas and a number of their leaders were not Communists did not prevent Tran Van Giau from attempting by force to neutralize, eliminate, or replace individuals who challenged Viet Minh domination of the resistance. The Viet Minh did not scruple to use terror not only against traitors but also against its political opponents; it was dangerous for a non-Communist to become too well known in the resistance. Thus when Ho Van Nga, one of the leaders of the United National Front, was jailed by the Viet Minh and a group of non-Communist intellectuals, among them men with leading positions in the guerrilla movement, petitioned for his freedom, the next word they had of him was that he was dead. Bui Quang Chieu, who had founded the moderate Constitutionalist Party in 1923, was also executed by the Viet Minh.

When in April 1946 the government in Hanoi ordered the Communist Nguyen Binh to attempt to unify the scattered resistance in Cochin China, he set up an administrative committee in the south of which the key positions, involving control of finances, the army, and the police, all went to Communists. He forced Huynh Phu So, the Hoa Hao leader, who threatened to become too powerful and too popular, into a minor position. But Huynh Phu So still remained an important political figure in the south and, finally, Nguyen Binh ordered his execution.

Almost despite themselves, however, the Cochin Chinese guerrillas were compelled to create a united front, not only against the French, but also against their separatist-minded compatriots in Saigon. The need to fight the common enemy leveled many differences and, under Nguyen Binh, Cochin Chinese nationalists and revolutionaries succeeded for a time in forming a working unity. Nguyen Binh took over while they were still disorganized and inexperienced, lacking arms and troops, and confronted with the difficult task of waging guerrilla warfare in the flat undefensible land of Cochin China. Gradually he built up a much-feared and effective fighting force in the south.

DISCUSSIONS AT DALAT

In the north, new negotiations were in progress. When Admiral d'Argenlieu returned from France after the signing of the March 6 accord and received Ho Chi Minh aboard the cruiser *Emile Bertin* in Ha Long Bay,[15] he showed himself in no hurry to summon the conference that had been promised in the March 6 Agreement. The Vietnamese were anxious to have it soon, while the Chinese were still in Indochina to give them a counterweight to the French if they needed one. And they wanted the conference in Paris, attended by wide publicity, so that they could bypass the backward-looking administrative and colonial groups which made policy in Saigon and enlist the support of the French Left as well as of international opinion.

Commissioner Sainteny had his own reasons for favoring Paris as the conference seat. He was anxious for Ho Chi Minh and the Vietnamese delegation to be as far as possible from the influence and pressure of nationalist extremists, as well as from the maneuvers of "certain Allied secret services" which "saw without pleasure Frenchmen and Vietnamese disposed to reach an agreement."[16] Certain French officials, however, concerned about the effect that Franco-Vietnamese negotiations might have on other parts of the empire, were not keen on publicizing the negotiations by holding them in Europe. They finally agreed to have a preliminary conference in the resort city of Dalat in southern Annam, which was to pave the way for a later and definitive meeting in Paris. At this time the Vietnamese were still optimistic and they showed their optimism by their choice of delegates to the conference, several of whom were known to be favorable to the French.

When the Dalat Conference opened on April 18, 1946, Vo Nguyen Giap rapidly emerged as the outstanding figure present, "a political man in every sense of the word," according to a French journalist.[17] In fiery language, Giap deplored the "tragic ignominy" of fighting still continuing in Cochin China. There was a bitter exchange between French and Vietnamese delegates, with accusations of treachery hurled across the conference floor. They finally agreed to appoint a mixed committee which would try to end the Cochin Chinese hostilities.

[15] The usage "Bay of Along" derives from the French. "Ha Long" is the Vietnamese name.
[16] Sainteny, *op. cit.*, p. 195.
[17] *Le Monde*, June 25, 1946.

The French and Vietnamese had three major problems on their agenda at Dalat: diplomatic relations between Viet Nam and foreign states, the future status of Indochina, and French economic and cultural interests in Viet Nam. After they had dealt with these, perhaps they could figure out the elusive meaning of "a free state . . . forming part of the Indochinese Federation and the French Union."

But on what basis could they deal with such problems? The March 6 accord threw no light on them. It was necessary to go back more than a year for the most recent statement of French policy on Indochina, to a time when the situation both in France and in Asia had been very different from what it was in 1946. The declaration issued by the French Provisional Government on March 24, 1945 had offered the Indochinese the right of participation in their own government and called for considerable changes in economic and administrative policy. Politically, however, the declaration changed very little.[18]

Six months later, when the time came to implement the March 24, 1945 declaration, it had already been outdistanced by events.

The March 6, 1946 Agreement, with its recognition of a "free state" of Viet Nam (however vaguely defined) and its acceptance of the unity of Tonkin and Annam, and possibly Cochin China as well, was incompatible with the declaration of March 1945, and French officials could not agree on which to apply. General Leclerc regarded the March 6 accord as superseding anything that went before, but Admiral d'Argenlieu did not; he vacillated between the two, and Franco-Vietnamese relations, as a result, were hampered and confused throughout 1946.

By the time the Dalat Conference met, the French already had had an opportunity to demonstrate what they had in mind when they spoke of the Indochinese Federation. They were powerful enough by 1946 to put behind their colonial policy the force they did not have when the 1945 declaration was first formulated; they were able to apply the declaration in Cambodia (as they did later in Laos).

After taking over Cambodia from the British, the French had signed a *modus vivendi* with the Cambodian Government on January 7.[19] Under its terms, the Commissioner of the French Republic, in his capacity as representative of France and of the Indochinese Federation, was directed to maintain public order in Cambodia, to issue regulations concerning Frenchmen, aliens, and Indochinese from other parts of the Federation, and to ensure observance of these federal regulations. He also headed the French services in the country.

The French Commissioner was expected to be personal adviser to the King as well, a position which gave him access to the King at all times. He was also assured of access to Cabinet meetings. It was he who nominated French experts

[18] See above, pp. 111–12.
[19] *Journal Officiel de la Fédération Indochinoise*, February 21, 1946, pp. 78–81.

to help in the operation of the country's technical services. In the sweeping language of the Franco-Cambodian Agreement, the Commissioner "shall give his approval to legislative and regulatory texts and acts, to proclamations and circulars or instructions of general application relating to the interpretation of such texts, as well as to decisions reserved, because of their importance, for the signature of His Majesty the King." Every Cambodian Minister had to have at least one French adviser (more when his work was particularly technical), and every Cambodian department head had to have a French technical adviser. At the same time, a broad number of services (including large-scale public works, federal justice, the treasury, higher and secondary education, customs, mines, railroads, and foreign immigration) were regarded as federal. They came under the control, not of the Cambodians, but of the French High Commissioner.

The lesson of French policy in Cambodia was that the Vietnamese were not the only people in Indochina to talk federation without practicing it. The intricate administrative structure envisaged by France for Indochina was as remote from federation as the loose economic understanding favored by the Vietnamese. Federation, implying a division of power between the various constituent units, on the one hand, and the federal government, on the other, did not exist in prewar Indochina, where supreme power was divided between the French Governor General and the French Government in Paris. Whatever powers were enjoyed by subdivisions of the federation did not belong to them by right, but were delegated from above by the French central government and were exercised directly or indirectly by French officials. Despite a somewhat wider participation in the administration of the country after 1945, the situation in Cambodia remained much the same as before the war. It was not easy to differentiate between what the French described as a federal structure and what was in fact the machinery of French rule.

For the French delegation at Dalat, the High Commissioner remained the key figure of the Federation. He was to be both president of the Indochinese Federation and representative of the French Union. He was to direct the federal services, assure execution of federal laws, and name federal commissioners and advisers who would be responsible only to him. Co-operating with him would be an Assembly of States, fifty of whose sixty seats would be held by the five traditional divisions of Indochina (ten to each), and the remaining ten seats by French interests; the Assembly would have limited powers over the federal budget and federal legislation. Under such an arrangement, Tonkin and Annam could have been outvoted by the French and the French-dominated regimes in Cochin China, Cambodia, and Laos. Even if the Cochin Chinese joined Viet Nam, the French (despite the numerical inferiority of the population who supported them) would control half the votes.

From the Vietnamese at Dalat the French could get agreement only that there should be some kind of federal assembly. For a time the Vietnamese insisted upon their own customs and on the right to coin their own money. They seemed finally to accept in principle the French position in favor of an Indochinese customs and monetary union, but they reserved the right to make their own commercial policy.

FOUR STATES OR THREE?

The policy which the French called federation was double-edged. It not only called for strong "federal" controls, but also for special treatment of minority groups. The French expressed great concern for the future of Indochinese minorities inside as well as outside Viet Nam. Admiral d'Argenlieu had said, "It is thanks to France that distinctive Laotian, Cambodian and other minority groups exist. It is thanks to us that they have not been absorbed by Annamese imperialism."[20]

At Dalat, the French went so far as to propose a special status for each of the important ethnic minorities of Viet Nam. For the Tho and the Nung in north Viet Nam, they asked an inspector of minorities and representatives in the government both of Viet Nam and of the Indochinese Federation. They wanted the Thai and Muong of Tonkin and northern Annam to have their own regimes, with large administrative autonomy inside Viet Nam controlled and guaranteed by the federal authorities.

In the southern part of Indochina, mostly on the High Plateaus of south Annam, lived the Moi, who numbered less than a million and were still partly nomadic and little civilized. Although relations between the Moi and Vietnamese of the coastal regions had been limited mainly to bartering mountain products for salt, the suzerainty of the Court of Hué over the area had been long established and the Moi were governed by Vietnamese administrators (*Quan Dao*). The French, however, wanted the Moi regions to be separated completely from Viet Nam, to become an autonomous territory within the Indochinese Federation.[21]

In Cochin China, particularly, the French demonstrated great concern for the wishes of all elements, no matter what their size, which wished to remain apart from Viet Nam. By the time of the Dalat Conference it was clear that the five separate states envisaged in the 1945 declaration no longer existed. The French were willing to admit that there were four—exclusive of south Annam. The Vietnamese insisted that there were three. Overshadowing the entire conference was the problem of the future of Cochin China.

The question at Dalat was whether the French would agree to breaking down the wall which separated Cochin China from the north. Cochin China,

[20] *New York Times*, October 14, 1945.
[21] Conférence Franco-Vietnamienne, Dalat, le 8 mai 1946, Commission Politique No. 7/N/CP, *Note sur les minorités ethniques.*

as the French were quick to point out, with its absentee landlords, extensive holdings tilled by tenant farmers, its landless agricultural laborers and small moneyed bourgeoisie, differed economically as well as administratively from Tonkin and Annam. The Vietnamese, however, claimed the rice and rubber areas of Cochin China and its strategic and commercial centers not only on ethnic, cultural, and historical grounds, but also on grounds of economic interdependence. Cochin China supplied the bulk of Indochina's rice and rubber exports. The richest area in Indochina, it contributed 40 percent of the country's revenue, although only three-quarters of its contribution was spent in Cochin China. Although there were two annual rice harvests in the north, as against one in Cochin China, they were insufficient to feed the northern population and the masses in the north were dependent for part of their food upon the rice of Cochin China.[22] Tonkin and Annam were overpopulated but Cochin China had a continuing labor shortage, due in part to the reluctance of Vietnamese to migrate to the south, but due also to French restrictions on such migration. As Cochin China supplied Tonkin with some of its rice, so Tonkin could supply manpower and coal and other minerals to the south.

The Vietnamese argued at Dalat that if Cochin China remained apart from Viet Nam, it would be another Alsace-Lorraine for which fifteen million Vietnamese would fight, to free from a foreign yoke. They insisted that the March 6 accord by implication had recognized the unity of Cochin China with Tonkin and Annam. And they questioned the honesty of any referendum which the French might hold.

For the French, Cochin China was the rice granary and the rubber center of Indochina, the location of the bulk of their investments in the country.[23] The big French economic interests, chief of which was the powerful Bank of Indochina, had every reason to wish it separate and safe from a Vietnamese government which would not be solicitous of their privileges. Nor could the French fail to be influenced by Vietnamese assertions of how indispensable Cochin China was to Viet Nam. The Vietnamese could not hope for an autonomous, much less an independent, existence without Cochin China. But with Cochin China they could easily dominate Cambodia and Laos, and the French might find it difficult to maintain their claim to be an arbiter among the Indochinese states.

The French asserted at Dalat that they were prepared to stand by their obligation to arrange a fair referendum, and that they would abide by its results.

[22] Cochin China differs from the north not only in "population density" but also in "nutrition density," the ratio between the number of inhabitants and of ricefields currently under cultivation. Here the differences show up clearly. Before the second World War there were 601 persons per square mile of ricefield in Annam and 653 in Tonkin; in Cochin China the figure was 219. See Karl J. Pelzer, *Population and Land Utilization*, p. 42.

[23] Three-fifths of all French-held concessions in Indochina were in Cochin China on the eve of the war, as were three-quarters of the cultivated areas in those concessions. *Ibid.*, p. 138.

But no referendum was possible, they said, until peace had been restored in Cochin China.

Economic, military, and cultural relations between France and Viet Nam also came up for discussion at Dalat. The Vietnamese welcomed French participation in the economic development of Viet Nam, an influx of French capital and specialists, and French training of Vietnamese technicians. Ho himself had said:

We are disposed to make many concessions, particularly economic. . . . What we want is collaboration with France, each giving what it has too much of. Impoverished France needs rubber and mining products; we will give them to her. She has too many technicians; let her send them here.[24]

At Dalat, in the spring of 1946, Viet Nam agreed to give preference to French technicians, and to employ foreign specialists only if France could not supply the skills they needed. The status of French enterprises and holdings in Viet Nam was more difficult to agree upon; it would have to wait upon the forthcoming conference in France.

Any military agreement between France and Viet Nam hinged upon a prior political understanding. The March 6 Agreement had recognized Viet Nam's right to its own army, but beyond that, nothing was decided. How would the Vietnamese army be organized? To what extent should other members of the French Union contribute to it? What part would it play in the defense of Indochina, in co-operation with other armed forces of the French Union? Would Viet Nam offer bases to the French Union? And what of the right of French Union forces to penetrate north of the sixteenth parallel, by now the unofficial military frontier of Viet Nam. The Vietnamese stood generally for the independence of their armed forces and against any over-all French control.

The Vietnamese did not cease to reiterate their attachment to French civilization. The French press, conservative as well as liberal, reminded its compatriots that France's colonial mission had changed, that now she must work in co-operation with her colonies, guiding them toward independence and keeping them within the French cultural community. With a kind of cultural imperialism which seems more typical of France than of other countries, it made much of France's civilizing influence, which it described as spreading from Indochina throughout the Far East.

The Vietnamese, for their part, insisted on their preference for compromise and negotiation, and on their great debt to French culture. They did not agree with the French on how to pay that debt. Willing though they were to recognize the importance of their cultural relations with France, they refused to give up their claim to ownership of the University of Hanoi, the French School of the Far East, and the Pasteur Institutes. Nor did they agree upon the place of

24 *Le Monde*, February 28, 1946.

the French language in Vietnamese education. The French, characteristically, placed great emphasis on this question but they could not persuade the Vietnamese to accept French as the required language in their secondary schools.

In the way of concrete achievement, there was not much to be said for this first Dalat Conference, although French and Vietnamese spokesmen did their best to view its proceedings in a favorable light. At least the delegates had arrived at the discussion stage. They had gone even further than that, according to Ho Chi Minh:

> Both our delegations have recognized the need to form an Indochinese Federation. In this federation all the states concerned will be linked not with hampering bonds, but with unifying and strengthening bonds. We agree on the principle of the creation of a federal organism providing it allows the members of the federation to prosper freely while remaining interdependent . . . We must still determine the methods by which this Federation is to be realized.[25]

But it was difficult to be optimistic after Dalat. The conference had only shown up more clearly the basic disagreements between the two peoples. Vo Nguyen Giap wept when it was over.

THE FONTAINEBLEAU CONFERENCE

The machinery of negotiation had nevertheless been set in motion. After Dalat a full-dress conference was scheduled for France, and Ho Chi Minh left for Europe at the end of May.

Marius Moutet, the Socialist Minister of Overseas France, asked Paul Rivet, another Socialist, to greet Ho at Orly airfield "as President of the Vietnamese Government and as a Socialist. At that time, either out of ignorance or by policy, they did not consider Ho Chi Minh a Communist. The affirmation of Ho Chi Minh's Communist affiliation was made only when the Franco-Vietnamese negotiations reached a dead end."[26]

When the Vietnamese arrived in France, they found that no place had yet been set aside for the conference. They went on to Biarritz, where they marked time for more than a week and Ho Chi Minh went fishing. "The conference was fishy from the start," one of the delegates later remarked wryly.

The last time Ho Chi Minh had come to France, it had been as an obscure seaman; in the summer of 1946 he was welcomed as a Chief of State, and thousands of people watched him curiously as he drove from the airport to his residence near the Etoile. He was cordially received by the Paris City Council; and in an official ceremony he laid a wreath on the tomb of the Unknown Soldier.

When the Franco-Vietnamese conference opened at Fontainebleau on July

[25] *Ibid.,* May 21, 1946.
[26] Paul Rivet, "Le Drame franco-vietnamien," *Cahiers Internationaux,* No. 6, 1949, p. 47.

6, the Viet Minh flag, the gold star on the red field, flew alongside the French tricolor. The composition of the Vietnamese delegation reflected the stiffening attitude of the Ho Chi Minh government after the disillusionment produced by the Dalat Conference. Although the Vietnamese sent to Fontainebleau a group of young men without much experience in diplomacy, most of them held Cabinet rank. Politically, they were mostly independents; two of them were Communists. By and large they were far less inclined to compromise than the men who had gone to Dalat.

The Foreign Minister of Viet Nam, Nguyen Tuong Tam, a member of the VNQDD, was supposed to head the delegation, but rather than share responsibility for any further concessions to the French, he fled to China; Pham Van Dong, the Communist Minister of Finance in the first Ho Chi Minh government, replaced him as chairman. Dong was a history teacher from Annam who had been jailed by the French for his revolutionary activities and released at the time of the Popular Front.

Another member of the VNQDD, Chu Ba Phuong, did not follow Tam into exile, but remained in the delegation. It included Nguyen Van Huyen, a prominent scholar who was associated with the French School of the Far East; and Hoang Minh Giam, the Socialist Vice Minister of the Interior, a teacher of French and French literature who had been active in the Vietnamese literacy movement, teaching Quoc Ngu before and during the war. The Vice Minister of Communications and Public Works, Dang Phuc Thong, was another delegate. An engineer and a liberal in politics, he had received his technical training in France where a younger brother of his, Dang Chan Lieu, was working with the Vietnamese parliamentary mission, also in Paris at that time.

One of the delegates, Ta Quang Buu, the Vice Minister of National Defense, had studied at Oxford; he had taught mathematics and English in Hué, and he headed the Vietnamese Boy Scouts. Vu Trong Khanh, another delegate, was a member of the Democratic Party, who had been Minister of Justice until the Cabinet reshuffle in March. Duong Bach Mai, a Communist, had spent time in Russia as well as in France.

The Vietnamese who was to bear the brunt of the negotiations, winning the respect of the French for his moderation and statesmanlike behavior, was Phan Anh. As Minister of Youth in the Tran Trong Kim Cabinet, Phan Anh had won great popularity and influence among the young people of Viet Nam, and in 1946 he was Ho Chi Minh's Minister of National Defense. The Minister of National Economy in the first Ho Chi Minh Cabinet, Nguyen Manh Ha, who had been active in the Catholic youth movement in Tonkin, was also at Fontainebleau, as were Huynh Thien Loc, Minister of Agriculture, who was reputed to have been one of the richest men in Cochin China, and Trinh Van

Binh, an expert on economic questions, who had also participated in the Dalat Conference.

The Vietnamese royal family was represented in the delegation by Prince Buu Hoi, a descendant of the Emperor Minh Mang and a cousin of Bao Dai. His father, Ung Uy, had headed the Private Council of the Imperial Family and had been Minister of Rites at Bao Dai's court until March 9, 1945. Buu Hoi himself was a scientist, not actively engaged in politics, an expert on cancer and Director of Research at the Radium Institute in Paris.

To deal with these men, who were among the best that Viet Nam could offer, the French selected an unimpressive delegation. Three of its members were representatives of the major French political parties. The others were from various government departments, including the colonial service, and some were allied with French business and financial interests in Indochina. They were mostly technical people, with little political importance or authority. Among them were several names familiar to the Vietnamese—General Salan, who had negotiated with the Chinese for their withdrawal and had participated with Leclerc in the landing at Haiphong; Pierre Mesmer, who had narrowly escaped death at Vietnamese hands when he parachuted into Tonkin in 1945; and Léon Pignon, who had just completed a term of office as political adviser to Sainteny, the French Commissioner in Tonkin (in 1947 Pignon was to become High Commissioner in Indochina).

Perhaps one of the ablest French delegates was Paul Rivet, the representative of the French Socialist Party and director of the Musée de l'Homme, who remained a member of the French delegation for two hours. He has told the story in his own words:

> The French delegation was presided over by Max André, who was my colleague on the General Council of the Seine and is the present Senator from the Seine. I have the greatest esteem for this affable and courteous colleague, and personally, the idea of working with him . . . was particularly agreeable to me. However, it is certain that the choice of M. Max André could not please the Vietnamese delegates, who were not unaware of his links with the Franco-Chinese Bank and, consequently, with the Bank of Indochina.
>
> However that may be, M. Max André invited to his home, on July 5, 1946, all the French delegates in order to make contact before the first official Franco-Vietnamese conference, which was to take place the next day at Fontainebleau. I accepted this invitation. I was surprised not to find among the delegates men whom I knew for their profound knowledge of the Indochinese scene. . . . I asked as soon as the meeting opened for the text of the agreements of March 6, which would serve as the basis of the discussions and I hoped to be able to study them that evening. My question appeared inopportune and I was told that this text would be communicated to me later. On the contrary, they insisted more on the necessity for strict discipline in the delegation and a rigorous adherence to decisions made by the majority of the members. From this moment, my role was a

silent one. I listened to the comments that the delegates exchanged and, when I took leave of M. Max André, I announced to him that I was resigning.

That evening I communicated this decision to M. Marius Moutet in a long letter in which I said that I intended to be neither dupe nor accomplice nor hostage, and in which I denounced the large-scale maneuver which was going to be undertaken with rare tenacity during long months: to bring the Fontainebleau conference to an impasse, to profit from the discredit that the failure of the negotiations was supposed to cast on the negotiators, in particular on Ho Chi Minh, and to propose the Bao Dai combination; if necessary, to impose it, by depriving Tonkin of rice supplies from Cochin China and thus provoking famine.[27]

French plans originally called for Admiral d'Argenlieu to preside at the opening session, when the Fontainebleau Conference met on July 6, but the Vietnamese refused to accept him as chairman. It was André, therefore, who opened the conference with a polite speech of welcome. Pham Van Dong replied with a bitter attack on French policy in Indochina. The March 6 accord had been violated time and again. Fighting was still going on in Cochin China. French troops, instead of remaining in their positions, had moved into the Moi Plateaux in south Annam. (They came, the French explained, in response to Moi requests for protection against the Vietnamese.) And they had taken over the palace of the Governor General in Hanoi. Most flagrant of all, in Vietnamese eyes, was French recognition of the "free republic" of Cochin China. They had recognized it on June 1, just as the Vietnamese delegation left for Fontainebleau.

THE COCHIN CHINESE "REPUBLIC"

The new Cochin Chinese government was a triumph not only for Admiral d'Argenlieu, but also for a Vietnamese colonel in the French army named Nguyen Van Xuan. The Japanese had offered Xuan the Ministry of War after March 9, 1945, but he had rejected it, insisting that he was a French officer; and he joined his French comrades in the Hanoi Citadel. In January 1946 he came back to Saigon and with a friend, Dr. Nguyen Van Thinh, like himself a French citizen, he worked out a plan for Cochin Chinese self-government. He went to Paris, where he found Marius Moutet receptive to the scheme (although Moutet later said that he did not agree with d'Argenlieu's action in recognizing a separate Cochin Chinese government).[28] Thinh became President of the "provisional government" of Cochin China, Xuan its Vice-President and Minister of National Defense. Of the nine members of the Cabinet, seven had acquired French citizenship.

The Cochin Chinese "'republic" was a popular protest against Vietnamese terrorism, according to the French. The Vietnamese saw it as a deliberate

[27] Rivet, op. cit.
[28] Marius Moutet, "Longues Négotiations," Politique Etrangère, April 1948, p. 133.

attempt to anticipate and bypass the promised referendum. To defend his government, Thinh cited the French declaration of March 1945, pointing out that the French had promised autonomy to each of the five countries of an Indochinese Federation. The March 6 Agreement had accomplished this for Tonkin and northern Annam, and now it was the turn of Cochin China, which he called the most advanced country in the Federation. Surely, Thinh argued, it could not be the only one to remain without a government.[29]

It was an interesting government that Thinh headed, if "government" was the proper word to describe it. His title was "President of the Provisional Government of the Republic of Cochin China." His ministers were to be not only appointed by him, but also responsible to him. "Nevertheless, the appointment of the Chiefs of the Technical Services shall require the previous consent of the Commissioner of the French Republic in Cochin China." The president was elected by two-thirds vote of the Advisory Council of Cochin China. The Advisory Council itself, however, was not an elected body; it had been appointed by the High Commissioner. Its membership was to be increased only if the "Provisional Government shall, in agreement with the Advisory Council, decide concerning increase of the Assembly and the terms and conditions of such increase." The government was expected to "render an account of its management before the Council," which had been selected, not by the people, but by the French. The Council was to approve the budget of Cochin China, but "'it shall not take action on expenditures appertaining to the government.'"[30] The general impression was of a dog chasing its tail, for the republic of Cochin China existed only on paper. In practice, Cochin China remained under close French control.

Admiral D'Argenlieu found the Cochin Chinese "republic" a convenient tool to play off against the Ho Chi Minh government, and when a Vietnamese parliamentary mission left for France, d'Argenlieu sent a Cochin Chinese delegation to Paris. (One of its members, Nguyen Van Xuan, was later to lead a Vietnamese government under the protection of French arms.) They called on Moutet, who declared his desire to see Cochin China find its proper place in the French Union.

Illuminating comment on events in Cochin China came from an unexpected source in August, when Colonel Xuan told the press that the separation of Cochin China, Tonkin, and Annam did not correspond to any national reality. The only thing, he said, that stood in the way of their union within the Viet Nam Republic was the Leftist tendency of the Hanoi government.[31]

[29] Ministère de la France d'Outre-Mer, *Bulletin d'Information*, August 12, 1946.
[30] *Notes Documentaires et Etudes*, No. 554. *Documents Relatifs au Problèmes Indochinois* II *Accords entre le France, le Cambodge, la Cochinchine et le Laos*.
[31] *Le Monde*, August 11–12, 1946.

FAILURE AT FONTAINEBLEAU

At Fontainebleau in the summer of 1946 there was little anyone could do about the Cochin Chinese "republic." The Vietnamese could protest but even if the majority of the French delegates had wished to reverse d'Argenlieu's policy, they did not have the authority to do so. They had no answer for Pham Van Dong's opening charges. Instead, the conference began a debate on the question of how much publicity their sessions should have. The Vietnamese wanted the sessions open, enabling Left-Wing groups in France to bring pressure on the French delegation. The French favored keeping all disagreements private and publicizing only their agreements. They reached a compromise, but that did not prevent the Fontainebleau Conference from becoming a French political issue, and in the long run the Vietnamese suffered from this more than anyone else.

The Vietnamese made the mistake of allowing their case to become identified with the French Left. According to a non-Communist Vietnamese delegate, the French Communists, operating less as revolutionaries than as members of a party which hoped to win in the next national elections, tended to advise the Vietnamese to yield to the French position on various issues. Nonetheless the Vietnamese put their faith in the Left, in the Socialists as well as the Communists, overestimating their strength and at the same time alienating powerful and more responsible elements in France.

Fontainebleau was no more successful than Dalat had been. Cochin China and the place of Viet Nam within the Indochinese Federation and the French Union were discussed once again, and once again there was no agreement.

The unsettled political situation in France, where a provisional government was still in power, did not make agreement easier. One draft constitution had already been rejected by the French people in May 1946; another was in the making while the Vietnamese delegates were at Fontainebleau. The form of the French Union, the new name for metropolitan France and its empire, had not yet been set.

The collapse of France in 1940 had acted as a catalyst on the prevailing discontents in the colonies. Indochina was not the only place where it laid bare French weakness to countries which the French had previously ruled—in large part because of the illusion of power which they had created among the subject peoples. It disrupted the structure of French control and led to the broadening and consolidation of nationalist movements. In 1944 Moroccan nationalists issued an abortive declaration of independence which was followed by widespread arrests. Riots in favor of a free Algeria broke out on May 8, 1945, and there were thousands of casualties. After the March 6 accord between France and Viet Nam, Malagasy deputies asked a similar

position as a "free state" for Madagascar. In August 1946 Tunisian nationalists, meeting at a congress in Medina, demanded independence.[32]

In France the draft constitution which would have based membership in
the French Union on "free consent" had been defeated, but for reasons of
domestic politics, not because of its provisions on the empire. Nationalists
throughout the empire were hopeful of broad reform.

During the summer of 1946, while delegates to the Constituent Assembly
in Paris, a number of whom came from parts of the empire outside France,
discussed the shape of the new French Union, the Vietnamese put forward
suggestions of their own at Fontainebleau. They proposed an assembly for
the French Union in which the different states would be represented according to their population; its powers would be limited to making recommendations to the member states.[33] Only if a member of the French Union were a
victim of aggression would the other members give it military aid.

The French delegation at Fontainebleau had a very different picture of the
French Union. They viewed it as a federation of nations led by France. The
unity of currency and of economic relations which they desired was not an
insuperable stumbling block to a Franco-Vietnamese agreement. But they
also insisted on unity of diplomacy and of the army under France, and that
was a subordination which the Vietnamese would not accept.

The structure thus outlined by the French delegation was in the traditional
pattern of the French Empire and, as it turned out, the one finally adopted
by the French people. But the summer of 1946 was an interregnum between
constitutions and there was no knowing how the idea of the French Union
might evolve. This was the more true because new elections were scheduled
for France in the fall. If the Left-Wing parties could win control of the government, it might be that the Vietnamese were not so unrealistic when they
talked about achieving a status for Viet Nam within the French Union like
that of Eire in the British Commonwealth.

The conference at Fontainebleau continued into August, when Admiral
d'Argenlieu dealt it a coup de grâce. He decided that the French Government was paying too much attention to the Vietnamese point of view. "You
must always remember all the people who drink the waters of the Mekong,"
he said several years later.[34] Taking it upon himself to remind Paris of the
existence of the non-Vietnamese peoples who also lived in Indochina, he
summoned a second Dalat Conference which opened on August 1. He in-

[32] Ellen Hammer, "The French Empire Today," in E. M. Earle, *Modern France: Problems of
the Third and Fourth Republics.*

[33] The Vietnamese plan also called for an annual conference of the various governments. Each
member of the Union would be represented in the others by a delegate with diplomatic functions
accredited to the Ministry of Foreign Affairs. There would be a court for the Union modeled on
the International Court of Justice, with the right of appeal to the International Court.

[34] In an interview with the writer.

vited to it delegates not only from Cambodia and Laos, but also from "southern Annam" and from the French-appointed government of Cochin China. It was d'Argenlieu's turn to invoke the March 1945 declaration in order to justify his action. The conference was logically called for by the 1945 declaration, he explained; it was a necessary follow-up to the first Dalat Conference which would give people outside Viet Nam a chance to discuss the future of Indochina.

The Vietnamese did not see the matter in that light. They had come to Europe to discuss the status of Cochin China and the place of Viet Nam within the Indochinese Federation. Now it appeared that these questions were being decided for them in Dalat and contrary to their interests. The appearance of Cochin Chinese "republican" representatives at Dalat was a poor augury for achieving any understanding on Cochin China at Fontainebleau.

And what exactly was South Annam? Although there was no legal justification for dividing up Annam, Admiral d'Argenlieu showed every intention of doing just that. In 1946 he set up the Moi regions as an autonomous area under a "Commissioner of the Republic for the Mountain Populations of South Indochina." Since this new administrative division included only the Moi who dwelled in South Annam, leaving the Moi populations of Cambodia, Cochin China, and Laos to be governed by their respective states, it was difficult not to regard d'Argenlieu's action as simply a political maneuver to weaken the authority of the Ho Chi Minh government.[35]

MODUS VIVENDI

In the summer of 1946 the Vietnamese, convinced that they could not accomplish anything by negotiations in France as long as the conference remained in session at Dalat, refused to continue the meetings at Fontainebleau. "The French High Commissioner has attained his end," wrote Oreste Rosenfeld, a prominent Socialist, in the Socialist weekly *Gavroche* on September 25. "The Fontainebleau Conference has failed. The break with Viet Nam has been achieved."

The French Leftist press generally gave the Vietnamese vocal sympathy, bitterly attacking d'Argenlieu and demanding his recall. Conservatives took issue with them. *Le Figaro* claimed that the French and the Vietnamese had been on the verge of an understanding. It was the attacks of "certain Left and extreme Left newspapers" that had caused the difficulty; they had given the Vietnamese the impression that they would be supported if they held out for more extreme terms.[36]

The Vietnamese delegation left for Viet Nam, but Ho Chi Minh stayed on

[35] Maurice Gassier, "Que faire en Indochine?" *Politique Etrangère*, May 1947. p. 141.
[36] *Le Figaro*, September 12, 1946.

in France. Even when the news of growing tension in Viet Nam reached Paris and his firm hand seemed necessary to restrain the extremists at home, Ho Chi Minh was reluctant to leave France with what he called "empty hands." But all that he succeeded in salvaging from his visit to Europe was a *modus vivendi* which he signed on September 14 after a stormy nighttime interview with Marius Moutet. The document was not at all what Ho Chi Minh had hoped for and he signed with grave misgivings. The French police inspector who escorted him from Moutet's residence, quoted him as saying, "I have just signed my death warrant." To Sainteny, who had come to Paris with him, and to Moutet, he said, "Don't let me leave this way. Give me some weapon against the extremists. You will not regret it."[37]

But all they could give him was the *modus vivendi* which skirted the vital issues between the two countries, confining itself to economic and cultural questions (on which the Vietnamese had made substantial concessions at Fontainebleau) and to immediate problems of public order. Frenchmen in Viet Nam, like Vietnamese in France, were to "enjoy the same liberty of establishment as the natives of the country, as well as liberty of opinion, of teaching, of trading and of traffic and, more generally, all democratic liberties." The agreement of the French Republic was required before the Vietnamese could change the status of French property and enterprises in Viet Nam, which were not to be "subjected to a more severe regime than that reserved for the property and enterprises of Vietnamese citizens."[38] French property was to be restored to its rightful owners. French schools were to function freely in Viet Nam.

The *modus vivendi* crystallized agreements already entered into at Dalat and Fontainebleau. The Vietnamese promised to give priority to French technicians and experts. There was to be only one legal currency throughout Indochina. A mixed commission including representatives of the different states of the Federation was to study the creation of a banknote-issuing agency to replace the Bank of Indochina; it was also to co-ordinate customs and foreign trade. There were to be no internal customs barriers, and there was to be an Indochinese customs union.[39] Another committee was to study the reestablishment and improvement of communications between Viet Nam and other countries in the Indochinese Federation and the French Union. And a Franco-Vietnamese commission was to arrange for Vietnamese consular representation in neighboring countries and for Vietnamese relations with foreign consulates.

Once again the French and the Vietnamese agreed to cease all acts of

[37] Sainteny, *op. cit.*, p. 209.
[38] *Notes Documentaires et Etudes* No. 548.
[39] The Vietnamese read this as providing for a customs union between states; the French, however, envisaged a federal customs.

hostility and violence in an effort to restore order in Cochin China. The two governments agreed to meet to negotiate a final treaty no later than January 1947.

For the third time, they had agreed only to postpone agreement. France was looking forward to general elections in November, after which, presumably, the French Government would be in a better position to make some final settlement. The Vietnamese, in the meantime, seemed to have given way on many issues. None of the members of the Vietnamese delegation to Fontainebleau would or could have accepted the responsibility for making such concessions to the French. Only Ho Chi Minh could do that. Ho explained: "We decided to facilitate the revival of French economic and cultural interests in Viet Nam in return for a promise that democratic liberties will be applied in Cochin China." He called the agreement "better than nothing."[40]

[40] *New York Herald Tribune,* September 16, 1946.

Chapter Eight

THE OUTBREAK OF WAR

Ho CHI MINH returned home aboard a French warship in October 1946 to find that events had moved swiftly in Viet Nam during his absence. He had left the venerable Minister of the Interior, Huynh Thuc Khang, at the head of the government. A nonparty man, Khang was a seventy-one-year-old scholar who had spent twelve years as a political prisoner in the French penal colony on Poulo Condore. It was not Khang however, but Vo Nguyen Giap, the young Communist chairman of the Supreme Council of National Defense, who had taken over actual authority in the country. Giap had consolidated the control of the Viet Minh over Viet Nam in the summer months of 1946.

Bao Dai had left the country by this time. For six months he had held the office of political adviser to Ho Chi Minh and had lived quietly in Hanoi as Citizen Vinh Thuy. When the March 6 Agreement was signed, he had been on hand to lend it his support. The transition from the old regime to the new had been made peacefully and, it seemed, successfully. Then Ho asked the descendant of the Nguyen Emperors to undertake a mission to China for the Republic, and Bao Dai left on March 18. He went first to Chungking, where the officials of the Chinese Government were, and then he went on to Hongkong, where there was no Chinese government. Weeks passed and lengthened into months, but he did not return. It became clear that necessity, not conviction, had persuaded Bao Dai of the virtues of working with Ho. Once out of the country, beyond the power of the Viet Minh, he was free to do as he pleased for the first time since the August Revolution, and it did not please him to play silent partner to Ho Chi Minh. Ho Chi Minh, for his part, was not sorry to see his strongest potential competitor for the leadership of Viet Nam outside the country. Bao Dai did not see Viet Nam again for three years; when finally he did return, he was chief of another government.

Bao Dai was not the only prominent Vietnamese to leave Viet Nam for political reasons in 1946. The March 6 Agreement had opened a breach in nationalist ranks. Viet Minh leaders, at first, tried to close it by peaceful means. In May, a number of leading Vietnamese set up in Hanoi what they called the Lien Viet, the League for the National Union of Viet Nam, a coalition broader and more inclusive than the Viet Minh and including representatives of various important political groups, among them the Viet Minh and the pro-Chinese parties as well as some independents. But leaders of the VNQDD and the Dong Minh Hoi refused to bury their differences with the

Viet Minh in the Lien Viet and insisted that the March 6 Agreement was a capitulation to France. (Judging by the behaviour of many of these leaders in later years when they elected to work with the French against the Viet Minh, such criticism was purely tactical; they appeared merely to have wanted power for themselves.) In many sections of northern Tonkin and in Hanoi itself, troops of the VNQDD and the Dong Minh Hoi clashed with Viet Minh forces. The Dong Minh Hoi set up its own insurgent government in the Hongay mining region.

General Leclerc's officers arrived north of the sixteenth parallel to find the pro-Chinese parties bitterly anti-French; the most faithful defenders of the March 6 Agreement seemed to be in the Viet Minh and the Ho Chi Minh government. And so the French became the temporary allies of the Viet Minh against the VNQDD and the Dong Minh Hoi. In Hanoi, French scout cars blocked streets leading to VNQDD party headquarters while Viet Minh troops attacked it. The French drove the Dong Minh Hoi out of Lang Son and Haiphong, permitting the Viet Minh to move in. In Hongay the French freed the local Viet Minh committee from jail.

When Chinese troops left Hanoi early in June, Vo Nguyen Giap was free to intensify military action against the opposition parties. He turned first on the Dong Minh Hoi, then on the VNQDD. His army tracked down their troops and cleared them out of the delta region; quantities of weapons were seized; members of the two parties were arrested on a variety of criminal charges ranging from counterfeiting to unlawful possession of arms. Some of their leaders fled to China, and then to Hongkong. The Vice-President of Viet Nam, Nguyen Hai Than, who belonged to the Dong Minh Hoi, had fled Viet Nam early in March, avoiding any responsibility for the March 6 accord. The VNQDD Foreign Minister, Nguyen Tuong Tam, crossed the frontier at the end of May and was joined in China by Vu Hong Khanh, the VNQDD member who had signed the March 6 Agreement; like Tam, he had been a member of the Vietnamese delegation at Dalat but had refused to go to Fontainebleau. Both parties, however, continued to have representatives in the Vietnamese Government: a member of the VNQDD, Chu Ba Phuong, remained Minister of National Economy and the Vice-Minister of Agriculture was Bo Xuan Luat of the Dong Minh Hoi.

By emasculating the opposition parties, Giap eliminated a major threat to Viet Minh control in the north; and with the war against famine already won, he took advantage of the respite from economic and military emergency during the summer of 1946 to build up the Vietnamese army.[1] He doubled its numbers and trained the men in modern military techniques; and he supplied them with weapons acquired mainly by way of the arms traffic with National-

[1] Giap supervised over-all policy while Ta Quang Buu assumed active leadership of the program.

ist China. The Vietnamese regulars were said to include 60,000 troops. Besides these there were the Tu Ve, partisans (mostly snipers) who functioned under a more elastic discipline. There were also Vietnamese youth enrolled in paramilitary operations. Vietnamese under arms were believed to exceed 100,000.

FRANCO-VIETNAMESE RELATIONS

In the summer of 1946 the implanting of the French army on Vietnamese soil led to Vietnamese charges of violations of the April 3 military accord. Franco-Vietnamese relations in the north were punctuated with clashes and incidents. Yet the average Vietnamese was not unfriendly when he met Frenchmen on city streets north of the sixteenth parallel. Companies of French soldiers circulated unhindered on Tonkinese roads. Work was resumed in French enterprises. By and large, relations were not bad; sometimes they were even cordial, while both sides waited to see what would emerge from the conference at Fontainebleau.

Some Vietnamese, however, like the Communist ex-Minister of Propaganda, Tran Huy Lieu, were not content to wait. Pointing to the success of the guerrillas in the south and counting on the army that Giap was building up in the north, they urged violent action against the French. Giap succeeded in holding them in check until the calling of the second Dalat Conference and the breakdown of the Fontainebleau Conference in August, when Viet Minh extremists launched a bloody attack against French troops at Bac Ninh. Giap and the local French commander both were in a mood to be conciliatory, however, and the incident was smoothed over.

During August, in Hanoi, delegates from Vietnamese religious groups—Catholics, Protestants, Buddhists, and Caodaists—set up a committee which joined other Vietnamese in protesting French infringements of the March 6 accord.

Then came news of the September *modus vivendi,* which, having settled neither the issue of Cochin China nor of independence, was greeted with little enthusiasm in Viet Nam. Extremists called meetings in Hanoi to announce their opposition to the concessions made to the French, and tracts were found in the Hanoi area attacking Ho Chi Minh. One of them read: "When a man remains in foreign countries for a long while, he becomes their slave." However, although the pro-Chinese and xenophobic groups, as well as the Trotskyites, were critical of the new agreement, most of the organized Vietnamese political groups continued to support Ho Chi Minh. They accepted the September *modus vivendi,* as he asked them to, just as before they had accepted the March 6 Agreement.

THE VIETNAMESE NATIONAL ASSEMBLY MEETS

Ho Chi Minh was back in the country in time for the second session of the National Assembly, which opened in Hanoi on October 28 with 291 members present. The largest single group in the Assembly were ninety independents. The Viet Minh was the largest party, holding eighty seats, and Pham Van Dong, just returned from Fontainebleau, was among its leaders. Other Communists sat together as the Marxist Group. They numbered only fifteen, but included such well-known figures as Vo Nguyen Giap, Tran Huy Lieu and Nguyen Van Tao (the Cochin Chinese veteran of the Indochinese Communist Party who had belonged to the Saigon Municipal Council before the war and, in August 1945, had become a member of the Committee of the South). The VNQDD and the Dong Minh Hoi were also represented, but the summer purge had taken its toll; thirty of the fifty VNQDD seats were empty, as were three of the twenty to which the Dong Minh Hoi was entitled. These were not the only parties in the Assembly. There was also a Democratic Party, founded in 1944 to organize Leftist students and intellectuals who, although unwilling to join an overtly Communist party, worked closely with the Viet Minh; it had forty-five seats. The Viet Nam Socialist Party, which had been established only in July 1946, had twenty-four seats.

Discussion was lively at this second session of the National Assembly, and apparently free. Although the speeches made and the questions asked were not always friendly to the government, they were given a hearing and were reported in the press. In the background, however, was a certain tension, an awareness that there was a point beyond which it was wisest not to go in criticizing the government. Police agents were in evidence and kept a watchful eye on opposition members, some of whose homes were searched. There were also reports that some dissidents disappeared while the meetings were going on. French sources said that of the thirty-seven VNQDD and Dong Minh Hoi members who managed to attend this second session, only twenty were on hand when it ended.

Two hundred and forty-two members were in the Assembly chamber on November 8 to vote on a constitution for Viet Nam. It was adopted by an overwhelming majority, only two members opposing it.[2]

This vote came less than a month after the people of France had adopted a new constitution for themselves which included articles outlining the new structure of the French Union and providing for Associated Statehood (the status envisaged for Viet Nam), a limited autonomy within a framework of

[2] Vice President Pham Van Dong said in 1950: "Our Republic possesses a constitution adopted by the National Assembly elected at the beginning of 1946. This fundamental law, however, has never been promulgated, because several of its provisions require for their application the cessation of the state of war." Quoted in Léo Figuères, *Je Reviens du Viet-Nam Libre*, p. 122.

French control. The constitution voted by the Vietnamese National Assembly, however, said nothing about Associated Statehood. It did not admit the possibility that Viet Nam might be subordinated to any foreign power.

It declared Viet Nam to be a democratic republic in which all power belonged to the people "without distinction of race, class, creed, wealth, or sex." Its territory, "composed of Bac-Bo or Northern Viet Nam (Tonkin), Trung-Bo or Central Viet Nam (Annam), and Nam-Bo or Southern Viet Nam (Cochin China) is one and indivisible. The national flag of Viet Nam is red centered with a five-pointed gold star. The national anthem of Viet Nam is the 'Tien Quan Ca.' The capital of Viet Nam is Hanoi."

The constitution guaranteed to Vietnamese citizens the usual democratic freedoms—of speech, assembly, association, religion, residence, and travel. It also guaranteed "the rights and interests of both manual and intellectual workers." It provided for free, compulsory primary education, and for state aid for "aged and infirm citizens unfit to work."

The Communist leaders responsible for the actual drafting of the constitution were unwilling to jeopardize the support of moderate groups at this time and drew up a fairly conservative document. Considerably to the Right of constitutions adopted by the new republics of Burma and Indonesia under Socialist leadership, which emphasized social welfare and planning and provided for regulation in the public interest of land ownership and private property in general, the Viet Minh constitution stated simply: "The rights of property and possession of Vietnamese citizens are guaranteed."

In view of the Communist predominance in the executive, however, much of this was rather academic. And in 1951, when political conditions inside and outside Viet Nam caused the Viet Minh to throw off the cloak of moderation, it announced plans to revise the constitution, and explained:

The Vietnamese constitution was created during a period in which the French colonialists were frantically preparing to occupy Central and North Viet Nam. Due to other weak points, principally because a gang of traitors depended upon the strength of Chiang Kai-shek's Kuomintang to carry out their activities, a progressive character was lacking, and consequently the constitution was not clearly defined.[3]

The constitution adopted in November 1946 provided for a single-chamber legislature, called the People's Parliament. Elections were to be by universal suffrage, by free, direct, and secret ballot open to all Vietnamese of 18 years and over, "except lunatics and those deprived of civil rights" (the latter an undefined category). Parliamentary elections were to be held normally every three years and Parliament was to meet twice a year in open sessions. "In exceptional cases, the People's Parliament is entitled to hold a secret meet-

[3] Voice of South Viet Nam (Viet Minh radio), May 4, 1951.

ing." The rights of members of Parliament were described by the constitution with a certain vagueness:

> The Government may not *ordinarily* arrest or pass sentence on any of the members of the People's Parliament without the prior permission of the People's Parliament or in case it is not meeting, of the Permanent Committee. A member of the People's Parliament may not be prosecuted for a speech or opinion expressed during the sessions. . . . [However,] when a member of the People's Parliament loses his right to vote, he loses at the same time all his rights and privileges as a member of the People's Parliament.

When Parliament was not in session, the Permanent Committee elected by it was to vote on government bills and decrees (subject to the subsequent approval of Parliament), to convoke Parliament, and to control and criticize the government.

If the term of office of the People's Parliament expires during such a crisis as time of war, the Permanent Committee is allowed to prolong its functioning for an indefinite time; however, the People's Parliament must be re-elected not later than six months after the end of such a crisis. . . . If the People's Parliament cannot meet, the Permanent Committee and the Government are together entitled to decide upon war or peace.

These provisions were to be particularly significant, as things turned out, for Viet Nam was plunged into crisis soon after the adoption of the constitution. The Vietnamese people had little opportunity to try out their constitution in time of peace.

Members of the ethnic minorities who inhabit Tonkin and Annam sat in the assembly which drew up the constitution, and the document recognized their special problems. Thus, "besides enjoying full and equal rights, the ethnic minorities are to receive every help and encouragement to enable them to reach the common level of advancement as speedily as possible." They were promised the right to study their own languages in local primary schools. For parliamentary elections the number of representatives from "up-country areas where there are ethnic minorities" was to be determined by law. Members of minorities were given the right to use their own language in law courts.

Finally, the constitution outlined the executive structure of the new government. A President, Vice-President, and Prime Minister were all to be chosen from among members of Parliament, the first two elected by parliamentary majority, the third chosen by the President and approved by Parliament. The Prime Minister, in turn, was to select his Ministers from Parliament, with its approval. But these constitutional provisions were never implemented. The Assembly never got around to approving a Prime Minister. Only in 1949 was a Vice-President appointed and he was chosen, not by Parliament, but by the President, Ho Chi Minh.

It was Ho Chi Minh who selected a new Cabinet in the fall of 1946, and before the Viet Nam Assembly disbanded its second session, it passed a vote of confidence in him and approved his Cabinet. The Communists more than doubled their strength in the government, holding five seats. Ho Chi Minh became Minister of Foreign Affairs as well as President, replacing the fugitive VNQDD leader, Nguyen Tuong Tam. Vo Nguyen Giap took over as Minister of National Defense; and the Cochin Chinese Communist Nguyen Van Tao became Minister of Labor. The Ministry of Finance remained in the hands of another Communist, Le Van Hien. Although the key Ministries of Interior, National Economy, and Education went to non-Communists, in each case the Vice-Minister was a Communist, in a position to exercise effective control over his department.

Other changes in the Cabinet were that the VNQDD lost two of their three seats and the Dong Minh Hoi one of their two. Socialist and Democratic strength remained unchanged, the Socialists keeping one seat, the Democrats two; and Bao Dai, although a resident of Hongkong of several months' standing, was renamed Supreme Political Adviser. But the decisive fact in the new Cabinet was that the Communists were no longer a small minority. They held more seats in the government than any other party.

THE ROAD TO WAR

The reshuffling of the Viet Minh government reflected the deterioration in Franco-Vietnamese relations which followed the September 14, 1946 *modus vivendi*. Frequent clashes occurred in the country, the responsibility for which was naturally disputed by the French and the Vietnamese; and the *modus vivendi*, which went into effect on October 30, did little to improve this state of affairs: few of its provisions were ever observed and the stipulation that there would be no further hostilities remained a dead letter.

Despite the September 14 agreement, no delegate of the Viet Minh was permitted to join the High Commissioner at Saigon in attempting to bring peace to the south. Admiral d'Argenlieu closed off the areas under his control in Cochin China from official Vietnamese representatives; and few political liberties were respected throughout the French-controlled sections of Cochin China. Although Dr. Thinh, the nominal President of Cochin China, tried to maintain the fiction that his government had some power, he could not close his eyes to its impotence. He told friends: "I am being asked to play a farce, and even after the Cabinet changes, the farce will continue."[4] Convinced that everyone had abandoned him—the French, the people of Cochin China, even

[4] *New York Times*, November 11, 1946.

his personal friends—he hanged himself on November 11, 1946.[5] This tragic event highlighted the political irresponsibility and unpreparedness of many well-meaning Cochin Chinese leaders who found themselves trapped in an impossible situation.

Undiscouraged by Dr. Thinh's suicide, however, High Commissioner d'Argenlieu installed a new Cochin Chinese separatist regime under Le Van Hoach, a leading member of the Cao Dai. Hoach took office in December, an event which further exacerbated the course of Franco-Vietnamese relations.

This was only one of several moves made by the French authorities in Indochina which discouraged the Vietnamese from hoping that much would come out of continuing their negotiations with France. On September 10, before the *modus vivendi* was signed, General Morlière, the French Commissioner in Tonkin, had set up a unilateral French control over imports and exports at the important Tonkinese port of Haiphong. The Vietnamese had looked forward to collecting much-needed customs revenue at Haiphong after signing the agreement, but the French refused to alter their control.

On November 16 Ho Chi Minh protested to French Premier Georges Bidault against the failure of the Franco-Vietnamese Customs Commission to meet, as prescribed in the *modus vivendi*. He objected also to the High Commissioner's action in levying taxes on French nationals in Viet Nam (notably on the cotton mills at Nam Dinh) as a violation of the September agreement, which stipulated that they would be under Vietnamese fiscal control.

The atmosphere in Viet Nam was tense in November 1946. On November 20 a French War Crimes Commission came to Lang Son to investigate a mass grave where a number of French soldiers, killed by the Japanese in 1945, had been buried. French troops escorting the commission clashed with armed Vietnamese and each side accused the other of provocation.

This incident at Lang Son, where the number of French dead was less than ten, was rapidly overshadowed by another incident of considerably more alarming proportions which began the same day. A French patrol ship seized a Chinese junk attempting to run contraband into Haiphong, where the French had established a virtual blockade. Vietnamese soldiers fired on the French ship from the shore, and shooting broke out within the city itself. General Morlière and Hoang Huu Nam, Vietnamese Undersecretary of State, intervened immediately; the French agreed to respect Vietnamese sovereignty

---

[5] According to General Xuan, in an interview with the writer, Dr. Thinh had a series of upsetting experiences in the hours preceding his suicide. In the morning, when he asked to see Admiral d'Argenlieu, he was told that the High Commissioner was too busy to receive him; shortly after, he saw his colleague, Tran Van Ty, leaving the High Commissioner's office. Then he was told that friends of his, who had refused to join his government, were willing to join a Cochin Chinese regime headed by someone else. On top of this, he learned that Cochin Chinese police, sent to remove Viet Minh placards, had been stoned by the local population. When General Xuan saw Dr. Thinh for the last time, on November 11, he found him distraught.

in Haiphong and both sides promised to keep their troops far enough apart in the city to avoid friction. In the afternoon of November 22 they succeeded in bringing the fighting to a halt.

This, however, was only the first installment of the incident at Haiphong. Admiral d'Argenlieu, who was in Paris at the time, making a report to the French Government, proposed using the Haiphong clash to give the Vietnamese a lesson; and his suggestion was approved. "Even going so far as the use of cannons?" he asked. "Even that," Premier Bidault replied, probably not realizing there was any question of immediate action.[6] D'Argenlieu cabled General Valluy, his deputy in Saigon, who ordered Morlière to use force against the Vietnamese. But peace had already been achieved in Haiphong, Morlière pointed out—the Vietnamese situation was grave and required not the exploitation of incidents but their settlement; any imprudent act might lead to widespread hostilities.

Unsatisfied by this reply, General Valluy telegraphed directly to Colonel Debès, commander of the French troops at Haiphong:

It appears clear that we are up against premeditated aggressions carefully staged by the Vietnamese regular army, which no longer seems to obey its government's orders. Under these circumstances, your commendable attempts at conciliation and division of quarters, as well as the inquiry that I asked you to make, are out of season. The moment has come to give a severe lesson to those who have treacherously attacked you. Use all the means at your disposal to make yourself complete master of Haiphong and so bring the Vietnamese army around to a better understanding of the situation.[7]

Debès delivered an ultimatum to the Vietnamese at Haiphong on November 23: he ordered them to withdraw from the French section of the city, the Chinese quarter, and the port; and he gave them two hours in which to reply.[8] When the two hours were up, the French turned the full force of their army and navy on the Vietnamese positions, subjecting Haiphong to air bombardment and heavy artillery fire. The Vietnamese quarter was completely destroyed; some six thousand Vietnamese were killed.[9]

Franco-Vietnamese relations grew steadily worse after November 23. The fighting at Haiphong and Lang Son destroyed the little confidence that still remained between the two peoples; the rumor spread among the Vietnamese

---

[6] Rivet, *op. cit.*, p. 51.

[7] Quoted in Institut franco-suisse d'Études coloniales, *France et Viet-Nam*, p. 42.

[8] At the time of the Haiphong incident, French officials invoked the Franco-Chinese Treaty of February 28, 1946 as a justification for what they explained as their desire to protect the large Chinese population of Haiphong.

[9] Rivet, *op. cit.*, p. 51. This seems a conservative estimate. "No more than 6,000 killed, in so far as naval bombardment of fleeing civilians was concerned," Admiral Battet, French naval commander, later told Paul Mus. (*Témoignage Chrétien*, August 12, 1949.) Total Vietnamese casualties as high as 20,000 have been cited.

that the French were planning to take Hanoi next.[10] The Tong Bo, the executive committee of the Viet Minh, demanded that the Vietnamese Government make a firm effort to safeguard its sovereignty. "We can negotiate only if we defend ourselves," it asserted.

The Haiphong incident remained unsettled. Early in December, in a letter to Vo Nguyen Giap, Vietnamese Commander-in-Chief, General Morlière demanded a full-scale Vietnamese withdrawal from the city—no military or paramilitary elements were to be allowed in the Haiphong zone; the transit of Vietnamese troops as well as the embarkation of Vietnamese army units within the zone was to be under French military control; French troops were to circulate freely on the Haiphong–Do Son road; and the various roads linking the French garrisons were all to be controlled by French troops. In reply, Giap proposed that they set up a mixed committee to discuss the question. But Morlière's instructions were precise; there was nothing further to discuss, he said. Haiphong and Lang Son remained under French military occupation.

On December 2 Commissioner Sainteny arrived in Hanoi. Once before, he had helped to achieve an accord between France and Viet Nam when there appeared little hope of agreement. If there was any way out of the Franco-Vietnamese impasse, he seemed the one man to find it. Unfortunately, however, his influence on the French Government seemed to have decreased at this time; and despite his efforts, Franco-Vietnamese negotiations were stalemated. Vietnamese leaders, under strong pressure from extremists and from Vietnamese public opinion generally, insisted that the September *modus vivendi* could be applied only after the situation had reverted to what it had been before the French occupied Haiphong and Lang Son. The French military refused to withdraw from either city.

The Vietnamese Government seemed anxious to avoid a complete rupture: it permitted French soldiers to join the Vietnamese who were guarding the electric plant of Hanoi against sabotage; and it also agreed to send a mixed commission to Hai Duong, which lay midway between Hanoi and Haiphong. But these concessions did not add to the confidence of the Vietnamese people, who were nervous and showed it. In large numbers they fled Haiphong and Hanoi for the relative safety of the countryside, while those who stayed behind began to dig foxholes and trenches. Above all, they barricaded the Hanoi–Haiphong road, fearful of French designs on their capital.

At the same time, Sainteny told French newspapers that a debate was going on in the Vietnamese Cabinet and that the future of Franco-Vietnamese relations depended on the outcome. Some of the members, he said, among them

10 For some time, Viet Minh leaders had been cognizant of the circular issued by General Valluy on April 10, 1946, directing each French garrison to undertake "the study of measures which would have the effect of progressively modifying and transforming the plan of action, which is that of a purely military operation, into a plan of action for a coup d'état." See *Journal Officiel, Assemblée Nationale*, March 18, 1947, p. 871.

Ho, wanted an understanding with France; others stood out for a more intransigent policy. In *Cuu Quoc,* the official paper of the Viet Minh Front, Tran Huy Lieu, Communist, member of the National Assembly and former Minister of Information, asserted, "The Vietnamese will neither renounce nor secede." From the Committee of Resistance of Haiphong came an appeal to "exterminate the French reactionaries. Let the nation resist to the end." A detachment of the French Foreign Legion moved into Haiphong from Cochin China.[11]

Ho Chi Minh sent an appeal to the French Government, insisting on the "sincere desire of the Vietnamese Government and people to collaborate fraternally with the French people" and on "the desire of Viet Nam to be part of the French Union." He warned against "a certain number of Frenchmen in Indochina who are acting contrary to the agreements concluded and pursuing a policy of force in regard to Viet Nam."[12]

Hanoi newspapers published a Viet Minh proclamation: "The grave hour has arrived. The Hanoi Committee of the Viet Minh Front calls on the people to be calm, to be united, and to be ready to rise when the government gives the order." Vietnamese troops strengthened their positions within Hanoi and the Vietnamese secret police were said to be arresting Vietnamese suspected of pro-French sympathies. The Vietnamese quarters of Hanoi were virtually deserted, and most of the stores closed their doors. Vietnamese newspapers attacked Admiral d'Argenlieu bitterly.

From China came a word of reassurance for the French in the form of a statement that the Chinese recognized French authority in Indochina and had no diplomatic relations with the Vietnamese Government.

In Tonkin, tension mounted. Americans in Indochina were told that if the Admiral returned, blood would flow. The French accused the Vietnamese of widespread terrorism; and Sainteny protested to Ho Chi Minh against a new violation of the September *modus vivendi* as the Vietnamese began to issue their own banknotes, contrary to the monetary unity for all of Indochina pledged in the agreement.

Sainteny told the press that conditions were as bad as during the worst hours before March 6. Asserting that France had remained faithful to the "spirit of 1946" and was ready to examine its common interests with Viet Nam and to discuss the customs status of Haiphong, he hoped that Ho Chi Minh, "with whom I have more than friendship," would be able to convince his colleagues of the grave consequences of a rupture.[13] Ho, for his part, went on record as desiring peace. The threat to it, if threat there was, he said, did not come from

11 The Foreign Legion had traditionally been considered by natives of French colonies as a symbol of oppression.
12 *Le Monde,* December 10, 1946.
13 *Ibid.,* December 12, 1946.

the Vietnamese, who did not want to fight but would do anything rather than renounce their liberty. "Neither France nor Viet Nam can afford the luxury of a bloody war," Ho Chi Minh said, "and to reconstruct on ruins would be catastrophic."[14]

The French landed seven hundred soldiers at Tourane, despite Vietnamese protests that this was a hostile act contrary to the *modus vivendi*. They came, the French explained, to protect French lives and property. In Hanoi the Vietnamese stepped up the pace of their "self-defense" preparations. They felled trees and used them as roadblocks, cut off streets by digging deep trenches at each end, made holes in walls through which weapons could be fired. Since they could not stop the French reinforcements from landing at Tourane, they cut the road between Hué and Tourane, isolating the French population in the capital of Annam.

In Paris, however, events seemed to take a turn for the better when Léon Blum became Premier of France on December 16 at the head of an all-Socialist Cabinet. Earlier that December, Blum had written in the Socialist organ, *Le Populaire,* that independence (later qualified to read "independence within the French Union") was the only solution for Viet Nam.[15] Ho Chi Minh immediately rushed off a message to the new Premier with proposals for relieving Franco-Vietnamese tension. But his telegram was delayed by the French censorship in Saigon and did not arrive in Paris until December 26, when it was too late to do any good.[16]

Even had Ho Chi Minh's message arrived in time, it is doubtful whether Léon Blum was in a position to reverse the Indochina policy over which the Socialist Marius Moutet had presided as Minister of Overseas France. Since the Liberation, the Socialists had been only one of three parties in the coalition governing France, poised precariously between the Communists and the MRP, too weak to impose a policy of their own upon the country. The new government, in any case, was simply a stop-gap regime appointed to serve out the few remaining days of the Provisional Government until the constitution of the Fourth Republic would go into effect.

In Indochina, meanwhile, events moved inexorably according to the pattern laid down at Haiphong and Lang Son. Frenchmen and Vietnamese were killed on the streets of Hanoi. The Vietnamese informed the French that they would no longer participate in the mixed patrols that had been on duty every night for the preceding several months in the city. They continued to build barricades in Hanoi, and to cut off important arteries leading to the city. Hai-

---

14 *Ibid.*

15 "There is one way and only one of preserving in Indochina the prestige of our civilization, our political and spiritual influence, and also those of our material interests which are legitimate: it is sincere agreement [with Viet Nam] on the basis of independence. . . ." Léon Blum, *Le Populaire,* December 10, 1946.

16 This delay, frequently alleged, is confirmed by Devillers, *op. cit.,* pp. 351–52.

phong was virtually isolated by Vietnamese roadblocks and in Hanoi only military patrols ventured out on the streets.

Admiral d'Argenlieu, still in France, declared that the Indochinese people must be convinced that France intended to remain in Indochina if they were not to lose confidence in the French. He urged the creation of a "real federation" and quoted Lyautey's maxim: "Show force so that you do not have to use it." Newspapers on December 18 reported that the Admiral was leaving Paris the following morning for Indochina. The French Government announced that Marius Moutet would also leave for Indochina to resume the negotiations he had begun with Ho Chi Minh in Paris, and to extend them to include the rulers of Cochin China, Cambodia, and Laos.

In Hanoi a hundred French parachutists moving into the Vietnamese quarter were attacked with grenades thrown from Vietnamese houses. French troops took over the Vietnamese Ministries of Communications and Finance to stop the Vietnamese from sniping from the buildings at French passers-by. Time was running out in Viet Nam.

On December 19, early in the day, General Morlière demanded the disarmament of the Tu Ve, the Viet Minh militia. For the Vietnamese, this was the final ultimatum. That night, on December 19, 1946, the fear and mistrust which had accumulated in the wake of all the bloodshed and broken promises erupted into open war. The Vietnamese turned on the French in Hanoi. They cut off the city's water supply and electricity, and attacked with machine guns, mortars, and artillery. From Hanoi the fighting spread rapidly throughout Tonkin and north Annam; and two days later Nguyen Binh launched a new attack in the south.

The largest number of casualties occurred during the indiscriminate repression which followed the occupation of Hanoi by French forces and cost the lives of several thousand Vietnamese civilians. The moral impact of this repression was so serious as to ensure the failure of subsequent French efforts to establish cooperation with the Vietnamese population in the north.

WHOSE RESPONSIBILITY?

After the events of December 19, the reality of the crisis in Indochina could no longer be ignored. This was considerably more than a series of mopping-up operations and "incidents"; the French and the Vietnamese were at undeclared war. The situation was perhaps best summarized by a conservative English newspaper in Singapore which, quoting in part from the Paris correspondent of the London *Times,* commented:

The French assert that they have shown the utmost restraint and have only resorted to arms under intolerable provocation. Certainly the reports of European civilians, men and women, murdered in their houses at Hanoi, are enough to arouse any white troops to fury. On the other hand, . . . the Times correspondent in Paris . . . wrote: . . . For weeks it has been evident that the consistent if defensive extension of French strong-points in Tonkin could scarcely fail to draw a full-scale attack from the Annamese sooner or later . . . [Rather than attempt to decide who was to blame,] the outside observer will be inclined to say that that is what must inevitably happen when a European army stands on the same soil with a militant and hostile nationalist movement . . .

The position in Indochina now is that France is on the verge of a full-scale colonial war—something that we hoped would never occur again in the history of Asia. . . . Any colonial power which puts itself in the position of meeting terrorism with terrorism might as well wash its hands of the whole business and go home. . . . Unless events take a very unexpected turn for the better, we are about to see a French army reconquer the greater part of Indochina, only to make it impossible for any French merchant or planter to live there outside barbed-wire perimeters thereafter. Whatever may be the solution of the problems of colonial Asia, this is not it.[17]

The Viet Minh refused to admit, either then or later, that Vietnamese forces precipitated the events of December 19, and many of the atrocity stories circulated by the French at the time have since been proved false. The official number of verified deaths was 43.[18] But the Vietnamese could not prove that they did not launch the actual attack, and in the French Assembly in December 1946 few deputies looked beyond this fact. Some of them were bitter at Ho Chi Minh. The MRP and the Rightist PRL (Republican Party of Liberty) argued that the Vietnamese Republic had broken the Agreement of March 6, that France could no longer negotiate with the Vietnamese. A number of informed Frenchmen favored another explanation—Ho had lost control of his government to more extremist elements headed by Vo Nguyen Giap. It is true that the failure of Ho Chi Minh's policy of negotiation did not make it very popular; but there is no reason to believe that he relied exclusively on negotiations. In the Viet Nam National Assembly, he had been accused of trying to play a double game, leaving Giap to take the decisive action while he supplied a peaceful façade. To this he replied that diplomacy was like military action, each maneuver being adapted to the particular circumstances.[19]

There was no need for a schism in the Viet Nam Government to explain why war came to Viet Nam. The Vietnamese chose the date on which it broke out, but the policy followed by members of the French administration in Sai-

[17] *Straits Times,* December 30, 1946.

[18] "The exact number of victims, Eurasians and Europeans together, was 37 and . . . the official list rose to 43 only by adding to it the soldiers and Sureté inspectors who fell . . . at the time of the taking of the city and of the repression." Paul Mus, *Témoignage Chrétien,* November 11, 1949. This observer also wrote: "I am today in a position to state and to prove that four-fifths of the stories or reports of awful atrocities inflicted by the Vietnamese on our compatriots in Hanoi, December 19, 1946 are either made up or in error." *Loc. cit.,* August 12, 1949.

[19] Léon Boutbien, *Franc-Tireur,* January 22, 1947.

gon made the war almost inevitable. They had systematically obstructed the carrying out of the March 6 Agreement. They had established a puppet regime in Cochin China, wrecked the Fontainebleau Conference, ordered the "pacification" of Haiphong; and the Vietnamese had had little reason to hope that their policy would change.

Long afterward, in the Assembly of the French Union, the French Socialist Oreste Rosenfeld said of the events of December 19:

> If we truly want to determine who was responsible, I do not hesitate to say that the great responsibility falls on the government of 1946 which let its High Commissioner formulate a policy contrary to government policy. You know very well that the High Commissioner, M. Georges Thierry d'Argenlieu, appointed by General de Gaulle, had exorbitant powers in Indochina. He was not even under the authority of the Minister of Overseas France, but directly under the President of the Council [the Premier, Georges Bidault] and so of the government. . . . The great responsibility of the government of M. Georges Bidault and M. Maurice Thorez was not to have had the authority to prevent Admiral d'Argenlieu from following a policy contrary to that of the French Government . . .
>
> On both sides—and there was the tragedy—there were guilty people, for if the French administration in Indochina in 1946 did not want to apply the policy decided by the government, on Ho Chi Minh's side there were also men who did not want to apply either the Agreement of March 6 or the *modus vivendi* of September 14 . . .[20]

Since the establishment of the Democratic Republic of Viet Nam in September 1945, Franco-Vietnamese relations had been conditioned by political currents inside France—by the weakness of the Socialists, who professed to favor Vietnamese demands, by the strength of the MRP, led by Georges Bidault, who opposed them; concerned particularly about repercussions in French North Africa, Bidault had consistently been against making concessions to the Vietnamese. General de Gaulle also wielded an influence on Indochinese affairs. No party in France denied the importance of national prestige and national power, but de Gaulle accorded these factors greater importance than did most, and was more ready than any but the Rightist parties to equate them with force. It was under de Gaulle that the March 1945 declaration was issued, and that fighting raged at the end of 1945 and early in 1946. French agreements with Viet Nam came during the presidency of Félix Gouin, the Socialist who succeeded him.

Although General de Gaulle had been absent from the center of the political stage during most of 1946, his political influence had continued. He had not yet founded a movement of his own at this time, and even many elements in the MRP regarded him as their spokesman. In speeches at Epinal and Bayeux, in which he attacked the two draft constitutions presented to the French people,

[20] *Journal Officiel*, Assemblée de l'Union Française, March 9, 1949, p. 337–38.

he had reiterated his policy of force and national greatness. In Paris on August 27, 1946 he had said: "United with the overseas territories which she opened to civilization, France is a great power. Without these territories she would be in danger of no longer being one."[21] Viewed in the context of the methods de Gaulle had favored to keep Indochina, this statement, made while the Vietnamese delegation was at Fontainebleau, had not encouraged them in their negotiations.

A French Catholic priest, after summing up the events of 1946, wrote:

> This succession of facts indicates a fairly clear general plan: to concede to Viet Nam a theoretical independence which no one is any longer in a position to refuse, but to reduce its territory as much as possible and to surround it with a belt of rival states in order to neutralize it . . . It cannot be denied that French policy in Indochina after March 6 was marked by Machiavellianism and that it ran counter to the most natural and most legitimate aspirations of the élite of the country. That leads us to regret that a priest and a monk—no one is unaware of the identity of Admiral d'Argenlieu—was willing, even with good intentions, to assume the responsibility for it. In fact, the succession of events proves that the policy of the Admiral brought France nothing and his presence at the head of the French administration in Indochina, unhappily, served to give credence to the legend that the Catholic priest and the missionary are agents of Western imperialism.[22]

Admiral d'Argenlieu, who had been appointed by General de Gaulle and to whom Premier Bidault had allowed such great freedom, was attacked by Vietnamese as epitomizing imperial force and breach of faith. The French Socialists and Communists, articulate in their criticism of him, campaigned vigorously for his recall.

The Communists, like the Socialists, favored negotiations with Ho Chi Minh; but they were emphatic that they did not want to see France reduced to what the Communist newspaper, L'Humanité, called "its own small metropolitan territory," which would happen, they warned, if the colonial peoples turned against the French. "Are we, after having lost Syria and Lebanon yesterday, to lose Indochina tomorrow, North Africa the day after?"[23] In the National Assembly a Communist deputy said: "The Communists are as much as the next person for the greatness of the country. But . . . they have never ceased to affirm that the French Union . . . can only be founded on the confident, fraternal and, above all, democratic collaboration of all the peoples and races who compose it."[24]

The Communists, in other words, overestimated their following among the

21 Le Monde, August 29, 1946.
22 "L'émancipation du sud-est asiatique. 2. Le Vietnam," Le Bulletin des Missions, 1948.
23 L'Humanité, July 24, 1946.
24 Journal Officiel, Assemblée Nationale, September 19, 1946, p. 3844.

French electorate and still hoped that they would rule France in the near future, at least as members of a Left-Wing coalition; they wanted Viet Nam within the empire when that time came. More immediately, they had to campaign on a nationalistic platform if they were to maintain and extend their following among the large numbers of nonparty members they needed to vote them into office. They would not risk an anticolonialist stand comparable to that assumed by the Dutch Communist Party on the occasion of Dutch military action against the Sukarno government in Indonesia.

As for the Socialists, they were not only weak, they were also split among themselves. It seems clear, for example, that although Marius Moutet, the Socialist Minister of Overseas France, did not like being ignored by Admiral d'Argenlieu, he was not nearly so critical of d'Argenlieu as were many of the Socialist rank and file. In the Assembly of the French Union, Oreste Rosenfeld went so far as to speak of the "crimes" of Admiral d'Argenlieu;[25] Moutet (and a minority of the Socialist Party), however, did not disapprove of much that the Admiral was doing in Indochina.

THE MOUTET MISSION

There was irony in the fact that a Socialist and long-time critic of French colonialism was Premier of France when the fighting began. No sooner were the Socialists in office, than they had to cope with the events of December 19, all the while trying to defend themselves against charges from the Center and Right that they were following a policy of weakness and national dishonor. To the extreme Left were the Communists, urging peace and negotiation.

Léon Blum acted in the emergency much as any man of the French political Center or Right would have done. He told the French Assembly:

We have been obliged to deal with violence. I declare that the men who are fighting out there, the French of Indochina, the friendly populations, may count unreservedly on the vigilance and resolution of the government.

It was our common task to try everything to spare the blood of our children— and also the blood that is not ours, but which is blood all the same, that of a people whose right to political liberty we recognized ten months ago, and who should keep their place in the union of peoples federated around France.

He stood by his principles: "The old colonial system founded on conquest and maintained by constraint, which tended toward exploitation of conquered lands and peoples, is finished today."[26] France's goal was still a free Viet Nam in an Indochinese Federation freely associated with the French Union.

And so, as Blum explained it, France went to war against Viet Nam, not in

25 *Ibid.*, Assemblée de l'Union Française, March 9, 1949, p. 338.
26 *Ibid.*, December 23, 1946, p. 320.

anger but in self-defense, its conscience clean of colonialism, its faith in the rightness of its cause barely questioned. "Before all, order must be reestablished," Blum told the Assembly, "peaceful order which is necessarily the basis for the execution of contracts."[27]

On December 23, loudspeakers in Hanoi proclaimed French martial law throughout Tonkin and north Annam, while French tanks and infantry were still battling for key buildings in the center of the city. The loudspeakers announced: "Every man not in uniform carrying arms or with arms in his possession will be shot. Any house not displaying the white flag will be searched. Any house from which shots are fired at Frenchmen will be attacked."

Ho Chi Minh, who had fled from Hanoi when the fighting started, announced a state of emergency throughout Viet Nam. He accused the French of having provoked hostilities. "The war will be long and difficult," he said over the radio. And he promised: "The possessions of foreign nationals will be protected and prisoners well treated." In Paris a delegation of the Viet Nam Government declared, "We do not want war." Viet Nam still hoped to collaborate with France "on the basis of an agreement concluded within the framework of the French Union."

. D'Argenlieu, returned to Indochina as scheduled, accused the Vietnamese of violating their agreements with France—of increasing the numbers and weapons of their army, of hate propaganda against the French, of terror against their opponents, of destroying the riches of the country and violating the democratic spirit. He said that France would not relinquish its hold on Indochina—"the maintenance and development of its present influences and of its economic interests, the protection of ethnic minorities with which it is entrusted, the care of assuring the security of strategic bases within the framework of defense of the Federation and the French Union." The Admiral declared: "France does not intend in the present state of evolution of the Indochinese peoples to give them unconditional and total independence, which would only be a fiction gravely prejudicial to the interests of the two parties."[28]

Two French emissaries arrived in Indochina on d'Argenlieu's heels—General Leclerc and Marius Moutet. They symbolized the two policies that Blum was trying to apply in Viet Nam: Leclerc the military man, and Moutet, a civilian who had negotiated the September 1946 *modus vivendi*.

Both men were on record as supporting the March 6 Agreement. The Frenchmen who had negotiated the agreement had been in close touch with Leclerc; and the General had stood by it during 1946, in striking contrast to Admiral d'Argenlieu. A man of high moral caliber and keen political intelligence, Leclerc enjoyed considerable respect among the Vietnamese. Recalled from his North African assignment, over Admiral d'Argenlieu's objections,[29]

[27] *Ibid.*, p. 321.
[28] *Le Monde,* December 27, 1946.
[29] Dansette, *op. cit.,* p. 213.

to investigate the military situation in Indochina, Leclerc wrote in his report: "In 1947 France will no longer put down by force a grouping of 24 million inhabitants which is assuming unity and in which there exists a xenophobic and perhaps a national ideal." Leclerc urged a peaceful solution, an agreement with all factions of the Vietnamese people: "*The capital problem from now on is political.* It is a question of coming to terms with an awakening xenophobic nationalism, of channelling it in order to safeguard, at least in part, the rights of France."[30]

Although the Moutet mission, it was underlined in Paris, was one of information not of negotiation, even more than Leclerc's visit, it held out the prospect of some rapid settlement of the Franco-Vietnamese war; Moutet, after all, was a Cabinet Minister with the power to make policy on behalf of the French Government.

Marius Moutet arrived in Indochina on December 25. Two days later he had already made up his mind about the impossibility of negotiating with Ho Chi Minh. When Moutet spoke at a dinner given in his honor by the Le Van Hoach "provisional government" in Saigon, it was difficult to see much difference between the point of view of the Socialist Minister of Overseas France and that of the Rightist High Commissioner of Indochina. Like d'Argenlieu, he found the "cruel disillusionment of agreements that could not be put into effect . . . We can no longer speak of a free agreement between France and Viet Nam."[31]

Moutet made a point of visiting Cambodia and Laos, which he described as examples of the order and friendship France hoped to find in Indochina. From Saigon he went to Pnom Penh, the Cambodian capital, where he was received by King Norodom Sihanouk and the Cambodian Assembly. "The role of France is to bring back order and peace in all countries where the French flag flies," he said. "France will not abandon her friends."[32] Moutet visited Siemreap and Angkor, also in Cambodia, and Vientiane, the capital of Laos, before he returned to Cochin China.

The French Government had never received any overtures from the Democratic Republic of Viet Nam, Moutet declared. He said: "If they have any proposals to transmit to us, they will be examined with care."[33] Then, suddenly, came the news that he had secretly left Saigon for Hanoi on January 3. The Viet Nam radio had been broadcasting messages asking negotiations with France; was it possible, after all, that Moutet was ready to negotiate?

The answer was no. Moutet spent little more than a day in Hanoi. He toured the city, talked with Sainteny, who had been wounded on December

---

[30] Quoted by Pierre Mendès-France, *Journal Officiel*, Assemblée Nationale, November 22, 1950, p. 8044; Dansette, *op. cit.*, p. 214. The italics are General Leclerc's.
[31] *Le Monde*, December 29–30, 1946.
[32] *Ibid.*, January 1, 1947.
[33] *Ibid.*

19, and with some local Frenchmen and Vietnamese, inspected military posts and hospitals and the sacked Pasteur Institute; and once he was fired upon. Before leaving Hanoi on d'Argenlieu's private plane, he said: "Before any negotiations today, it is necessary to have a military decision. I am sorry, but one cannot commit such madness as the Vietnamese have done with impunity."[34]

Before he left Indochina he made an assertion which he was to repeat many times. He said that no attempt had been made by the Ho government to enter into contact with him. He said this again when he returned to France, in speeches and in interviews. It is a matter of record, however, that Marius Moutet had opportunities for seeing men associated with the Viet Minh government. Evidence of this lies not only in the radio appeals made by the Vietnamese to Moutet, which he ignored, but also in the statements of a member of the Moutet mission, Dr. Léon Boutbien. Boutbien, who belonged to the Executive Committee of the French Socialist Party, brought back from Indochina a report totally at variance with that of the Minister of Overseas France. When he landed at Orly airfield with Moutet, he told newspapermen that the French as well as the Vietnamese were to blame for the fighting. He was bitterly critical of Admiral d'Argenlieu, and he dated the beginning of hostilities, as the Vietnamese did, not from December 19 but from November 20 and the Haiphong affair.

In a series of articles published in *Franc-Tireur* in January, Léon Boutbien elaborated his conclusions with enough impartiality to enable Ho Chi Minh later to recommend the series as showing "the real cause of the present conflict."[35] Boutbien based his report on unofficial talks he had had with Vietnamese nationalists; not only, it seemed, had the Viet Minh government contacted the Moutet Mission, but Boutbien had actually met some of its representatives. It was Moutet, apparently, not the Vienamese, who did not wish to negotiate. In France some politicians laid the responsibility for Moutet's consistent refusal to negotiate on pressure from his MRP colleagues. If such pressure was exerted, it did not fall on an unwilling victim.

OPINION IN FRANCE

With Admiral d'Argenlieu under intensified attack from the French Left after the December outbreak of fighting, Premier Blum proposed to General Leclerc that he take over command of the French troops in Indochina and, in time, succeed d'Argenlieu. Leclerc refused; and he refused again when Paul Ramadier, Blum's successor, offered him the post of High Commissioner with broad powers.

[34] *Ibid.*, January 5–6, 1947.
[35] *New York Times*, February 10, 1947.

Leclerc told Ramadier what his conditions for acceptance would have been: full civil and military power for himself and an army of 100,000 men, 90,000 of them Europeans; eventual negotiations with the Viet Minh; and independence for the Vietnamese within the French Union with safeguards for French interests and military bases.

"They want to use you," General de Gaulle warned Leclerc. "You don't know politics . . . They will make you take the responsibility for abandoning Indochina . . . They will make you an instrument of capitulation."[36] Even more influential than General de Gaulle, in Leclerc's final decision to refuse the post of High Commissioner, was his feeling that whatever he might attempt to do in Indochina would be hamstrung in Paris; and he advised Ramadier to give the job to a civilian who could count on having political support.[37] However, for the time being, d'Argenlieu stayed on as High Commissioner.

It was difficult to reconcile the continued warfare with French government protestations of their desire for peace. But Marius Moutet, who remained Minister of Overseas France when a coalition Cabinet came to power in January 1947 under Paul Ramadier, another Socialist, professed to find no incompatibility between them. The government's position was that the Viet Nam Republic was in the hands of a group of extremists who had gotten out of control. It described the Viet Minh as terrorist, pro-Japanese, Communist, totalitarian, bitterly anti-French, and totally lacking in good faith.

From Saigon, Admiral d'Argenlieu proposed a common policy among the great powers to arrest the progress of Communism in Asia, beginning with Viet Nam. But it was no solution to the Vietnamese problem to blame it entirely on Communism, as Frenchmen fighting Vietnamese nationalism had done so often since the 1920's. General Leclerc said in January 1947, "Anti-Communism will be a useless tool as long as the problem of nationalism remains unresolved."[38]

In his ministerial declaration before the French Assembly, Premier Ramadier declared himself in favor of independence and unity for Viet Nam—"independence within the French Union," and "union of the three Annamese countries, if the Annamese people desire it."[39] Ho Chi Minh welcomed this statement. In a radio address, he said: "When France recognizes the independence and unity of Viet Nam, we will retire to our village for we are not ambitious for power or honor."

But no attempt was made to put Ramadier's declaration into practice. The Rightist press by then was criticizing the weakness of the French military effort in Viet Nam while Leftists attacked the government for failing to carry

[36] Quoted in Dansette, op. cit., p. 216.
[37] Ibid., p. 217.
[38] Devillers, op. cit., p. 367.
[39] Journal Officiel, Assemblée Nationale, January 21, 1947, p. 29.

out past French promises of autonomy. The Viet Minh radio appealed for peace, asking independence and unity for Viet Nam within the French Union. The Vietnamese delegation which Ho Chi Minh had left behind in Paris, profiting from the French tradition of liberalism toward colonial peoples in France, was able to go on publishing its propaganda after December 19, and it remained in touch with the French Government. Early in February this delegation proposed a cease-fire on all fronts, the appointment of an armistice commission, the withdrawal of troops to positions defined in the March 6 Agreement and its April annex, and negotiations with the "legal government presided over by Ho Chi Minh" on the basis of the accords.

Premier Ramadier told a press conference that he could not take seriously this bid for negotiations. He doubted that it was authentic, he said; although it had been made in the name of Ho Chi Minh, the signature was typewritten and the message came from Paris. This was rather a feeble excuse; even at that time the Viet Minh government had radio transmitters in full operation, and it would have been a simple matter to get them to confirm any proposals put forward by their delegation in Paris.

In any case, Ramadier said, he could not accept a return to the March 6 Agreement as the basis for an armistice: that Agreement, having been broken by "the aggression of Hanoi," no longer existed.[40] The Viet Minh radio retorted: ". . . if the agreement of last March 6 is to be considered void by France, we renounce any integration into the French Union and will fight for absolute independence."

Growing doubts of the methods of French policy were voiced in France. The results of a public opinion poll were announced in February: 42 percent of the people queried favored negotiations with Viet Nam; 36 percent favored force; 8 percent thought that France should leave the country; 14 percent had no opinion.[41]

Toward the end of March, the independent Left-Wing newspaper, *Combat,* published an interview with Max André, who had headed the French delegation at Fontainebleau. In a later article in *L'Aube,* the organ of his own party, the MRP, André denied some of the statements attributed to him, but he stood by the central thesis that Ho Chi Minh had wanted peace and that, as of two months earlier at least, Ho was the only man to deal with in Viet Nam. Looking back over the recent history of Franco-Vietnamese relations, André deplored the second Dalat conference, found it regrettable that French troops had moved into the Moi Plateaux, and questioned the wisdom of establishing the Cochin Chinese "Republic." The Viet Minh was not purely Communist, he said; it was a national front which included Socialists and Catholics. Nor did it receive arms from Russia—Nationalist China was a much likelier

[40] *Le Monde,* February 15, 1947.
[41] *New York Times,* February 4, 1947.

source. As to fanatically anti-French elements, these were more likely to be found among the Dong Minh Hoi and the VNQDD than the Viet Minh.[42]

Also in March, the British *New Statesman and Nation* described a secret report from General Morlière which asserted that it was with Ho Chi Minh that negotiations must begin and, also, that the large majority of the people of Cochin China favored union with Viet Nam.[43]

In various quarters in France the warning was heard that if the French continued on their present course, they might lose Indochina. The Socialists and Communists continued their press campaign against d'Argenlieu. The Ramadier government seemed fearful of giving the impression that it would be yielding to Leftist pressure if it removed him; but early in March, it gave way. Emile Bollaert, Radical Socialist, civilian and parliamentarian, was appointed to succeed Admiral d'Argenlieu. His appointment, said Ramadier, inaugurated a new "constructive phase."[44]

THE FRENCH ASSEMBLY DEBATES

In the second week of March 1947, domestic tensions in France reached a climax as the National Assembly debated the government's Indochina policy. It was a fiery debate. The Communists clashed on three separate occasions with their opponents, each time walking out of the Assembly chamber; once they actually came to blows.

A dramatic incident occurred when former Premier Paul Reynaud, in the middle of a speech about atrocities supposed to have been committed by the Vietnamese, pointed his finger at Duong Bach Mai, head of the Viet Minh delegation in Paris, and said: "This is the criminal." Mai was seated in the distinguished visitors' gallery, in a box not far from Emile Bollaert, the new High Commissioner. Right-Wing deputies demanded that Mai be expelled; the Communists told him to stay. Edouard Herriot, the President of the Assembly, sent a guard to the box, asking him to leave, but Mai stayed on; it was the Communists who walked out when Reynaud continued his charges.[45]

For the first time in the debate, the Third International was accused of having at least a share in Indochina's difficulties. The charge came not from the extreme Right, but from Maurice Viollette, Radical Socialist specialist on the empire. "Nationalism in Indochina is a means," he said. "The end is Soviet imperialism." The Communists protested angrily and Marcel Cachin called "an abominable lie" the assertion that such a thing as Soviet imperialism

---

[42] *Combat,* March 25, 1947; *L'Aube,* March 27, 1947.

[43] *New Statesman and Nation,* March 22, 1947.

[44] *New York Times,* March 7, 1947.

[45] Duong Bach Mai was arrested several days later and subsequently deported to Viet Nam. He was succeeded as chief of the Viet Minh delegation in Paris by Tran Ngoc Danh, also a Communist.

existed. Ramadier rose finally in an effort to clear the air. He reminded the Assembly that an important international conference was then taking place in Moscow, discussing the future of Germany. "We must seek a common meeting ground on which France can show herself united in defense of her ideals," he urged.[46] The Premier asserted that no one meant to hurt French relations with the Soviets or to mitigate French gratitude to the Red Army. "I will add that on the question of Indochina, we have always noted the correctness of the government of the Soviet Union."[47]

There was no speaker who did not say that France should stay on in Indochina, but from the Left came criticism of French policy and demands for immediate negotiations with Ho Chi Minh. When Pierre Cot called for negotiations, Ramadier intervened to say that no proposal for negotiation had been received either from the Vietnamese Government or from Ho Chi Minh. It was true that letters had been addressed to the French Government, one of them to Léon Blum when he was still Premier. "That letter bore a signature, Ho Chi Minh. The signature has been analyzed by experts and it is false."[48]

Marius Moutet rose then, to justify his past actions. Regardless of the succession of governments in Paris, he said, French policy remained the same: "to affirm the necessity of maintaining the presence of France, the defense of its interests, the protection of its friends." He spoke warmly of those friends.

I traveled through Cambodia and that marvelous country of Laos where the whole population welcomes you with flowers in their hands. What a contrast with Hanoi, where after our visit to the [de Lanessan] hospital, men in ambush on the roofs fired at us . . . Nearly a third of the population of Indochina is not Annamese . . . I can bear witness that, among all these people, there is not one who does not fear the Annamese.

For Moutet the outbreak of December 19 was another Pearl Harbor, and he subscribed to the theory that Ho Chi Minh had lost control of his government. "When Ho left Paris, I was convinced that he wanted to collaborate with us," but fifteen days after Ho's return, before the National Assembly, he was repudiated by certain extremists who reproached him for not bringing back independence and unity.

"Viet Nam is not all Indochina," Moutet said, "and I wish to say that the Viet Minh is not all Viet Nam . . . We have to defend our work out there and pursue it in the interests of the populations." Who, after all, could talk of independence? Look at the United States in the Philippines. "They evidently have certain means for maintaining themselves economically in this territory; but I must say that they possess an impressive number of military bases there." True the English had left India, but considering the many victims of com-

46 *Journal Officiel*, Assemblée Nationale, March 14, 1947, pp. 848, 851–52.
47 *Ibid.*, p. 848.
48 *Ibid.*, March 18, 1947, p. 875.

munal warfare between Moslem and Hindu, this, said Moutet, was simply isolationism.

Unity, too, was a thing to be seriously qualified, so far as Moutet was concerned. There could be no referendum in Cochin China until there was an end to terrorism. "I do not reproach Admiral d'Argenlieu for not having followed the directives of the government. I reproach him for having anticipated them."

Moutet was willing to admit the possibility of union of the three Vietnamese areas, but they had to "find the formula which, while satisfying the desire for unity, will allow the existence of autonomous governments which are a necessity for the peaceful life of this country." France, in other words, could not permit the establishment of a single Vietnamese state.

Moutet was worried about the future of French control over Laos and Cambodia, which could easily be overwhelmed by 20 million united Vietnamese. "From the moment when they feel that this union is accomplished and that they are not truly protected, we can say goodbye to Cambodia and Laos, which will turn toward other unions and toward other political bonds."[49] He did not mention Siam as a possible pole of attraction for Laos and Cambodia once the fiction of an Indochinese federation was demolished, but observers agreed that it was a serious possibility.

"I ask only to return to the accords of March 6," Moutet said. "But I would like to be certain . . . that with these accords of March 6 we will not relive the terrible hours that brought us to December 19."[50]

There was in any case, a serious obstacle to carrying out the March Agreement. The new French constitution, adopted in October 1946, provided for common military defense and diplomacy for the French Union, with the French Republic directing both in the common interest. "That without doubt was not marked clearly in the treaty of March 6," Premier Ramadier said "The constitution was not approved then. It was not even written. Today it can no longer be a question of the framework of the treaty of March 6. There can only be the new constitutional framework which is imposed on us and which will offer us the possibility of constructive work."[51] The accord with Viet Nam, it seemed, was something that the French Government had granted for the moment and that it felt free to withdraw at will.

"We must protect the life and possessions of Frenchmen, of foreigners, of our Indochinese friends who have confidence in French liberty," Ramadier said in March 1947. "It is necessary that we disengage our garrisons, re-establish essential communications, assure the safety of populations which have taken refuge with us. That we have done."[52]

49 *Ibid.*, pp. 879–82.
50 *Ibid.*, p. 902.
51 *Ibid.*, p. 905.
52 *Ibid.*, p. 904.

In vain did nationalists from other parts of the French Union urge negotiations with the Vietnamese. "The French Union has been baptized in blood," said the Madagascan deputy, Joseph Raseta, "the fresh blood of young Frenchmen and of our brothers in Viet Nam. All the overseas people hope for an end to a fratricidal war which, if it is prolonged, risks creating an unbridgeable abyss between people who can and should live in peace." He asked that the French Government "put an immediate end to the war and look again for the bases of a just and necessary peace."[53]

In Madagascar, revolt broke out against the French during this same month, March 1947. Tens of thousands of Madagascans as well as a number of the small French population of the island were dead before the rebellion was put down. Raseta himself was condemned to death, a sentence which was later changed to life imprisonment.

In the French Assembly on March 18, 1947 an Algerian joined Raseta in support of the Viet Minh. The Vietnamese, according to Mohammed Khider, were revolting against an often brutal colonialism. The use of force was no longer a solution.[54] And Félix Houphouet from West Africa, who belonged to the African Democratic Rally (RDA), said that no one in Parliament or in the French Union wanted France to leave Indochina. What they wanted was an immediate cessation of hostilities.[55]

Ramadier refused to promise either peace or negotiation. On March 18 he received a vote of confidence from the Assembly of 410 to 0. One hundred and ninety-five members abstained, among them the Communists and the deputies from Overseas France. The Communists, however, evidently were not seriously interested in the Vietnamese struggle for independence except as it served their own purposes; and in 1946, despite frequent denunciations of past French policy in Indochina coupled with appeals for negotiations with the Vietnamese, they were considerably more concerned to make a nationalist appeal to the French electorate than to give overt support to the Ho Chi Minh government. As a result, only the Communist deputies withheld their votes; the Communist Cabinet members voted with the government in support of the war. A directive ordering military action against the Vietnamese was countersigned by the Communist Vice-Premier of France, Maurice Thorez.

Premier Ramadier promised the French Assembly: "Now that French force is affirmed, I have said so, the Minister of Overseas France has said so, it is necessary to construct, and the civil era must succeed the military era."[56] On March 22 the Assembly approved increased military credits asked by the government.

[53] *Ibid.*, p. 905.
[54] *Ibid.*, p. 906.
[55] *Ibid.*
[56] *Ibid.*, March 21, 1947, p. 1024.

INDIFFERENCE ABROAD

While the politicians were debating in France, the war went on in Viet Nam. There was little international interest in Indochina during 1946 and 1947. The rights and wrongs of the Dutch and the Indonesians were already being hotly debated before the United Nations, but a curtain of silence seemed to have dropped over Viet Nam.

The Viet Minh delegates to the Asian Relations Conference held in India during March 1947, reported that twice their messengers had been killed before the Ho government succeeded in smuggling out their credentials to Bangkok, where the delegates waited. They attacked as French puppets the Cambodian and Laotian delegates who also came to New Delhi. With the Indonesians, they appealed for Asian support.[57] But Pandit Nehru, presiding over this first assemblage of Asian states, was anxious not to antagonize the West by any political pronouncements. And the emergent states of Asia were too preoccupied with their own problems in achieving self-government to give the Vietnamese more than verbal interest, the more so because they did not want to be tarred with the Communist brush.

The Soviet Union, which was not backward in championing other colonial peoples, notably the Indonesians, preferred not to raise the question of Viet Nam. During the meeting of the United Nations General Assembly in London in 1946, Soviet Delegate Manuilsky made clear to a Vietnamese visitor that the USSR, at that time, was not directly interested in Viet Nam.[58]

Early in 1947, as in the fall of 1945, the issue of British support of the French military effort in Indochina was raised in the British House of Commons. A Labor member asserted that Britain's governing party was not just a Socialist party, but an international Socialist party which, as such, had an interest in Vietnamese affairs. But Foreign Minister Ernest Bevin rejected the suggestion that Britain should find out French intentions in Indochina before proceeding with negotiations for a Franco-British alliance. The sole purpose of the treaty, he said, was to prevent German aggression. Indochina was a problem for the French alone.[59]

[57] The Vietnamese and Indonesian delegates proposed a five-point program, after the conference ended, for action by the countries of Asia against colonialism:
   (1) Place the issue of colonialism and particularly the issue of Viet Nam on the Security Council agenda.
   (2) Immediate recognition of the Indonesian Republic and the Viet Nam Republic.
   (3) Joint Asian action to force the withdrawal of foreign troops from all parts of "occupied" Asia.
   (4) Joint Asian action to prevent Dutch and French reinforcements from going to Indonesia and Viet Nam.
   (5) Sending Asian medical aid and volunteers to Asian battlefields.
[58] This statement is based on an interview with a Vietnamese nationalist in Paris.
[59] *Parliamentary Debates,* House of Commons, February 12, 1947, 361.

Agence France-Presse, the semiofficial French news agency, revealed in Paris in March 1947 that more than £17,500,000 worth of army equipment had been sold by the British to the French troops in Indochina during the previous sixteen months and that a further agreement had just been concluded by which Britain would turn over to France equipment valued at £1,760,000, enough to put into the field an airborne division of 16,000 men.[60]

Was the Minister of State aware, asked an MP, of the report that no less than £20,000,000 worth of equipment had been delivered by the British to French forces in Indochina for the specific purpose of quelling the Vietnamese rebels? Hector McNeil, to whom the question was addressed, said only: "No aid specifically designed for Indochina has been given to the armed forces."[61]

The United States kept hands off the Viet Nam conflict. It was not yet deeply concerned about the strategic position of Indochina in Southeast Asia. Despite its tradition of anticolonialism, the United States had moved only cautiously and after delays in the Indonesian affair; and in 1946–47 Indonesia seemed to American policy-makers to offer far better reasons for intervention than Viet Nam. For one thing, both Americans and Englishmen had substantial investments in Indonesia, while Indochina was almost exclusively a French economic preserve; no other nation had any serious economic interests in Indochina to involve it in the country's affairs.

More important, the United States did have a tremendous stake in France, which American policy-makers considered a key to the defense and the recovery of western Europe. The State Department, as a result, was sympathetic when Frenchmen argued that if they lost Viet Nam, they would lose North Africa and most of their empire as well, with disastrous economic and military results to France. Further, a "soft" policy toward Ho Chi Minh, according to French opponents of such a policy, would lead to the overthrow of any "Third Force" government in France and bring to power either General de Gaulle or the Communists.

When to this line of reasoning was added the fact that Communists played a key role in the Vietnamese resistance, the American Government was not inclined to be openly critical of French policy in Indochina. It contented itself with expressing a wish for peace in Viet Nam. In February 1947, Secretary of State George C. Marshall said that he hoped "a pacific basis of adjustment of the difficulties could be found."[62]

[60] *New York Herald Tribune*, March 10, 1947.
[61] *Parliamentary Debates*, House of Commons, March 24, 1947, 827.
[62] *New York Times*, February 8, 1947.

Chapter Nine

FAILURE OF A BAO DAI–HO CHI MINH
SOLUTION

WHEN THE HO CHI MINH government left Hanoi when the fighting broke out, it was at the head of a nationwide resistance movement, as the French discovered when they tried to set up an opposition government. The Vietnamese closed their ranks when the fighting began. Men like Ngo Dinh Diem and Ho Chi Minh's former Minister of National Economy, the Catholic Nguyen Manh Ha, who had remained behind in Hanoi, refused to lend themselves to any French political maneuvers against the Viet Minh. And from Hongkong, refugee leaders of the Dong Minh Hoi and the VNQDD announced that they were ready to join in the common struggle against the French.

The Viet Minh put off any action which might have uncovered fundamental divergences of doctrine or policy among the various groups opposing the French—Catholics and Communists, Socialists and Democrats, former members of the imperial court at Hué, peasants and bourgeoisie. It was also important not to antagonize China and Siam, both of which were friendly to the Vietnamese, or any other foreign country which might one day help Viet Nam. And so they concentrated on the war with France, on growing food, combating illiteracy, and maintaining the dike system in Tonkin against the ever-present menace of flood. With the war the first concern of the central government, much of the day-to-day administration of the areas controlled by the Vietnamese reverted to nationalist local authorities, many of whom were anti-Communist.

At the same time, and for the same reason—to rally support at home and abroad—government spokesmen insisted that the Viet Minh regime was neither extremist nor anti-French. Ho Chi Minh wrote a cordial personal letter to Sainteny, promising that the war would cease as soon as independence was proclaimed. The Vietnamese, Ho Chi Minh told a correspondent, desired only

. . . independence and unity, freedom and happiness for the Vietnamese people and the raising of Vietnamese cultural levels. The first aim of Viet Nam when the war is over is to wipe out misery and ignorance; then we will increase production and to do so we need capital, technicians and manpower. The Vietnamese people will provide technicians and manpower and the Vietnamese Government large amounts of raw materials, but we will readily welcome French and foreign capital in the common interest.[1]

1 République Démocratique du Viet-Nam, Service d'Information, Bureau de Paris, *Bulletin,* July 8, 1947.

The need for a broad national front to fight the war was reflected by various changes in the Cabinet during 1947. Ho Chi Minh gave up the Ministry of Foreign Affairs to a Socialist, Hoang Minh Giam, and two prominent Communists—Vo Nguyen Giap and Pham Van Dong—were dropped from the Cabinet. Giap remained Commander-in-Chief of the Viet Nam army, but he was replaced as Minister of National Defense by an independent, the Oxford-educated Ta Quang Buu, his Vice-Minister, who had been a member of the Vietnamese delegation at Fontainebleau; and Pham Van Dong was replaced by a member of the Democratic Party as Vice-Minister of National Economy. When the elderly Huynh Thuc Khang died, his post as Minister of the Interior was filled only temporarily by an adherent of the Viet Minh and then by Bao Dai's former viceroy in Tonkin, Phan Ke Toai. A new Ministry of War Veterans and Invalids was set up, and both the Minister and the Vice-Minister were Catholics. And a militant Buddhist was also named Minister without Portfolio. All of this seemed part of a concerted effort to underline the moderate character of the Ho Chi Minh government: however little faith Viet Minh leaders may have had in the readiness of the French to give them either unity or a genuine independence, they still seemed to be courting international and French opinion, as well as the non-Communist majority at home.

Ho Chi Minh appealed to the French Government and the French people on March 1, 1947:

Once again, we declare solemnly that the Vietnamese people desire only unity and independence in the French Union, and we pledge ourselves to respect French economic and cultural interests . . . If France would but say the word to cease hostilities immediately, so many lives and so much property would be saved and friendship and confidence would be regained.[2]

The new Foreign Minister of Viet Nam, Hoang Minh Giam, tried again the following month:

The French Government, by nominating the new High Commissioner of France in Indochina, seems to have evidenced a desire to orient its policy toward Viet Nam along a different road, one worthy of the new France. I am persuaded that the motion of the National Council of the Socialist Party, dated March 21, 1947, deciding not to miss any opportunities to enter into negotiations with Viet Nam, expresses not only the sentiments of the French Socialists, but those of all the people of France. In order to prove the sincere attachment of Viet Nam to peace and its friendship for the people of France, the Vietnamese Government proposes to the French Government the immediate cessation of hostilities and the opening of negotiations for a peaceful settlement of the conflict.[3]

2 Ibid., Messages de Paix adressés par le Président Ho-Chi-Minh au Peuple et au Gouvernement française, p. 11.
3 Ibid., pp. 12–13.

This diplomatic appeal to the Socialists produced no result: if some French Socialist leaders spoke out quite strongly in favor of negotiations and Socialist Party congresses annually demanded them, they did not succeed in persuading their Socialist colleagues, Premier Ramadier and Overseas France Minister Moutet, to veer to any extent from their uncompromising attitude.

It is true that a majority of the Frenchmen living in Indochina did not like the idea of negotiating with the Viet Minh. Eugène Thomas, a former Socialist Cabinet Minister, back from a trip to Indochina, expressed the opinion that many Frenchmen in administrative and economic posts there could not understand that they were living in the year 1947.[4] He said that there was a need for men who believed in justice and that they were difficult to find among French civilians in the country, while the French military had a record of pillage, violence and assassination, the burning of villages and the execution of innocents. "At the risk of angry disagreement from certain people, I will say that the presence of General Leclerc and his divisions, the presence of the Foreign Legion, has not served French interests."[5]

When Emile Bollaert, d'Argenlieu's successor, arrived in Saigon in April 1947, a new era of conciliation seemed to have opened. Bollaert declared an end to the censorship in Saigon and lifted the state of siege in Hanoi and Haiphong. He issued new rules to guide French officials, stating, "We will no longer intervene in native administration."[6] When the Vietnamese asked for an armistice that April, he replied by sending a personal emissary, Paul Mus, to see Ho Chi Minh.

But Bollaert's freedom of action was hedged with limitations. His appointment was only a temporary one which was supposed to last no more than six months. He could not take the slightest action on the spot without prior approval by the French Cabinet. And when he was in Indochina, he operated out of Saigon, where French financial and administrative circles were linked closely with French Right-Wing political parties and the French military wielded an important influence on local Indochina policy. French army leaders were determined to see the Vietnamese capitulate and it was their readiness to use force against the Viet Minh rather than make concessions to it which was responsible for the failure of what has been called the Mus mission.[7]

[4] *Le Populaire,* April 6–7, 1947.
[5] *Ibid.*
[6] *Bulletin* du Ministère de la France d'Outre-Mer, July 14, 1947.
[7] The opposition of the military to negotiations with the Viet Minh appears to have been reinforced by that of the MRP. "The MRP Minister of War, M. Paul Coste-Floret, was . . . on an official visit to Indochina (April 26–May 3). A witness has assured me on his honor that in the car which brought him from the Hué airfield to the city the Minister asked General Valluy 'to do everything to dissuade Bollaert from negotiating with Ho Chi Minh'." Devillers, *op. cit.,* p. 387.

Paul Mus had been General Leclerc's political adviser until May 1946 when he resigned to become director of the government School of Overseas France in Paris. The mission of this expert in Oriental civilizations, who had grown up in Indochina and had many friends among the Vietnamese, could have been used to discuss the political situation frankly with Ho Chi Minh and to explore the possibilities of a settlement. Instead, Mus was used only as a messenger; he brought French terms for a cease-fire amounting to unconditional surrender: the Vietnamese were to lay down their arms and to permit French troops to circulate freely in Vietnamese territory.

A number of men, mostly Germans and Austrians, had deserted from the Foreign Legion to join the Vietnamese; Japanese were also fighting on the side of the Viet Minh; and many of these foreign veterans had become officers and instructors. The terms Mus carried also called for turning over to the French all this non-Vietnamese personnel in the Vietnamese army.[8] In addition, Vietnamese troops were to be confined to zones designated by the French command. The only nonmilitary demand—and one to which the French Government attached great importance—was that all French hostages be surrendered.

When Paul Mus was later criticized by the Vietnamese and their friends for agreeing to deliver such terms, constituting in his own words "a request for guarantees equivalent to surrender,"[9] he tried to justify himself by explaining that some other messenger might not have brought back an honest account of his interviews with Viet Minh leaders. Also, Mus wanted to check on rumors then current that Ho Chi Minh was dead, rumors which the French Government on several occasions had endorsed, alleging that Ho Chi Minh's messages were forged and did not deserve any reply.

In the company of two young Vietnamese, Mus travelled on foot from the French outposts, six miles north of Hanoi, to Ho's headquarters. Mus was not an official negotiator, having no contact with the Ministry of Overseas France, but word spread among the Vietnamese that he was coming, and he was greeted in Vietnamese-controlled areas with hope, for the people thought that he was bringing peace. He met Hoang Minh Giam at the Bridge of Rapids in Tonkin and asked him to arrange an interview with Ho; and some sixty kilometers from the French advance posts, he finally met the Vietnamese President.

Ho Chi Minh appeared disappointed when he heard Mus' message; the

8 Paul Coste-Floret told the French National Assembly: "The failure of this negotiation [the Mus mission] resulted from the clause on the surrender of foreigners in the ranks of the Viet Minh." *Journal Officiel*, Assemblée Nationale, March 11, 1949 p. 1569.

9 This and other direct quotations relating to Paul Mus' trip are taken from his letter published in *Le Monde* March 15, 1947. The following description of the trip, however, is also based on interviews with M. Mus, as is the description below of his interview with Bao Dai in Hongkong.

Viet Minh could not accede to the French terms and survive. Ho Chi Minh flatly rejected the French terms. "If you were in my place, would you accept them?" Ho asked Mus, and the Frenchman admitted that he would not. Ho said to Mus, "In the French Union there is no place for cowards. If I accepted these conditions, I should be one."

The war went on. When Paul Coste-Floret, Minister of War, returned to Paris in May after a visit to Indochina, he had glowing things to say about the French war effort. There was no longer a military problem, he said; the success of French arms was complete. The expeditionary corps, 115,000 strong, occupied the major cities and controlled the means of communication; and not a single French garrison remained encircled. It is true that he immediately added: "It is evident that the greater part of the country remains in the hands of the Viet Minh. I do not think that we should undertake the conquest of French Indochina. It would necessitate an expeditionary corps of at least 500,-000 men."[10]

THE FRENCH CONCEPT OF THE BAO DAI POLICY

The spring of 1947 ushered in a military impasse. General Leclerc estimated in his report that the French needed an extra division to return the military situation in Viet Nam to what it had been in March 1946.[11] This division actually set sail in the spring of 1947. Its destination, however, was not the war in Viet Nam but the revolt in Madagascar. Because of that new sore spot in the empire, the French had to put off their hope of large-scale reinforcements in Viet Nam. This was a turning point in the Franco-Vietnamese struggle which marked its transformation into a war of attrition: the Vietnamese lacked the force to expel the French, and the French, from this time on, were unable to dislodge the Vietnamese resistance.

Once again the only way out seemed to be that of negotiation. But the events of December 1946 had altered the situation radically; the whole delicate problem of re-establishing diplomatic contact between the two sides, with the attendant bargaining and negotiation, would have to be undertaken anew. Ho Chi Minh's terms were well known—the Republic must include Cochin China and must have most, if not all, of the attributes of independence. The French Government was no more willing to concede these demands than it had been a year earlier.

But was there perhaps someone other than Ho Chi Minh with whom to negotiate? In Indochina, many of the French military, along with the more influential French administrators, had never recognized the necessity of dealing with Ho. They had sought other Vietnamese leaders from the start.

[10] *Combat,* May 14, 1947.
[11] Dansette. *op. cit.,* p. 213.

They had abetted, when they had not inspired, recognition of the Cochin Chinese "republic." And they had never accepted Bao Dai's abdication as final.

Even before the signing of the March 6 Agreement, d'Argenlieu had turned to the royal family of Viet Nam in the hope that they could be persuaded to set up a government in opposition to the Viet Minh. That attempt proved premature, but d'Argenlieu did not abandon hope of restoring the monarchy. In January 1947, less than a month after hostilities had begun, he wrote:

> If we examine the problem basically, we are led to inquire whether the political form unquestionably capable of benefiting from the political prestige of legitimacy is not the traditional monarchic institution, the very one that existed before the Japanese surrender . . . The return of the Emperor would probably reassure all those who, having opposed the Viet Minh, fear that they will be accused of treason.[12]

The royal family enjoyed a considerable prestige among the Vietnamese people, who had fought with Ham Nghi against the French in 1885–88 and conspired with Duy Tan against them in 1916. Both these Emperors had died in exile only a few years apart, Ham Nghi during the second World War, Duy Tan in a plane crash soon after it. In Hué, as the boatmen paddled their sampans along the Perfumed River in the shadow of the mountains which loomed above the city, they still sang a song about Duy Tan and how he had struggled for independence and lost. Duy Tan's father, ex-Emperor Thanh Thai, was still alive but he was too old to return to politics.[12a] The most logical candidate for the Vietnamese throne remained Prince Vinh Thuy, the ex-Emperor Bao Dai. Although personally a controversial figure whose acquiescence to French rule seemed more like that of his father, Khai Dinh, than of their nationalist-minded predecessors, Bao Dai still wielded influence among Vietnamese. The French recognized this when they forbade him to enter Cochin China until the time of the second World War; and the Viet Minh acknowledged Bao Dai's influence in its turn when Ho Chi Minh appointed him Supreme Political Adviser to the revolutionary government.

In the spring of 1947 Ho Chi Minh was in Viet Nam and in apparent control of the resistance, while Bao Dai, still nominally a member of the Viet Minh government, was in Hongkong. The French were confronted with a choice: either they might negotiate with the man who was leading the war against them and demanding radical concessions, or they might try to replace him with another who, despite his flirtation with nationalism under the Japanese, would, they believed, be content with much less. The French conception of the Bao Dai policy rested on two controversial assumptions: that Bao Dai would accept terms which France would not be unwilling to grant; and that, if he

---

12 Quoted in *Journal Officiel*, Assemblée de l'Union Française, January 19, 1950, p. 49.
12a Thanh Thai died in 1954.

did accept them, he would be in a position to impose them on the Vietnamese people.

In Hongkong the men around Bao Dai were suspicious of French overtures to the ex-Emperor, uncertain as to whether d'Argenlieu really wanted to deal with Bao Dai or was simply trying to frighten the Viet Minh into making concessions. So Bao Dai held aloof early in 1947, leaving d'Argenlieu to spend his last weeks as High Commissioner in building up the "republic" of Cochin China, the only French-controlled government in existence in territory claimed by the Viet Minh.

But with the whole of the territory claimed by the Viet Minh in dispute between the French and the Vietnamese, the tactic of splitting up the country seemed outdated. The French had already inflated the Cochin Chinese autonomy movement out of all proportion to its natural size by supporting the minority groups in the south which had most to lose in a unified Viet Nam ruled by the Viet Minh. It was time for a bolder French maneuver—an attempt not merely to weaken the new Vietnamese state, but to supersede it. It was time for Bao Dai.

The future of the French Union appeared to be at stake: not only was there war in Indochina, but there was revolt in Madagascar and growing unrest in North Africa. To many Frenchmen it seemed that if France did not stand firm in one part of the empire, she might lose it all.

BAO DAI'S SUPPORTERS

"France will remain in Indochina and Indochina will remain within the French Union. That is the first axiom of our policy," High Commissioner Bollaert announced in May. But "let the representatives of all parties come to us. I say all parties because we do not admit that any group has a monopoly on representing the Vietnamese people."[13]

The French had not yet entirely turned their backs on the Ho Chi Minh government, but they were more than willing to encourage contenders for leadership of the nationalist movement who were outside the Viet Minh coalition. They contacted Bao Dai early in 1947; and by March 1947 it was generally known that French emissaries were in touch with Bao Dai in Hongkong. He did not, however, commit himself publicly to any policy.

During May the Viet Minh sent its own emissary to Bao Dai in an attempt to re-establish national unity. He was Ho Dac Lien, a prominent nationalist, and he came to ask the ex-Emperor to carry on joint negotiations with the French in the name of the Ho Chi Minh government as well as his own.[14] This sensible plan was wrecked by Bao Dai's advisers.

[13] *Le Monde*, May 17, 1947.
[14] *Journal de Saigon*, August 25, 1947. Quoted in *Notes Documentaires et Etudes* No. 752, *Positions indochinois: Bao Dai*.

When Paul Mus, Bollaert's political adviser, saw Bao Dai in Hongkong that month, Bao Dai told him that he would ask as much of France as Ho Chi Minh, possibly more. He would never return to Viet Nam to lead a police state, Bao Dai said, but if his people wanted him, he would feel differently about going home. High Commissioner Bollaert himself went to Hongkong in June.

By the summer of 1947 it was already evident that certain Vietnamese would welcome an opportunity to use Bao Dai as a rallying point for opposition to the Viet Minh. Although some were outspokenly nationalistic, most were opportunists, eager to accept power from anyone who cared to share it with them. Among them were members of the Dong Minh Hoi and the VNQDD, which in 1946 had competed with the Viet Minh for control of the nationalist movement and lost. Some VNQDD and Dong Minh Hoi leaders in exile in China had actually talked of joining forces with Ho Chi Minh when they learned of the outbreak of fighting against France; they soon changed their minds under the influence of Chinese Nationalist politicians who, at war with Mao Tse-tung at home, were suspicious of the Communist leadership of the Vietnamese resistance. A "National Union Front" in support of Bao Dai was established in China in February 1947 under VNQDD and Dong Minh Hoi auspices, and was later organized inside Viet Nam. It was the first of several such fronts formed from time to time by pro-Bao Dai groups during 1947. These shifting coalitions were never able to achieve any effective unity. Even the founders of the first National Union Front were at odds with each other: the Dong Minh Hoi leaders favored a constitutional monarchy, the VNQDD a republic. The first National Union Front claimed to represent both parties, but the majority of the rank and file of the VNQDD and the Dong Minh Hoi continued to support the Viet Minh because it alone was engaged in the struggle against France.

In Cochin China, the Cao Dai and the Hoa Hao joined the National Union Front, bringing their troops with them. Their split with Ho Chi Minh had long been in the making, ever since the two politico-religious groups had clashed with the Viet Minh in September 1945. Although both groups had continued in uneasy alliance with the Committee of the South during 1946, sections of them had broken away even before the war became general in December. In the fall of 1946 the French brought back the Cao Dai "pope," Pham Cong Tac, from his Madagascan exile. Later that year, Le Van Hoach, a leading member of the Cao Dai, was made president of the French-appointed regime in Cochin China. When Tac called upon his followers to join the French early in 1947, most of them did, although a minority of the Cao Dai continued to fight alongside the Viet Minh.

The Hoa Hao changed sides at about the same time. The strength of the Hoa Hao lay, above all, in the singleminded devotion of its members to their young leader and the founder of their movement, Huynh Phu So. In April 1947 Huynh Phu So was captured on Nguyen Binh's orders and executed for alleged treason. Infuriated by this action, his followers joined forces with the French against the Viet Minh.

Less than a year later, in January 1948, the Cao Dai and the Hoa Hao signed an agreement in which they pledged their support to Bao Dai and agreed on separate zones of action. Their pact was approved by the French without enthusiasm, it was reported, for it aimed at independence for Viet Nam, a close unity for the three Vietnamese countries and an end to separatism; and the words "within the framework of the French Union" were added only after the agreement was signed. On occasion the Cao Dai and the Hoa Hao clashed with each other as well as with the Viet Minh. They did not offer strong or disciplined support to the Bao Dai movement.

Support from another quarter came from Annam and Tonkin, where a number of former mandarins and monarchists proclaimed their adherence to Bao Dai. When the French established Vietnamese committees with limited administrative functions in areas of Tonkin and Annam captured from the Viet Minh during 1947, they staffed them with men willing to support the ex-Emperor. Despite the fear of assassination, which kept back some people who might have accepted office under the French, a member of the VNQDD, Truong Dinh Tri, once a Minister in the Ho Chi Minh government, agreed to head such a committee in Tonkin; and in Hué, Tran Van Ly, a Catholic and former mandarin, headed the Administrative Committee of Annam.

A number of other Vietnamese, some of them Catholics, took their cue from Ngo Dinh Diem. A Catholic and strongly anti-Communist, Diem was profoundly nationalistic and a believer in complete independence for Viet Nam. If there were any prospect of realizing his nationalistic ends, he was ready to join the movement in favor of Bao Dai.

The reasons for which men turned to the ex-Emperor thus differed widely. Some hoped to use him to oust the French from Viet Nam. Others looked to him to act as a mediator between Ho Chi Minh and the French. Still others counted on him to protect them against Vietnamese nationalism rather than against French paternalism. This was particularly the case with the small unrepresentative minority which supported the Le Van Hoach government in Cochin China and favored autonomy within Viet Nam in order to protect their own special interests, an arrangement which they believed would be more feasible under Bao Dai than under Ho Chi Minh.

From his vantage point in Hongkong, Bao Dai watched the emergence of these diverse groups which looked to him for leadership. In July he announced that he was neither for nor against the Viet Minh but above political quarrels, and that he would not go home unless his people wanted him. A new National Union Front, formed in the summer of 1947, urged all political, religious, and social groups to unite under Bao Dai. It exhorted the ex-Emperor to lead a militant movement for Vietnamese unity and independence, and to fight what it called the red terror.

BOLLAERT SPEAKS AT HA DONG

Emile Bollaert had not yet given up his hope of achieving a truce with the Viet Minh as a preliminary to negotiations both with the Viet Minh and with pro-Bao Dai groups. "We intend that neither victors nor vanquished will emerge from this conflict," he said in July. "It is with all parties and groups in a vast upsurge of patriotism that we will work out a lasting peace."[15]

The Viet Minh radio replied: "If this clear view of the situation guides French policy, a peaceful solution can certainly be found."[16]

But Bollaert was finding it difficult to gain support from his own compatriots. His plan was not only to offer a cease-fire to the Viet Minh, but also to recognize the independence of Viet Nam within the French Union. This would have been in line with developments elsewhere in Asia: the Dutch had already signed the Linggadjati Agreement with the Indonesians the previous March, guaranteeing them substantial autonomy; and on August 15 India and Pakistan were due to receive their independence from Great Britain. Bollaert had decided to make his speech to the Vietnamese that same day; French unit commanders had already received sealed envelopes marked "not to be opened until August 15 at 12 o'clock," with detailed instructions for a cease-fire. But this project was not at all to the liking of high-ranking French military men in Saigon. General Valluy departed suddenly for France, where he alerted MRP members of the Cabinet, among them Georges Bidault and Paul Coste-Floret, and they prevailed upon Premier Ramadier to summon Bollaert home for consultation.[17]

When Bollaert arrived in Paris, the French Cabinet was called into session and the MRP members made clear their firm opposition to taking any action from which Ho Chi Minh might profit. It would be the Viet Minh which would be strengthened, not Bao Dai, if there were to be a truce in Viet Nam, they reasoned, and therefore France could not afford peace. As to the inflam-

[15] *Le Monde,* July 25, 1947.
[16] In August the Viet Minh made new peace overtures. Tran Van Giau, chief of the Viet Minh delegation for Southeast Asia, talked with the French Minister in Bangkok and emphasized the desire of Ho Chi Minh for peace and negotiation. He said that Ho was willing to consider terms which offered unity and independence to Viet Nam within the French Union, with close cultural and economic Franco-Vietnamese collaboration; no French garrisons in the interior of the country but bases for the defense of the French Union at Lao Kay, Lang Son, Hongay, Tourane, Cam Ranh, and Cap Saint Jacques, with free communication among them; and a close association with France in foreign affairs and diplomatic representation. These conditions were immediately cabled to Paris where little attention was paid to them. *L'Express,* December 19, 1953.
[17] *Ibid.*

matory word "independence," how could the French Government talk of independence when the Viet Minh might be in a position to insist that it be realized? Other members of the Ramadier government were not prepared to risk the life of the Cabinet on the question of Indochina policy, and Bollaert's terms were revised and watered down in Paris. On September 10, when Bollaert finally made his speech at Ha Dong, calling it a final offer which "must be rejected or accepted as a whole," he did not offer a truce and he said nothing of independence; he mentioned only liberty within the framework of the French Union. France, he said, renounced control over the internal administration of Viet Nam, but not of the Vietnamese army nor of Vietnamese foreign relations, both of which were to remain in French hands. Bollaert promised that the Vietnamese alone would decide the future of Cochin China. The French High Commissioner, however, was to be the arbiter among the three Vietnamese regions, and he was to control the federal budget.[18]

"The government and the people of Viet Nam are dissatisfied with the narrow-minded policy outlined in the High Commissioner's speech at Ha Dong," the Viet Minh Foreign Minister, Hoang Minh Giam, told a press conference; and the Viet Minh radio rejected the Ha Dong offer. The official organ of the Viet Minh in Cochin China suggested that the Viet Minh might look elsewhere for friends. "We ask internal and external sovereignty, the freedom to establish friendly economic and cultural relations with all the democratic countries—particularly with France from which we accept the status of Associated State—and with the United States."

In a letter dated "near Ha Dong, September 12, 1947," Dr. Pham Ngoc Thach, Viet Minh Undersecretary of State, wrote to United Nations Secretary General Trygve Lie "to request the Security Council of the United Nations to put an end to the war of aggression that France has undertaken these last two years against Viet Nam." Thach proposed "the opening under the auspices and guarantee of the United Nations of peace negotiations between France and Viet Nam represented by the Ho Chi Minh government, on the basis of [Vietnamese] independence and territorial integrity" and "respect of French cultural and economic interests;" and the withdrawal of French armed forces from Viet Nam. Thach received no reply.

The pro-Bao Dai groups greeted the Ha Dong declaration with little more enthusiasm than the Viet Minh. A number of Bao Dai's supporters had been meeting in Hongkong when Bollaert made his offer, and they also rejected it. They were receptive, however, to one passage in the speech—his appeal not only to Ho Chi Minh but to "all the political, intellectual and social factions of Viet Nam." The Bao Dai supporters in Hongkong appealed for leadership to the ex-Emperor as the only true representative of the Vietnamese people.

18 Services Français d'Information, Hors Série No. 117, *Discours prononcé par M. Bollaert à Hadong (Tonkin), le 10-9-47.*

They had done just what the French officials who allowed them the passports and the dollars to go to Hongkong had hoped that they would do. Instead of joining forces to take advantage of the shift to the Right in the Viet Minh government and of Viet Minh overtures for a united front, instead of trying to broaden still further the political basis of the Viet Minh government and at the same time preserve Vietnamese unity, they had decided to break openly with the existing government and ally themselves with the French.

Bao Dai replied to their appeal:

To avoid bloodshed, I renounced the throne of my ancestors. Since you wished to entrust the destiny of the country to new leaders, I decided to withdraw . . . Now, in spite of the dictatorship which forbids freedom of speech, I hear your appeals and your cries of distress. You have revealed to me the whole picture of your misery . . . In your distress you came to me. Answering your appeal, I accept the mission which you entrust to me and am ready to contact the French authorities . . . I want first of all to get independence and unity for you . . . Then I shall exert the full weight of my authority to mediate in the conflict which has put you one against the other.[19]

FRANCE CHOOSES BAO DAI

Another man who was to play an important role in the Bao Dai movement cut short his sojourn in France to return to Saigon in September 1947. He was Nguyen Van Xuan, who had recently and opportunely been promoted from colonel to brigadier general in the French Army, a rank which no officers of Vietnamese blood had ever before achieved even when, like Colonel Do Huu Chan, they were heroes of the first World War.

A cofounder with the late Dr. Thinh of the Cochin Chinese "republic," by 1947 Xuan had dropped his insistence on total separation of Cochin China from the rest of Viet Nam and favored instead a substantial autonomy for each of the three Vietnamese areas; he liked to regard himself as a possible arbiter between Ho Chi Minh in North Viet Nam and Bao Dai in Central Viet Nam, with Xuan himself ruling in Cochin China. A crisis in the Cochin Chinese government presented the General with the opportunity to try out this scheme. In Saigon Le Van Hoach was under attack in the Advisory Council for his failure to win popular support and to prevent widespread insecurity; his critics doubted his ability to protect the interests of the Cochin Chinese government in any future Franco-Vietnamese negotiations. When the Hoach government resigned following a vote of nonconfidence, Xuan, his way prepared by his political friends, became on October 1 the third president of Cochin China.

The vague overtures he made to local resistance elements did not seem con-

19 Ministère de la France d'Outre-Mer, *Bulletin d'Information*, October 6, 1947.

vincing to them and he was sharply rebuffed by the Viet Minh. Bao Dai, for his part, was troubled by Xuan's known separatism and asked the High Commissioner to liquidate the Cochin Chinese Advisory Council and replace it with an Administrative Committee like those in Tonkin and Annam. General Xuan tended to regard Cochin China as an independent republic entitled to its own form of government, but he tried to reassure Bao Dai by giving his regime a more nationalist character, proclaiming it the Provisional Government of South Viet Nam.

In October, members of the different pro-Bao Dai groups traveled to Hongkong for audiences with the ex-Emperor. Among them were Le Van Hoach, other members of the Cao Dai and the Hoa Hao, and people from the Cochin Chinese government. Ngo Dinh Diem went too, but only because of a personal telegram from Bao Dai asking him to come.

The Viet Minh replied with force to these attempts to organize an opposition to Ho Chi Minh. It ordered the execution of two prominent men who might have become rallying points for antagonists of the Viet Minh—Nguyen Van Sam, whom Bao Dai had sent as his delegate to Cochin China after V-J Day, and Dr. Truong Dinh Tri, chairman of the North Viet Nam Administrative Committee. Both men were killed in October by agents of the Viet Minh, one in the south, the other in the north, within twenty-four hours of each other.

But the organization of the Bao Dai movement, once started, went ahead with the active encouragement of French officials. Bao Dai finally agreed to see Bollaert again and early in December he left by plane for Ha Long Bay to meet the High Commissioner aboard a warship. Although members of the ex-Emperor's entourage had warned him against signing anything, on December 7 Bao Dai gave way to the insistence of Bollaert and put his signature on a statement of terms which offered Viet Nam a status far short of independence.

Back in Hongkong, Bao Dai found some of his advisers highly critical of these terms. When Diem, Tran Van Ly, and General Xuan arrived to consult with the ex-Emperor, they all declared themselves strongly opposed to making concessions of independence. Bao Dai himself soon agreed that the terms were inacceptable and all of his subsequent negotiation with Bollaert was directed to demanding more generous ones. At the same time, by taking the position that he was only a private individual, speaking just for himself, Bao Dai tried to avoid having what he had unthinkingly signed regarded as a political commitment.

This aptitude for maneuver on the part of the ex-Emperor was something that French officials had not bargained upon when they had urged him to return to political life. But in the fall of 1947 the most important thing, so far as they were concerned, was that they had found in Bao Dai and his supporters both a political weapon and a justification for military action against the Viet

Minh. The French Government, in which the political balance had shifted further to the Right, saw less reason than ever to make concessions to Ho Chi Minh. The Communists had left the Cabinet (because of disagreement on domestic political issues, not on Vietnamese policy), and the Minister of Overseas France was no longer a Socialist but Paul Coste-Floret, an MRP member strongly opposed to the Viet Minh. Under the influence of Coste-Floret, the decision was made to abandon the idea of negotiations with the Viet Minh. On December 23 the French Cabinet announced that it had instructed High Commissioner Bollaert "to carry on, outside the Ho Chi Minh government, all activities and negotiations necessary for the restoration of peace and freedom in the Vietnamese countries."[20]

Bao Dai left for Europe several days later. The Bao Dai solution had become the official policy of the French Government.[21]

FRENCH-VIETNAMESE IMPASSE

But was Bao Dai to be mediator or ruler? Many Vietnamese still talked of what they called a "Bao Dai-Ho Chi Minh solution" in the hope that the country could thereby avoid bloodshed and present the French with a united picture of Viet Nam. Only such a joint solution, they believed, would make possible the establishment of a democratic regime and prevent a shift in power within the Viet Minh camp to the extremists. And such a solution might in fact have achieved a certain stability in Viet Nam for none of the great powers at that time was anxious to become involved in Indochina.

When the ex-Empress Nam Phuong arrived in France late in 1947 and proposed to Buu Hoi[22] that he rally nationalist support behind Bao Dai, he told her that he would be glad to do so on condition that the ex-Emperor envisaged unity of action with the resistance in order to halt the drift of the Viet Minh toward Communism. But this the men who were around Bao Dai at that time were not prepared, for personal reasons, to undertake. It was only months later that a diplomat of some stature, Prince Buu Loc, a cousin of both the ex-Emperor and of Buu Hoi, became Bao Dai's chief adviser.

[20] *Bulletin d'Information de la France d'Outre-Mer,* January 15, 1948.

[21] Some of the responsibility for this policy was attributed in certain quarters to an American, William C. Bullitt, wartime United States Ambassador to France, who had visited Indochina in the fall of 1947 and had seen Bao Dai in Hongkong. Bullitt had gone on to Europe, where he was received by leading officials of the French Government; and in Geneva he saw Bao Dai again. In December 1947, *Life* magazine carried an article by Bullitt detailing the merits of a policy directed at winning the majority of the Vietnamese nationalist movement away from Ho Chi Minh and the Communists to Bao Dai ("The Saddest War," *Life,* December 29, 1947). Bullitt's prestige was great in France and his words were invested by Frenchmen with a semiofficial character; his support for Bao Dai was interpreted by a number of people, particularly among the French Left, to mean American support for Bao Dai and it contributed to the conviction, widely held among Frenchmen, that the United States had taken an initiative in launching the Bao Dai policy.

[22] See above, p. 167.

Bao Dai found himself caught between the French and the Vietnamese. The French, it was evident, intended to stay on in Viet Nam and regarded Bao Dai as a means to that end. Although some Vietnamese shared this aim, the great majority did not. Bao Dai's task was thus not merely to try to conciliate the more nationalist-minded of his few followers; he had to broaden substantially the political base from which he operated.

The peasants, the intellectuals, and the young people of Viet Nam either supported the resistance or remained aloof from politics; it was among them that Bao Dai had to build up a following if he was to compete seriously with Ho Chi Minh for leadership in the nationalist movement. But it was difficult to rally support to a man who, having first abdicated his throne, seemed to be trying to return to Viet Nam on the shoulders of the French. There was only one way in which Bao Dai conceivably might win them over—if he could get from France the unity and independence which had been refused to Ho Chi Minh.

This was the basic conflict inherent in the French conception of the Bao Dai policy, for Bao Dai was valuable to the French only as long as he did not insist upon as much as Ho Chi Minh; they supported Bao Dai because they believed he could be counted upon not to be too intransigently nationalistic. The only possible hope for Bao Dai's success, however, lay in his ability to sell himself as a genuine nationalist to the non-Communists who constituted the bulk of the resistance.

Early in January 1948 Bao Dai arrived in Geneva, where he had several interviews with Bollaert and found the High Commissioner determined not to modify his position on the terms he had offered the previous December at Ha Long Bay. Bao Dai then went on to Paris. Bollaert flew to Rome, reportedly in an unsuccessful attempt to enlist the influence of the Vatican among Vietnamese Catholics in order to win them away from Ho Chi Minh.[23] The Church, it seemed, was unwilling to take a firm stand against the Viet Minh as long as most Vietnamese Catholics as well as the native clergy favored the resistance.

In Bao Dai's former capital of Hué, articles appeared in the press in favor of the creation of a monarchist party to be formed under the leadership of Buu Hoi, but the ex-Emperor's cousin, like most Vietnamese, saw no logical reason for any effective nationalism to develop against the resistance at this time. When Ho Chi Minh renewed his proposal to Bao Dai for joint action—this time in a letter to Bao Dai signed by Pham Khac Hoe, former secretary to the Emperor and later secretary at the Fontainebleau Conference—Buu Hoi agreed to deliver the message. This overture failed, however, like the preceding one, and for the same reason. With this incident, any hope for the early achievement of national unity in Viet Nam disappeared and the way was

[23] *New York Times,* January 18, 1948.

open for the coming alignment of the Viet Minh with the international Communist bloc.

Bao Dai and Bollaert had made an appointment to continue their discussions at Ha Long Bay the following month, but in Paris Bao Dai discovered anew the complexity of the French political scene. He heard talk that Bollaert would be replaced. General de Gaulle by then had formed his Rally of the French People (RPF), which asserted that it would not accept any agreements on Indochina signed by a Third Force government, and it seemed possible that the RPF might be the next government of France. Under the circumstances, Bao Dai decided to prolong his stay in Europe and waited in Paris through February and into March; and while he waited he talked with a number of French politicians and officials of the Ministry of Overseas France.

In Indochina Bollaert was disquieted at news of these conversations. He protested to the French Government, and the Radical Socialist Party, to which he belonged, supported his protest. He had been given the authority to negotiate with Bao Dai, he pointed out, and that authority had been confirmed on December 23; as High Commissioner it was his job and his alone to negotiate with Bao Dai. Premier Georges Bidault, whose determination not to make concessions to the Vietnamese had not lessened, agreed, and Bao Dai returned to Hongkong in March 1948. Other familiar faces also appeared on the streets of the British crown colony—Ngo Dinh Diem and Le Van Hoach, members of the Cao Dai and of the Hoa Hao, people from the Administrative Committees of Tonkin and Annam.

Bao Dai's supporters had not been idle during his absence. Their problem was to find the political formula which would enable Bao Dai to return to Viet Nam. General Xuan, finding it impossible to sell to the Viet Minh the idea of himself either as arbiter or as leader of a Third Force movement, proposed calling a special congress which would bring together representatives of the anti-Viet Minh nationalist movement. Bollaert took up this idea, hoping to use such an assembly to formalize political support around the ex-Emperor and create a backbone for Bao Dai's political action, in order to gain an endorsement of Bao Dai and of the terms he had accepted the previous December. Nationalists, however, made it clear that they would not permit any such congress to be used to rubber-stamp French policies (nor were they prepared to allow it to serve the ends of any ambitious Vietnamese politicians). The separatist Cochin Chinese Council, fearful of being overruled and outvoted in any national assembly, regarded the very idea of a congress with a marked lack of enthusiasm.

Ngo Dinh Diem, who had been much spoken of as the man to head Bao Dai's first government, went to Saigon to see if Bollaert was prepared to offer more liberal terms. He came back to Hongkong reporting failure.

The reply of Bao Dai and his advisers to this French intransigence was that he could not return to power as long as the aspirations of the Vietnamese people remained unsatisfied. Ngo Dinh Diem proposed the establishment of a national study committee uniting representatives of the various elements in the country, including the resistance, to draw up a list of demands on the basis of which Bao Dai could negotiate with the French. Diem pointed out that Bao Dai could then have set up a truly national government. But this statesmanlike plan did not appeal to members of Bao Dai's entourage who preferred to see a government established immediately, regardless of its necessarily unrepresentative character. They persuaded Bao Dai to advise his followers to realize Vietnamese unity themselves by forming a national government. Clearly influenced by the stiffening opposition to Communism in the West, Bao Dai made a bold claim to speak for the entire resistance: "The present resistance is aimed at supporting negotiations that the present revolutionary government, given the condition of world affairs, is no longer able to direct. It is necessary to create a provisional central government more in conformity with the international situation."[24]

The French, however, were reluctant to make concessions to Vietnamese nationalism, whether demanded by Bao Dai or Ho Chi Minh, and in Paris Bao Dai was attacked by Right-Wing politicians as well as by the Left. Leftists called him a puppet unqualified to speak for the Vietnamese people; Rightists were bitter over his refusal to yield on the issues of unity and independence. Negotiations with the French had reached an impasse.

THE DEADLOCK IS BROKEN

The situation was worsened by a sudden French maneuver. The French announced that a Thai Federation had been founded on March 4 in upper Tonkin: the Great Thai Council, which united the principal Notables of the Thai minority living in the northern mountains, had decided to declare its autonomy, with its own administration, justice, police, and government.

Since there was scant evidence of any real Thai autonomy movement, French officials had undoubtedly played an active role behind the scenes; the new "Federation" seemed just another step in the policy which had been marked by such actions as recognition of the Cochin Chinese "republic" and establishment of a separate Moi state. It seemed to indicate a French desire to weaken any government which came to power in Viet Nam, under the cloak of protecting ethnic minorities.

In a letter to the French Socialist Party at this time, Louis Caput recalled that

... the French authorities have long been exploiting the Moi particularism of the High Plateaux. The mountain people of these regions include numerous primitive and unorganized tribes (Rhadés, Djaras, Bahhars, Roho, etc.) who certainly did

[24] *Bulletin d'Information de la France d'Outre-Mer,* June 15, 1948.

not like the more enterprising Vietnamese, but are beginning to detest singularly the French who recruit them as soldiers, subject them to exactions and impose forced labor upon them. As a result, there has been a growing malaise, an abandonment of work and land, a retreat into the forest, and the least that one can say is that the situation in the High Plateaux of the Indochinese South begins to become very disquieting.

According to Caput, "the Moi question has moreover been one of the principal reasons for the bitter-sweet discussions between Bollaert and Bao Dai, the latter refusing to abandon these regions which France intends to turn into its central fief."

The new Thai Federation further exacerbated Franco-Vietnamese relations. Caput reported to his Socialist colleagues:

The Thai affair has led to a profound reaction in Viet Nam and has been considered a French provocation and a new menace. The Administrative Committees of Hué and Hanoi, and the Provisional Government of South Viet Nam have sharply protested: unanimity has been recreated among all Vietnamese regardless of their political tendency (and in the last analysis they are all against France); the recent conversations in Hongkong have been largely concerned with this point and it has weighed heavily in the reticent if not hostile attitude of the [Vietnamese] delegates in regard to resuming negotiations between Bollaert and Bao Dai.

Faced with the deadlock between Bollaert and Bao Dai in March 1948, the French made a new move. News was allowed to leak out that they had sent Louis Caput as an emissary to Ho Chi Minh. Viet Minh supporters were later highly critical of Caput, asking why, if he wanted to meet people from the Viet Minh, he did not simply go into guerrilla-held territory instead of flying to Hongkong. They interpreted the Caput episode as an attempt by Bollaert to bring pressure on Bao Dai and his entourage, a method of indicating the High Commissioner's willingness to reopen negotiations with Ho Chi Minh if Bao Dai did not prove more amenable. Caput himself came finally to share this view. In a letter dated September 18, 1948 he wrote, "I am more and more convinced that I was asked to go to Hongkong only in order to facilitate his [Bollaert's] rapprochement with Bao Dai and hasten the conclusion of the accords of June 5 [1948]."

But in April 1948, Caput seems to have gone to Hongkong in good faith. He had been an honest exponent of negotiations with Ho Chi Minh, and was so still. As he wrote at the time, "There was not a plane which did not bring to or take back from Hongkong French and Vietnamese emissaries. But I was certainly the first who undertook this famous 'pilgrimage' while being firmly hostile to negotiations with Bao Dai."

Caput had hoped to meet Pham Ngoc Thach or perhaps even Hoang Minh

Giam, but no member of the Ho Chi Minh government appeared in Hong-kong. News of his visit became public, however, throwing Bao Dai's sup-porters into a panic. They resumed negotiations with Bollaert soon afterward. And the French gave their reluctant consent to the formation of a provisional central government.

FORMATION OF A CENTRAL GOVERNMENT

With Bollaert's conditions substantially unchanged from what they had been the previous December, Bao Dai remained aloof from the new govern-ment and Ngo Dinh Diem refused to lead it. It was General Xuan, who several months earlier had been highly critical of the French terms, who now decided to head a government which would accept them. During the spring of 1948, General Xuan travelled through the country to round up support among Bao Dai's followers. His efforts bore fruit on May 20 when a number of men from different sections of Viet Nam gathered in his palace in Saigon. Eleven of them were from Tonkin, seven from Annam, twenty from Cochin China. Among them were members of the Administrative Committees of North and Central Viet Nam, and of the Provisional Government of South Viet Nam. They in-cluded members of the Cochin Chinese Council as well as Le Van Hoach, the Cao Dai Pope Pham Cong Tac, and Tran Quang Vinh, Commander-in-Chief of the Cao Dai.

These men were supporters of Bao Dai rather than of Xuan and many of them, particularly those from the north, were not overly enthusiastic about the General. But he produced a trump card, a letter from the ex-Emperor. Bao Dai wrote:

The constitution of a provisional central government is at present a necessary first step toward resolving the Vietnamese problem in regard to France and to international opinion. The people have asked me to resume power, but I do not be-lieve that would be in the national interest at the present time. It is for that reason that I give my approval to your plan to form a provisional central government.[25]

Armed with this letter, Xuan had no difficulty in being elected president of the new government. The vote was 37 to 0 with one abstention. Xuan formally announced to Bollaert that Viet Nam had declared its unity and that he was charged with forming its first government. Then he flew to Hongkong to consult with Bao Dai.

It was Bao Dai who picked the flag of the central government—a back-ground of yellow (the imperial color) with three red horizontal stripes across the middle. The first ordinance of the new regime, which appeared in the *Journal Officiel* of South Viet Nam on May 31, provided that, "because of the

[25] *Ibid.*

present state of war, the exercise of sovereignty by the Vietnamese people, who are the source of all legal power, is suspended." The new government was expected "to negotiate with France, restore peace, organize the public powers, and prepare when possible for elections to a Constituent Assembly charged with elaborating the future constitution of Viet Nam."

On June 6, in Hanoi, at the Pagoda of the Sword, Tran Van Huu, Xuan's successor as Governor of South Viet Nam, read a proclamation announcing the establishment of a provisional central government of Viet Nam.

It was difficult for people, either in France or in Viet Nam, to be very enthusiastic about the Xuan government. Bao Dai himself was not wholly committed to it. His official spokesman in Hanoi said that he would negotiate in the name of the Xuan government only when it was recognized by France; and that he would not return to Viet Nam until the French had granted the country unity and independence.

In the Saigon newspaper, *L'Echo du Viet Nam,* Nguyen Phan Long, who supported Bao Dai, pointed out that General Xuan did not, after all, have the power or the prestige to restore peace; all he could do was try to find some acceptable terms for an armistice between the Viet Minh and the French.

It turned out that the Xuan government could not even do that. One man after the other refused Xuan's invitation to join his Cabinet. He had difficulty in finding people to work with him and when finally he succeeded in drawing up a ministerial list, it included few men of any political experience, no one who commanded any large following.

The Xuan government was neither representative nor popular and had little power; no Vietnamese of any stature, whatever his politics, would serve in it. But through its very subservience to the French it did make one contribution to Viet Nam. It won from France concessions on an issue which had been the major cause of the failure of the Fontainebleau Conference—admission of the unity of Cochin China (South Viet Nam) with Tonkin (North Viet Nam) and Annam (Central Viet Nam).

Chapter Ten

THE ELYSEE AGREEMENTS

In 1948, for the first time, there were two Vietnamese governments in Indochina. When the Xuan regime came into existence, the Ho Chi Minh government was already in its third year and a new system was slowly taking shape in the regions controlled by the Viet Minh. It was characterized at this time more by the absence of the French colonial administration than by any radical innovations of its own. There was no redistribution of land; no attempt was made to divide up the large estates of the south or to collectivize the tiny holdings in the north.

The Viet Minh concentrated on improving production, increasing the food crops, and encouraging local industries. Cut off by the war from trade with the outside world, it aimed at economic self-sufficiency as it directed its efforts toward supplying the needs of the army and raising the living standards of the peasantry, upon which the resistance depended for support. The Ho government returned to the proven techniques with which it had staved off famine in 1946. It called on the peasants to supplement their normal rice crops with others, such as sweet potatoes, corn, and manioc. It organized the protection of the dike system. To rally the people in support of the national effort, it launched a "patriotic emulation campaign," encouraging each individual, each group, each district to try to outdo one another in fighting famine, illiteracy, and the French. This "patriotic competition" ranged from digging foxholes to reducing rents.

At the same time, the Ho government decreed the lowering of land rents by 25 percent. It set up an Office of Production Credit to supply capital to peasant families, to artisans, and to small industries. It encouraged the formation of co-operatives in industry and agriculture.

The Vietnamese moved whole factories into the forests and the workers lived in barracks close by. There, in the wilderness, they manufactured paper, chemicals, and pharmaceutical products. The Viet Minh encouraged the planting of cotton and mulberries and the raising of silkworms in order to help out the textile industry. Textile production was said to be nearly enough to meet the people's needs. And the greatest achievements were reported in the arms industry, which produced bazookas and other weapons, as well as explosives.

There was wide popular participation in the government and administration of the Viet Minh zones. It came in part from the enthusiastic adherence of the non-Communist majority to this program which was geared to popular needs and which, in fact, was carried out by non-Communist intellectuals and technicians. It came also from techniques of control and organization through which the Ho government reached down into the peasantry, rallying support and eliminating opposition; and in this, despite the background of nationalist activity, the hand of the Communists could already be felt heavily. Only one labor organization was permitted in Viet Minh territory, the Viet Nam Federation of Labor; closely linked with the Ministry of Labor, it was affiliated with the Communist-controlled World Federation of Trade Unions. The Vietnamese organizations of women and youth were associated with the Communist World Federations of Democratic Youth and Democratic Women. Throughout the Viet Minh areas the literacy campaign went on the more actively as the people who had learned to read became more open to political indoctrination; and politically-oriented courses of popular education were instituted for the newly literate.

The Viet Minh, soon to fall behind the iron curtain as it severed its relations with the West, still controlled the hinterlands and the eastern forests of South Viet Nam, most of the Central Vietnamese coast (where Chinese junks smuggled war material to the guerrillas), and the greater part of North Viet Nam. More than half of the population of Viet Nam lived in areas controlled by the Viet Minh, which at this time was strong enough to launch a campaign aimed at cutting off the French zones from the interior. The French occupied only the cities and a few fortified points in the hinterland (including, since the summer of 1947, frontier posts along the Chinese border), and they depended for food on regions controlled by the Viet Minh. Saigon and Hanoi, supposed to be centers of French strength, were honeycombed with supporters of the resistance who collected taxes from the Vietnamese and Chinese inhabitants.

The new Xuan government, by contrast, had no territory of its own, and little following. What strength it possessed lay in its diplomacy and in its ability to use the alternative presented by the Viet Minh and the Viet Minh military effort to extort concessions from the French. The Xuan government marked the first stage in the policy which centered on Bao Dai and which consisted in trying to win enough from the French by political action to enable Bao Dai and his supporters to supplant the Viet Minh and rule over a united Viet Nam.

AGREEMENT AT HA LONG BAY

On June 5, 1948 two planes arrived within minutes of each other at Ha Long Bay, where strangely shaped greenish-gray limestone cliffs edge the water and little rocky islands jut up in the Bay. One plane came from Hongkong carrying Bao Dai; aboard the other plane were General Xuan and several of his colleagues from North, Central, and South Viet Nam. They all boarded the

French warship, the *Duguay-Trouin,* anchored in the Bay, where High Commissioner Bollaert was waiting to receive them, and there they signed what came to be known as the Ha Long Bay Agreement. It was eighty-six years to the day since France had signed the treaty with Emperor Tu Duc which recognized French control over three Cochin Chinese provinces—the opening wedge in French domination of Indochina.

In the Ha Long Bay Agreement, France recognized the independence of Viet Nam as an Associated State within the French Union, "which is now free to realize its unity."[1] The Xuan government, for its part, promised to protect the rights and interests of French nationals, to respect democratic principles, and to give priority to French advisers and technicians in filling its needs. The Ha Long Bay Agreement was very short, but it provided for a series of separate accords on cultural, diplomatic, military, economic, financial, and technical questions to follow.

It was an unusual document: for the first time the word "independence" appeared in a Franco-Vietnamese accord; and the French had at last accepted the idea that Cochin China was a part of Viet Nam. But the Ha Long Bay Agreement (with a secret protocol attached) was nothing more than the accord which Bao Dai had signed and regretted at Ha Long Bay the previous December. The independence it recognized was hedged with qualifications and the unity to which it referred had yet to be translated from principle to practice; also, the accord was signed with a government which did not control the country.

The reaction of the Viet Minh was to discount the new agreement, attacking its Vietnamese signatories as having been handpicked by the French, and the Viet Minh announced a sentence of death against General Xuan. Ho Chi Minh said:

Today the French colonialists have set up a puppet central government ready to commit every kind of treason in the service of its foreign masters. The Government of Viet Nam reserves for itself the right to try these quislings in accordance with national laws. In the name of the government and the people of the Democratic Republic of Viet Nam, I pronounce null and void any document signed by these puppets with any foreign country.[2]

The important fact, however, was not who these men happened to be but that for the first time a group of Vietnamese had won French acceptance of independence and unity, however limited; and Bollaert counted on the Ha Long Bay Agreement to cut the ground politically from under Ho Chi Minh, making it impossible for the Viet Minh to continue the fight in the name of

[1] *Journal Officiel,* March 14, 1953, p. 2409. Technically, the agreement was signed "in the presence of" Bao Dai, who countersigned it.
[2] Viet Nam News Agency, June 7, 1948.

nationalism. That he was disappointed in this goal was due less to the propaganda of the Viet Minh than to the obvious reluctance of the French Government to take the agreement seriously, substantiating widespread Vietnamese doubts of French good faith. Thus, on June 8, just three days after the agreement was signed, the Minister of Overseas France, Coste-Floret, rose in the French Assembly to explain that, after all, the Ha Long Bay Agreement could change very little. France had promised not to oppose the union of the three regions of Viet Nam, if that was what their people wanted, he said, but Cochin China was still a French colony; its status could not be altered without the permission of the French Parliament.[3] The secret articles which were signed at the time of the encounter at Ha Long Bay were reported to place serious limitations on Viet Nam's control of its army and foreign policy; and on June 8 Coste-Floret reminded the Assembly that the French government insisted on a single foreign policy and a unified army for the entire French Union.

The Ha Long Bay Agreement required ratification in France before it could become formal and this was slow in coming. In vain did the High Commissioner urge immediate action. France was in the midst of Cabinet crisis; Bollaert returned to France to argue personally the importance of the agreement, determined not to go back to Indochina without an endorsement of his policy from the French Government.

Only on August 19, 1948 did the French Government declare that it supported its High Commissioner.[4] Even then, from the Rightist Republican Party of Liberty (PRL) came complaints that France had abdicated its rights and interests at Ha Long Bay. At the same time the Socialists attacked Xuan as having no authority to speak for Viet Nam; and a Communist, who urged negotiations with the Viet Minh, accused the General of being an American cat's-paw. It was from the MRP and the Radical Socialists that Bollaert gained support. The MRP had been identified with French postwar Indochina policy from the start, and with MRP leader Georges Bidault temporarily out of the Cabinet, a probable obstacle to acceptance by the party of even this qualified independence was removed. The Radical Socialists at this time were not particularly inclined to make concessions to the Vietnamese; however, the agreement signed at Ha Long Bay was general enough to permit a variety of interpretations and, if Paul Coste-Floret was a member of the MRP, Emile Bollaert was a Radical Socialist whom his party did not want to abandon. Premier André Marie, himself a Radical Socialist, announced the "entire and solemn" adherence of his government to the Ha Long Bay Agreement.

"Furthermore," said the Premier, his government "believes that the existing

---

[3] *Journal Officiel,* Assemblée Nationale, June 8, 1948, p. 3290.

[4] During that summer of 1948 the Ho government invited Louis Caput as the delegate of the French Socialist Party in Indochina to meet with resistance officials in Tonkin. This initiative was ignored by the French Government.

regime in Cochin China no longer corresponds to current needs, and that it is up to the populations themselves to determine freely their definitive status within the framework of the French Union. The government renews the appeal of the High Commissioner to all the intellectual and political factions of Viet Nam to co-operate on this basis in this work of independence and peace."[5]

Did this mean that the French Government intended to deal only with Bao Dai? asked René Pleven, a prominent deputy. The Premier did not reply, but made a gesture that was taken by some to mean yes. However, the Socialists, who for reasons of domestic politics had agreed to endorse the Ha Long Bay Agreement, chose to believe that André Marie's appeal to all the intellectual and political factions of Viet Nam could leave the way open to further negotiations with the Viet Minh. His declaration, meaning different things to different people, was approved by the French Assembly by a vote of 344 to 185, with the PRL abstaining and the Communists in opposition.

But the resistance did not lay down its arms. "How do you explain that guerrilla war did not stop in Viet Nam after the Ha Long Bay accord and the approval of the accord by the French Government?" Bollaert demanded a month later. "How do you explain that the Viet Minh, instead of rallying to those who had realized its slogans, has redoubled its violence against a government which has obtained independence and unity?" Bollaert endeavored to account for this state of affairs with the explanation that the Viet Minh was Communist-dominated and acting in accordance with Cominform strategy.[6]

However, the "psychological shock" predicted by the High Commissioner did not materialize anywhere in Viet Nam; even in French-controlled areas there was little enthusiasm for the Ha Long Bay Agreement, although the French administration tried to stir it up. The French prefect of Saigon issued the following order which was reprinted with critical comment in the Saigon press:

A demonstration will be held next Thursday, September 9, at 9 o'clock before the Saigon City Hall in favor of the Ha Long Bay Agreement. All officials and regular or daily employees of the regional services of Saigon and Cholon must attend. The head of the Technical Services and the head of the Hygiene Service are particularly asked to warn the nonpermanent personnel . . . that they must attend and that a check will be made. They will get their pay for the working day if they are present.[7]

Instead of rallying nationalists in the Viet Minh front to Bao Dai, the Ha Long Bay Agreement crystallized more support around Ho Chi Minh. The conservative nationalist leader Ngo Dinh Diem had called upon Bao Dai before the agreement was signed to tell him, as he had told him earlier, that he

[5] *Journal Officiel*, Assemblée Nationale, August 19, 1948, p. 5988.
[6] *Bulletin* du Ministère de la France d'Outre-Mer, October 15, 1948.
[7] *L'Union Française*, September 11, 1948.

would not co-operate with the French until Dominion status was guaranteed to Viet Nam. In Paris, Buu Hoi, the member of the royal family who had taken part in the Fontainebleau Conference, declared to the press early in 1949, on behalf of the many members of the family who were fighting the French alongside the Viet Minh in the maquis:

The former Imperial Family of Viet Nam regards with profound sadness the spilling of blood which is taking place in Viet Nam because of the refusal of the French authorities to negotiate with the national government of President Ho Chi Minh. There will be no end to this fratricidal war while the French authorities continue the policy of creating and supporting artificial "governments" without any roots in the Vietnamese people. . . .

Considering the democratic aspirations of the Vietnamese people and the present evolution of events, the former Imperial Family expresses the wish that if the French Government wants to keep some influence in Viet Nam, it should enter into relations with the government of President Ho Chi Minh, in order to seek with it a peaceful solution of the conflict based on justice and fraternity.[8]

In Viet Nam, at about the time that Buu Hoi made his statement, his father, Prince Ung Uy, left the French-controlled areas to join Ho Chi Minh. Ung Uy, who had resigned from Bao Dai's Cabinet in March 1945 when the Japanese took over the country, was head of the Council of the Imperial Family and a great-grandson of the Emperor Minh Mang.

WEAKNESSES OF THE XUAN GOVERNMENT

Viet Nam was rife with nationalism by 1948, a nationalism from which Bao Dai's supporters, as has been shown, were not immune. The country was united by neither fear of nor fondness for Communism, but solely by a determination to expel French colonialism; the Vietnamese wanted independence, they cared little about who won it for them. The Xuan government was the immediate test of French willingness to see an independent or even an autonomous government in Viet Nam.

It was soon evident that the French were not at all willing to permit the establishment of a strong government under General Xuan. Each day laid bare the glaring inconsistency between French assertions that they had granted independence to Viet Nam and the reluctance of French administrators to give Xuan even the most limited powers. They continued to rule directly most of the areas under the control of the French forces; even where a Vietnamese administration did exist, the French federal services (the 1948 version of the prewar administrative structure directed by the Governor General) continued to wield most of the substance of power. Xuan had at his command neither an army, a police force, nor independent finances. Hanoi, Haiphong,

[8] *Combat*, February 16, 1949.

and Tourane were still French enclaves. The Moi country in southern Central Viet Nam, which the French had taken over in 1946, was still under French control, and the "autonomous" Thai Federation was a point of bitter dispute between the Vietnamese and the French.

North, Central, and South Viet Nam each had its own Governor, whom separatists with French support had prevented General Xuan from placing under the control of the new central government. In the south particularly, Governor Tran Van Huu openly flouted the authority of the central government. Cochin China remained a juridical monstrosity; it was at one and the same time a French colony, an autonomous republic, and one of the three divisions of the country ruled by the central government. It was under a triple network of administration: the French High Commissariat, the French army, and the Provisional Central Government of Viet Nam all had services in the south; and there was also the organization maintained by the Viet Minh. Although General Xuan had a certain following among the Cochin Chinese middle class, he received little authority from the French, was the object of active enmity from the Viet Minh, and even encountered hostility in the Council of Cochin China, which in December 1948 had renamed itself the Assembly of South Viet Nam and remained as a far from moribund survival of Admiral d'Argenlieu's separatist policy. Twenty-five Vietnamese members of the Assembly had resigned in July 1948 to further the unification of the country, but a hard core of separatists, mostly French, refused to follow their example; regardless of the Ha Long Bay Agreement, they continued to stand firm against Vietnamese unity.

By the end of 1948 the structure of French control over Viet Nam did not differ markedly from what it had been in the time of Admiral d'Argenlieu. Max André addressed a complaint on this score to Coste-Floret:

I know well, Mr. Minister, that you and the High Commissioner are fully aware of the duties of France toward the Associated States, but are you sure that this new revolutionary concept of independence, of sovereignty of the Associated States has penetrated to all your administrators, to all your services in Paris, to all the local administrations in Indochina?[9]

And Paul Rivet informed the French Assembly that "a high official who, on his return, came to share his apprehensions with me, told me that at the present time, when we occupy only the cities in Indochina—I insist on this fact—there are four times more officials than in 1940."[10]

A few men became members of General Xuan's government only to resign when they recognized its weakness. Xuan's sole converts were a small group called the Binh Xuyen, widely described as bandits by both Frenchmen and

[9] Journal Officiel, Assemblée de l'Union Française, March 9, 1949, p. 320.
[10] Journal Officiel, Assemblée Nationale, March 10, 1949, p. 1516.

Vietnamese, and it was said that considerable sums of money had changed hands before even they consented to join General Xuan. Some members of the Xuan government still liked to think of themselves as intermediaries between the resistance and the French; and Xuan and Bao Dai both looked to the time when resistance elements would join them. But nationalists fighting with the Viet Minh had little reason to change sides when the subservience of the Xuan government to the French was so patent. Furthermore, a unified line of action between Bao Dai and the Viet Minh was obviously not the aim of French policy.

Having neither power nor popular support, the Xuan government was poised precariously between Bao Dai and the Viet Minh. Aware that their tenure of office was short-lived, some ministers were not above exploiting their position to their own personal profit; and the impotence of the government was aggravated by the widespread corruption among its members.

The aloofness of Bao Dai from the Xuan government rapidly became a bone of contention between the ex-Emperor and the French. High Commissioner Bollaert's view, which was that of the French Government, was that Bao Dai must return home and assume personal responsibility for the Ha Long Bay Accord and for further agreements desired by the French; Bollaert and the French Government blamed the weakness of the Xuan regime upon the reluctance of Bao Dai to associate himself with it. Bao Dai, however, was cautious; he regarded the Xuan government as an object lesson and would not compromise his own position by identifying himself with it. He refused to go home until he could bring with him an agreement on unity and independence.

There the matter rested at the beginning of October 1948, when Emile Bollaert left Indochina as High Commissioner for the last time. Originally fixed at only six months, his term of office had stretched to eighteen. He had presided over the beginnings of the Bao Dai policy. For a while he had tried to keep the door open to negotiations with Ho Chi Minh as well as with the Bao Dai groups, but in this attempt he lacked both boldness and authority. The Ha Long Bay Agreement was his triumph; and by the time he resigned it was already clear that it had been a hollow one.

In the fall of 1948 Indochina welcomed the third High Commissioner it had had in little more than two years. He was Léon Pignon, the man who more than any other had inspired and directed the policy which took shape under Admiral d'Argenlieu. Despite his association with the negotiations leading to the March 6 Agreement and his membership in the French delegation at Fontainebleau, Pignon had consistently maneuvered behind the scenes to sabotage negotiations with the Viet Minh; his objective was to make use of Bao Dai in order to reconsolidate French authority over Viet Nam. One of Bollaert's first steps as High Commissioner, in attempting to improve Franco-

Vietnamese relations, had been to get rid of "the two great inspirers of the policy of the Admiral, Léon Pignon, Political Adviser, and Albert Torel, Commissioner of the Republic in Cochin China. . . . The first was named Commissioner of the Republic in Cambodia, the second was 'authorized' to take a vacation in France."[11] But Bollaert's policy of negotiation had failed. The appointment of Léon Pignon marked the triumph of the clique of French colonial officials (headed by himself and Torel) who since 1945, in opposition to Sainteny and General Leclerc, had been determined not to make peace in Indochina until they could do so on their own terms, which were nothing less than the restoration of colonialism.

NEGOTIATIONS IN FRANCE

In France, although to the general public Viet Nam seemed fairly remote, less vital an issue than the cost of living at home or the situation in Europe, there was articulate dissatisfaction with the course of the Vietnamese war. The Communists urged negotiations with the Viet Minh, attacking what they called "the filthy war" and demanding "peace for Viet Nam!" The independent Left-Wing newspapers, Combat and Franc-Tireur, were similarly critical of the refusal of the government to negotiate with Ho Chi Minh, as were several influential magazines, notably the liberal Catholic Esprit and Jean-Paul Sartre's Les Temps Modernes. A minority in the MRP also favored negotiations with Ho Chi Minh.

The French Socialist Party had already gone on record at successive party congresses in support of such a course, despite the unwillingness of their representatives in Parliament and in the Cabinet to risk their membership in the coalition government by attempting to translate party declarations on Viet Nam into action. From Indochina, Louis Caput had written to his Socialist comrades during August 1948:

In Viet Nam, the prestige of the [Socialist] Party is almost ruined; the great hopes that it awakened in 1945 and 1946 have been most cruelly deceived by the policy of Schuman, Bidault and Moutet, a policy of which the Socialist Party appears to have been the prisoner and—they say it openly here—the accomplice.

In January 1949 Guy Mollet, secretary of the party, addressed a letter to President Vincent Auriol, saying:

Negotiations with Bao Dai cannot lead to an accord with the people of Viet Nam. . . . The ex-Emperor does not enjoy any authority in the country, the armed forces of Viet Nam do not obey him and are not under him . . . the Directing Committee [of the French Socialist Party] has charged me to ask the government to put an end to the war by negotiations with all the political and cultural factions of

11 Devillers, op. cit., p. 384.

the Vietnamese people—and in the first place, with the Ho Chi Minh government.[12]

From the Assembly of the French Union came a similar appeal. This was the body created by the constitution of 1946 in which half the members came from sections of the empire outside metropolitan France. Although its powers were limited to advice, it was developing as a forum for discussion of imperial questions where the views of the indigenous peoples received a generally more sympathetic hearing than elsewhere in the governing bodies of the French Union. In January 1949 the Political Affairs Commission of the Assembly of the French Union adopted a Socialist proposal asking the government, in the spirit of agreements already signed, to reopen discussions on as broad a basis as possible in order to apply a policy of fraternal collaboration between France and Viet Nam in the French Union.

However, the French Government had no intention of deviating from its conception of the Bao Dai policy. And the Socialist deputies and Ministers, when the time came, were still not prepared to oppose actively the decision of their MRP and Radical Socialist colleagues.

The French Government pinned its hopes on Bao Dai's return to Viet Nam and, by the winter of 1948–49, it did so with a certain urgency. For several years the Vietnamese had been fighting in relative isolation. They had smuggled guns and supplies from China across the northern frontier and by ship from Hongkong. There was also considerable traffic of this kind with the Philippines; and Siam had maintained a benevolent neutrality. Beyond this, the Vietnamese had no allies. Since 1946 they had fought the French army alone.

The victories of the Communists in China threatened radically to change this situation; they meant that the Viet Minh would soon have powerful friends on its northern border. Vo Nguyen Giap described 1948 as a year of great victories and told the Vietnamese that their military successes combined with the changed international situation made it possible for their armies to prepare for a general offensive. The timetable was in the hands of the Chinese Communists: Bao Dai had to split the mass of the resistance away from Ho Chi Minh before the Chinese arrived within helping distance. There was not much time left.

But could Bao Dai, simply by going home, accomplish this split? The tug of war in France continued. Yes, said the French Government, and government officials, impatient with Bao Dai's nationalist demands, appealed to him to go back to Viet Nam. His answer then, as before, was a flat negative. His political future already seriously compromised by the weakness of the regime General Xuan had founded under his aegis, Bao Dai could not go back with-

[12] *Le Populaire*, March 10, 1949.

out terms generous enough to give him something to bargain with against the Viet Minh. He insisted on a definitive treaty with France before he would leave Europe, with a more real independence and unity than that conceded to the tottering Xuan government.

In January, General Xuan himself came to France to see Bao Dai and to urge him to become active head of a central government of Viet Nam. The Governor of Central Viet Nam, Phan Van Giao, also saw Bao Dai, as did the Governor of South Viet Nam, Tran Van Huu, who received assurances that Cochin China could be autonomous within a united Viet Nam.

Bao Dai's supporters in Viet Nam, meanwhile, were disturbed by the interminable and apparently fruitless negotiations dragging on month after month in Europe. When Phan Van Giao came back from France, he tried to reassure them. He told a crowd gathered in Hanoi:

With regard to the fear that the Emperor might make mistakes in his negotiations with France, I can affirm that from the political and diplomatic points of view, there is no Vietnamese who has a talent [and] a farsightedness . . . comparable to that of the Emperor. . . . We can only say that if Emperor Bao Dai is delaying his return, it shows that he is resolved to attain results satisfactory to his purposes and in conformity with the aspirations of the people, and that he will return only after attaining them.[13]

Everything depended on the resistance, and Giao followed the lead of others of Bao Dai's supporters in trying to wean its members away from Ho Chi Minh:

National resistance members, your feats are indeed magnificent. It is for the country that you have taken up arms and it is also for the country that you are now ready to join the Vietnamese National Army . . . and when the Emperor returns and his success is unquestionable . . . the people will not make a mistake and Ho Chi Minh will be the enemy of the people.

The Vietnamese soon had a chance to put this prophecy to the test. On March 8, 1949, Bao Dai and Vincent Auriol, President of France, exchanged letters at the Elysée Palace in Paris, at last achieving a detailed agreement. And Bao Dai told the press that he would soon return to Viet Nam. He said:

Soon an era of reconstruction and renovation will open in Viet Nam. The country will be given democratic institutions which will be called on primarily to approve the present agreement . . . profound economic and social reforms will be instituted to raise the general standard of living and to promote social justice, which is the condition and guarantee of order. These national objectives of peace suppose the union of all Vietnamese regardless of their political or religious tendency, and the generous support of France on which I know I can count.[14]

[13] Radio South Viet Nam, February 15, 1949.
[14] Le Monde, March 9, 1949.

AN ASSOCIATED STATE

The next step was up to the French Government. The French eventually had to ratify the Elysée Accords signed on March 8, but first the French Parliament had to act on Cochin China, which was still legally a French colony. Unless it did, and formally declared Cochin China a part of Viet Nam, the new agreement would be null and void, and Bao Dai would not go back to Viet Nam. And until it did, the French Government would not publish the text of the Elysée Accords.

The March 1949 agreements gave Viet Nam not only the promise of unity but also what they described as independence within the French Union. They made clear, however, that this independence would not be permitted to jeopardize the French position in Indochina. With the Elysée Accords, Bao Dai accepted terms which had been rejected by the Vietnamese delegation at Fontainebleau when they were put forward by the French Government in 1946.

In March 1949 Viet Nam officially joined the French Union as an Associated State, and France promised to support a Vietnamese application for membership in the United Nations. Under the French constitution, however, Associated Statehood was far removed from independence; in this respect comparisons between the British Commonwealth of Nations and the French Union, so often made by foreigners, were highly misleading. The provisions on the empire in the constitution of 1946 were drawn up according to the traditions of French imperial practice; within the newly named French Union the constituent parts of the empire were accorded varying degrees of subordination to metropolitan France. The old protectorates, which were offered the position of Associated State, received the largest degree of autonomy, and in the Elysée Accords Viet Nam was granted the right to have its own diplomats in a few specified countries—China, Siam, and the Vatican. (Because of the establishment of the Mao Tse-tung regime, India was later substituted for China, a purely technical change, as it turned out, because the Indian Government did not recognize the Bao Dai regime.) At the same time, however, Viet Nam recognized the right of France to control both its foreign policy and its military affairs. Laos and Cambodia accepted a similar status later in 1949, but Tunisia and Morocco, which were also expected to do so, have not yet seen fit to sign the treaties which would transform them into Associated States.

In the Elysée Accords, Viet Nam also agreed to send representatives to the Assembly and the High Council of the French Union, the two new advisory bodies provided for in the constitution of 1946. Despite the unique qualities of the Assembly, which met for the first time in December 1947, bringing together delegates from all the overseas territories as well as from metropolitan France, it was regarded with marked lack of enthusiasm by a number of

Vietnamese nationalists who did not see why Vietnamese should sit in the same assembly as representatives of various French colonies which no one pretended to regard as autonomous. They were hardly more enthusiastic about the High Council of the French Union, which was supposed to assemble representatives of the Associated States and of France, and to assist in the general direction of the French Union; the High Council did not meet until 1951 and, when it did, appeared considerably more formal than functional. The first President of the French Union, Vincent Auriol, demonstrated a desire and a readiness to strengthen the new framework of the French Union, but the President of the French Union is also the President of the French Republic and it was difficult for nationalists to escape the conclusion that the real center of power in the French Union was, as it had always been, in the French Government.

The Elysée Agreements, which promised Viet Nam its own army responsible for the maintenance of order and internal security, required the Vietnamese army to come to the defense of the empire and to have French military advisers and French equipment. At the same time, a French Union army was to be stationed in Viet Nam and French soldiers were given the right to circulate freely among the bases and garrisons assigned to them. In wartime a French officer was to command Vietnamese as well as French Union forces.

Although the agreements stated that Bao Dai had received broad administrative autonomy ("The Government of Viet Nam should exercise fully all of the attributes and prerogatives implied by internal sovereignty"),[15] the French economic regime imposed on the country when Indochina was still part colony, part protectorate, was carefully preserved. Viet Nam required the permission of the French Government before it could change the status of any French property and enterprises in its territory. And when the Vietnamese Government employed foreign advisers and technicians, they were to be from France or the French Union whenever possible and had to be approved by the French Government. The Indochinese piastre remained tied to the French franc, although the French Government agreed that the parity between the piastre and the franc would only be modified after consultation with the Associated States.

The French kept a special legal status for their own nationals and passed on to the Vietnamese Government the obligations which France had incurred to Nationalist China under the treaty of February 28, 1946: whenever Frenchmen or foreigners protected by special treaty with France were involved in legal cases, they were not to be tried under Vietnamese law but under French law, and before mixed courts in which Frenchmen as well as Vietnamese would sit.

15 *Journal Officiel*, March 14, 1953, pp. 2410, 2413.

236 THE STRUGGLE FOR INDOCHINA

The idea of a strong federation in Indochina had become so indistinguishable from French attempts to control the country that it had lost most of the little Indochinese support it may once have had, and in the Elysée Agreements it gave way to the concept of Associated Statehood for each of the three Indochinese States. But the project for an Indochinese Federation was far from dead. The areas in Viet Nam inhabited by minorities like the Moi and the Thai remained for the time being under French administration.[15a] In 1948 the French Parliament had passed a law to establish an Indochinese bank to issue the Indochinese currency, the piastre, taking over this important power from the private French-controlled Bank of Indochina; the Elysée Accords confirmed that there would be such an Indochinese Bank of Issue and that the piastre would be the currency of all Indochina. Viet Nam, Cambodia, and Laos were to be joined in a customs union as well as a monetary union. And the important questions of the degree of control that Viet Nam was to have over its own treasury, communications, foreign trade and customs, immigration, and economic planning, were reserved for a later "interstate" conference.

Had French policy altered fundamentally toward Viet Nam? After the signature of the Ha Long Bay Agreement, Coste-Floret had taken pains to reassure the French Assembly that this was not the case. Paul Ramadier, who had become Minister of National Defense in the government of Henri Queuille, did virtually the same thing after the Elysée Accords. On March 9, just after they were signed, he told the Council of the Republic: "Expenditures for Indochina are more necessary than ever because a new phase is beginning which does not permit us to slow down our military efforts."[16]

In the French Parliament, the Left again demanded direct negotiations with the Viet Minh and criticized the government for trying to turn the fighting into a civil war. The Communists blamed the Bao Dai policy on the United States, quoting Le Monde reports from Washington that the American Government believed a national Vietnamese regime under Bao Dai could halt the spread of Communism.

Paul Rivet, who broke with the Socialists because of his disagreement with their Indochina policy, also raised the specter of American intervention. With considerable imagination, he saw it as taking many forms—religious (because Cardinal Francis Spellman had stopped off in Indochina during a tour of the Far East, Rivet professed to see evidence of a plan among American Catholics to organize a great crusade from Japan to Indochina); diplomatic (by which he meant William C. Bullitt[17]); and economic (the reason, said Rivet, that an American senator had recently paid a visit to Saigon was to bring in American finance capital). However, "I believe that the departure of France

---

[15a] These regions were subsequently recognized as Vietnamese crown domains.
[16] Ibid., Conseil de la République, March 9, 1949, p. 613.
[17] See above, p. 216, footnote 21.

from Indochina would be a disaster for us and for the Vietnamese," Rivet said.[18]

The Socialists stood by Guy Mollet's letter to President Auriol. Oreste Rosenfeld said in the Assembly of the French Union:

> It is said "Ho Chi Minh is a Communist." I know it, I don't doubt it; but he is at the head of an important faction of the Vietnamese people. If we can come to an understanding with him to end the war, what importance has it for us that he is a Communist? We are not in Indochina to establish a regime that pleases us; we have declared since the month of March 1946 that we want to leave to the Indochinese the right to administer and to govern themselves.
>
> It is also said—and this is much more serious—that one cannot have confidence in the word of Ho Chi Minh and that, moreover, one cannot negotiate with him because he will shun us. . . . But if you are so certain that Ho Chi Minh does not want to negotiate with us, you have to force his back to the wall, you have to put him in the position of refusing your proposals. Then you will be able to address yourself to the Vietnamese people and say to them: we have given you satisfaction in all your national demands; Ho Chi Minh does not want to negotiate because he is a Communist, because he is pursuing another policy. At that moment the Vietnamese people could perhaps turn toward Bao Dai or toward any other personality with whom you negotiate.[19]

Rosenfeld tried in vain to persuade the Assembly of the French Union to adopt a course proposed by the Socialists a year earlier—that the Assembly of the French Union proffer its good offices to the French and the Vietnamese to bring them together in an attempt to find a solution to the conflict. The year before, the Assembly of the French Union was too young, he said. "We did not have what I might call the spirit of the French Union." But the Assembly of the French Union, it seemed, was still too young in the spring of 1949, too much an extension of the political divisions and attitudes in metropolitan France, too little imbued with the French Union spirit, to take up Rosenfeld's challenge.

Kind words for Ho Chi Minh came from an unexpected source in the Assembly of the French Union. "If I found before me again the Ho Chi Minh of 1946, the man who signed the March 6 convention, the man whom I saw in Paris, I would negotiate with him." The speaker was Albert Sarraut, veteran Radical Socialist, onetime Governor General of Indochina and an ex-Premier of France, the former father-in-law of Jean Sainteny who had negotiated with Ho Chi Minh in 1945 and 1946.

"I have known him since 1923, the time when as Minister of Colonies I had a rather lively interview in my office at the Rue Oudinot with Ho Chi Minh, who then called himself Nguyen Ai Quoc, after which Ho Chi Minh decided

[18] *Journal Officiel*, Assemblée Nationale, March 10, 1949, p. 1513.
[19] *Ibid.*, Assemblée de l'Union Française, March 9, 1949, p. 339.

that it was better to leave French territory." When Sarraut confronted him with the record of his revolutionary activities in 1923, Ho Chi Minh replied, "I am fighting for the independence of my country."

The two men did not meet again for twenty-three years. And then, at the time of the Fontainebleau Conference, "from personal conversations that I was able to have with Ho Chi Minh in this period of July-August 1946, I got the strong impression that he had a sincere desire at that time for an understanding with us." Sarraut said:

If the Ho Chi Minh whom I knew could really act freely, on witnessing today the realization by the French Government of what has been the object of his entire life, the independence of his country, the reason that he has fought for forty years with a personal disinterestedness that we have the fairness to recognize, don't you think that this man would say, that he would write: "My dream is realized, my country is independent, I have done my job. I am going to help, with French cooperation, to raise up my country from its ruins and to bind its wounds"?[20]

The problem is not with which man to negotiate, Sarraut told the Assembly of the French Union, but rather the conditions necessary to realize independence. The policy of the French Government, said Coste-Floret, MRP Minister of Overseas France, "has always been to negotiate with all the intellectual and political factions of Viet Nam because we believe that peace will only be made there by the rallying together of all Vietnamese nationalist elements, no matter where they come from or who they are."[21]

Although this may have been the theory of French policy, in practice it added up to Bao Dai. Men who might have worked with Ho Chi Minh during the summer of 1946 had been shocked by the events of December 19, 1946 and closed their eyes to the responsibility of Frenchmen in precipitating the outbreak. They made up their minds that no matter the cost they could not achieve an agreement with Ho Chi Minh. Sarraut, for one, subscribed to Marius Moutet's old theory that Ho Chi Minh had lost control of his government. "I am certain," he said, "that Ho Chi Minh is not free, that Ho Chi Minh is a prisoner. . . . The Giaps, the Giams, the Dongs, the Tran Van Lieus . . . do not want this cooperation with France at any price . . . and have as the cornerstone of their program the expulsion of France and the French."[22]

The French Parliament addressed itself to the problem of Cochin Chinese unity according to the procedure laid down by the French constitution. Article 75 stated that "the respective status of members of the Republic and of the French Union are susceptible of evolution. Modifications of status and the passage from one category to another within the framework fixed by Ar-

[20] Ibid., pp. 343-44.
[21] Ibid., p. 308.
[22] Ibid., pp. 343-44.

ticle 60[23] can only result from a law voted by Parliament after consultation with the territorial assemblies and the Assembly of the Union."

No such territorial assembly existed in Cochin China and it was to create one that the French Government presented a bill to Parliament in March 1949. From Rightists were heard fears for the future of French citizens in Cochin China, doubts as to the constitutionality of unifying Viet Nam, warnings that it would mean the end of French rule in Indochina. They were disturbed by the nationalism of Bao Dai as well as by that of Ho Chi Minh. A member of the PRL quoted from a letter written by Xuan's political adviser in Paris:

"The elected members of the Socialist Party, faithful representatives of the French working class, have a choice: to rally to the Bao Dai solution or to recommend a new entente with Ho Chi Minh. The first solution, as well as the second, will free Viet Nam from what we call imperialist and colonialist domination."[24]

In March 1949 the position of the French was far removed from what it had been three years earlier when they had promised to hold a referendum on the status of Cochin China. "In 1946 the referendum should have taken place," Oreste Rosenfeld said. "But in the present state of our legislation, it is no longer possible. . . ."

"Very good," said the Minister of Overseas France.

Rosenfeld continued:

. . . The constitution which dates from the month of October 1946 does not allow for the procedure of a referendum.

Consequently, even if the March 6 Accords are not considered—rightly or wrongly I don't want to discuss here now—as null and void, even in that case, after the adoption of the constitution of 1946 the government no longer had open to it the possibility of proceeding by referendum. It had to have recourse to the device of article 75 . . . and as the territorial assembly does not exist in Cochinchina, it is necessary to act under Article 77 and create a territorial assembly.[25]

The Cochin Chinese territorial assembly thus offered the possibility of unity to Viet Nam—any Viet Nam, regardless of its rulers—by what were apparently the only possible means under the French constitution. For this reason even a number of people who were not eager to see France deal with Bao Dai approved the government's plan. The assembly, it was decided, was to have 64 members, 16 of them French nationals and 48 Vietnamese (the same proportion of 1 to 3 that prevailed in the South Viet Nam Assembly). Each of the various provincial councils in Cochin China was to elect two Vietnamese,

23 "The French Union is formed, on the one hand of the French Republic which includes metropolitan France, the overseas departments and territories, and on the other hand, of the associated territories and states."

24 *Journal Officiel*, Assemblée Nationale, March 11, 1949, p. 1547.

25 *Ibid.*, Assemblée de l'Union Française, March 9, 1949, pp. 335–36.

and the Saigon-Cholon council of administration was to elect eight. The French members were to be chosen by representatives of the liberal professions and of the syndical and corporative organizations of Cochin China. Although the Socialists were overruled in their attempts to have the assembly elected by direct and secret universal suffrage, with the French represented only in proportion to their numbers, the Socialists found the prospect of Vietnamese unity sufficiently attractive to accept the restricted and weighted electorate favored by the government.

On March 12, by a vote of 339 to 201, the bill became law. A territorial assembly was to be elected in Cochin China, its sole function to vote on changing the territorial status of Cochin China, either by attaching it to the Associated State of Viet Nam or by choosing some other status within the French Union.

This bill was passed almost 150 years after the Emperor Gia Long, then a disinherited prince fighting for his throne, had lost all of his country except the south; over a period of years, using Cochin China as a base, he had succeeded with French help in unifying the three regions of Viet Nam. After the efforts of successive generations of nationalists to restore the unity that Gia Long had achieved by arms and that the Vietnamese had lost to superior French force during the 1860's, the legalistic atmosphere in which formal unity was attained in 1949 came as a distinct anticlimax.

"ELECTIONS" IN COCHIN CHINA

Despite all the serious and sometimes angry debate which laid the framework for it, the territorial assembly of Cochin China had a curiously unreal character. On paper it represented only a small number of the people who lived in Cochin China; and it represented even fewer in practice.

Tran Van Huu was confronted with the problem of what councils were supposed to elect the Vietnamese representatives. Were they to be those elected under the Third Republic? Those set up by Vichy? Those established in 1946? Huu had to ask the French Commissioner in Cochin China and he, in turn, the Minister of Overseas France. Coste-Floret, who had told the Assembly of the French Union that the elections would be "eminently representative," that they would be by indirect universal suffrage based upon the system of Notables and hence upon popular consent, ruled in favor of the provincial councils appointed by the various provincial administrators during 1946, with little reference to popular consent. Many of the councils had long since ceased to function or even to exist. They had lost members by resignation, disinterest, and death—the last mostly because of the Viet Minh's offensive against Cochin Chinese Notables willing to collaborate with the French. As a result, the administration had to appoint a number of councilors before these in turn could choose members of the territorial assembly. Forty of the sixty-four men who sat in the assembly (a clear-cut majority) were thus appointed by the administration.

On the eve of the elections, General Xuan sent a message to the South Viet Nam electors, reminding them that the Elysée Accords would be void if they did not vote for unity, and assuring them that their special interests would be respected in a united Viet Nam.

The elections were held on April 10. Viet Minh spokesmen urged people to stay away from the polls and there were considerable abstentions, even among the few people qualified to vote. Nguyen Phan Long, one of the more prominent abstainers, attacked the whole procedure as a farce in the *Echo du Viet Nam*. Only some 5,000 Vietnamese in Cochin China had the right to vote and, of these, little more than 700 actually did so.[26] Almost 500 Frenchmen also voted.

These were the men who chose the sixty-four members of the Cochin Chinese territorial assembly which met on April 19 in a highly charged atmosphere. A Rightist critic declared:

Its members were the object of the most diverse pressures. Twenty million francs had been distributed at friendly meals presided over by General Xuan in person. Threats of death had been reserved for the irreconcilables. To the French delegation the services of the Commissariat of the Republic had presented various arguments: collapse of the ministry, resumption at the instigation of the Socialists of relations with Ho Chi Minh, and finally, the coming of a United Nations commission of good offices.[27]

The French members of the assembly hoped to have Cochin China achieve a separate status and a direct relationship with France, with the possibility then open to it of a vote on whether or not to join Viet Nam; the Vietnamese members wanted immediate unity. They agreed after a heated series of discussions that Cochin China should be attached to the Associated State of Viet Nam. The stumbling block was an article proposed by the French providing "that the effective and legal attachment of Cochin China be . . . null and void in case of a change in the status of Viet Nam within the French Union." Twenty-three Vietnamese members refused to accept this proviso. An Algerian nationalist deputy remarked:

Despite the precautions taken in the choice of official candidates, there was in the Cochin Chinese assembly a majority among the Vietnamese element which opposed the paragraph. Thus even for those people elected who were friends of the administration, and who were compromised in the eyes of the majority of the Vietna-

[26] The official French report that 80 percent of the qualified Vietnamese electorate outside Saigon-Cholon voted was highly misleading in view of the fact that the qualified electorate in the provinces was limited to 185 people, as contrasted to 4,899 in Saigon-Cholon.

[27] General Aumeran of the PRL, *Journal Officiel*, Assemblée Nationale, May 22, 1949, p. 2767.

mese people, this Article 3 appeared suspect, to say the least . . . a permanent menace to the national unity of Viet Nam and a clear obstacle on the road to full liberty
and sovereignty.[28]

On the 23rd, Henri de Lachevrotière, a Right-Wing journalist who was
later assassinated by the Viet Minh, bitterly attacked the Vietnamese for their
intransigence on Article 3. "Is it Ho Chi Minh you want?" he demanded.
"If that is so, have the courage to say so, for I have always had the courage of
my convictions." He said, "If you take this position now, it is because of an
evil genius. Is it General Xuan? Does he desire to replace His Majesty Bao
Dai?"[29]

When the Vietnamese stood firm, General Xuan had to add his voice to
the debate and personally urged them to give way. They finally capitulated
and the joining of Cochin China to Viet Nam, modified by the disputed article, was approved on April 23 by 55 of the 63 members present, with six in
opposition and two abstaining. At the same time, the assembly reminded Bao
Dai of his promise that South Viet Nam would be autonomous.[30]

"The only loser is Ho Chi Minh," High Commissioner Pignon declared at
the closing session of the Cochin Chinese territorial assembly.[31] This did not
prevent General Xuan from saying several days later, "Places will be reserved
in the future government for resistance elements which rally to the new regime. The participation of Ho Chi Minh is not excluded a priori. It will de-
pend on the proof that the head of the Viet Minh can give as to the purity of
his nationalist sentiments."[32]

The Cochin Chinese assembly having declared itself, Bao Dai did not wait
for the French National Assembly to act on its advice. He left for home, as
he had said he would, on April 25. His three years of exile were over. When
he arrived in Indochina, quietly and without fanfare, he went immediately
to the resort city of Dalat in the hills of the Moi country in south Central
Viet Nam, there to await final action by the French Parliament on Vietnamese unity.

UNITY

When the French Cabinet presented Parliament with a bill to make Cochin China a part of Viet Nam, critics from the Right and Left joined forces
in attacking the Cochin Chinese elections. It was not easy to make out a case

[28] Mohammed Khider, ibid., p. 2778.

[29] Quoted from the record of the Cochin Chinese assembly, Journal Officiel, Assemblée de
l'Union Française, May 19, 1949, p. 521; see also Le Monde, April 24–25, 1949.

[30] The Cochin Chinese assembly formally recalled a letter Bao Dai had written to Tran Van
Huu, President of the South Viet Nam government, on March 16, promising to reserve for South
Viet Nam a special status within Viet Nam, taking into account "its present situation and its
most sincere desire to conserve in the South its old habits of life by a large administrative de-
centralization." He had promised also that French nationals residing in South Viet Nam would
be able to express themselves freely on all matters concerning their property and business.

[31] Le Monde, April 26, 1949.

[32] Ibid., May 3, 1949.

for fair elections having been held in Cochin China. But the very fact of the highly restricted suffrage and the undoubted pressure exercised by the French administration only served to underline the desire for unity in Cochin China, even among Vietnamese most under French influence.

The Cambodians also raised objections to unification. The Cambodian Government had consistently opposed the move. It had made its opposition clear to the French since before the signing of the Ha Long Bay Agreement. The Cambodian Government was anxious for guaranties of the rights of the more than 450,000 Cambodians still living in Cochin China as well as of the right of Cambodia to free navigation on the Mekong River and to free use of the port of Saigon, Cambodia's indispensable outlet to the sea. A fourth claim involved disputed frontiers. "We ask simply that our interests in Cochin China be considered before the attachment of Cochin China," Cambodian Princess Yukanthor said in the Assembly of the French Union, "because we fear the imperialistic designs of Viet Nam and fear that if the attachment of Cochin China is made without reservations in regard to Cambodian interests, we will not be able to get these concessions from Viet Nam."[33]

Coste-Floret assured the Cambodians that the rights of their minorities in Cochin China would be protected, as would those of all minorities in Viet Nam; one of the provisions of the Elysée Accords was that each of these minorities would be protected by agreements between France and Viet Nam. Cambodian outlets to the sea were to be safeguarded by later agreements. Coste-Floret discounted the Cambodian territorial demands, and he read a letter to the Council of the Republic in which Léon Pignon bluntly told King Norodom Sihanouk that the only reason he was raising the question of frontiers was because the French had been conciliatory on other issues.

The French Assembly adopted the bill to make Cochin China a part of Viet Nam by a vote of 352 to 208, with the Communists among the opposition, and it became law on June 4. The disputed article which French members of the Cochin Chinese territorial assembly had forced into its final motion, was dropped. If the status of Viet Nam within the French Union were to change, unification would not automatically be voided: in the event of such a change, the status of Cochin China would be discussed anew by the assemblies called for in Article 75 of the French constitution.

With Vietnamese unity no longer a promise but a fact, the Elysée Accords could go into effect, and on June 14 Bao Dai and High Commissioner Pignon met at a formal ceremony in Saigon to exchange letters bringing to Viet Nam the independence agreed to at the Elysée Palace. Later that month the Cochin Chinese government offered its resignation to Bao Dai and formally terminated the experiment in Cochin Chinese separatism begun under Admiral d'Argenlieu.

[33] *Journal Officiel*, Assemblée de l'Union Française, May 19, 1949, p. 517.

Once Bao Dai had talked as if he intended to act as a mediator between the Vietnamese people and France. There had even been speculation that through Bao Dai's good offices Ho Chi Minh and the French Government might succeed in achieving some basis of agreement. Bao Dai returned home bound by an agreement with France; he had no parallel understanding with the Viet Minh. He announced his intention of retaining provisionally the title of Emperor "in order to have a legal international position but," he said, "I solemnly proclaim that the future constitution of Viet Nam will be decided by the people who have fought heroically for the independence of their homeland." In the meantime he declared himself Chief of State.

Chapter Eleven

THE ROAD TO INDEPENDENCE:
BAO DAI VERSUS THE VIET MINH

LÉON PIGNON had succinctly defined the prevailing French policy toward Viet Nam even before he became High Commissioner. While still adviser to Admiral d'Argenlieu, he wrote:

Our objective is clear: to transpose to the field of Vietnamese domestic politics the quarrel that we have with the Viet Minh, and to involve ourselves as little as possible in the campaigns and reprisals which ought to be the work of the native adversaries of that party.[1]

Although this policy of divide and rule came inevitably to be linked with the return home of Bao Dai, if it was to be successful it required considerably more than the physical presence of the Emperor in Viet Nam; it required his active co-operation along with that of at least a substantial fraction of the Vietnamese people, and this co-operation was not forthcoming. The continued presence of French troops on Vietnamese soil and of French officials in the Vietnamese administration was enough to convince the average Vietnamese and the Emperor that they all had still to achieve independence. Even those nationalists who realized that the changeover could not be accomplished in a day, waited to see how real were the concessions that Bao Dai had won from France and were not prepared to compromise on a shadow independence. As a result, most of the intellectuals and young people either continued to work with the Viet Minh or remained aloof from politics, and in the summer of 1949 Bao Dai was unable to attract many outstanding Vietnamese, even among those most opposed to Ho Chi Minh.

Ngo Dinh Diem again assumed leadership, speaking for the nationalist majority who refused to commit themselves either to Bao Dai or to Ho Chi Minh. Diem turned down offers to head Bao Dai's Cabinet and declared:

The national aspirations of the Vietnamese people will be satisfied only on the day when our nation obtains the same political status which India and Pakistan enjoy. . . . I believe it is only just to reserve the best posts in new Viet Nam for those who have merited most of the country: I speak of the resistance elements.[2]

Lacking any other suitable candidate in the summer of 1949, Bao Dai finally had to take over the post of Prime Minister himself. Few of the members of his Cabinet had ever served in government positions, few were representatives

---

[1] Orientation note, No. 9, January 4, 1947. Quoted by Devillers, *op. cit.*, p. 364.
[2] *L'Echo du Viet Nam*, June 16, 1949.

of anyone other than themselves. General Georges Revers, French Chief of Staff, who was sent to study the situation in Indochina during May and June 1949, was highly critical of this state of affairs. He wrote: "If Ho Chi Minh has been able to hold off French intervention for so long, it is because the Viet Minh leader has surrounded himself with a group of men of incontestable worth." It was up to Bao Dai, then, to line up a group of comparable worth. General Revers was justified in his complaint; the fault, however, was less with Bao Dai than with the French who left to him so few of the attributes of independence that he could only set up "a government composed of twenty representatives of phantom parties, the best organized of which would have difficulty in rallying twenty-five adherents."[3]

South Viet Nam (Cochin China) was the place where Bao Dai's political and military support was most strongly organized and, compared with other parts of Viet Nam, it was allowed to be overrepresented in his government. It is true that the Ministries of Foreign Affairs and Interior both went to Nguyen Phan Long, an influential unionist journalist from Saigon who edited the *Echo du Viet Nam*. But the Vice-President of the government was General Nguyen Van Xuan, whose year as puppet president of Viet Nam and whose earlier history as the separatist leader who contributed to the failure of the Fontainebleau Conference had not added to his popularity.

In view of the anarchic political situation in Viet Nam, Bao Dai seemed to have been wise to decree that there would be three governors for North, Central, and South Viet Nam, each of them appointed, not by the Prime Minister as General Xuan had desired (intending thereby to subordinate them firmly to the central government, which was more vulnerable to French influence), but by the Chief of State, an arrangement which had the effect of leaving relatively broad powers of expenditure and patronage in the hands of the three governors. Another ordinance envisaged the eventual creation of an advisory national assembly appointed by the Chief of State, to be replaced when peace came by a freely elected constituent assembly. Bao Dai even promised social reforms leading to a just and humane regime.

In the meantime a number of posts in the Emperor's Cabinet were optimistically reserved for men from the resistance, and when Bao Dai visited Hanoi in the summer of 1949 he laid a palm branch on the monument to the Vietnamese who had been shot by the French after December 19, 1946. Members of Bao Dai's household talked of the guerrillas as "our heroes." This was something that General Revers could not understand. "Is Viet Nam at war or not?" he demanded in his report. "If it is, one does not have to exalt the resistance as the Bao Dai government does."

But if nationalists spoke with different voices after Bao Dai returned home,

---

[3] The quotations are from General Revers' supposedly secret report, the wide circulation of which was the occasion of the political scandal, "the affair of the generals," in 1950.

all of them demanded independence. During the winter of 1949 an almost forgotten voice came out of Asia, asking help for Viet Nam. The elderly Prince Cuong De appealed from his Japanese exile, in the name of the Phuc Quoc, for the immediate withdrawal of French forces. He called on the free world for aid in realizing Vietnamese independence—from the "French colonialists" and the "Viet Minh Communists"—under the aegis of the United Nations (particularly the United States).

Cuong De was a voice from the distant past; but he did not speak very differently from Ngo Dinh Diem (who, however, never publicly criticized the Viet Minh). And Ho Chi Minh told a reporter that the immediate aim of his government was to get French troops out of Viet Nam. After that they would discuss the next step. "Each thing in its turn," he said.[4]

THE DECISIVE SHIFT INTO THE COMMUNIST CAMP

Unfortunately for the Vietnamese national cause, the Viet Minh at that very time hurried to pay a price for Communist domination of the resistance movement. It blundered across the no-man's land of the cold war into a position where it found itself confronted by the Communist-containment policy newly formulated by the United States. The Vietnamese Communists thereby made a military victory impossible for themselves, and for the nationalist elements who had relied upon them in their fight for independence.

Although few nationalists were willing to join an active opposition to the Viet Minh if divisions among the Vietnamese would only be exploited by the French, many nationalists had been antagonized by the Communists in the period since August 1945; even before the outbreak of the cold war, the Viet Minh had encountered some difficulty in justifying itself as a wholly nationalist movement like the Indonesian. By 1949 the international situation was strained and the Western sensitivity about Communism intensified. Marshall Plan dollars were already being sent to France for use in Europe, releasing francs for expenditure on the Vietnamese war; and in June 1949 the State Department welcomed the formation "of the new unified state of Viet Nam" and expressed the hope that the March 8 Elysée Accords would "form the basis for the progressive realization of the legitimate aspirations of the Vietnamese people."[5]

Vietnamese Communists had been present when three conferences were held in Calcutta the previous year—of the Indian Communist Party, New Democratic Youth League, and Southeast Asia Students—attended by representatives of the Far Eastern countries and the Soviet Union. These conferences had been followed in quick succession by Communist risings in Burma,

[4] *Franc-Tireur*, December 10–11, 1949.
[5] *Department of State Bulletin*, July 18, 1949, p. 75.

Malaya, and Indonesia. The Far Eastern correspondent of the London *Times* wrote:

> Beyond certain coincidences and a common pattern of action which manifested itself throughout Southeast Asia, suggesting a coordinating agency, there has been no concrete evidence of Russian instigation of complicity. What has happened has, of course, been in the Russian interest, but it is difficult to imagine that the Kremlin could have "ordered" direct action unless it had seemed to the local Communist leaders to be the right tactic.[6]

For Vietnamese Communists, who alone of the groups represented at Calcutta were leading what was still a broadly national resistance movement, it had seemed a tactical error to emphasize the class struggle in 1948. But in 1949, after three years of war during which no foreign power had intervened to establish peace, the French seemed to be finding friends in America; and at the same time an ideologically friendly China was taking shape across the Vietnamese frontier. In exchange for help from abroad, the Viet Minh prepared to barter both the broad policy of national union which it had professed when it went to war in 1946 and the independent diplomacy grounded on a more realistic view of the national interest which Ho Chi Minh had pursued since 1945.

It seems highly questionable that the Chinese ever demanded such a radical shift in Viet Minh policy: Communist China had every reason to support nationalist revolutionary elements on its frontier even if they did not choose to make themselves over entirely in its image. Even the Chiang Kai-shek regime had helped Ho Chi Minh during the second World War and as late as 1946. There is no question at all, however, that Ho Chi Minh and his supporters played into the hands of the French; at a time when the French were stalemated in Indochina, weakened militarily and economically, and with little prospect of extensive foreign support, the Viet Minh made them a present of large-scale American aid against the Vietnamese nationalist movement— not to maintain French colonial rule, which the United States had no particular reason to do, but to fight Communism. In so doing, the extremists in the Viet Minh movement incurred a grave responsibility to the Vietnamese people.

Viet Minh leaders broke with the non-Communist world, declaring openly their allegiance to international Communism and proceeding with much fanfare to proclaim the primacy of Communist institutions and techniques in the zones under their control. This process began as the continuing fighting brought to the fore extremists in the Viet Minh coalition; and the pressure of international events enabled them to consolidate their power as the Chinese Communists won a series of decisive victories over Chiang Kai-shek's armies

[6] Ian Morrison, "The Communist Uprising in Malaya," *Far Eastern Survey*, December 22, 1948, p. 285.

during 1949. It is true that Ho Chi Minh told an American newspaperman in August 1949 that the new situation in China did not bring Viet Nam into the Soviet camp. He said that the Communist victories meant "a change in the center of gravity of power in Asia" but "Viet Nam is relying, as always, on its own strength to win its independence."[7] But the behavior of the Viet Minh in regard to both internal and external problems did not substantiate Ho Chi Minh's words.

In Viet Nam, the Communists strengthened their control over members of non-Communist groups working with them. When Ho Chi Minh sent his personal representative, Pham Ngoc Thach, to watch over the South Vietnamese resistance, the President also sent along a message praising the southern Viet Minh troops for their military successes, but adding that "from the political point of view the combatants have committed errors. The political instruction of the army still leaves something to be desired. Individualism still exists in certain regions, even among certain leaders."[8] It was believed that Thach's job was to eliminate such "errors"; and, in fact, the administrative committee of resistance in the south was reorganized while he was there. To Central Viet Nam, Pham Van Dong was sent to do what was believed to be a similar job of tightening the grip of Communist control; and then he returned to the north to become Vice-President of the Viet Minh government. More and more important posts in both the administration and the army were taken over by the Communists. They were, by then, holding the reins of power in all the various organizations through which the Viet Minh controlled the people, such as the movements of peasants, workers, women, and youth. Party committees paralleled all the administrative committees and held the real power behind them, and more political commissars were attached to the army, linking its scattered units into a framework of ideological orthodoxy.

From abroad, radical Chinese Communist leaders called the tune for these moves. In November 1949 the Viet Nam Federation of Labor sent delegates to the Asian and Australasian Trade Union Conference in Peking at which the Communist line for Southeast Asia was laid down. Liu Shao-chi, a leading Chinese Communist and an exponent of immediate revolutionary expansionism throughout Southeast Asia, said in his keynote speech: "The national liberation movement and the people's democratic movement in the colonies and the semi-colonies will never stop short of complete victory . . . The great victory of the Chinese people has set them the best example." He then proceeded to lay down the methods to achieve this victory:

[the] nationwide front must be led by and built around the working class, which opposes imperialism most resolutely, most courageously, and most unselfishly, and its party, the Communist Party, with the latter as a center. It must not be led by

[7] *Le Monde,* August 24, 1949.
[8] *Combat,* July 23–24, 1949.

the wavering and compromising national bourgeoisie or the petite bourgeoisie and their parties. . . . It is necessary to set up wherever and whenever possible a national army which is led by the Communist Party. . . . The existence and development of the organization of the working class and of the national united front are dependent upon the existence and development of such armed struggles.[9]

This program of action was alien to the Vietnamese scene; it was a prescription for dividing the country, not for uniting it. But the Viet Minh chose to follow the Communist line blindly, and thereby lost the support of leading elements of the population.

Back in Viet Nam, the Federation of Labor held the first national conference of Vietnamese trade unions throughout the Viet Minh zone, with the announced intention of carrying out the plans and decisions of the Peking Conference. Leading Communists attended: Vice-President Pham Van Dong, General Vo Nguyen Giap, and Minister of Labor Nguyen Van Tao. Also present were Truong Chinh, at this time General Secretary of the Marxist Group, and Hoang Quoc Viet, who became Chairman of the new Central Executive Committee of the Federation of Labor; both of them Communists who, although perhaps not as well known as some others, wielded great influence in the Viet Minh.

As the Chinese Communists moved closer to the Vietnamese frontier, the Viet Minh radio hailed their victories. In December 1949 they arrived at the Tonkinese border and raised their red flag at the international bridge linking Mon Cay with Tunghing. The Viet Minh rushed to recognize the new regime and early in 1950, when the Viet Minh sent out requests for recognition to a number of countries, Communist China was naturally the first to recognize it.

On January 30, 1950 the Soviet Union also recognized the Ho Chi Minh government on the ground that it represented the overwhelming majority of the population of the country. This Soviet move deserves some comment; it has generally been misinterpreted by the West and by the Viet Minh itself. It did not necessarily mean that the Soviet Union had chosen to recognize the Ho government because of its Communist leadership, but rather appeared to have been undertaken within the framework of the Soviet policy of supporting anti-imperialist-minded regimes. Another illustration of this policy was the recognition of the Sukarno government in Indonesia a little more than a year after it had crushed a Communist revolt in Madiun and executed its principal leaders. American Secretary of State Dean Acheson apparently did not take into account such Soviet subtleties when he gave the coup de grâce to Western sympathy for the Viet Minh by declaring that Russian recognition should remove "any illusions as to the 'nationalist' nature of Ho Chi Minh's aims and reveals Ho in his true colors as the mortal enemy of native inde-

[9] New China News Agency, November 23, 1949.

pendence in Indochina."[10] Marshal Tito of Yugoslavia, having only recently been weaned from Stalinism, understood the Soviet action better and agreed to recognize the Ho Chi Minh regime. It is true that overzealous Viet Minh spokesmen rebuffed him several times, and the Viet Minh radio reported sharp criticism of Tito by the Communist-controlled Federation of Labor.[10a] In 1952 the Viet Minh sent an ambassador to Moscow.

If Secretary Acheson's remarks about Ho were not completely valid at the time of the Soviet recognition, Viet Minh leaders did their best to give them more substance; by the time the Viet Minh celebrated the fifth anniversary of the August Revolution which had brought it to power, it had clearly chosen to antagonize the United States. Ho Chi Minh said in August 1950, when American aid to the French army was just beginning to trickle into Indochina:

Since the beginning of the war the Americans have tried to help the French bandits. But now they have advanced one more step to direct intervention in Viet Nam. Thus we have now one principal opponent—the French bandits—and one more opponent—the American interventionists ...

On our side, a few years of resistance have brought our country the greatest success in the history of Viet Nam—recognition of the Democratic Republic of Viet Nam as an equal in the world democratic family by the two biggest countries in the world—the Soviet Union and democratic China—and by the new democratic countries. That means that we are definitely on the democratic side and belong to the anti-imperialist bloc of 800 million people.[11]

The Viet Minh radio said: "If the Communist Party did not exist, it is certain that there would have been no August Revolution and no Democratic Republic of Viet Nam."[12]

Marxist indoctrination permeated the directing elements in the Viet Minh zones. In 1950 Tran Van Giau, Communist veteran of the Committee of the South and recently returned from a mission in Southeast Asia, was appointed to the important post of Director of the Viet Nam Central Information Service. The Viet Nam Youth Association and the Viet Nam Peasants Association gave courses in political ideology, and the Federation of Labor announced as one of its goals "the raising of the political and moral standards of the laboring masses according to the revolutionary spirit." In July 1950 a Cabinet decree ordered government personnel in state-owned factories to devote six hours a week of office time to the study of such subjects as dialectical and historical materialism. In south Central Viet Nam a training program was announced to teach officials and workers in the factories that "the administrative machine

---

10 *Department of State Bulletin*, February 13, 1950, p. 244.

10a The pointlessness of this excess of zeal cannot be better illustrated than by the Russian moves in 1953 to alter their policy toward Tito and seek a diplomatic rapprochement with Yugoslavia.

11 Voice of South Viet Nam, August 16, 1950.

12 Viet Nam News Agency, August 17, 1950.

of Viet Nam is a machine serving the people, the basis of which is the peasantry. Leadership is reserved for the proletarian class."

Among the peasant masses, on the contrary, the Viet Minh emphasized the nationalist character of the war. The campaign against literacy went on, and the Ho Chi Minh government claimed to have reduced the illiteracy rate to 20 percent in 1950. The Vietnamese press, almost nonexistent in 1945, five years later was said to have a circulation of two million copies daily in the Viet Minh zones. But, above all, the new literacy opened the way to more intensive indoctrination in the ideology of the Viet Minh revolution. Friendship with China was emphasized, and the United States was attacked as well as France; in Viet Minh propaganda Bao Dai often appeared as an American puppet.

With the end of the summer rainy season, the fighting became bitter, as it had year after year; it was the pattern of the war in Indochina. But in 1950, for the first time, Chinese Communist troops were just across the border. The Viet Minh dropped its guerrilla tactics to open a full-scale attack on French positions along the Chinese frontier. It was a sudden and victorious offensive. Cao Bang was the first frontier post to fall and over 3,000 Frenchmen died in the evacuation. In rapid succession That Khe, Na Cham, Dong Dang, Lang Son, Dinh Lap, and Thai Nguyen fell to the Viet Minh.

In Paris, Premier René Pleven told the disquieted National Assembly that 20,000 Viet Minh troops had been trained and fully equipped inside Chinese territory. He said that the Viet Minh had received from Communist China a large quantity of mortars, artillery, automatic weapons, and radio equipment.

From this time on the specter of full-scale Chinese intervention on the side of the Viet Minh hung over all French and American discussion of the Vietnamese war. Chinese aid increased during 1951 when the Chinese apparently feared that the Korean War might lead to a United Nations attack on China. When no such attack materialized, the extent of Chinese aid diminished and in 1952 it was reliably reported to have been considerably less than the previous year.[13] Apart from the very important training of Vietnamese soldiers on Chinese soil and the sending of Chinese advisers, technicians, and officers to Viet Nam, Chinese aid was made up of relatively limited supplies of arms and materiel; it was economic, including such items as machinery and tools, as well as military. With the substantial exception of coal, most of the mineral resources of North Viet Nam were in the hands of the Viet Minh, which nationalized them; and wolfram, tin, manganese, and zinc, along with rice, opium, rubber, and timber, were reportedly being sent to China in at least partial payment for Chinese aid.

Perhaps the most significant aspect of this aid was not the increase in strength that it brought to the Viet Minh, but rather what it failed to bring. Most conspicuously lacking was Chinese help in building and supplying a

[13] *Times* (London), January 28, 1953.

Vietnamese air force, without which each Viet Minh offensive was bound to end in a bath of blood as was the case with the ill-fated Viet Minh attack in the Tonkin delta in 1951. In 1953 a London *Times* correspondent commented: "Assaults such as those against Nghia Lo and recently against Na Sam and Phat Diem would not have been possible without artillery from China. Nevertheless, neither in quantity nor in the nature of the weapons supplied has Chinese aid been decisive."[14] The main objective of Chinese policy seemed to be not so much to enable the Viet Minh to win a military victory as to maintain it at fighting strength; Pham Le Bong, formerly an important Lien Viet official, who fled to the Bao Dai zone late in 1952, told of the existence of an agreement providing for Chinese intervention only in case the Viet Minh suffered a decisive defeat.[15]

Courting Chinese help, however, Vietnamese Communists in the meantime had arrived at the logical conclusion of their political maneuvers. On March 3, 1951 a congress was reported to have been held in Viet Minh territory. Ho Chi Minh was present as were a number of leading Vietnamese and Ho Tung Mau, one of the founders of the Indochinese Communist Party, made a short speech. Then there mounted the rostrum not one of the popular and well-known Communist leaders but a man who was relatively unknown, Truong Chinh, a veteran of Ho Chi Minh's old Revolutionary Youth League who had been made General Secretary of the underground Communist Party in 1941. At this meeting ten years later, Truong Chinh announced the formation of the Viet Nam Lao Dong (Workers) Party, which he called "the vanguard and general staff of the working class and working people of Viet Nam."[16]

The Indochinese Communist Party, formally abolished in the fall of 1945, had been openly reconstituted under a new label, and Truong Chinh was its General Secretary. Rightly or wrongly, many Vietnamese regarded the rise of men like Truong Chinh, who had not played a particularly heroic part in the early days of the Democratic Republic of Viet Nam, as indicating a shift in power within the Viet Minh, away from the militant leaders and in favor of bureaucratic elements relatively removed from the people and more inclined to political extremism.

At the same time, the Viet Minh, which had found itself losing much of its coalition character as the war went on, decided to reassert the unity of the various groups resisting the French. It tried to broaden its political base by completing a long-announced merger with the Lien Viet, the national front formed in the spring of 1946, and the Viet Minh radio claimed that 8,000,000

[14] *Ibid.*
[15] *Le Monde*, January 28, 1953.
[16] Viet Nam News Agency, April 10, 1951. Truong Chinh is the assumed name of Dang Xuan Khu.

people were united in the new front under the presidency of Ton Duc Thang, a veteran revolutionary. It is permissible to regard this alleged unity with skepticism.

In March 1951 the Communist Party, now the new Lao Dong Party, announced its membership in the Lien Viet. To preserve the façade of democracy, the various political and social groups operating in the Viet Minh zones also went through the forms of declaring their allegiance to the Lien Viet. The Democratic Party was even designated as the official party of the petite bourgeoisie, the intellectuals, the landowners, and the "progressive bourgeois" classes. However, the arrogant manner in which the Lao Dong Party had declared its existence to the other parties in the Lien Viet left no doubt as to where the real power lay.

NATIONALISM IN CAMBODIA AND LAOS

Even as the Viet Minh consolidated its control over the resistance zone in Viet Nam, it reached out into Laos and Cambodia. These countries also had their nationalists, some working with the French, some openly against them.

Both Laos and Cambodia had Issarak or "Free" movements which dated back to the war years. After the arrest of Cambodian Prime Minister Son Ngoc Thanh in 1945, some Cambodians had fled to Siam, at this time still under a regime friendly to Indochinese nationalists. Aided by the Vietnamese and the Siamese, the Khmer Issarak (Free Cambodians) organized a small military force in Battambang, one of the Cambodian provinces seized by Siam during the war and still under Siamese rule.[17] Other Cambodians, who had taken refuge in Cochin China, appealed from Vietnamese territory to the Cambodian people to rise against the French. There was fighting throughout the Battambang region by the end of 1946 and it was no longer safe to visit the famous ruins of Angkor Wat, a massive and impressive reminder of the vanished splendors of the Khmer Empire, which lay in the forests of Siemreap not far from the Siamese border.

Bangkok became the foreign capital of the Indochinese nationalist movement. The Viet Minh had an active delegation in Bangkok which issued propaganda and smuggled home arms and supplies for the Vietnamese army. The Free Cambodians reorganized in the Siamese capital, although they never succeeded in uniting among themselves, and in Cambodia each Issarak chief maintained his own private army and ruled his own piece of territory. The Free Laotians brought their government to Bangkok after their defeat in the spring of 1946, and thousands of their compatriots came with it.

To foreign visitors, Free Laotian leaders deplored the traditional stereotype

---

17 By the Treaty of Washington, signed in November 1946 by Siam and France, the three Cambodian provinces and the sections of Laos on the right bank of the Mekong which had been seized by the Siamese in 1941, were returned to the two Indochinese states.

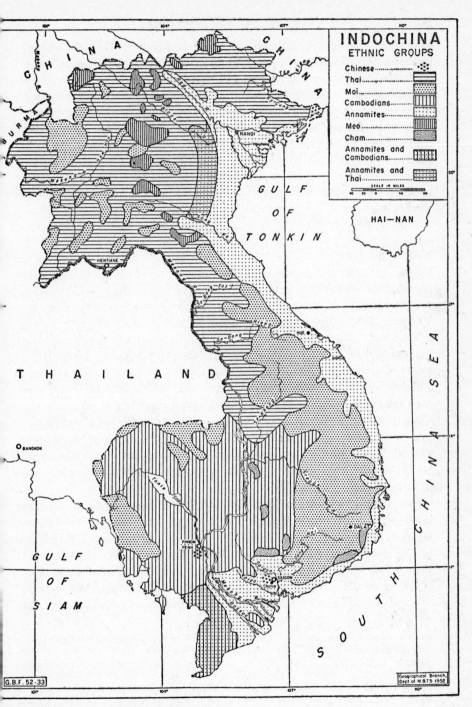

of the Laotians—as a simple and happy people who spent their days playing music and making love. Prince Petsarath had a plan for developing the natural wealth of Laos, its mines, forests, and waterfalls. To attract the foreign capital necessary for such an undertaking, he proposed to lease the natural resources of Laos on forty-year concessions, with the Laotian Government holding a majority of the stock. Petsarath headed the Free Laotians, surrounded by an elaborate protocol and flanked by his two brothers, Souvanna Phouma, more friendly to the French than the others, and Souphanouvong, commander of the Free Laotian guerrillas, who was known to be pro-Vietnamese. Another wing of the Laotian Issarak was led by Thao Oun, who had worked with the Allies against the Japanese during the war.

In 1946 and 1947 the word came along the Mekong that the French were sending Laotian and Cambodian troops into action against the Vietnamese. Neither the Laotians nor the Cambodians were particularly friendly to the Vietnamese; they were sensitive to old memories of Vietnamese expansion to the West, and nationalists were inclined to be critical of the many Vietnamese used by the French as administrators in Cambodia and Laos before the war. The Free Laotian government indeed had plans to place a quota on both Vietnamese and Chinese immigration into Laos (and the Laotian Government has, in fact, restricted the immigration of both peoples). However, the Issarak were prepared to make common cause with the Vietnamese against the French and they were bitter at seeing their compatriots drafted. This attitude was not confined to the exiles. At home, in Cambodia, the newly formed Democratic Party urged the withdrawal of Cambodian troops from Cochin China in order to avoid friction with the Vietnamese. In national elections held in December 1947 the Democrats, who also stood for larger autonomy for Cambodia and broad democratic rights for the people, won more than two-thirds of the seats in the new Cambodian assembly.

Cambodia and Laos had both held elections to constituent assemblies the previous year—the first elections in their history. The old absolute monarchies, which had long existed more in memory than in reality, were abolished; and in 1947 under the active sponsorship of their Kings, in collaboration with the French, both countries became constitutional monarchies, guaranteeing democratic rights with popularly elected assemblies and responsible Cabinets.[18] They joined the French Union as Associated States early in 1948, although they

---

[18] The two governments were much alike, although the Laotian constitution gave somewhat more power to the King than the Cambodian. There was in the Laotian constitution no blanket provision like that in the Cambodian which required the King to have all his public acts countersigned by the Prime Minister and at least one other Minister. The Laotian King, unlike the Cambodian monarch, was permitted, on exceptional occasions when the deputies could not assemble, to issue legislative acts by royal decree, subject to eventual assembly ratification. The Cambodian assembly had to be convened at least twice a year for three-month sessions; in Laos only one such session was provided for, and this the King could either extend or terminate.

did not sign treaties formalizing their new status until after the signing of the Franco-Vietnamese Elysée Accords the following year, and sent representatives to the Assembly of the French Union.

Although in both countries the Kings retained substantial powers, not all of which were delineated in their constitutions, the change in political forms was nonetheless a sweeping one, giving opposition elements for the first time a legal medium for the expression of their views. But the new constitutions did not appease the Issarak. Some of the popular unrest was simply banditry and some was derived from personal rivalries, but much of it was rooted in nationalism: the new constitutions had to function within the framework of the *modi vivendi* signed with France in 1946, and although Laos and Cambodia had achieved a considerable political autonomy, the two countries continued to live under a nationwide network of French control.

Predominantly peasant countries with virtually no middle class, Laos and Cambodia were undeveloped industrially, their economy was in the hands of the French, the Chinese, and the Vietnamese, and much of their administration, where it was not French, was Vietnamese. They had only a small upper class of landowners, intellectuals, officials, and nobility. They had, as a result, few trained administrators to take over the posts left open to them by the French. Their financial resources were inadequate (leaving them dependent upon French economic aid), and corruption was widespread in the government and the administration. But of all their internal problems, the most serious was the insecurity prevailing in both countries.

Laotian and Cambodian government appeals to the Issarak to surrender were left unanswered. After November 1947, when Pibul Songgram, the pro-Japanese wartime dictator, returned to the Premiership of Siam, the Siamese Government became less tolerant of Indochinese nationalist movements in exile and placed numerous restrictions on their activities. (It seemed particularly fearful of Vietnamese Communism, both inside and outside Viet Nam, and in 1950, after a Cabinet crisis on the issue, it recognized the Bao Dai government, one of the few Far Eastern states to do so.) When the Pibul Songgram government made it difficult for them to operate in Siam, Khmer Issarak leaders fled to Western Cochin China, where they sought Viet Minh help. Several thousand of the Issarak even allied themselves with the Viet Minh which apparently made every effort to dominate the Free Cambodians, even sending political commissars to attempt to indoctrinate them in Communism. In 1949, when King Norodom Sihanouk again offered an amnesty to the insurgents if they would lay down their arms, warning them against the Communism of the Viet Minh, a certain number nevertheless continued to collaborate with the Vietnamese and were eventually organized under Viet Minh auspices into a United Issarak Front and a Provisional Committee of National Liberation. Some Issarak, however, accepted the King's offer.

Even while they challenged the established governments in Laos and Cambodia, the Issarak maintained connections with legal political movements in both countries. In Laos they even claimed the sympathy of King Sisavong Vong, pointing out that he had never revoked any of the agreements he had signed with the Free Laotians. In Cambodia, where in 1948 French authorities uncovered the so-called Black Star conspiracy leading to the arrest of several Democratic Party members because of their anti-French activities, the Khmer Issarak had close ties with elements of the Democratic Party.

Not unaware of the close correlation between their internal difficulties and their position in the French Union, Cambodian Government circles began to demand a treaty to supersede the unpopular *modus vivendi* of 1946 with a new and more real independence. In the Assembly of the French Union at Versailles, Cambodian representatives asked for a new treaty. And at Pnom Penh, in November 1948, King Norodom Sihanouk said at a public ceremony attended by the High Commissioner: "I spoke of independence because I am fully convinced that this word and everything it implies constitutes the key to our problem."[19]

The Cambodian Government did not conceal its displeasure as it watched the Vietnamese win concessions from the French with the Elysée Agreements which seemed to be denied to the other Associated States. Only later in 1949 did Cambodia and Laos sign similar accords with France, the Laotians on July 19, the Cambodians (delayed by a series of French Cabinet crises) not until November 6, 1949.

As a result of the July 19 agreement, the Free Laotian government in Bangkok announced its dissolution; it declared that independence had been achieved. In November 1949 High Commissioner Pignon's plane left Bangkok for Vientiane, the Laotian capital, with twenty-five members of the Free Laotian government aboard. Attempts by Laotians on both sides to reach an agreement had finally been successful; and less than two years later Prince Souvanna Phouma became Prime Minister in the government of King Sisavong Vong.

Neither Prince Petsarath nor Prince Souphanouvong went back with the others. Petsarath apparently decided to withdraw from politics, but Souphanouvong threw in his lot with the Viet Minh, and in the fall of 1950 the Viet Minh radio announced that a Laotian People's United Front had been formed, headed by Souphanouvong.

By 1950 Viet Minh supply routes from Bangkok crossed Laos, stretching to Vinh in north Central Viet Nam. The Viet Minh also brought its arms and medical supplies across southern Cambodia into South Viet Nam and controlled much of the Cambodian coast on the Gulf of Siam. Several Issarak bands remained at large in Cambodia, some, but not all, in alliance with the

[19] Radio Saigon, November 14, 1949.

Viet Minh, and the Cambodian Government was anxious to increase its armed forces and take over from the French the job of pacification. The French frequently promised arms for a large Cambodian army, but they did not materialize according to Prime Minister Yem Sambaur, who said in March 1950, "We hope this is a matter on which we can get American help."[20]

When political squabbles among its members caused the King to dissolve the Cambodian National Assembly in 1949, new elections were put off because of the prevailing insecurity; they were not held until the summer of 1951 when the Democratic Party won another victory.[21] In the two intervening years Norodom Sihanouk ruled without a parliament and appointed Cabinet after Cabinet, each of which fell because it could not command support. And each new Prime Minister placed at the top of his program the need to put down the spreading unrest. Conditions became so bad that there was no safety for the traveler outside the cities. Production of rice and rubber fell, leading to deficits in tax receipts which the government needed to support its administration.

The Issarak leader, Dap Chhuon, had surrendered not merely to receive an amnesty, but also to have his several hundred followers integrated into the Khmer forces as a "free corps," and they brought peace to western Cambodia; for the first time in years it was possible to visit Angkor Wat unmolested. Prime Minister Yem Sambaur pointed to the peace that Dap Chhuon had imposed on Siemreap as showing what Cambodian troops could accomplish when left to themselves, but French officials were not nearly as confident and General des Essars, commander of French troops in Cambodia, was seriously concerned over Dap Chhuon's activities. A British writer described an interview he had with the French commander in 1950:

It seemed that a certain, quite unforeseen element had suddenly cropped up. It was to be feared, in fact, that Dap Chhuon was no decent, reliable, straightforward bandit after all. Either he had never been one of the old school of dependable tiger's-liver-eating thugs, or in some mysterious way he had been corrupted, being now, indeed, suspected of having turned Communist. The latest news of him was that he had put one of his men in each of the villages, who had presented the Notables with a list of reforms to be carried out. That was the state of affairs. Apart from all the bother the Viet Minh gave, they now had their own people, who used to be satisfied with looting pigs and rice, going in for all this silly nonsense. The General wondered how long it would be before he had to send his planes to Siemreap.[22]

[20] New York Times, March 26, 1950.

[21] Since their victory in 1947 the Democratic Party had been split by dissension and various individuals and groups had broken away from it, paralyzing constructive political activity. In the 1951 elections, however, the Democrats won 53 seats out of a total of 78. The second party in the assembly, holding 19 seats in 1951, was the more conservative Liberal Party, which was inclined to be less critical of the French than the Democrats and which gave the King more unquestioning support.

[22] Norman Lewis, A Dragon Apparent, pp. 205-6,

The Cambodian Government, for its part, was not at all satisfied with its new treaty with France. It objected to the special rights that the treaty gave to Chinese and Frenchmen, placing them above Cambodian law and exempting them from Cambodian courts. Cambodian nationalists also objected to having French troops so active on Cambodian soil. Early in 1950, Prime Minister Yem Sambaur said:

'We can take care of the Issarak without French help. . . . If the country were really independent there would be no Issarak. There would be no reason for them.'

It was the French air force [Yem Sambaur said, which], on the mere report that Issarak had been seen in them, bombed Cambodian villages off the face of the earth, or the Foreign Legion went into them and massacred the villagers; men, women and children. . . .

And as a result, he said, the country people were turning to Communism. Communism, Yem Sambaur thought, was singularly unsuited to the people of Cambodia; a country without industries and an urban proletariat, and with few rich landowners. But now it was being presented to the people as a way of salvation. That was why you had the phenomenon of Cambodian Issarak chiefs coming to terms with the hitherto detested Vietnamese—a totally unprecedented state of affairs. The best way to convert a villager to Communism was to burn his house down and kill one or more members of his family. In this way you abolished a man's inducements to lead a quiet, respectable existence. When you cut the bonds that tied a man to the existing order, he naturally became a bandit, and if you could persuade him that the Communists would fight his enemies more ruthlessly than the others, well, he would be a Communist too. And that was how the Issarak bands grew, and that was also why they were quite ready to provide themselves, if the Viet Minh suggested it, with political commissars. 'But then, of course [Yem Sambaur said] the transition to Communism is less difficult for an Asiatic, even for members of the upper classes. Perhaps we have less to lose. In any case, the prospect does not alarm us. There are times when one feels that perhaps it would be even better to be a little poorer, if at the same time one could be a little freer.'[23]

Yem Sambaur meant freedom from the French. Like so many Indochinese, he did not seem as much concerned with the other freedoms that would be lost under Communism.

Two years later Yem Sambaur, no longer Prime Minister but still a warm supporter of the King, was arrested in Pnom Penh by order of the Democratic Party government; he was accused of conspiring against the Cambodian Government. This was the same year, 1952, in which Son Ngoc Thanh, who had declared Cambodian independence under the Japanese and ruled as Prime Minister until arrested by General Leclerc, returned to the political limelight.

Son Ngoc Thanh had been permitted to return to Cambodia the previous year and had immediately plunged into politics. Early in 1952 the nationalist newspaper which he had founded in Pnom Penh was closed down by the Cam-

[23] *Ibid.,* p. 208.

bodian authorities and he was accused of fomenting disorders in the country. Apparently fearful of arrest, he fled in March to join the Khmer Issarak, who were still active near the Siamese frontier. They named him president of their Cambodian Committee of National Liberation and he soon entered into close relations with the Viet Minh.

He left behind a disturbed and tense city. The Democratic Party had already been split by divisions within its ranks and some of its members had resigned from the government, accusing it of subservience to France. King Norodom Sihanouk, himself openly critical of French restrictions on Cambodian independence, by then had taken a firm stand against the Issarak. He said:

> These rebels have done nothing which could permit us henceforth to treat them as nationalists, as patriots. On the contrary, they have turned into enemies of the nation and are leading the people toward ruin and slavery. We must consider them as traitors to the constitution and the nation.[24]

When the flight of Son Ngoc Thanh precipitated tension throughout Pnom Penh and student demonstrations against France, the King requested the Democratic government to take strong action against the disorders. Instead, the government promptly arrested one of the King's leading supporters, Yem Sambaur, the former Prime Minister. The King responded in June by dismissing the entire Democratic Cabinet headed by Prime Minister Huy Kanthoul. Norodom Sihanouk took over active leadership of the government and pledged himself to achieve order and independence in three years, after which he would submit himself to the judgment of a people's court with six foreign nations as observers. Under the threat of dissolution, he prevailed upon the Cambodian assembly to grant him full powers. And while the Issarak radio insisted that the King was not a free agent because of the presence of French troops in the country, he assumed personal direction of a military campaign against Son Ngoc Thanh.

In his own capital, Norodom Sihanouk continued his political battle with the Democratic Party and in January 1953 he dissolved the National Assembly, which was dominated by the Democrats, on the grounds that it included numerous elements hostile to the King and linked to the rebels. Then he announced a new attack against the Issarak.

The Viet Minh had strengthened its control over elements of the Issarak in both Laos and Cambodia. The Viet Minh radio announced that in March 1951 delegates from the Cambodian People's United Front, the Laotian People's United Front, and the Viet Minh had met to set up a Joint National United Front for Indochina. For the first time the Free Cambodians and the Free Laotians joined the Viet Minh in attacking the United States as well as

24 *Chroniques d'Outre-Mer*, November 1951.

France. Souphanouvong was reported to have come from Laos, Ton Duc Thang from Viet Nam, and Sieu Heng Young, described as the leader of the "Liberation Army," from Cambodia. The Viet Minh radio issued the United Front manifesto which read:

The French colonialists and the American interventionists are making all-out attempts to conquer Viet Nam, Cambodia and Laos and to enslave these three peoples once again ... The American interventionists are not only plotting to turn these three countries into their colonies but to use them as bases for aggression in China, to suppress the liberation movement of the peoples in Southeast Asia, and to plunge the world into a new World War.

One of the resolutions of the conference declared:

The basic task of the Viet Nam, Cambodian and Laotian revolutions is to drive out the French aggressors and the American interventionists, so as to achieve the genuine independence of Viet Nam, Laos and Cambodia.

For the immediate future the Issarak provided a certain nuisance value against the French. They were, however, of potential political importance to the Viet Minh: whenever the Viet Minh was ready, the Issarak would be the native movements through which the Vietnamese could extend their authority over Laos and Cambodia.

VIET MINH DIFFICULTIES

Until the spring of 1953, when it began its sweep into Laos, the Viet Minh concentrated on the fighting at home. "Increase production!" was the watchword throughout the Viet Minh zones. The "patriotic competition campaign" continued, and "Labor Heroes" were hailed for their accomplishments. The government gave out bonuses and the title of "Model Peasant" for production achievements in agriculture.

At a conference of the Peasants' Association, Truong Chinh said:

The Viet Nam Lao Dong Party confirms the slogan 'The land belongs to the people who work it' as perfectly legitimate. When conditions are right, the Party will resolutely lead the peasant masses to carry out this slogan. However, if conditions do not permit and if any peasant wants to make haste with land reform, the Party will tell him, 'Please wait' ... for the time being, however, the agrarian reform must be carried out smoothly so as to maintain a broad national unity in view of a long-term resistance.[25]

And so the Ho Chi Minh government continued in its efforts to establish cooperatives, to reduce land rents, to regulate usury, and under certain special conditions to cancel all debts. Lands belonging to French "colonialists" and Vietnamese "traitors" were confiscated and redistributed. However, if a Viet-

[25] Viet Nam News Agency, May 8, 1951.

namese landlord was simply living in the French zone but not collaborating with the French, the Viet Minh radio announced that his land would eventually be restored to him. Any land left uncultivated was open to seizure by the government and distribution to the peasants. Only in Cochin China, where most of the big estates were located, could there have been any widespread redistribution of land, but no such redistribution occurred. However, wealthy landlords living in the Viet Minh zones made frequent "contributions" of land to the Ho government, which were sometimes divided up and given to the poorer peasants.

The 25 percent reduction in land rents announced earlier in the Viet Minh zone did not seem to have worked very successfully. In 1950 the order went out for each village to form a Committee for the Implementation of the Land Rent Cut, in which peasants most in need were to have representatives.

In the matter of taxes the Viet Minh encountered even more difficulty. It imposed a multiplicity of levies on the people under its control—taxes on trade, agriculture, industry, imports and exports—many of these taxes called "contributions" or "loans." The government was supported mainly by an agricultural tax in kind. The average peasant, however, had to pay three different taxes to the central government, in addition to a wide variety payable to the regional authorities. He paid a land tax, a contribution in grain to the public stores, another for mass education, another for maintaining regional troops, still another to support the gangs of workmen who repaired the roads. There was also a 10 percent tax on yearly rents. And a price was set at which the peasant had to sell his grain to the government.

Encountering widespread opposition among the peasants to paying all these taxes, the more so because inflation had made the currency issued by the government virtually useless, the Viet Minh declared a sweeping reform in May 1951—it decreed the end of all taxes on agriculture except for an agricultural tax in kind, to be estimated in accordance with the average annual income from lands and ricefields. A one percent regional tax was to go to the regional budget.

As late as 1950, foodstuffs were still said to be cheaper and more abundant in the areas controlled by the Viet Minh. Rice and dried fish were actually shipped from the Viet Minh–held hinterland into Saigon itself, through the intermediary of Chinese merchants who also sold gasoline to the Viet Minh. Even at that time, however, there was extreme austerity in the Viet Minh zones, civilian and military personnel were generally restricted to two meals a day, and manufactured goods were in short supply.

By the following year the situation had deteriorated radically. There were serious shortages of food, salt, cloth, and consumer goods. There was much dysentery, malaria, and tuberculosis; when people fell ill there was no medicine to treat them unless they belonged to the high-level Communist hierarchy, and one of the best-known victims of the soaring tuberculosis death rate was Dang Phuoc Thong, Vice-Minister of Public Works, a nationalist who had followed the government since the early days of the Ho Chi Minh regime. Infant mortality was appallingly high. Air raids added much to the plight of the population, and the napalm bomb did not spare civilians. The fighting also took a heavy toll of the able-bodied and the young; Nguyen Binh, the one-eyed commander of the resistance in South Viet Nam since 1945, was killed during the fall of 1951 fighting in Cambodia.

"We have many defects," Ho Chi Minh said on December 19, 1952, on the sixth anniversary of the Viet Minh attack in Hanoi. He admitted that neither the agrarian policy of the government nor the promised reduction of rent and usurious interest had been completely realized; and that the peasants, who constituted by far the greater part of the Viet Minh armed forces and paid the bulk of the taxes levied by the Viet Minh, were in a precarious position. "For these reasons," he said, "in the coming year our government, our party and the Lien Viet will mobilize the peasants in order to apply strictly the policy of reduction of rents and interest, in order to safeguard the rights of the peasants."[26]

The central committee of the Lao Dong Party reiterated Ho's statements in a report which the *Times* described as reading very much as though it might have been issued from Yenan in 1939; like the Chinese Communists before the war, and unlike the Russians, it emphasized that it was concentrating on a peasants' rather than a workers' revolution. This was only natural in view of the absence of privately-owned industry in the Viet Minh zone. The Lao Dong Party, in any case, had clearly not yet captured the peasant masses, and the name of Truong Chinh, so publicized in 1951 as a leader of the revolution, was not even mentioned in the Peking radio report of the Lao Dong central committee meeting which announced the intention of the party to concentrate on "agitation among the masses" and on strengthening the leadership of the party. It promised not only to reduce land rents and interest rates, but also to secure political supremacy for the peasantry.[27]

However, despite periodic talk about a great counteroffensive that would sweep the French from the country, all the Viet Minh could offer its adherents was more of the same misery and the continuing prospect of an unending and destructive war. This kind of life, with the political police omnipresent, was not of the sort to attract people living in the Bao Dai zones, where they had food and even were able to enjoy some measure of political freedom.

Rebelling against the desperately poor living conditions and the increasingly oppressive orthodoxy of the Viet Minh areas, a number of Vietnamese made their way out of the resistance zones. Some of them came with exit permits

---

[26] *Le Monde*, December 20, 1952.
[27] *Times* (London), February 26, 1953.

issued by the Viet Minh. Others escaped by their own means. Many intellectuals slipped away from the Viet Minh, as did many members of the professional and upper classes—doctors, teachers, lawyers, engineers, landowners, merchants.

In view of the terrible circumstances of life in the Viet Minh zones, the striking fact is not the number of people who left, but the number who stayed behind. They seemed dedicated to a single purpose. "All the prisoners we question are unanimous," Nguyen Van Tam, Prime Minister of the Bao Dai government, said; "they are fighting for the independence of Viet Nam."[28]

When he went on to claim that independence already existed in the Bao Dai zone, however, few Vietnamese believed him. The people who came to the French-controlled areas by and large did not join the French-sponsored government. Like most of the people in the regions ruled by Bao Dai, they became what the Vietnamese called by the picturesque designation of *trum chan* (people who hide under a blanket), and what the French called *attentistes*—men who waited, taking no sides, to see whether it would be possible to find a better answer to Communist dictatorship than the handful of corrupt men who formed the core of the Bao Dai regime at that time.

MORE FRANCO-VIETNAMESE AGREEMENTS

Despite the fact that French officials regarded Bao Dai as the key to their policy of divide and rule, it was still not impossible for the Emperor to turn his position to the advantage of the Vietnamese people and make a Bao Dai policy of his own. He could not do this alone; but in 1949 and early in 1950, the Emperor and his supporters believed that the United States was prepared to help them by bringing pressure to bear on the French to grant them the concessions that Ho Chi Minh demanded on the battlefield. This faith in American policy was incarnated in Nguyen Phan Long, who, as Foreign Minister, urged the application of the Elysée Accords in their broadest sense.

The joint Franco-Vietnamese commissions called for by the Elysée Agreements were slow in getting started with their task of drawing up specific accords, some to implement the master agreements of March 8, some to supplement them; and slower still in reaching agreement on the new conventions. Only on December 30, 1949, were the final agreements signed at a ceremony at the City Hall in Saigon, the provisional seat of the Bao Dai government. High Commissioner Pignon and Bao Dai addressed the crowds from the balcony, and some 50,000 people paraded through the streets, waving red and yellow flags, while church bells and pagoda gongs sounded. *Le Monde* hailed the day as "an important event not only in the evolution of Franco-Vietnamese relations, but also in the history of French policy in the Far East. . . ."[29]

[28] *Chroniques d'Outre-Mer*, November 1952.
[29] *Le Monde*, December 31, 1949.

However, the framework of agreement laid down on March 8, with all its limitations, still held good. The minority areas in Viet Nam were still under French control. The police was still in French hands and was expected to remain there until a French victory over the Viet Minh. Although various armed groups supported it, the Bao Dai regime itself had no army and no independent finances. And the future of the "interstate" organs concerned with such vital matters as foreign trade, customs, finance, and immigration, and still under French control, would only be determined by an "interstate" conference of the French and the three Indochinese governments. (This conference, which was projected for January 1950, did not in fact take place at Pau until six months later.)

All of these factors, and above all the presence of French soldiers and officials on Vietnamese soil, contributed to the conviction of Vietnamese, regardless of their politics, that the French High Commissioner was still in effective control of the country. Even when the French made concessions on paper, French officials were slow in implementing them. They were slow in substituting Vietnamese officials for Frenchmen, slow in delegating power to the Vietnamese government that did exist.

The few able men who rallied to the Bao Dai regime, like Nguyen Huu Tri, Governor of North Viet Nam, did so in the hope that they might yet transform the Elysée Agreements into a more genuine independence. "The Vietnamese regard the March 8 agreements as only a stepping stone," Tri told a reporter early in 1950. "We want full, complete independence. Many intellectuals are waiting because they are afraid to trust the March 8 agreements. We have had many promises in the past. We want now to see real transfer of power." He said that in North Viet Nam there had been a considerable transfer of administrative functions from France to the Vietnamese in education, public welfare, agriculture, public health, public works, and some police powers. But, he said, "in every sphere the French keep back something."[30]

Under these circumstances, it was not surprising that appeals to resistance elements to join the Bao Dai government fell generally on deaf ears. The "psychological shock," for which Frenchmen were always searching in their efforts to split the resistance, failed to materialize. There was pessimism in the Bao Dai camp, pessimism too in the High Commissioner's office, which neither by force nor by political action had succeeded in bringing peace to Indochina. But it seemed that they were to have another chance. The changing international situation brought French officials aid at a time when they were sorely in need of it, and for this they could thank the Viet Minh and the Chinese Communists. As events laid bare the meagerness of France's resources, the successes of the Communists in China transformed the Vietnamese war into a major international problem; and when the Viet Minh made clear its

[30] *New York Times*, March 6, 1950.

friendship for China, the French, no less than the Vietnamese, turned to the United States for help.

RATIFICATION AND RECOGNITION

The United States was deeply concerned by the Communist threat to the balance of power throughout Southeast Asia. During the summer of 1949, Secretary of State Dean Acheson stated unequivocally:

Should the [Chinese] Communist regime lend itself to the aims of Soviet Russian imperialism and attempt to engage in aggression against China's neighbors, we and the other members of the United Nations would be confronted by a situation violative of the principles of the United Nations Charter and threatening international peace and security.[31]

Did this herald a new and vigorous American policy in the Far East? Foreign Minister Nguyen Phan Long told the Associated Press: "I am happy to note the good disposition of the American State Department in regard to the peoples of Southeast Asia. It cannot fail to bring to these people effective guarantees of liberty and security."[32]

Certainly the urgent need of the French for American aid operated to the immediate advantage of Bao Dai early in 1950. If the French were to justify their claim to be fighting in defense of the Bao Dai government, they had little choice but to ratify the Elysée Agreements to which that government owed its existence; only then could they ask the United States for material support in Indochina. Bao Dai himself came to Paris to urge ratification and in January 1950, after ten months of delay which served to weaken further the Emperor's already weak position, the French Parliament began its debate on ratification. The Assembly of the French Union, where delegates from Viet Nam sat for the first time, heard Overseas France Minister Jean Letourneau urge speedy action. "It is evident," he explained, "that as long as Parliament does not recognize this independence, no foreign and friendly state will be disposed to recognize them [Viet Nam, Laos and Cambodia] and thus permit their entrance into international life."[33] Viet Nam needs aid which France itself cannot supply, Paul Devinat, Radical Socialist, told the National Assembly. "It is important, therefore, to give Viet Nam, by the independence that we guarantee it, the means of finding a complementary aid on the international level from the United Nations or from governments which will grant it credits."[34]

Lest there be any doubt that such governments did exist, ready and waiting

[31] Department of State, *United States Relations with China*, p. xvii.
[32] *Le Monde*, August 12, 1949.
[33] *Journal Officiel*, Assemblée de l'Union Française, January 19, 1950, p. 32.
[34] *Ibid.*, Assemblée Nationale, January 27, 1950, p. 586.

to help Bao Dai, United States Ambassador-at-Large Philip C. Jessup took the unusual step, while the French parliamentary debate on ratification was still going on, of extending to Bao Dai in Hanoi on behalf of Secretary of State Acheson, the "confident best wishes" of the American Government "for the future of the State of Viet Nam with which it looks forward to establishing a closer relationship."[35]

Laotian and Cambodian members of the Assembly of the French Union spoke favorably of the agreements that their countries had signed with France in 1949, which were also under consideration (although the Cambodian Government actually was not at all satisfied with the new accord). The agreements were perhaps not perfect, said the Laotian Ourot Souvannavong, because they did not grant full independence. However, he said, the Laotians did not want to overreach themselves, and he expressed the gratitude of the Laotian people for this "gift that France has offered to Laos."[36] He was followed by Princess Yukanthor, who recalled that Cambodia had already been invited to attend international conferences in India and the Philippines, but went on to criticize certain aspects of French policy in Cambodia.[37]

Letourneau declared that the three Associated States had already achieved "internal sovereignty." He said that "France no longer has any direct part in the administration of one or another of these territories."[38] Already, he added, France had surrendered to the Vietnamese the direction of most of the public services of their country: only certain essential public works remained to be transferred. And all fiscal receipts except customs were being collected by the Vietnamese themselves.

Alain Savary set forth the Socialist position. He deplored the limitations in the agreements in regard to foreign affairs and defense, and spoke of:

... clauses which will be superfluous if, as I hope and believe, the relations between our states are good, but useless and dangerous germs of difficulties if, by some misfortune, for lack of reciprocal efforts, tension grows. ... I think also that in regard to the legal and economic conventions, these texts are stamped with too great a distrust and that in independent states you cannot expect to keep for Frenchmen a regime which, whether you like it nor not, recalls that of capitulations.

But in substance the Socialists accepted the treaties with Viet Nam, Laos, and Cambodia. Savary said: "It only remains to ask the government to apply

35 *Department of State Bulletin*, February 13, 1950, p. 244.

36 *Journal Officiel*, Assemblée de l'Union Française, January 19, 1950, p. 52.

37 "I recall," the princess said, "that last August I was invited by the Minister of Overseas France to travel with him in Indochina. When we were in Cochinchina, in Saigon, the Minister had to make a trip to Soc Trang where, you are not unaware, the Cambodian population is dominant. I asked to accompany the Minister on his trip. I was informed that Madame Coste-Floret had invited me to spend the day with her on a plantation." *Ibid.*, p. 53.

38 *Ibid.*, p. 33.

them in the spirit of the constitution and without losing sight for a single instant of the aspect of the new Asia."

At the same time, however, Savary called upon the French Government to act in Indochina by the most effective means and, if need be, by recourse to international authorities.

> In a future which is perhaps not far off, the international aspect of the conflict is likely to become more important than local conditions. This then will be the ultimate solution. For the present, we say to the government that the first condition for reestablishing peace is to launch an immediate appeal for a military truce and then to realize it.[39]

A Socialist proposal for a truce was overruled by the National Assembly, as was a similar proposal introduced by Paul Rivet.[39a]

From the Communist benches, Raymond Barbé protested against what his party regarded as half measures. "It can only be a question of one thing, I say, not of a truce which would be a trap, but of withdrawing the expeditionary force from Indochina, of repatriating it in order to permit the Vietnamese people to direct freely their own affairs."[40] Barbé served notice on the French Government that the Communist Party intended to do everything it could to force this withdrawal by instigating strikes, particularly among sailors and dockyard workers.

The Communists and their friends professed to be concerned about French interests in Indochina. If the war goes on, "what becomes of the interests of French planters, French merchants, French industry?" asked *Progressiste* Jacques Mitterand. He raised the favorite Communist bogey of American imperialism, saying: "The trade is for the United States. The raw materials are for the United States. It is the ruin of French interests which the present government majority represents. . . ."[41]

The debate in the National Assembly was violent and reached a noisy climax when Madame Jeannette Vermeersch, the wife of Communist leader Maurice Thorez, thumbed her nose at the government benches when the Ministers were leaving the hall; when Edouard Herriot, President of the Assembly, reprimanded her, she repeated the gesture.

"It is necessary that the French people know that at the present time the only true enemy of peace in Viet Nam is the Communist Party," said René Pleven, Minister of National Defense. "Because the members of the Com-

---

[39] *Ibid.*, pp. 55–56.

[39a] The Socialist proposal was defeated by a vote of 483 to 109. During the Assembly debate the previous May, Rivet's motion in favor of a truce and general elections in Viet Nam under United Nations control had been defeated by 392 to 196 votes. In January 1950, a similar proposal made by Rivet and a group of Socialists was defeated in a voice vote.

[40] *Ibid.*, p. 57.

[41] *Ibid.*, p. 61.

munist Party know that peace in Indochina will be re-established by the policy of independence that we are following."[42]

"Peace with Viet Nam! Peace with Viet Nam!" the Communists shouted, trying to drown him out.

Men of the Right and Center rose to insist on the importance of the Vietnamese war on the international scene. Summing up, Letourneau said:

It is not at all a question of approving or disapproving a government; we are very far beyond the transitory life of a government in an affair of this gravity. It is necessary that, on the international level, the vote that takes place tonight reveals truly the major importance that this event should have in the eyes of the entire world.[43]

Said Frédéric-Dupont:

The Indochina war has always been the test of the French Union before international Communism. But since the arrival of the Chinese Communists on the frontier of Tonkin, Indochina has become the frontier of Western civilization and the war in Indochina is integrated into the cold war.[44]

Premier Georges Bidault had the last word. "The choice is simple," he said. "Moreover, there is no choice."[45]

After that stormy debate the French National Assembly rallied and voted just after midnight on January 29, 396 to 193, to approve the agreements with Viet Nam, Laos, and Cambodia, the Socialists unenthusiastically joining the majority. From the extreme Left there were cries of "Down with the war!" Paul Coste-Floret retorted: "Long live peace!"

No sooner had the French Government ratified the three treaties on February 2, 1950, than the Western powers swung into action, and on February 7 the United States and Great Britain both recognized Bao Dai; they also recognized the Associated States of Cambodia and Laos. The British Government explained its action with the assertion that the Bao Dai regime was the only one controlling large areas of Viet Nam, with a capital city and a visible government. The British were, however, "anxious that rather more independence should have been given to the Bao Dai government than had, in fact, been given."[46] The State Department said: "This recognition is consistent with our fundamental policy of giving support to the peaceful and democratic evolution of democratic peoples toward self-government and independence."[47] Although the Elysée Agreements had not listed the United States among the

[42] Ibid., Assemblée Nationale, January 27, 1950, p. 625.
[43] Ibid., Assemblée de l'Union Française, January 19, 1950, p. 79.
[44] Ibid., Assemblée Nationale, January 27, 1950, p. 607.
[45] Ibid., January 28, 1950, p. 697.
[46] Parliamentary Debates, House of Commons, February, 1950, 2099.
[47] Department of State Bulletin, February 20, 1950, p. 291.

nations with which Viet Nam was permitted to have direct diplomatic relations, President Truman said that his country looked forward to exchanging diplomatic representatives with the Associated States.

Before the month of February was out, the French Government had put in a formal request to the United States for military and economic aid to Indochina.

Much as the French needed this aid, French officials were prepared to accept it only on their own terms: regardless of the Elysée Agreements, their primary concern was still to strengthen their own position in Indochina, and this was inevitably at Bao Dai's expense. The French distrusted American policy toward the French Empire, fearing American economic inroads into the French colonies. They also feared what they regarded as traditional American anticolonialism, and it was this fear that was uppermost in regard to Indochina. They insisted that if American economic aid were to be delivered directly to the Vietnamese, American military aid at least should go only to the French. General Marcel Carpentier, Commander-in-Chief of the French forces in Indochina, said:

I will never agree to equipment being given directly to the Vietnamese. If this should be done I would resign within twenty-four hours. The Vietnamese have no generals, no colonels, no military organization that could effectively utilize the equipment. It would be wasted, and in China the United States has had enough of that.[48]

When two American warships dropped anchor off Saigon in March 1950 to show American support for Bao Dai, Viet Minh–directed riots broke out in the city. Vietnamese police who arrived on the scene were unwilling to move against the rioters, many refusing even to get down from their trucks; and Governor Tran Van Huu had to call on the French for help. French officials welcomed such practical demonstrations of the weakness of the Bao Dai regime; in all their negotiations with the Americans the French insisted that their strong hand was indispensable in Indochina.

In May, Secretary Acheson announced that the United States would grant military and economic aid to restore security and develop "genuine nationalism" in Indochina. He made a point of saying that this aid would go not only to France but also directly to each of the Associated States, a claim which, by and large, was not immediately substantiated. With the outbreak of war in Korea the following month, President Truman promised that the furnishing of military assistance to the forces of France and the Associated States in Indochina would be accelerated, and an American military mission was dispatched to provide close working relations with those forces. American officials talked of strengthening the Bao Dai government; they even talked to

48 *New York Times*, March 9, 1950.

the French about granting it a more real independence. However, Vietnamese nationalists who had interpreted American recognition as a promise to protect Bao Dai, not merely from the Viet Minh but also from France, soon discovered that their optimism was premature.

THE FAILURE OF NGUYEN PHAN LONG

No one was more aware of the weakness of his position than Bao Dai himself. During all the months of negotiation with the French, relatively little effort had been expended on channeling support behind the Emperor inside Viet Nam and he returned home to find himself in what amounted to a political vacuum. In contrast to the resistance zones, where political life had been efficiently organized by the Viet Minh for its own purposes, the areas under French control were distinguished by their apparent lethargy in political matters.

This could not be explained simply by the fact that the Viet Minh had its clandestine network everywhere, dissuading Vietnamese from collaboration with the French. In this very family-conscious country where blood ties were traced back through many generations and numerous people living in the French-controlled regions had relatives in the resistance with the Viet Minh, communications were never really cut between the different zones; the division between those who fought and those who did not was never absolute nor even clear cut. Superimposed upon and reinforcing the effect of this intricate maze of personal loyalties was the traditional Vietnamese feeling for the unity of the state. Even the many individuals, generally from the professional classes, who were strongly critical of the Viet Minh, would not openly turn against it if the only result of their action would be to divide the country. They did not want to be branded as traitors, or *viet gian*. Instead, with few exceptions, they preferred to withdraw entirely from political life, swelling the ranks of those elements so characteristic of post-1946 Viet Nam— the *trum chan* or *attentistes*.

Nevertheless, there was feverish activity among certain Vietnamese in the areas controlled by the French army, who took advantage of the artificial prosperity engendered by the war, notably the over-valuation of the piastre in reference to the franc. This situation, with the piastre fixed at 17 francs as contrasted with its real purchasing power which was less than half that amount, led to a flight of capital on highly favorable terms from Indochina to France. With the help of a flourishing black market, it permitted the accumulation of vast sums by individuals who bought up dollars with francs and changed the dollars first into piastres and then back into francs, more than doubling the original investment in the process. Nominally the inflation-ridden Indochinese economy, its foreign exchange and its foreign trade, was strictly controlled, but in practice the lack of public morality on the part of a number of Frenchmen and Vietnamese who exploited this period of national tragedy to their own profit led to widespread corruption and speculation. Scandal after scandal produced angry criticism in France and demands for investigation and reform. In Viet Nam, where political office and economic advantage were inevitably linked, the resultant profiteering helped further to discredit the regime in the French zone, to strengthen the *trum chan* in their abstention, and to raise the prestige of the Viet Minh, even among its opponents.

Not only was there no national assembly in the zones nominally ruled by Bao Dai, but there were no political parties—merely self-interested groups, like the Cao Dai and the Hoa Hao in the south or the newly formed Dai Viet in the north, which carved out their own zones of influence in exchange for lending their support to Bao Dai. There was not even a free press. Ostensibly this absence of popular organs gave to Bao Dai a degree of absolute authority he would not otherwise have had; but at the same time it weakened his position in the country, and, although his isolation from the people may have allowed him a certain freedom in making public appointments, it also left him defenseless against French pressure whenever French officials chose to exert it. The limitations inherent in this situation swiftly became apparent when Bao Dai, in January 1950, gave up the post of Prime Minister to Nguyen Phan Long, editor of the *Echo du Viet Nam* and already Minister of Foreign Affairs and Minister of Interior.

Nguyen Phan Long tried to win over members of the resistance, but he did not succeed. He did not even succeed in winning over Vietnamese personalities living outside the Viet Minh zones who refused to collaborate with the French; and in Saigon thirty-one moderate intellectuals signed their names to a manifesto demanding independence for Viet Nam guaranteed by the United Nations, a status equivalent to that of Pakistan, the withdrawal of French troops to certain bases as a preliminary to evacuating the country, and national unity in Viet Nam based on progressive democratic principles—much the same terms as those demanded by Ngo Dinh Diem.

So far as his appeals to the resistance were concerned, all Nguyen Phan Long accomplished was to alienate the French authorities who were concerned, above all, to prevent the country from uniting against them. He did something even more dangerous to his political career than that; no sooner was he in office than he appealed for American military and economic aid direct to Viet Nam without the benefit of French intermediaries. He made no secret of his desire to build up a Vietnamese army. The people wanted their own troops, not Frenchmen, he said, to occupy regions taken over from the Viet Minh. Let the United States give him some $146,000,000 for economic reconstruction and for a national army, and he said he could defeat Ho Chi Minh in six months.

The Dai Viet in North Viet Nam, which supported Governor Nguyen Huu Tri and was made up largely of former mandarins, chose this time to assert its power in the new central government. In March 1950 three Dai Viet Ministers—the only Tonkinese in the Long Cabinet—resigned, and issued a statement accusing Nguyen Phan Long of an equivocal attitude toward Communism; they said that he was playing into the hands of the "ultra-nationalists."

Nguyen Phan Long's pro-American policy had antagonized the French administration; and he had no political party or movement from which he could draw strength. When French officials directed Bao Dai to dismiss him, the Emperor did so, in May 1950.

The dismissal of Nguyen Phan Long demonstrated the impossibility of making an independent policy in Viet Nam without popular support. It marked a new stage in the politics of the Bao Dai regime, which, as it continued to maneuver to win more concessions from the French, was characterized by three features:

First, an end to attempts to woo the Communist-led resistance, and the institution of the "campaigns and reprisals" against the Viet Minh toward which Léon Pignon had directed French policy for so long.

Second, appointment of men who had been active in the Cochin Chinese separatist movement to almost all of the key posts in the Bao Dai government (with the notable exceptions of Prince Buu Loc, Vietnamese High Commissioner in Paris, and his associate, Nguyen Dac Khe). The spokesman of Cochin Chinese separatism, Tran Van Ty, had expressed their opinion very frankly when he said: "Independence? If France offered it to us tomorrow, I would refuse it."[49]

Third, however, and the most significant for the future of Viet Nam, was the emergence of an articulate public opinion in all levels of Vietnamese society, which forced even such men to assume an increasingly nationalistic position.

TRAN VAN HUU AND THE PAU CONFERENCE

Nguyen Phan Long was succeeded as Prime Minister by Tran Van Huu, a wealthy landowner and a French citizen, who resigned as Governor of South Viet Nam to accept the post. In his inaugural speech Huu appealed to "the lukewarm, the hesitant, to take a position. The equivocation must stop." He said:

Those who, inspired by their devotion to Communism, believe they can have recourse with impunity to terrorism to force the people to submit will not benefit from any indulgence. Those who become their accomplices by abusing the liberty

[49] Devillers, op. cit., p. 393.

of the press in this country, will also be dealt with so that they cannot do any harm.[50]

But these words, backed up though they were by police action against individuals suspected of relations with the Viet Minh and by rigorous control of the press to end "subversive propaganda" and "lying or tendentious campaigns," did not awaken much of a response among the many who remained uncertain and critical of the Bao Dai regime.

In 1950 the rumor spread that Prince Cuong De might return home after almost half a century of exile. In the name of the Phuc Quoc, Cuong De had taken an independent nationalist stand ever since the beginning of the Franco-Vietnamese war. He had even appealed to Ho Chi Minh, in a letter to the Vietnamese press, acknowledging his patriotism but urging him to take into account the international situation and step down in favor of others who would be more acceptable to the West. Critical though Cuong De was of the Communist leadership of the Viet Minh, when Bao Dai sent him a message through the French Embassy in Tokyo, inviting him to come back to Viet Nam, Cuong De refused to support the Bao Dai government, convinced that it was still under French control. In 1950, however, he tried to go to Bangkok; but the Siamese Government did not permit him to land, and he went back to Japan. Cuong De died in Tokyo the following year. For decades his name had been synonymous with the dream of many Vietnamese for independence; and once it had been a rallying call for risings and revolutionary organization. But Cuong De had been away too long and the news of his death made little stir in Viet Nam. New political forces had crystallized in his homeland since his departure and new leaders, in closer touch with the people, had come to the fore.

For Bao Dai, laboring under the political burden of continuing French control over the regions he was supposed to rule, it was difficult enough to make contact with these forces and leaders. Early in 1951, when the Emperor directed Tran Van Huu to broaden his Cabinet in order to bring into it more representative elements, only the Dai Viet accepted his invitation; and its association with Tran Van Huu lasted a much shorter time than even its abortive collaboration with Nguyen Phan Long. Hardly had news of the new Cabinet been bruited, than Tran Van Huu clashed openly with Nguyen Huu Tri.

Formerly a mandarin under the French administration, Nguyen Huu Tri had gravitated naturally toward the ex-mandarins and government officials united in the Dai Viet; and they, in turn, had proceeded to consolidate their political position in the north under the protection of Governor Tri. Nguyen Huu Tri's administrative experience had stood him in good stead; he had brought some efficiency to the government of North Viet Nam. But when he

[50] *Bulletin d'Information de la France d'Outre-Mer,* June 1950.

challenged the autonomous bishoprics of Phat Diem and Bui Chu, two pre-dominantly Catholic regions in central North Viet Nam, he found that he had overreached himself.

Phat Diem and Bui Chu had been autonomous even under the Viet Minh which, at first, had been very careful of Catholic sensibilities, and Le Huu Tu, Bishop of Phat Diem, had been named Supreme Advisor to the Ho Chi Minh government in 1946 after Bao Dai left for China. In other sections of the country the revolution had been marked by a wholesale overthrow of the old village councils and their replacement by supporters of the Viet Minh, but in the Catholic areas the Viet Minh had left intact the village com-mittees and the Catholic hierarchy. However, the Viet Minh had become more demanding with the passage of time and had insisted on introducing its own men into the government of even the largely Catholic villages. This had become a matter of serious concern for Le Huu Tu, and when Bao Dai invited him to accept his authority, the Bishop agreed, on condition that no white troops would appear in his diocese. In October 1949 French land troops moved in force on Phat Diem and on the neighboring diocese of Bui Chu —the home of some 350,000 Catholics—but only Vietnamese parachutists were dropped.

Le Huu Tu had maintained wide freedom of action even under the Viet Minh; and his regime and that of the Bishop of Bui Chu remained autono-mous under Bao Dai. They raised their own troops and ruled their own do-mains, holding both civil and religious power in their own hands. And the church spires continued to stand out over the devastated landscape for, in that, at least, the Viet Minh had seen no reason deliberately to antagonize the Catholic community. As for the French, the Most Rev. Peter Ngo Dinh Thuc, like his brother Ngo Dinh Diem highly critical of the Bao Dai government, remarked that the French did not ignore "the strategic importance of the area, controlling as it does a section of the route to rice-producing Tonkin, nor the opportunity of consolidating the territory in non-Communist hands. Bao Dai followed the example of Ho Chi Minh and appointed the Bishops as *his* representatives in the area. An odd situation, surely."[51]

Nguyen Huu Tri, however, supported by the Dai Viet, tried to encroach upon the semi-independent status of the two Bishops and to bring them di-rectly under his authority as Governor of North Viet Nam. This attempt to increase his power played into the hands of Prime Minister Tran Van Huu. While Huu was still Governor of South Viet Nam, an equal in rank with Tri, he had missed no opportunity to assert the independent rights of Cochin China. But such tactics were no longer to his taste when he became Prime Minister; like his predecessor, General Xuan, his concern was now to subordi-

<hr>

[51] Most Rev. Peter Ngo-Dinh-Thuc, "Viet-Nam Through Vietnamese Eyes." *World-mission,* February 1951, p. 70.

nate the three Governors to himself, and he was wary of seeing Nguyen Huu Tri and the Dai Viet become strongly entrenched in the north. To break their hold on North Viet Nam at a time when their dispute with the Bishops had already caused them to be criticized in many quarters, he offered to Tri the post of National Defense in the central government and then, with Tri's conditional acceptance, proceeded to appoint to other Cabinet posts various separatists who were unacceptable to Tri. When Tri refused to join this Cabinet, Huu forced him to resign his Governorship as well; and other Dai Viet members who had just been named to the Cabinet also resigned.

The Tran Van Huu Cabinet, even after its reshuffle in 1951, in the tradition of previous Cabinets in the French-controlled areas consisted of a group of men with neither power nor parties behind them. But the practice of national authority seemed of itself to create a national point of view and Tran Van Huu soon found himself in the position of asserting Vietnamese rights. He encountered great difficulty in winning concessions from the French on internal affairs, but in the field of international relations he found them not adverse to making concessions which might strengthen their claim to be concerned primarily with the fight against Vietnamese Communism. His tenure of office was thus marked by various diplomatic achievements. Under Tran Van Huu, for example, the new regime progressed a definite step beyond the Elysée Agreements and announced its intention of establishing diplomatic relations not only with India, Siam, and the Vatican, but also with the United States and Great Britain. All limitations on its right to diplomatic representation were eventually dropped and Viet Nam was granted the privileges of full diplomatic status in each country which recognized it.

Tran Van Huu went to France in June 1950 to join representatives of France, Laos, and Cambodia for discussions at Pau on the "interstate structure" of Indochina, which had been provided for in the Elysée Agreements. This conference, originally scheduled to end in August, dragged on until the end of November. It was the first time since the Fontainebleau Conference four years before that Vietnamese delegates had confronted Frenchmen across a conference table in metropolitan France. The Vietnamese political situation had altered so much since 1946 that Nguyen Dac Khe and Nguyen Quoc Dinh, the same Vietnamese legal advisers who, with Phan Anh and in the name of the Ho Chi Minh government, had carried a major share of the work at Fontainebleau, were active at Pau on behalf of the Bao Dai government.

The three Indochinese delegations were at Pau to decide, in agreement with the French, on the forms and powers of the organs which would take over from the French administration the postal, telephone, and telegraph services of Indochina; immigration control; foreign trade and customs; finance and economic planning. There was no question of France reassuming on the federal level the powers that it had recognized as belonging to the

Associated States, Letourneau assured the assembled delegates. But it was important, he said, that each of the three states strengthen itself by supporting interstate bodies which could operate in liaison with the French Government.

Was there much difference between the old Indochinese Federation and the new interstate organs? In the six months that the conference went on, it was sometimes difficult to know. Vietnamese delegates complained that the French were trying to reassert their control over Indochina; and Prime Minister Huu, who had rushed home to Viet Nam on the occasion of the serious French reverses on the northern frontier in the fall of 1950, went so far as to demand a new and more equal treaty to supersede the Elysée Agreements. "It is not necessary for young men to die so that a French engineer can be director of the port of Saigon," he said. "Many people are dying every day because Viet Nam is not given independence. If we had independence the people would have no more reason to fight." Huu appealed to the United States "as the leading democratic nation" and said, "We hope America and Britain will bring pressure on France in order to achieve democratic freedom. We want the right to decide our own affairs for ourselves."[52]

Other delegates at Pau were suspicious of what they regarded as Vietnamese attempts at domination. The Cambodians brought up the questions of free navigation on the Mekong River and of administration of the port of Saigon, both of which had been under the control of the French High Commissioner. They were important to Cambodia and, to a lesser extent, to Laos; both countries depended on them to carry much of their trade through South Viet Nam to the sea.

The Vietnamese had hoped to leave these questions to direct talks with Cambodia; but the Cambodians claimed French support at Pau and discussions went on for six difficult weeks. The delegates finally agreed to set up a consultative commission of the four states to direct navigation on the Mekong; it was to sit at Pnom Penh and be presided over by a Cambodian. The Vietnamese protested the presence of Frenchmen on the commission as a survival of the old federal structure, but they protested in vain when Frenchmen pointed out that 100 percent of the military fleet using the Mekong was French, as was 80 percent of the commercial shipping.

For the port of Saigon they worked out a similar agreement. Vietnamese sovereignty was to be respected but the three other states were to be granted free and equal rights in the port. In effect, at Saigon as on the Mekong, the French were left in control of navigation and the police.

The various items on the agenda of the Pau Conference took much longer to deal with than had been expected. It was not difficult to dispose of the Indochinese postal, telephone, and telegraph systems, which reverted to the control of the state in which they operated. They were to be linked by a study com-

[52] *New York Times*, October 20, 1950; *Le Monde*, October 19, 1950.

mittee composed of delegates of France and the three Indochinese states, as well as by conferences on communications in which France would participate whenever a question came up of concern to the rest of the French Union.

On immigration, it was agreed that each country would have its own national services and that the French would join the three Indochinese states in conferences on Indochinese immigration problems. The three states accepted serious limitations on their sovereignty: the French Government was given free access to Indochinese immigration files; and the French High Commissioner received the right to propose the expulsion of any foreigner whose presence he regarded as harmful to the security of French troops.

Problems arose at Pau when the remaining items on the agenda came up for discussion; although technical and economic matters, they were all basically political. It took six weeks, for example, to thresh out the future organization of customs and foreign trade. The delegates agreed finally on an Indochinese customs union in which the three states would divide the total customs receipts among them. For the time being, 71 percent of the receipts would go to Viet Nam and 22 percent to Cambodia, with the remaining 7 percent to Laos. The Indochinese customs would be directed by an interstate technical committee and an intergovernmental conference on both of which the French were to have representatives. To draw up import and export plans for Indochina, two separate bodies were provided for, with Frenchmen again sitting alongside Vietnamese, Cambodians, and Laotians. The new Bank of Issue for the piastre, to which the three Associated States had agreed in the accords which they signed with France in 1949, was also to be under quadripartite direction. Finally, there was to be an Indochinese committee to draw up economic development plans. In this, too, the French Government was to participate.

Within the framework of the interstate controls outlined at Pau, Viet Nam, Laos, and Cambodia were each to have its own customs, foreign trade, export and import plan, treasury, immigration service, development plan, and postal and communications system.

The Vietnamese delegation particularly, under the leadership of Finance Minister Nguyen Trung Vinh, stood firm at Pau for broad delegations of power to the three states and made a determined effort to win more of the independence which had been only partially conceded in the Elysée Accords. They tried to broaden the then generally accepted conception of the French Union by putting forward a version of quadripartitism which called for absolute equality among France and the three Indochinese states, with the French assuming not merely in the three Associated States but at home, in metropolitan France, the same obligations that Viet Nam, Cambodia, and Laos assumed in Asia. "The central idea," said Nguyen Dac Khe, "is that France should harmonize its interests—not those which it has in Viet Nam and which are important and perfectly legitimate, and which are regulated by Vietnamese laws and regulations . . . but rather its continental interests, with those of the three Associated States."[53]

Some French observers regarded the Pau Conference as a disastrous abdication of French authority and a well-known specialist on Indochinese economic questions, who saw it as the death knell of France's position in Indochina, wrote:

By accepting the eventual restriction of trade within the French Union, by losing all effective authority over the issuance of money, by renouncing control over foreign trade, by permitting a system of controlled prices for exports and imports, we have given the Associated States all the power they need if they wish to assure the ruin of our enterprises and compel their withdrawal without in any way molesting our compatriots.[54]

A Vietnamese writer read the agreements reached at Pau very differently:

All these conventions conserve in Indochina a privileged position for French capital, supported by the presence of a powerful fleet and army. Even if no one talks any more of an Indochinese Federation, it is still a federalism both administrative and economic (Monetary Union, Customs Union, Communications Union, etc.) which co-ordinates the various activities of the three Associated States. France always exercises control through the representatives she has in all the organs of planning or of federal surveillance, and through what is in effect the right of veto, because the president or the secretary general of these committees is always elected by joint decision of the four governments and, further, because most of the decisions of the committees are made by unanimous agreement.[55]

On the whole, however, the Vietnamese delegation was satisfied with what it had accomplished, convinced that it had made an advance on the Elysée Accords. But it had made this advance at Pau only to lose it afterward as specific conventions were drafted to implement the Pau agreements and French officials demonstrated an inclination to withdraw in practice the concessions they had made in principle. For example, when the Vietnamese had accepted the existence of interstate committees, it had been with the understanding that these would in no way replace the old federal structure but would be simply advisory, with the power to make recommendations to the four states but without the power to enforce them. French officials seemed desirous of changing this interpretation, making obligatory on each of the Associated States the decisions of the various economic committees in which Frenchmen, Cambodians, Laotians, and Vietnamese were all represented. Furthermore, Vietnamese foreign trade remained completely under French control; and even

53 Conférence Inter-États, Plenary Session, October 14, 1950.
54 Paul Bernard, "Bilan de la Conférence de Pau," *Documents de France Outre-Mer*, Supplement to No. 256, p. 3.
55 Tran Minh The, "Les Conventions de Pau guarantissent-elles l'indépendance du Viet Nam," *Mondes d'Orient*, April 1951, p. 11 (75).

American economic aid to Viet Nam was channeled through this French monopoly. Some of the Vietnamese who had been most optimistic during the Pau negotiations privately expressed grave doubts as to the possibility of dealing with French officials at all under the existing circumstances.

Tran Van Huu, who said in December 1950 when the three Indochinese Prime Ministers signed the Pau conventions, "I solemnly proclaim that our independence is now perfect,"[56] went to the United States the following year to sign the Japanese Peace Treaty. This was a diplomatic triumph for Viet Nam as for the other Associated States, which also sent representatives to join the delegates of the sovereign nations gathered in San Francisco. Tran Van Huu had gone a long way since his days as separatist Governor of South Viet Nam, and his American trip had the effect of reminding him, if he needed to be reminded, that the United States represented a possible counterweight to France in the diplomatic struggle for Vietnamese independence. He gave indications that he was following the example of Nguyen Phan Long, looking over the shoulders of the French for American support and trying to make an independent policy of his own. Like Long, he found himself alone and exposed to the consequences of French disapproval. Although Huu subsequently tried to appease French officials, notably on the occasion of the first meeting of the High Council of the French Union in December 1951, it was too late, and in June 1952 he was dismissed.

It was just three years since Bao Dai had become Prime Minister without adequate political spadework to prepare the way for him, and found that the new title meant little new power. If his successor, Nguyen Phan Long, could not incarnate national unity to the same degree as Bao Dai, he was at least both a nationalist and a unionist. Tran Van Huu, with his separatist background, had not at first seemed a dangerous nationalist, but even Huu proved in time too nationalist-minded to survive as Prime Minister. He was replaced by Nguyen Van Tam, who was known as "the tiger of Cai Lay" because of the zeal with which he had participated in the French repression of Vietnamese revolutionaries at Cai Lay in 1940.

THE NGUYEN VAN TAM GOVERNMENT

Nguyen Van Tam was a French citizen, a former police official and administrator who in 1945 had volunteered to join General Leclerc's army, then engaged in "mopping-up" operations against the Vietnamese, and had later been appointed head of a province in Cochin China. At the forefront of the Cochin Chinese separatist movement, Tam held posts in both the Thinh and the Hoach governments. When Tran Van Huu became Prime Minister, Tam headed the political police, in which capacity he fought the terror of the Viet Minh with terror of his own. Tran Van Huu, himself not without experience

56 *Chroniques d'Outre-Mer*, January 1951.

in collaborating with the French, said of him, "Tam is not a Vietnamese patriot; he is a French patriot."[57]

Certainly Nguyen Van Tam had ample opportunity to continue his close association with the French when he became Prime Minister. The administration which he inherited was still strongly under French influence. Its economic services, to the extent that they existed at all, were subordinated to the French and could not act. Even though it derived a substantial portion of its revenues from customs duties and from the old monopolies of opium, alcohol, and salt, it remained dependent on French economic, as it was on French military, support. Although Vietnamese officials were active at the village level and other Vietnamese held high offices in the Bao Dai government, the provincial and regional administration was still generally supervised by Frenchmen.[57a] To many Vietnamese, the symbol of continuing French control over the entire Bao Dai administration was the consistent refusal of French officials to hand over to the Vietnamese Government Norodom Palace in Saigon, the traditional seat of the French Governor General. And it was a fact that the French Government had instituted a more direct supervision over the Vietnamese administration after the dismissal of Léon Pignon, following the Chinese Communist-supported Viet Minh victories in the fall of 1950 and the appointment of General Jean de Lattre de Tassigny as both High Commissioner and French Commander-in-Chief in Indochina. De Lattre, a Free French hero of World War Two, succeeded in stemming the Viet Minh advance and dispelling the panic which had broken out among the French population of North Viet Nam. But in January 1952 De Lattre died, and Jean Letourneau, who had been in charge of Indochinese affairs since 1949, first as Minister of Overseas France and then as chief of the new Ministry of Associated States, was appointed High Commissioner while still retaining his post in the French Cabinet. This combining of the duties of High Commissioner in Indochina with the broad powers of a French Cabinet Minister, an unprecedented arrangement for the government of a supposedly independent country, gave Letourneau more sweeping authority than either Bollaert or Pignon had had; no matter how carefully Bao Dai secluded himself at Dalat, far removed from the High Commissioner's office in Saigon, where Prime Minister Tam also had his seat of government, the Vietnamese Government was left little freedom of action.

The full weight of Letourneau's presence in Indochina was not felt during the first year, which he spent commuting between Saigon and Paris. But in January 1953, a new Cabinet shift in France which brought Radical Socialist

[57] *Paris-Match*, July 12–19, 1952.

[57a] Until the Buu Loc government assumed office in January 1954, most official government documents were written in French "because of the presence of numerous French officials in the administrative services." *Viet Nam*, February 15, 1954.

René Mayer to the Premiership, led to the appointment of Joannès Dupraz, also a member of the MRP, to act as Letourneau's deputy in Paris, leaving Letourneau for the first time free to devote his full energies to watching over and manipulating Indochinese affairs on the spot. It was not a happy arrangement for Bao Dai and other Vietnamese who had hoped for greater freedom from French control.

A French Parliamentary Mission of Inquiry which visited Indochina in 1953 deplored "the accumulation of powers [which] has replaced the force of prestige. The Minister, who has become resident and High Commissioner, has also assumed responsibility for the conduct of military operations. A veritable dictatorship has been instituted, without limit and without control. Dictatorship not of a man but of government bureaus . . ."

The Parliamentary Mission went on to indict the Letourneau administration:

The artificial life of Saigon, the temptations of power without control, the security of a judgment which disdains realities, have isolated the Minister and his entourage and have made them insensible to the daily tragedy of the war . . .

It is no longer up to us to govern, but to advise. The big thing was not to draw up plans irresponsibly, but to carry on daily a subtle diplomacy. In Saigon our representatives have allowed themselves to be inveigled into the tempting game of power and intrigue.

Instead of seeing the most important things and acting on them, instead of making on the spot investigations, of looking for inspiration in the village and in the ricefield, instead of informing themselves and winning the confidence of the most humble people, in order to deprive the rebels of their best weapon, the Norodom Palace clique has allowed itself the luxury of administering *à la française* and of reigning over a country where revolution is smouldering . . .

The press has not the right of criticism. To tell the truth, it has become official, and the principal newspaper in Saigon is at the disposition of the High Commissariat. Letters are censored. Propaganda seems to be issued just to defend the High Commissariat. Such a regime cannot last, unless we are to appear as people who are determined not to keep their promises.

The Parliamentary Mission spoke of Saigon "where gambling, depravity, love of money and of power finish by corrupting the morale and destroying will-power." And it observed: "The Ministers of Viet Nam appear, in the eyes of their compatriots, to be French officials. The Prime Minister, despite his finesse, does not escape their condemnation."[58]

Nguyen Van Tam never succeeded in dispelling this impression which was widely held by the Vietnamese public. Even when he took action which in another man might have been regarded as nationalistic, his close collabora-

[58] *L'Express*, May 23, 1953. The four authors of this report were: Frank Arnal (Socialist), Louis Christaens (Independent), Paul Devinat (Radical Socialist), and André-François Mercier (M.R.P.)

tion with French officials and his arbitrary control of the press and the police made his motives suspect. In the Tam government, as in the governments of his predecessors, the south was overrepresented in relation to the north, and separatists still held the key posts. The *directeur de cabinet,* or chief secretary, of Nguyen Van Tam, like that of Tran Van Huu, was a Frenchman; however, unlike the professional administrator who had assisted Huu, the Frenchman assigned to Tam was a member of the *Sureté,* the French police.

Prime Minister Tam failed signally to rally popular support. One evidence of this failure was the continuing ability of the Viet Minh to receive from the peasant population detailed information about French military movements. The war against the Viet Minh could not be won until this flow of information was reversed to the advantage of the Bao Dai regime.

Another evidence of the unpopularity of the Tam government was that the only people willing to accept office under Tam, with few exceptions, were politicians without parties, individuals who had been elected by nobody and represented very few, a fact which gave an unreality to the announcements of political reshufflings and new appointments that emanated periodically from Saigon and Dalat. Actually, throughout the year and a half that Tam remained Prime Minister, he was engaged in a continual struggle for power, and always with elements which never entirely accepted jurisdiction of his administration—not only with the Viet Minh, but with the entrenched political groups which had taken shape in the French-controlled zones, with the nationalistic *trum chan,* who did not hide their keen dislike for the new Prime Minister, and, in the end, even with the Emperor himself. And to each of these elements he lost out in turn.

The political organization of the Bao Dai zones, such as it was, was not based upon parties but was centered on five virtually feudal units.[58a] The diverse elements which had supported Bao Dai in the early days when he was in Hongkong and in Europe were no less diverse now that he was home but they had tended to coalesce around the Cao Dai, the Hoa Hao, and the Binh Xuyen in the south and the Dai Viet and the Bishops of Phat Diem and Bui Chu in the north. And each of the five was gradually building up its own state within a state.

In the south, the Cao Dai and the Hoa Hao controlled large areas of the countryside, maintaining their own armies, collecting tolls from the local population, and proclaiming their allegiance only to the Emperor. It is true that some Cao Dai groups were entirely religious, playing no active role in politics save as their members might individually choose. Other members of

[58a] To use the word "feudal" in this connection, as is commonly done by French journalists, seems justified by the fact that these various groups, as distinguished from political parties, had their own military forces, controlled distinct areas of territory, and collected tolls from the local population.

the Cao Dai, led by Colonel Trinh Minh The, Chief of Staff, had announced their opposition to the French and the Viet Minh and proceeded to independent military action as a third force movement in 1951. Still others, the so-called Eleven Unified Sects headed by Cao Trieu Phat, continued in alliance with the Viet Minh. Elements of the Hoa Hao also clashed with the French on occasion.

The majority of the Cao Dai, however, like the Hoa Hao, drew substantial material benefits from their support of Bao Dai. Prime Minister Tam attempted to consolidate their private armies into the national army, which would have threatened their privileged position in the country and brought them more directly under his control. But they were strong enough to rebuff Tam. The Cao Dai troops were estimated to number anywhere from 15,000 to 20,000 and the Hoa Hao 8,000 to 10,000. They were joined in the south by the troops of the Binh Xuyen, estimates of which varied between 1,000 and 3,000. The Binh Xuyen had been generally recognized as bandits when they joined the central government of General Xuan, and there was no particular reason to believe that they had changed in character. However, under the leadership of Bay Vien, who became well-known as the owner of the "Grand Monde," one of the most famous gambling establishments in the Far East, they brought their support to Bao Dai, and the Emperor appointed Bay Vien to the rank of general.

In the north, where Nguyen Huu Tri resumed his old post of Governor, the fact that the Viet Minh occupied the region between Hué and the Tonkinese delta had the effect of giving him a considerable freedom from the government in Saigon; and the mandarinal Dai Viet, whose power waxed and waned with his, consolidated its own sphere of influence. In Phat Diem and Bui Chu, however, the Bishops continued to rule unhindered.

It would be erroneous to give the impression that the Catholics who lived outside Phat Diem and Bui Chu had any special political organization or took any special political position. Several Catholics happened to be members of the Tam Cabinet but they were there, like Le Van Hoach, the veteran Cao Dai separatist, and Vu Hong Khanh of the virtually defunct VNQDD, in their personal capacity. A number of Catholics continued to live in the Viet Minh areas, generally abstaining from political activity. Some others were tacitly encouraged by their bishops to organize local "self-defense" militia against the Viet Minh with arms supplied by the French. In South Viet Nam, in the region around Bentre, some Catholics joined the "Mobile Units for the Defense of Christendom," local militia raised against the Viet Minh by the Franco-Vietnamese Colonel Leroy. Generally, however, there was nothing of a political nature to distinguish Catholics from the non-Catholics among whom they lived.

If Nguyen Van Tam was unable to assert the authority of his regime over the "Big Five" groups, he also encountered competition with his government at Dalat, where what amounted to still another government had formed around Bao Dai. Regardless of changes in the Cabinet in Saigon, a few men remained close to the Emperor: Nguyen De, his *directeur de cabinet,* whose intrigues were generally believed to have led to the dismissal of Tran Van Huu as Prime Minister in favor of Tam; Phan Van Giao, Governor of Central Viet Nam; and Pham Van Binh, sometime Governor of North Viet Nam, who had favored the restoration of Bao Dai as early as 1946. Also close to Bao Dai, as the Emperor's interest in building a national army grew, was General Nguyen Van Hinh, son of the Prime Minister.

All these disparate groups and individuals had one thing in common: they maneuvered and intrigued much more for the sake of their own personal interests than for any political issue. It was for this reason that the majority of the population in the Bao Dai zone looked toward more nationalist-minded leaders, of whom the most prominent was Ngo Dinh Diem. Because they regarded the Tam regime as inadequate, the people remained aloof from political life; and although they had been alienated by the Communism of the Viet Minh, they did not publicly criticize the resistance because it was fighting in the name of independence.

Ngo Dinh Diem, who had held no post under the French since his resignation as Bao Dai's chief Minister in 1933, left Viet Nam in 1950. He went first to Japan where he saw Cuong De shortly before the death of the old prince, and then he went on to the United States, where he found refuge with the Maryknoll Fathers in New Jersey. Other Vietnamese of varying political complexions came to France; they ranged from Hoang Xuan Han, Minister of National Education in the Tran Trong Kim Cabinet and a member of the Viet Minh delegation at the Dalat Conference, to Nguyen Manh Ha, Minister of National Economy in the first Ho Chi Minh government and a delegate to the Fontainebleau Conference.

Ngo Dinh Diem waited in the United States, and later in Europe, as other Vietnamese nationalists waited at home and in Paris; they were prepared to settle for nothing short of independence. And in 1953, despite the limited powers of the Tam regime and the unrepresentative nature of its personnel, many of whom would disappear from the Vietnamese political scene with the achievement of independence, nationalists had reason for optimism. Neither Bao Dai nor the French could close their eyes to the fact that the existence and activity of the Viet Minh since 1945 had radically changed the temper of the country; it might in time be possible to rally the people against the Communists, but first they had to be convinced that they had won their independence. In response to this popular opinion, the Bao Dai regime undertook the implementation of two long-announced policies—the building up of a national army and the holding of national elections.

TOWARD A VIETNAMESE NATIONAL ARMY

The Vietnamese national army owed much to the efforts of General Jean de Lattre de Tassigny. The two generals (both of them posthumously named Marshals of France) who played an important role in Viet Nam in the period after the Japanese surrender had, on the whole, a salutary effect on French policy, in that they tended to see beyond the vested interests of the French colonial service and the French colonials to the more basic realities of the Vietnamese situation. In 1945 and 1946 General Leclerc had succeeded in temporarily holding at bay the divisive projects of Pignon and Torel, and negotiating directly with the Viet Minh. In 1951, when that no longer seemed feasible, General de Lattre arrived to lay the foundations of what, under the influence of Pignon, had been consistently withheld—an independent Vietnamese army. He acted on the assumption that it was both good politics to build up a national army, so that the Vietnamese could feel that they were fighting their own battles, and also good military policy—the stronger were the Bao Dai troops, the more of the burden they would take off the French forces.

In 1953, the Viet Minh army, including regulars, regional troops, and local militia, numbered somewhere between 300,000 and 400,000.[58b] Aligned against it were some 420,000 troops of the French Union: the expeditionary corps, including Frenchmen, Africans, Legionnaires, and Indochinese; native auxiliaries like the Cao Dai, the Hoa Hao, and the Binh Xuyen; and the Vietnamese national army headed by General Nguyen Van Hinh, Chief of Staff. Vietnamese fighting with the expeditionary corps were transferred to the Vietnamese army which at the end of 1953 numbered some 200,000 men.[58c] However, this army was still far from adequate. It had not yet begun to attract the large numbers of Vietnamese that proponents of a national army hoped to bring under its colors in order to relieve the French Union Army. And even the Vietnamese who were enlisted in the Bao Dai army did not all prove themselves entirely reliable. If a number of Vietnamese troops fought well, there were reports of others who did not hold their own against the enemy; sometimes they had to call on French troops for aid, sometimes they even deserted to the other side. When General Hinh said that it would be several years before his army would be capable of taking over the country from the French, former Premier Edouard Daladier protested in the National Assembly:

Are we to continue the war until 1956 as the Chief of Staff of the Vietnamese army says? ... Are you sure that in 1956 there will be a Vietnamese army capable of relieving the French army? I doubt it. I know, we all know, that in many regions

58b *L'Express,* February 27, 1954.
58c According to Vietnamese official sources, the army numbered 205,700 men on December 31, 1953. *Viet Nam,* February 15, 1954.

this army is subjected to enemy propaganda which is not lacking in effectiveness, that numerous desertions, notably of non-commissioned officers, have resulted, and there is no evidence that the predictions of M. Hinh are being realized and that in 1956 the Vietnamese army will be in condition to take over the battle alone and allow us to leave.[59]

Daladier had put his finger on a vital problem. The Vietnamese army would doubtless increase its numbers as its supplies and its finances became more adequate to its needs. It lacked trained and experienced Vietnamese officers, but presumably these would eventually be supplied with the help of the new officers' training schools established by the Bao Dai government in collaboration with the French. The weakness of the Vietnamese army could not be explained simply by such operational problems. When members of the French High Command went out of their way, as did General Carpentier, to insist that Vietnamese troops could not be trusted by themselves, that they did not have enough good officers of their own, it was difficult to avoid the conclusion that French military men were talking more about French policy than objective facts. After all, to determine the ability of Vietnamese to fight, it was only necessary to consider the men who had been fighting the French for eight years. Chinese aid to the Viet Minh had arrived only in the last few years; and the Japanese, Germans, and Austrians who had helped to train the Viet Minh army in its early days were far fewer in number than the Frenchmen who had been active from the beginning in the French-controlled zone. Yet civilians like Vo Nguyen Giap became generals, officers were trained as they were needed, and the men who followed them fought under the most difficult conditions.

Evidently, if Vietnamese wished to go to war, they could hold their own against any troops. There were even a number of trained Vietnamese officers, prewar veterans of the French army, who had so far abstained from participation in the war, but who could have been recruited to serve in a genuinely national army. There was still much to do, however, before such an army could be established. Emphasizing the importance of a Vietnamese army in the struggle for independence, nationalists insisted on greater freedom, not simply as the price of a national army, but as the prerequisite for one: and here they were on firm ground, for few Vietnamese would join the army unless they had a real incentive to do so.

In the first instance, this meant more freedom for the army itself, which nationalists complained remained too closely under French control. Nguyen Van Hinh himself was a French citizen, like his father, and had been a major in the French air force until he was brought back to Viet Nam to be named Chief of Staff. With greater freedom for the army achieved, nationalist leaders

[59] *Journal Officiel*, Assemblée Nationale, October 27, 1953, pp. 4578–79.

were inclined to be less interested in attempting the all-out conquest of Viet Nam than in consolidating freedom in the areas already under nationalist control, guarding them with Vietnamese troops exclusively, placing them under Vietnamese administrators, and instituting social, economic, and political reforms. Were independence clearly demonstrated to exist in the Bao Dai zone, there was at least the possibility that it might serve as a sufficient attraction to win over non-Communist adherents of the Viet Minh and help to isolate the Communist diehards. In any case, even if priority were given to military considerations, the military problem would remain essentially a reflection of the political problem; and no one had stated this more clearly than General Raoul Salan, French Commander-in-Chief in Indochina, when he said: "We shall win ... when all the vital forces of the nation, from the peasant in the ricefield to the bourgeois in the cities, participate."[60]

ELECTIONS

Social and economic reforms, to ease the living conditions of the peasantry and to end the corruption in the cities, seemed indispensable if Viet Nam was to have a sound and popular administration, and for this reason there was much talk of reform on the part of the Vietnamese Government, particularly of projected agrarian reforms. Under normal conditions, such measures would certainly have won the support of the population, but even if the Prime Minister had not been Tam, but a less compromised individual who demonstrated a genuine desire to improve social conditions, it seemed unlikely that an agrarian reform program could be implemented to any reasonable extent in a country where so many of the peasants lived under the dual jurisdiction of French troops during the day and Viet Minh troops at night. Certainly Nguyen Van Tam's promises of agrarian reform had little effect on the people. They did not even serve the purpose of making friends for Tam among the population which openly accused him of corruption and which had not forgotten the very active role he had once played as a member of the former colonial police organization in Cochin China. All that was lacking was convincing evidence of the popular attitude toward Tam, and that was provided by the national elections which Tam announced for January 25, 1953. The results of these elections doomed his administration.

These national elections—to municipal and communal councils in the French-controlled zone—were particularly significant because so few of the normal channels for the expression of public opinion had been open to the people; they still had neither political parties, a representative assembly, nor a free press. In the Bao Dai zone, where there was little popular enthusiasm for the war and little confidence in the French, abstention from political ac-

60 *Paris-presse-l'intransigeant*, January 20, 1953.

tivity by key elements of the population had become a major characteristic of political life. The elections demonstrated, however, that vigorous political forces had never been far beneath the surface even in regions where French control was strongest.

The elections were announced only for areas under the authority of the Bao Dai government, which was said to administer 25 percent of the territory of Viet Nam and roughly 50 percent of its estimated 27 million citizens; and only one village out of three in the Bao Dai zone was regarded as sufficiently "pacified" to be permitted to vote.[61] Further, the right to vote was given only to those who had registered in the census taken in 1951 for purposes of general mobilization. It was limited, in other words, to people who had already acquiesced in some measure to the authority of the Bao Dai regime. Altogether, some one million Vietnamese were qualified to vote.[62]

The Viet Minh, which had hoped to sabotage the elections, found itself in no position to stop people from going to the polls. In Saigon, where the fact that the city was the seat of both the Tam government and the office of the French High Commissioner was not conducive to free political activity, little interest in the elections was openly demonstrated, despite the emergence of a Socialist group which stood for a truce, negotiations with the Viet Minh, and general elections controlled by neutrals. Elsewhere, however, there was a marked recrudescence of a political activity, notably in North Viet Nam. And in South Viet Nam, Bishop Ngo Dinh Thuc, the brother of Ngo Dinh Diem, declared in a pastoral letter that any Vietnamese Catholic who did not exercise his right to vote would be guilty before God, before the Church, and before the country.

The most striking fact about the elections was the participation of so many of the *trum chan* or *attentistes* on a strongly nationalistic platform. This was notably the case in Hanoi, where 60 percent of the population voted and elected a list headed by Nguyen The Truyen, an old revolutionary comrade of Ho Chi Minh who had been freed from French imprisonment in 1946 through the intercession of Ho. The Nguyen The Truyen list was elected with Catholic support and was made up of so-called nationalists of the Left—doctors, lawyers, journalists, and intellectuals generally. They were critics of the Tam government and stood for a genuine unification of the country, for free national elections, and for an end to the war.

The elections, which the London *Observer* headlined as "Blow to Premier," were a repudiation of the French policy of divide and rule, and a demand for independence and unity which, according to the popular belief, even in these restricted and controlled elections, had not been achieved by Nguyen Van

---

[61] *Le Monde*, January 24, 1953.

[62] Of these some 400,000 were in the north, 400,000 in the south, and 240,000 in Central Viet Nam. *Ibid.*

Tam. However, such a popular protest could not, of itself, end or even alter the relative isolation of the Bao Dai regime in the country. The French conception of the Bao Dai policy as it was implemented in Saigon—to use the Emperor to divide the country in order to consolidate French control over it —had clearly failed. But political life in the Bao Dai zone was still an uneasy equilibrium in which the "Big Five" groups, the personal entourage of the Emperor, the government of Prime Minister Tam, and various French officials and military men each played their part, while the population at large went about its daily life in apparent passivity. The January 1953 elections gave some indication of what people were really thinking but nationalist opponents of the Viet Minh had still to build up the organization and rally to the leaders who could transform the popular desire for unity and independence into political reality. And to do this, they were still inclined to look for help abroad; even as they pinned their hopes on the development of a national army, they looked, as they had done before, to the United States in their efforts to counterbalance the French. Curiously enough, however, it was not from Washington but from Pnom Penh that help came. For a short time, during the spring and summer of 1953, King Norodom Sihanouk became the spokesman of all Indochinese nationalists in their struggle for independence.

Chapter Twelve

"PERFECTING" INDEPENDENCE

IN 1953 the Franco-Vietnamese war was in its seventh year and neither the French nor the Viet Minh had yet succeeded in breaking the military stalemate in which their struggle had been bogged down from the beginning. If the French held the richest and most populous areas of the country (the Red River delta in the north and the Mekong River delta in the south), sections of the coast of Central Viet Nam, and isolated outposts, the countryside was a no-man's-land infested by the Viet Minh. The French-held cities were islands in Viet Minh territory; Hanoi, Hué, and Saigon were all in the Bao Dai zone, but there were no land communications between them; only by air or sea could the traveller circulate in Viet Nam.

The Tonkinese delta had become a major battlefield with the arrival of the Chinese Communists on the northern frontier. In the fall of 1950, newly strengthened with aid from China, the Viet Minh had threatened to engulf the delta. But then General Jean de Lattre de Tassigny arrived to hold back the Viet Minh tide and secure the region for France by building a wall of forts and blockhouses around it. Finding it impossible to take the delta by direct assault, Vo Nguyen Giap developed an alternative strategy and began gradually to infiltrate his men into this crucial area. Some 20,000 regular Viet Minh soldiers were soon believed to be active in the delta, and they were said to have trained some 50,000 others virtually under the eyes of the French. In 1953, a year after the death of General de Lattre, this territory, supposed to be a center of French strength in Viet Nam, had become a center of Viet Minh strength as well. At harvest time, Viet Minh troops carried off rice from the rich delta fields, while the recruiting of men and the spreading of Viet Minh propaganda from village to village went on unendingly as the Viet Minh employed among the peasants, with telling effect, its two most useful weapons, nationalism and terror. Even regions of the delta which in the daylight were nominally under French control, reverted under the cover of darkness to the Viet Minh. Not surprisingly, French journalists began to describe the situation prevailing in the Tonkinese delta as a "condominium."

Elsewhere, in the mountainous, sparsely populated hinterland, the Viet Minh ranged widely, operating in Cambodian and Laotian territory as well as in Viet Nam. In effect, there were not only two governments in Viet Nam, there were also two wars. The French Union army fought its war from entrenched positions with strong air and sea support and generally could concentrate enough solid force on any one spot to defeat the enemy in a large-scale encounter. But the troops of General Giap rarely sought large-scale encounters. Although year after year Viet Minh spokesmen talked of the third stage of revolutionary military strategy, the all-out offensive which would drive the French into the sea, this never materialized and the Viet Minh remained in the second stage, close to its guerrilla origins, based on the population, fighting a war of movement and maneuver, with brief sharp encounters with the enemy, harrying the French Union army at its exposed points but avoiding its full force. When there was a prospect of winning a local encounter, Giap fought; rather than risk his men in larger actions, he withdrew them to look for more likely victories elsewhere. In view of the considerable extent of the Indochinese peninsula, it was little wonder that these two wars, fought side by side, had gone on so long.

In the fall of 1952 the Viet Minh launched an offensive in the strategic Thai mountain country, the northernmost section of North Viet Nam, and rapidly assumed control of it down to the Laotian frontier. Then, early in 1953, several Viet Minh divisions moved in force on Laos. Immediately the spotlight of international attention was turned on them.

Giap chose to move into Laos in the midst of the Communist peace drive following the death of Stalin. The Viet Minh offensive was the one dissonant note in world Communism's protestations of peace, and it occasioned cries of alarm from the West which purported to see in it evidence of Viet Minh aggressive designs against Siam and all of Southeast Asia. The United States sent special aid to the French forces, the Siamese Government talked of bringing the Viet Minh threat to international peace before the United Nations, the Laotian Government, not itself a member of the United Nations, upset French officials by appealing directly to the U.N. But still the Viet Minh came on, four divisions strong, moving steadily and unchallenged into the heart of Laos. As the old King Sisavang Vong waited in his capital with Prime Minister Souvanna Phouma, the Prime Minister's brother, Souphanouvong, was approaching with the Viet Minh; along with its weapons and military equipment, the Viet Minh brought its political arsenal, Pathet Lao (the Free Laotian movement) and the Laotian prince who led it.

As the world watched, the Viet Minh continued its advance and then, suddenly, still unchallenged, it turned in its tracks and retreated back to Viet Nam, leaving a Laotian revolutionary government behind at Sam Neua and a small number of troops. Why had it come, and why did it go? The question was never satisfactorily answered. Had Giap been seeking the appearance of military victory in an area which was virtually undefended because of its meager strategic importance to satisfy public opinion at home? Had the move been directed at encouraging the growing French desire for peace, or at reaping the Laotian opium harvest, so useful to the Viet Minh in providing currency for foreign trade? Had he left because of his inability to keep his men supplied? Had his Chinese advisers urged him to leave before he brought the weight of the free world down on their heads?

Colonial strategists asserted that the invasion of Laos, like all previous Viet Minh moves, was part of the Communist plan of international aggression, and they turned up a man named Nguyen Van Long, who was supposed to be the architect of Viet Minh Thai policy. But there was no need to credit the Communists with undue Machiavellianism. The major interest of the Viet Minh was still Viet Nam, as Prime Minister Winston Churchill pointed out, and Viet Minh leaders were not unaware that French military strategy called for assaults against the Viet Minh strongholds in the provinces of Thanh Hoa and Nghe An, not only by landing operations against the Central Vietnamese coast but also by attacks from French-held Laos.

When French Premier René Mayer stated that no Frenchman could accept the view that the fighting in Southeast Asia was inspired by popular movements for liberation and called the invasion of Laos another example of aggression "ordered from abroad," he could not find many Indochinese to agree fully with him. Although the Communism of the Viet Minh has been a major disaster for the Vietnamese people, they were almost invariably seduced by the nationalistic guise assumed by the movement. The Laotians had been more fortunate: the Viet Minh had not chosen to remain in force in the country and, despite its attempt to use the Issarak movement for its own ends, it had apparently failed to stir up popular discontent or even anti-French sentiments among the Laotians. But it served little purpose to deny the popular basis of the Vietnamese war so long as the question of independence was permitted to remain a live issue in Indochina. The person who dramatized this fact most convincingly was not a Vietnamese at all, but the young King of Cambodia, who had personally taken command of the Cambodian forces which were fighting against insurgents in his own country.

KING NORODOM SIHANOUK TAKES A TRIP

What would happen if the Viet Minh were to turn next on Cambodia where some 10,000 insurgents were at large, perhaps half of them already associated with the Viet Minh which controlled the western reaches of the country, and all of them justifying their resistance on the grounds that they were fighting for Cambodian independence? King Norodom Sihanouk considered this eventuality and was not at all sanguine about the reaction of his people. He went to France to put his problem before the French Government; gaining no satisfaction in Paris, he paid a visit to the United States and in New York he released a statement to the press. He declared, according to the *New York Times*:

that unless the French gave his people more independence 'within the next few months' there was real danger that they would rebel against the present regime and become a part of the Communist-led Viet Minh movement . . . the demand for further independence was consistent with his support of the theory of a French Union in which member states would enjoy the same independence as do, for instance, Pakistan and India within the British Commonwealth . . .

Speaking in French, the King said sadly: 'If we have an invasion of the sort that Laos has suffered recently, I am not at all certain that I can call for a general mobilization as did Laos. If there is a menace, the people will say that the French are encircled and that their end has come.'

He recalled that when he signed the treaties that bound Cambodia to the French he told his people that they would gain real independence.

'I am the man responsible for joining the French Union,' he said, adding that if his people did not get what was promised to them, 'I deserve punishment.'

He added that during the past few years 'there has been growing support among the thinking masses of the people of Cambodia to the theory that the Communist-led Viet Minh is fighting for the independence of the country.'

'They do not want to die for the French and help them stay here,' he said.

King Norodom . . . said he had been called to Paris by the French 'to see if it is possible to save the French Union.' He remarked that the French Government was 'not very happy' at his airing his grievances publicly, but he felt he had to follow the wishes of his people.

The King said the principal difficulites in Franco-Vietnamese relations were the insistence of the French on having most of the Cambodian troops under their command, and restrictions on judicial and economic sovereignty.

'Cambodian justice does not apply to the French,' the King said, 'and our police cannot touch them. In economic matters they have our hands and feet tied; we cannot import and export freely and we have no freedom of taxation.'

King Norodom said the French Government had suggested that his attitude was playing into the hands of the Communists by dividing non-Communists and that other Paris sources had suggested that he was attempting to gain support in the United States on the ground that American business might like to supplant French investments in Indochina.

The first suggestion, he said, is worthless on the ground that continued French adamance toward Cambodian demands probably would mean the fall of Indochina. The second he called 'ridiculous.'

'Cambodia is very sorry that her wishes do not please France, and so we don't quite know what to do,' he said. 'If France does not understand us, we will not ask anything of other nations. I will simply go home and ask my people what they want to do.'

'Paris does not like my coming to America,' the King said, 'because it says I am applying pressure here. I cannot be doing that because I represent a very small nation that cannot very well apply pressure on anyone.'[1]

From the United States, the King returned home via Japan, where he appeared at public ceremonies, a not very subtle reminder that if Cambodia was

[1] *New York Times*, April 19, 1953. For a fuller account of the Cambodian situation see *L'Express*, July 4, 1953; *Chroniques d'Outre-Mer*, July–August 1953.

a member of the French Union, it was first of all an Asian and a Buddhist country. Then he went on to Cambodia but only for a brief stay; it was announced that the King had left suddenly for Bangkok and that he would not return until he had achieved independence. As it happened, things did not work out that way. The Siamese Government was unwilling to shelter a Cambodian government-in-exile, even if it was headed by a king, and Norodom Sihanouk returned to Cambodia but he did not go back to his capital of Pnom Penh. He established his headquarters at Siemreap and announced his intention of remaining there until his country was given independence.

The entire episode was as remarkable as it was unexpected, and it was one which no other ruler in the French Union could have risked; the Sultan of Morocco was deposed for considerably less than that. Bao Dai, least of all, was in a position to emulate Sihanouk. It was true that both men had been placed on their thrones by the French but Norodom Sihanouk had been selected as King by Admiral Decoux, in preference to the late king's eldest son, in order to resolve a dynastic question and reconcile the younger and older branches of the Cambodian royal family, whereas Bao Dai still bore the onus among his people of having been chosen by the French in an attempt to weaken what was then still a broadly national movement. The Cambodian, recognizing that his position was imperiled by the strength of popular nationalist sentiment, moved to master it and make himself the spokesman of it. In Paris, the Cambodian Prime Minister Penn Nouth explained the position of the King and his government, saying:

For my part, I am high on the blacklist of the nationalists. The Communists would behead me if they took power. His Majesty is promised the same lot because of his pro-French sentiments. We are caught between two forces. France regards us as traitors because we do not always say 'amen,' and our adversaries accuse us of working for you. It is true that we want to work with you, but in conditions which preserve our sovereignty and independence.[2]

The King himself went even further: "If Cambodia does not obtain satisfaction by peaceful means, she will have recourse to other methods. For that she is ready to sacrifice even her existence."[3]

In this fashion Norodom Sihanouk was able to rally even Cambodian extremists behind him. A number of Issarak joined him and, over the clandestine radio of the rebels, Son Ngoc Thanh declared that he had been mistaken in regarding the King as a traitor, that in view of the position he had taken against France, he was a true patriot. Even some members of the Cambodian forces fighting under the French deserted to join the King.

Balancing precariously between the pro-Viet Minh elements and the French (whom he needed, and from whom he nevertheless tried to differentiate

2 *Paris-presse-l'intransigent*, May 6, 1953.
3 *New York Herald Tribune*, July 25, 1953.

himself), Bao Dai's position was not at all comparable to that of the Cambodian King. Bao Dai could not abandon his post, even temporarily, without the certainty that the Viet Minh would take over the country. And he did not feel free to risk French disapproval by making political trips to other countries. In time, however, the Vietnamese profited, as did the Laotians, from Sihanouk's intransigence, for the French Government was in a mood to make concessions on independence; the King's dramatic flight had coincided with a growing demand for new policies and decisive actions to deal with Indochinese problems.

"A SERIES OF LOST OPPORTUNITIES"

Considering that France had been fighting in Indochina for seven years, that in the fall of 1952 President Vincent Auriol announced that French expenditures on the war had reached 1,600 billion francs, twice the amount of American Marshall Plan aid to France,[4] and that by the end of that year French casualties since 1945 including dead, wounded, missing, and prisoners totaled more than 90,000,[5] there was a startling amount of confusion in France about Vietnamese policy.

Jacques Raphael-Leygues, a young Radical Socialist leader whose views on the Vietnamese problem have recently won a considerable audience, said:

The war in Indochina is the culmination of a considerable historical evolution which has been hindered by stupidity, by fear, by many mistakes. It is certain that at the time of the Liberation everything could have been saved. It would have been enough to have been very clear about our objectives and quite fluid in implementing them. Instead, we have been very uncertain about our objectives and very harsh in implementing them. Since 1946 the war in Indochina has been a series of lost opportunities.[6]

Apart from such sensible opinions expressed by individuals in French political life, the behavior of the various political parties in Parliament added considerably to the confusion characterizing Indochinese problems. It is still difficult for people abroad to understand how the coalition French government of 1945 to 1947, in which two of the three member parties belonged to the Left and insisted on their friendship for Ho Chi Minh, was never able to come to terms with him. And certainly there is good reason to regard the professedly anticolonialist Socialists and Communists as seriously culpable in regard to Indochina ever since 1945.

The French Communists, characteristically, pursued a ruthless policy of

---

[4] *Chroniques d'Outre-Mer*, December 18, 1952.

[5] *Le Monde*, December 18, 1952.

[6] At the Radical Socialist Party Congress held in Bordeaux, October 1952. *L'Information Radical-Socialiste*, October 1952.

Realpolitik. They were key members of the government which appointed and supported Admiral d'Argenlieu, which permitted the failure of the Fontainebleau Conference and the attack at Haiphong, and which refused to negotiate with Ho Chi Minh after December 19, 1946. Although then the largest party in France, the Communists did not lift a hand in defense of Vietnamese independence, which they were later, in their weakness, to champion so vociferously; and when they left the government in 1947, it was on a domestic issue unconnected with the Vietnamese question. Only in 1950, when it was obvious even to them that they had no chance of winning control of the government by an appeal to the electorate, and when Ho Chi Minh and the Viet Minh were moving openly into the Cominform camp, did the French Communists move from words to action and start a campaign of strikes and demonstrations aimed at obstructing the transport of soldiers and war materiel to Indochina. When this proved completely ineffective, the Communists were left to content themselves with verbal attacks on the French Government (for which the Vietnamese question served as a convenient text) and with emotional demands for the evacuation of Indochina, a move which they knew could not possibly be made in the context of events. Observers of the Soviet scene saw the French Communists adopting the so-called "Zhdanov line," which subordinated Asian problems to European; by the time they were ready to change, finding that, if they were unable to seize power in the West, Asia offered a fertile field for revolutionary action, the French Communists were no longer in a position to do anything about it.

The Socialists, for their part, equally opposed in theory to imperialism, were hardly less opportunistic in practice. The decline of the French Socialist Party, and with it the disappearance of the postwar mirage of a strong anti-Communist Left grounded on the Socialist Party, was nowhere more evident than in regard to Viet Nam. Not only was the party divided between supporters of empire like Marius Moutet and their opponents, but it too was interested more in retaining nominal political power as a member of the governing coalition, which it did not leave until February, than in any program of principle or of action. Political conscience lost out to political expediency, and if the Socialists never found it easy to reconcile the war with their Marxist anticolonialism, they found it even less easy to translate their anticolonialism into effective practice. They tried to define their vacillating role. "It was said that I declared from this tribune three and a half years ago: 'neither reconquest nor abandonment.' That is correct!" the Socialist Daniel Mayer told the National Assembly. "We have always been opposed to a policy of exclusive force and we have always spoken against the withdrawal of the expeditionary corps."[7] But when they tried to explain what they actually did stand for, the Socialists also retired into a cloud of ineffectual rhetoric, revealing themselves with few exceptions as a group of well-intentioned men with

[7] *Journal Officiel,* Assemblée Nationale, October 19, 1950, p. 7001.

a fatal weakness for invariably voting in the end in favor of the very policies they had criticized in debate.

With the anticolonialist wing thus immobilized out of opportunism and weakness, the MRP was left to make Indochinese policy for the tripartite coalition which governed France after the Liberation. It seems a long while since the idea was voiced in France that the MRP was certain to be Leftist in regard to colonial questions because its members had few vested interests in the colonies, unlike the Radical Socialists, who had built up the empire under the Third Republic. Although this forecast did prove true of an uninfluential anticolonialist minority of the MRP, no sooner had the party superseded the Radical Socialists (as it did during the first years of the Fourth Republic, when the Radicals were still too closely identified with the failure of the Third to play a major political role), than a majority of the MRP swiftly acquired substantial interests in Indochina, not so much of an economic as of a political nature. Contrary to expectations, the MRP did not support its coreligionists in the empire, but acquired a vested interest in the somewhat doctrinaire and certainly inelastic policies, which allowed concessions to the Vietnamese only reluctantly and when forced to do so, of Georges Bidault, Paul Coste-Floret, and Jean Letourneau.

In the crucial years directly after the Liberation of France, there was little public interest in France in Indochinese questions. The outbreak of war in December 1946 did not do much to dispel this general apathy, in part, at least, because the French army fighting in Indochina is not a popular conscript army as, for example, the American army in Korea, whose fate so aroused American opinion as to be a vital factor in the Eisenhower victory in 1952; the French expeditionary corps is made up of regulars, and the majority of these are drawn not from metropolitan France but from other parts of the empire. There was thus no public opinion to force the Indochinese problem from the obscurity of the political limbo to which the three major parties by common consent had consigned it; and, in practice, French government policy toward Viet Nam was left to be formulated and implemented by a surprisingly small group of men in key positions—professional administrators, men with large economic interests in Indochina, and politicians dreaming of power and empire—who were able to have their own way because of the peculiar nature of the French political scene.

As the war dragged on, this state of affairs came in for increasing criticism and in 1953 even the colonialist weekly, *Climats,* demanded the recall of Letourneau as resident Cabinet Minister and High Commissioner in Indochina. The French Parliamentary Mission which visited Indochina early in 1953, reported:

It is grave that after eight years of *laisser-aller* and of anarchy, the presence in Indochina of a resident Minister has not been able to put an end to these daily scandals in the life in regard to the granting of licenses, the transfer of piastres, war damages, or commercial transactions. Even if our administration is not entirely responsible for these abuses, it is deplorable that one can affirm that it either ignores them or tolerates them.[8]

Commenting on this report, J. J. Servan-Schreiber, the influential editor of the independent weekly, *L'Express,* observed in *Le Monde:*

The generally accepted theory is that the prolongation of the war in Indochina is a fatality imposed by events, one of those dramas in history which has no solution. The theory of the skeptics is that the impotence or the errors of the men responsible for our policy in Indochina have prevented us from finding a way out of this catastrophic enterprise. The truth is that the facts now known seem to add up to a lucid plan worked out step by step to eliminate any possibility of negotiation in Indochina in order to assure the prolongation without limit of the hostilities and of the military occupation.

He blamed this on the "natural tendency of the military proconsulate to perpetuate itself" and on "certain French political groups who have found in the war the principal source of their revenues . . . through exchange operations, supplies to the expeditionary corps and war damages. . . ."[9]

There appeared to be a growing revulsion among the French public in 1953 against what had been done in its name in Indochina, as plain speaking and unpleasant facts were heard for the first time by the average Frenchman. The René Mayer government tried to take both the political and military situation in hand. It offered new concessions to Norodom Sihanouk. It announced the appointment of General Henri-Eugène Navarre as the new French Commander-in-Chief in Indochina, replacing General Salan. And on May 10, it devalued the currency of Indochina, revaluing the piastre at ten francs instead of seventeen.

Popular criticism had fastened with special tenacity on the piastre traffic which was known to fill not only the pockets of speculators but also the military arsenal of the Viet Minh, whose agents bought up on the black market dollars which they used for buying arms and supplies. In 1949–1950 a scandal connected with the piastre traffic had been the occasion of the notorious "affairs of the generals" which had attracted wide publicity and public denunciation of the traffic; but nothing had been done to end it. Press attacks continued, and in May 1953 the Left-Wing organ, *L'Observateur,* printed documentary evidence against individuals profiting from the traffic, citing names and dates. A few days later the government announced the devaluation.

For a move which had been so long anticipated, this came as a decided anticlimax. Actually, the piastre was still over-valued, and the dollar-piastre-franc

8 *L'Express,* May 23, 1953.
9 *Le Monde,* April 30, 1953.

exchange went on, although at a somewhat less remunerative rate. At the same time, the inflation-ridden Associated States were confronted with further inflation and had to curtail their expenditures sharply. Foreign observers noted a popular reaction against the French in Indochina. Most serious of all, however, was the failure of the French Government to do more than formally notify the governments of the three Associated States of the impending devaluation only several hours before it went into effect. This was a clearcut violation of the agreement signed with Viet Nam, Cambodia, and Laos in 1949, in which the limitation on Indochinese financial autonomy, the linking of the piastre to the franc, had in some degree been compensated for by the obligation assumed by France to consult with the three Indochinese states prior to making any changes in the relationship between the two currencies. At a time when France was concerned more than ever to present itself as the champion of Indochinese independence, its actions once again seemed to counteract its words; worse than that, it weakened the position of the very men and the very governments in the Associated States which it was to the advantage of France to support.

The reaction of the three states, which was quick in coming, was one of protest against this unilateral action; each state in turn objected to it. And Prime Minister Nguyen Van Tam, who was not known for his nationalist statements, asserted that the whole concept of the French Union should be revised, that Viet Nam did not want to be "the tenant of a house built without us." Relations between France and the three Associated States were at a new low when the René Mayer government fell in May 1953, and France entered several weeks of Cabinet crisis.

"A NEW LOOK" IN FRENCH POLICY

Joseph Laniel, conservative Independent, who was elected Premier at the end of June, addressed himself immediately to the Indochinese situation. He dismissed Letourneau who, for the first time since 1949, no longer had an influential voice in Indochinese policy. The new Premier separated the posts of High Commissioner and Cabinet Minister: a diplomat, rather than a soldier, was named Commissioner General,[9a] Maurice Dejean, former French Ambassador to Japan; and Marc Jacquet became Secretary of State in charge of relations with the Associated States.

Laniel moved from personalities to the broader question of French relations with the three Associated States. One of his first official acts, on July 3, was to inform the governments of the three Associated States that France was prepared to "perfect" their independence and sovereignty by transferring

[9a] In each of the three Associated States the French also maintained a High Commissioner, and each of the Associated States was represented in Paris by a High Commissioner.

to them various functions which had remained under French control. He called on each of the three to settle with France whatever problems it might have in the fields of finances, justice, and military and political affairs.

To the Indochinese, this offer naturally could not appear either novel or startling. Years before, the offer of independence—the word which French officials were afraid to mention in 1945, 1946, and 1947—would have had a telling impact on Vietnamese opinion. But since that time, independence had been offered on so many occasions—in the Ha Long Bay declaration, the Elysée Accords, the conventions signed on December 31, 1949, the Pau Agreements—while economic, military, and many administrative services remained under French control, and such symbols of Vietnamese independence as Norodom Palace in Saigon were still in French hands, that the skepticism of the Vietnamese was not surprising. In this respect, the French Government suffered from the mistakes of its predecessors; it seems clear that the French did actually envisage a substantial broadening of the autonomy of the Associated States but, after all that had gone before, their problem was to persuade the Associated States of their sincerity. After years of intereference with the independence of the various governments, only one last mistake remained to be made and this was to go to the other extreme, to allow Bao Dai's entourage to simmer in its own juice of inexperience and intrigue without offering them what no government has ever resented, advice drawn from a much wider experience which could help them to solve their various problems.

In reply to Premier Laniel's offer of July 3, each of the three governments agreed to new negotiations with France. The Cambodians offered a series of counterproposals and then settled down to difficult discussions. In the course of their military talks, when the French challenged Norodom Sihanouk's right to command all troops stationed on Cambodian soil, arguing that they had to defend the country from the Viet Minh, Prime Minister Penn Nouth appealed to the Viet Minh to withdraw its troops from Cambodia, saying that his government had no quarrel with Communism as long as it did not impose itself by force on the Vietnamese people. But the Cambodians subsequently worked out a military accord with the French and Norodom returned to his capital in November and declared his support of the French view that "the true danger for Cambodia is the Viet Minh."

The course of Franco-Laotian negotiations was much smoother and on October 22, 1953, King Sisavang Vong signed a treaty of friendship and association with France in which Laos was recognized as "a fully independent and sovereign state," and Laos reaffirmed its membership in the French Union.[10] On the occasion of the ceremonies attending the signature of the

[10] *Notes et Etudes Documentaires* No. 1,811 *Traité d'Amitié et d'Association et Conventions annexes entre la République française et le Royaume de Laos* (Paris, le 22 octobre 1953).

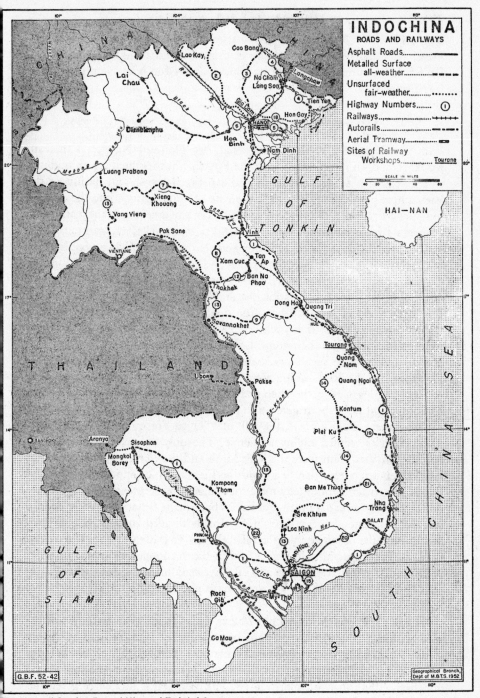

INDOCHINA
ROADS AND RAILWAYS

Asphalt Roads................
Metalled Surface
   all-weather...............
Unsurfaced
   fair-weather..............
Highway Numbers.........①
Railways.......................
Autorails.....................
Aerial Tramway.............
Sites of Railway
   Workshops...............Tourane

SCALE IN MILES

By courtesy of Canadian Dept. of Mines and Technical Surveys

Note. In recent years many sections of the railways and roads, especially in the north, have been cut, destroyed or closed to traffic because of hostilities.

treaty, President Auriol, after paying tribute to Laos and to the new agreement, deplored the expressed desire of some individuals to leave the French Union. He was referring to events which occurred in Viet Nam during the summer of 1953.

THE NATIONALIST UPSURGE IN THE BAO DAI ZONE

In Viet Nam, the announcement that Bao Dai and Nguyen Van Tam would soon open negotiations with the French was the signal for an outburst of political activity. Until this time, the political fervor and daring of the Vietnamese people seemed to have been sucked pretty much into the orbit of the Viet Minh with the result that, with certain exceptions, the nationalist elements which supported Bao Dai tended to be relatively cautious men, neither bold in their conception nor very effective in rallying popular support, fearful of antagonizing the French and finding it easier to look for help abroad rather than inside Viet Nam. This was perhaps the inevitable result of a policy which was antinationalist and antirevolutionary in its inception. But seven years of war had left little doubt that Vietnamese on both sides wanted independence; if French reluctance to grant it had encouraged extremists to consolidate their control over the Viet Minh, at the same time it had discredited each successive Vietnamese regime to take shape in the Bao Dai zone. As the Right-Wing French newspaper *Climats* pointed out in a series of articles in 1953, the "Bao Dai experiment" could not be judged fairly because it had never been given a fair chance to work.

Under these circumstances, the talk of a Third Force heard in some Vietnamese circles seemed highly academic. The only political factions of importance in Viet Nam were the Viet Minh and the elements which more or less actively supported Bao Dai—and the French. "We cannot have a 'Third Force,'" a prominent Vietnamese nationalist said recently, "because we don't want it to be a Fourth Force." What was necessary, in other words, was not to create new divisions in an already divided country, but to operate through the organized political life already in existence; and, where possible, to encourage shifts in power within the two opposing camps in order to bring to the fore responsible and effective nationalists whose primary concern was the welfare of the Vietnamese people, and who thus would be acceptable to the West.

Whether the Viet Minh would follow such leaders even if they still existed within its ranks, only its response to a French and Vietnamese policy frankly oriented in the direction of Vietnamese independence would demonstrate. But it was already certain that there were competent and honest nationalists willing to work more closely with Bao Dai if they were given the opportunity, and anxious to take advantage of the growing American role in

Viet Nam to try to make a more genuinely Vietnamese Bao Dai policy. In this they would doubtless have had the support of the Emperor, who so far had maintained his own form of *attentisme*—rebuffing French efforts to compromise him with the various pro-French regimes functioning under his authority. Bao Dai, in his own way, stood for the unity and independence of Viet Nam; and already he had spoken publicly of his desire for increased independence, and of his hope for American support.

Against this background, Ngo Dinh Nhu, a trade union leader and a brother of Ngo Dinh Diem, assumed a leading role in organizing an unofficial "congress of national union and peace" which assembled in Cholon on September 6, 1953. It demanded unconditional independence for Viet Nam and, on the domestic level, the immediate summoning of a national assembly, freedom of press and association, an end to corruption, and reforms of the army and the administration. This congress took such a strong stand that Bao Dai felt the need to summon his own official congress the following month to meet in two-day session and endorse his position by choosing twenty men from among whom Bao Dai could select six to carry on the forthcoming negotiations with France.

Although the methods by which the members were selected and the limited duration and purposes of the congress led many nationalists (among them Ngo Dinh Nhu) to refuse to participate in it, the second congress, as it turned out, did not differ radically in attitude from the first. Under the leadership of Dr. Pham Huu Chuong, who had recently left the Viet Minh zone where he had been director of public health services, this congress refused to appoint any delegates to negotiate with France, rejecting all responsibility for the negotiations. It also demanded a constitution and a national assembly and moved that all treaties with France be approved by a national assembly elected by universal suffrage. And it declared that Viet Nam, when independent, would not participate in the French Union (although the members were later persuaded to modify this motion to refer to "the French Union in its present form").

The congress had sharp repercussions in France, where newspapers and politicians of widely divergent political groups demanded to know what France was fighting for in Indochina. French opinion had never regarded the war primarily or even essentially as a war against Communism. Communism had not even been an issue when the French Government negotiated with Ho Chi Minh in 1946, when the French army and French officials refused to make peace with him in 1947, when they built up Bao Dai as an alternative to him in 1947 and 1948. The idea that they might be engaged in a struggle against international Communism only occurred to Frenchmen later and never assumed any great popularity in France. In Indochina French policies had long played into the hands of the Communists; by rejecting the idea of independence for any Vietnamese regime, regardless of its politics, French officials for years had made it impossible for the Bao Dai government to have any hope of success against the Viet Minh. It is true that by 1953 much of the old spirit of colonialism had died, but it had been replaced not by anti-Communism, but by an emotional attachment on the part of Frenchmen to the concept of the French Union. It was for the French Union that France was fighting in Indochina, Premier Laniel told the National Assembly in October 1953, as he had already told Bao Dai; if the Vietnamese chose to leave the French Union, France would have no more reason to fight. "France will never abandon her friends," he said, "but she has no reason to prolong her sacrifices if the very people for whom they are made disdain those sacrifices and betray them."[11]

Once having insisted on the principle of the French Union, however, French leaders declared their willingness to broaden its meaning. The new Franco-Laotian Treaty was a step in this direction. And in November 1953, the first statesman of the French Union, President Vincent Auriol, in a valedictory address on the occasion of the final session of the High Council of the French Union, laid down an extremely liberal interpretation of the French Union, as "a great fraternal community constituted by France and its *départements* and overseas territories, as well as by the freely associated, independent and sovereign states, free and equal in rights and duties, which solemnly pledge themselves to pool their resources, to coordinate their efforts in order to develop their respective civilizations, to increase their well-being, and to assure their security."[12]

The French reaction to Vietnamese demands was thus not nearly as uncompromising as it may first have seemed, but Vietnamese nationalists had only begun to make known their demands which reflected widespread popular dissatisfaction with the domestic situation in the Bao Dai zone. In the face of the upsurge of nationalist sentiment, the Tam government, headed as it was by a French citizen, could not last very long. Although Tam made a last-ditch bid for nationalist leadership, demanding elections and more independence for Viet Nam, he was obviously unacceptable to the nationalists and Bao Dai himself took the initiative in asking for his resignation in December.

All of this was evidence of new life in the long stagnant Vietnamese political scene. Even the "Big Five" groups, which had filled more than half the

11 *Journal Officiel*, Assemblée Nationale, October 27, 1953, pp. 4602–3.

12 *Le Monde*, November 29–30, 1953. Following President Auriol, Commissioner General Maurice Dejean pointed out the two conceptions on which the French Union was based: "One, set forth in the preamble of the constitution, is essentially liberal and egalitarian; the other, in section eight [of the constitution], is essentially federative and confers on one of the partners a role of coordination and direction. One can now say that it is the first that France is following in her relations with the Associated States." *Ibid.*, January 19, 1954.

seats in the October congress, had joined in voting resolutions which were contrary to the desires of Bao Dai; but they were bound to the existing regime by such strong ties of material advantage that they stood in practice as the strongest supporters of the status quo, corrupt, ineffectual, and unrepresentative though it might be. Aligned against them were a variety of individuals and nascent groups. If many Vietnamese still registered their disapproval of the regime by refusing to participate in it (a practice they had learned from the years of French rule, when so many people who did not choose to indulge in revolutionary activities had withdrawn from all political life), certain small political groupings were taking shape in the Bao Dai zone, like that formed in Saigon by Ngo Dinh Nhu and his friends and certain Socialist groups. In the north, Dr. Chuong and other men who had recently left the Viet Minh shared many of Nhu's ideas but were prepared, as he was not, to establish an authoritarian regime in order to direct a national and social revolution.

How these heterogeneous elements could be organized into some sort of working unity represented a major problem for Vietnamese nationalists. Even for those who tended to be critical of Bao Dai because of his apparent reluctance to establish representative institutions and his support of individuals not conspicuous for their nationalism, the Chief of State seemed to be the one personality around whom the country might rally were he to assume active leadership of the nationalist movement. This was a difficult role to wish on anyone: it was possible and reasonable to expect a reform and cleaning up of the Vietnamese administration, but the problem of the relationship with France was not easily solved. It was all very well to demand the withdrawal of the French; there was no question but that that was the way to rally popular support. The difficulty was that, as yet, no Bao Dai regime could exist without France; if it were left alone, it would be overwhelmed in a matter of days by the Viet Minh.

Under these circumstances, it was not surprising that Vietnamese nationalist elements regarded with a watchful eye the growing desire on the part of Frenchmen to make peace in Indochina.

NEGOTIATIONS WITH THE VIET MINH?

At first, it was mostly French Socialists and independent Leftists (as well as Communists) who, soon after the war had begun, urged negotiations with the Viet Minh. They wielded little political influence, and the reasons they gave—humanity, political morality, the right of people to determine their own government in their own interest—did not find a receptive audience in France. But then members of the influential Radical Socialist party began to question the utility of the war.

Although as late as 1948 and 1949 the Radicals seemed generally even more intransigent than the MRP and less inclined toward reform and concessions, the only member of the party who had held an important post in regard to Indochina prior to this time was Emile Bollaert; and in spite of his failure, Bollaert played a more constructive role as High Commissioner than either his predecessor or his successors (with the exception of General de Lattre). As a result, when the Radical Socialists re-emerged as a major political party, it was the only one which had not shared a serious responsibility for, and hence was not committed to defending, French government policy in Indochina since 1945. The Radical Socialists quite naturally joined the MRP and the Independents in the various Center-Right coalitions which governed France after the Leftist parties went into the opposition, and Radical Socialists like René Mayer became official spokesmen for the Indochina policy of the French Government. It was not surprising, however, that when new and responsible voices were raised in the French Parliament in criticism of the Vietnamese war, these also came from the Radical Socialist benches, where sat the men who, not having to defend their own political record, were free to consider objectively the effect of the war on French national interests.

In October 1950 former Cabinet Minister Pierre Mendès-France first stated in the National Assembly what was to become the position of an important segment of the Radical Socialist Party.[13] He said:

Without doubt technical errors have been committed and it has been right to condemn them from this tribune; but it is the global concept of our action in Indochina which is false because it is based at once on a military effort which is insufficient and powerless to assure a solution of force and on a political policy which is insufficient and powerless to assure the support of the population.

Mendès-France insisted that no military solution was possible. Not only would a military effort have to be an enormous undertaking, remote from France, he held, but

... further, we have today the burden of reconstruction, the necessities of a modern social policy, a standard of living to safeguard, and a European situation which it is also necessary to watch over. . . . Let us have no illusions . . . that we can do everything at the same time . . . assure rearmament in Europe and make

13 Even earlier, during December 1949, in L'Aurore, the official organ of the Radical Socialist Party, O. P. Gilbert concluded a series of articles on Viet Nam with a recommendation for the evacuation of the country. Although reprimanded for this view on another page of the same journal, Gilbert declared his lack of confidence in what was then French policy and wrote: "We must stop the war in Indochina. Indochina is too far away for us to have a true, a single chance of winning. And even if we did, they would not let us profit. We must leave Indochina . . . Let us accept, as the English accepted in India, the material loss of Indochina . . . Indochina will no longer be French; it will be Annamese and perhaps, for a time, Communist. But those whom our élite have trained and perfected will remember France, will speak French and will forget, little by little, the mistakes of colonialism and will think only of the merits of our civilization." L'Aurore, December 15, 1949.

war in the Orient. . . . I repeat in conclusion, one thing in any case is sure: it would be an unpardonable crime to pursue in Indochina a policy of which the uncertainty, the equivocation and the mediocrity have already cost us so dear. . . .

There was just one way out, he said,

. . . a political agreement, an agreement obviously with the people we are fighting. . . . That means concessions, large concessions, beyond a doubt more important than those which would have been sufficient long ago. And the differences between the losses which are now unavoidable and those which would have been sufficient three or four years ago is the price that we will have to pay for our unpardonable errors.[14]

Although when Mendès-France made this speech, members of his party insisted that he was speaking only for himself, other Radical Socialists soon echoed his sentiments. They were concerned by the continuing financial drain of the war, by the number of graduates of Saint-Cyr military academy (the French West Point) and of noncommissioned officers who were being killed each year, by the fact that France was dissipating vainly in Indochina the military strength it needed to counterbalance the reviving military power of Germany and to maintain its control over other sections of its empire, by the certainty that unless French policy were soon changed in Viet Nam, the French would reap a harvest of hate throughout the country.

At the Radical Socialist Congress held in Bordeaux in October 1952, prominent members of the party hammered away at the fundamental importance of the Indochinese question to the situation in France and to its position abroad. "Whatever the government of France and whatever its financial policy," prewar Premier Edouard Daladier said, "it will be very hard to resolve the difficulties until the Indochinese problem is resolved." They tell us, he said, that in Indochina we are defending the French Union, but "The future of France is in Africa. Rabat, Dakar, Algiers have as much importance for us as Strasbourg and Metz." Instead of wasting men and materiel in Indochina, he said, it was important to have 100,000 French soldiers in North Africa "at a time when attacks are multiplying in Tunisia, when foreign influences are developing in Morocco and all of Africa."[15]

The Indochinese war was also a serious drain on the contribution of France to the North Atlantic Community and to the defense of Western Europe. "The war in Indochina is at the heart of the European question," said Edgar Faure in October 1952; he had been Premier of France several months earlier.[16]

This sort of reasoning led logically to attempts at reopening contacts with the Viet Minh; a country of the political maturity of France could not carry

14 *Journal Officiel*, Assemblée Nationale, October 18, 1950, pp. 7003–04.
15 *L'Information Radical-Socialiste*, October 1952.
16 *Ibid.*

on a war indefinitely without making some effort on the political level to break the military deadlock in Viet Nam. Late in 1952, under the conservative Cabinet of Antoine Pinay, government circles decided to attempt an informal exchange of views with the Viet Minh about the possibility of bringing the war to an end by the methods of diplomacy. It was important that the man who was to lend his good offices to such an exploratory mission should be above suspicion of partiality so that the free world, and particularly the United States, should have no reason to believe that this would be the prelude to any political surrender to the Communists. For this reason, the choice fell on Prince Buu Hoi, a staunch nationalist who had lent his support to the Ho Chi Minh government during its nationalist period and severed relations with the Viet Minh when the extremist elements gained control.

In February 1953, after René Mayer had become Premier, Buu Hoi delivered to the Ho Chi Minh government through its representatives in Rangoon[16a] assurances that the French Government was not opposed to the principle of negotiations and would welcome contacts which would bring about a clarification on both sides.[17] The prince was accompanied by Jacques Raphael-Leygues, a member of the moderate Radical Socialist group which was not eager to see the war go on without at least trying to achieve such a clarification. Subsequently Albert Sarraut, veteran Radical Socialist statesman and President of the Assembly of the French Union, came out in favor of negotiations with the Viet Minh provided that it would not insist on communization of the country. A similar interest in seeking contacts with the Viet Minh was expressed by leading political figures in France, and in June 1953 Pierre Mendès-France failed by only thirteen votes to be elected Premier of France. The Viet Minh, however, merely acknowledged Buu Hoi's message without comment, and no explicit reply was received until November 29, when Ho Chi Minh belatedly informed the Swedish newspaper *Expressen*, in answer to a series of questions that had been put to him, that he was prepared to consider negotiating with France. At that time, in view of the new Soviet line under Malenkov, Ho Chi Minh's answer, which was couched in doctrinaire Communist rhetoric, was widely considered as merely a part of the international Communist campaign of peace propaganda and without any intrinsic political importance.

Only certain Vietnamese nationalists, misled by the growing unpopularity of the war in France, took Ho Chi Minh's statement at all seriously. They were fearful that the French might decide to abandon them to face the Viet

---

[16a] Since 1950, when the Siamese Government recognized Bao Dai, the Viet Minh has maintained in Burma a diplomatic mission, which has not been formally recognized.

[17] *La Vie Française*, October 23, 1953. For later information see: *L'Express*, March 6, 1954; *Journal Officiel*, Assemblée Nationale, March 9, 1954, p. 771; *ibid.*, Assemblée de l'Union Française, March 11, 1954, pp. 230–231; *Le Figaro*, March 13 and 15, 1954.

Minh alone with only the doubtful protection of an inadequate army and an ineffectual administration, the shortcomings of both of which they attributed to French policy.

The French Government, however, did not intend to abandon its commitments in Indochina. Its position was well summed up by Roger Priouret in an article in *La Vie Française,* obviously inspired by official sources:

The adversary wants us to sue for peace as though we were defeated, it wants to impose conditions which are not unknown . . . .: proclamation of the Popular Republic of Viet Nam, evacuation of the expeditionary corps, and protection of French interests.

We know what would become of these interests with nothing to guarantee them any more, and which are not only material interests. But we know also and above all that a truce at that price would be for our allies, even for the non-Americans, the proof that they should no longer have any confidence in us, and for North African extremists it would be a signal for disorders. Who knows even what 'precautions' the United States might be led to take in Morocco?[18]

Before the parliament Premier Laniel explained the French position at length, placing it within its international context and making it clear that France envisaged negotiations only in full agreement with the governments of the Associated States. He said:

The war will not end by extermination but, rather, with the discouragement of one of the two belligerents; and the reasons for discouragement, in the long run, are greater on their side than on ours. . . . Of course, negotiations are to be hoped for. No one has ever made war for the pleasure of making war, certainly not for seven years. It would be inadmissable for anyone in this Assembly to imagine that the French Government does not always think of peace as its supreme objective in this affair.

But to make peace, it is necessary to be at least two, and those who speak of peace and negotiation are saying nothing so long as they fail to say with whom it is necessary to negotiate, with whom it is necessary to make peace. With China? It goes without saying that no matter what happens, we will never falter in our loyalty to our Allies, but with that reservation a negotiation with China in order to facilitate the settlement of the war in Viet Nam does not appear to us as a pact with the devil.

France has given the most tangible proofs of the sincerity of her intentions in regard to Viet Nam. These proofs are recognition of total independence and acceptance of unity sanctioned by the vote of the French Parliament concerning Cochin China. It is impossible to believe that Vietnamese nationalists, even if they were Communists, could have chosen freely to prolong the war, to pursue the devastation of their country, after all that France has done to respond to the aspirations of Vietnamese patriotism. Everything points to the conclusion that the

18 *La Vie Française, loc. cit.*

great Communist powers have compelled the Viet Minh to continue the war. For Vietnamese nationalists, the war can no longer have national objectives. I do not know of any Franco-Vietnamese accord which limits our liberty of negotiations or which would hamper our efforts for peace. There are unknown agreements which doubtless oblige the Viet Minh, in exchange for the arms it receives, to utilize them as long as the Communist camp esteems it to be in their interest.

But why do we think that the chances of a solution today are greater than a year ago? It is because a great change has occurred since then. That change derives from the armistice in Korea. The armistice is the sign that when the Communist world is certain that it cannot achieve a military victory without risking a general conflagration, it accepts at least a pause, at least a truce.

Well, what do we observe since the armistice? Until last August, the *mots d'ordre* of Russian and Chinese propaganda were the total victory of the Viet Minh and the crushing of the imperialists. Since that time, numerous allusions to the possibilities of negotiation have been made in Moscow and Peking. On September 19, in a speech delivered in the Kremlin, M. Malenkov expressed his desire to see the armistice in Korea become 'the point of departure for new efforts aimed at lessening international tension in the entire world, and notably in the Far East.' An analogous declaration was made on August 24 by M. Chou En Lai, Chinese Minister of Foreign Affairs.

M. Foster Dulles, on his side, on several occasions has publicly declared himself ready to participate in such a negotiation. In a speech at St. Louis, on September 2, he declared that from the political conference on Korea 'could come, if Communist China desired it, the end of aggression and the return of peace in Indochina.' He confirmed this idea on September 24 before the United Nations. The British Government also has gradually rallied to this thesis.

Is it necessary for me to say what France thinks? Who among us would object to the idea of negotiations, in an international framework, in order to reestablish peace in Indochina? Unhappily, there is someone who does not seem to be in agreement, it is Ho Chi Minh, it is the general staff of the Viet Minh, it is the small group of leaders of a movement which is no longer able to make compromises. . . .

Summing up, Laniel said:

My government is ready to seize all occasions to make peace, whether in Indochina or on the international level. . . .[19] I must repeat in the clearest and most categorical fashion that the French Government does not consider the Indochinese problem as necessarily requiring a military solution. No more than the Americans in Korea do we demand an unconditional capitulation of the adversary in Korea in order to discuss with him. No more than the United States does France make war for the sake of war, and if an honorable solution were in view, either on the local level or on the international level, France, I repeat, like the United States in Korea, would be happy to welcome a diplomatic solution of the conflict.[20]

[19] *Journal Officiel*, Assemblée Nationale, October 27, 1953, p. 4606.
[20] *Ibid.*, Conseil de la République, November 12, 1953, p. 1748.

CHALLENGE TO AMERICANS

Whatever the formula for peace, the French Government recognized that it was no longer entirely a free agent in Viet Nam. It is true that France had consistently resisted formal internationalization of the war, refusing to appeal to the United Nations to take action in regard to a war which, beyond a doubt, is a threat to international peace and security. Even in 1953, at the time of the Viet Minh invasion of Laos which occasioned so much alarm abroad, when certain members of the French Cabinet were reported to favor a request to the United Nations for help, they were overruled—partly to avoid foreign discussion and intervention in the affairs, not only of Indochina, but of the French Union generally; and partly out of fear that United Nations intervention would precipitate Chinese intervention on the side of the Viet Minh, creating a situation similar to that which had prevailed in Korea. At the same time, however, the French Government sought and received from its allies (from the signatories to the North Atlantic Treaty in 1952 and from the British and American Governments on various occasions and at Bermuda in 1953) an endorsement of its war effort as vital to the defense of the free world. And it also sought and received substantial military and economic aid, mostly from the United States.

Certain highly placed French officials were once reported as fearful of allowing American aid to reach fifty percent of the total French military effort in Indochina, on the theory that the United States would then be in "the zone of political demands." Such fears were somewhat unrealistic; at the moment when American aid, whatever its percent, became indispensable to France, as it did long ago, the United States reached that zone. The French Government had to take into account the determination of the United States to defend Indochina against Communism.

By 1954 the American Government was paying about eighty percent of the total French military expenditures in the Associated States.[20a] American aid, which began in 1950, had averaged $500 million annually and included ammunition, vehicles, aircraft, naval vessels, small arms and automatic weapons, hospital supplies and technical equipment, which were delivered directly to the French Union forces under the supervision of an American Military Assistance Advisory Group (MAAG). In 1953, on the basis of military plans drawn up by General Navarre and a French pledge "to intensify prosecution of the war" and make "every effort to break up and destroy

[20a] Christian Pineau, spokesman of the Finance Committee of The National Assembly stated that "The distribution of expenditures for the Indochinese war is as follows: . . . out of a total expenditure of 626 billion francs, the share of the United States is 490 billion (about U.S. $1,400 million) or 78.25%, and that of France, 136 billion or 21.75%." Aid to the Associated States, 135 billion francs, was charged entirely to the United States. *Journal Officiel*, Assemblée Nationale, March 16, 1954.

regular enemy forces in Indochina,"[21] the United States promised France an extra $385 million.

This "Navarre Plan" was directed at infusing the French Union forces with a new dynamism and a spirit of attack. It called for French reinforcements and for increasing the armies of the Associated States. In 1953 and 1954 the French commander undertook to pursue the strategy which General de Lattre had formulated but which he had not had the time to carry out fully before his death. With the Tonkinese delta ringed by French defenses, Navarre tried to root out the Viet Minh from its positions in the delta. At the same time, he launched a series of operations directed at consolidating French control over other regions from which the Viet Minh had been only nominally expelled. And he attempted to meet the Viet Minh on its own ground by training Vietnamese "commando" battalions adapted to the guerrilla tactics of Giap's men.

This was not positional warfare; there were no political boundaries and no front lines; the battlefield was constantly shifting and few areas were under the exclusive control of either side. The problem for the French was less to win land than to win battles. In the fall of 1953 they concentrated on the Tonkinese delta region until just before Christmas, when the Viet Minh launched a new attack on Laos, moving swiftly from Vinh on the Central Vietnam coast, over mountains and across jungle country, until they reached the Siamese frontier on the Mekong. This time, however, their advance occasioned relatively little alarm in informed quarters, which recognized the unreality of sensational newspaper reports that the Viet Minh was trying to cut Indochina in two; elements of the Viet Minh army, ranging through the broad expanses of sparsely settled Laos, had cut the country in half years before; only sea and air routes linked the north and south.

The war went on on various fronts in the winter of 1953-54. A key point for the entire French military position in Indochina was the French stronghold at Dien Bien Phu in the Vietnamese Thai country on the Laotian frontier. With the region heavily beseiged by the Viet Minh, it seemed for a time that the future of the entire war might be at stake there; in Washington, the National Security Council anxiously discussed the situation in January 1954 and considered a French request for four hundred American air mechanics and maintenance men to be sent to Indochina.[22] Also in January, while the French position in the Thai country was still menaced, Vietnamese battalions under General Navarre's command landed at Tuy Hoa on the Central Viet Nam coast, an area which for years had been under Viet

21 *Department of State Bulletin,* October 12, 1953.

22 Joseph and Stewart Alsop, *New York Herald Tribune,* January 27, 1954. They agreed finally to send 200 American technicians. When this move occasioned concern in the United States that it might be a prelude to a large-scale involvement of American manpower in the Indochinese war, President Eisenhower denied that this would be the case.

Minh control. This landing, which necessitated the weakening of French positions in other, more important sectors in Central Viet Nam, seemed to have been dictated more by motives of propaganda than of strategy, although the swift success of the French attack, which was duplicated in March at Qhi Nhon, seemed to demonstrate that French strategy had erred in concentrating on the delta regions while leaving the Viet Minh free to recruit its manpower in and consolidate its political control over large areas of central Viet Nam.

Later that month, the Viet Minh struck on another front. It withdrew a substantial number of the troops threatening Dien Bien Phu and advanced in force on Luang Prabang, the Laotian capital, renewing the earlier attack which it had halted in the spring of 1953, a move which was variously explained as motivated by a possible desire on the part of the Viet Minh to extend its lines over as wide an area as possible in preparation for any cease-fire negotiations, and perhaps even by a determination to forestall any shifts in Communist policy which might lead the Chinese to abandon the Viet Minh. Indeed, as the Big Four Foreign Ministers met in Berlin in January–February 1954, every military move in Indochina, on the part of the French as of the Viet Minh, seemed to be undertaken with an eye to its effect on their allies.

In the midst of the confused military situation, one thing at least seemed clear. Despite certain limited successes achieved under the "Navarre Plan," French forces still appeared unable to cope with the continuing infiltration of the Viet Minh into the key delta regions; this infiltration recently extended even to the High Plateaus of the Moi region in the southern part of Central Viet Nam, an area which had been considered as safe by the French and the Bao Dai government. The day when the French Union forces would be able to seize the initiative from the Viet Minh, if it were to come at all, seemed remote.

On another and less publicized front, the United States continued to extend its aid directly to the governments of the Associated States. The prospect of having no French intermediaries between the Americans and the Indochinese, with its implication of closer Indochinese relations with the United States and of greater independence for the Associated States, had been accepted only with reluctance by empire-minded French officials. Only a few years ago Robert Blum, former chief of the American aid program, had even been described by French colonial administrators in Viet Nam as "the most dangerous man in Indochina." But the American aid program went on; the United States spent $96 million in the years 1951–54 on technical and economic aid, and an additional $30 million on a military support program. Administered by STEM (Special Technical and Economic Mission), this aid was given not only to strengthen the military effort against the Viet Minh, but also to increase the effectiveness and broaden the popular support of the governments of the three Associated States so that they could hold their own against the Communists; and to increase agricultural and industrial production.

After the years of war, the Indochinese were in sore need of such help. If the French did not have the resources to do all that was necessary, the Associated States had considerably less, just enough, a Mutual Security Agency report observed, to cause them to be "best known to the people in the capacity of policeman and tax collector."[23] In prewar years, Indochina, despite depressed conditions at home, had been able to present a prosperous face to the world with a consistently favorable balance of trade; but that vanished with the war, and Indochina now imports more than twice as much as it exports. To the usual economic and social problems of the region, which in Viet Nam are compounded by the density of the population in several key areas, were added new and serious complications brought on by the war, such as the hundreds of thousands of refugees who crowded into the cities and French-controlled coastal areas, and the breakdown of communications and transport facilities. STEM interested itself in a wide variety of fields: rebuilding highways and bridges; resettling refugees; regrouping unprotected villages into larger defensible units;[23a] improving conditions of public health, carrying on the large-scale treatment of such diseases as trachoma and malaria, and constructing sanitary wells; sponsoring a low-cost housing program; and assisting in a program to reduce illiteracy.

In view of the ambitious nature of this program, it may seem surprising that so little has been accomplished, both in improving the military situation and in strengthening the Vietnamese regime. Vietnamese themselves find several explanations for this state of affairs. They are inclined to attribute it to a lack of preparation; to inadequate contacts with the local population and an insufficient knowledge of local conditions, the heritage of the many decades of American indifference to Indochinese affairs; and to unwarranted confidence in the façade of Vietnamese officials behind which widespread corruption has flourished.

This enormous American investment in Indochina, nevertheless, bears witness to a decisive shift in United States policy toward Southeast Asia in a period of a few years. Just as American indifference, not so long ago, resulted in a passive attitude toward Vietnamese aspirations for independence and thereby contributed to the present havoc, so today it is to be hoped that the keen interest of the United States in this region of the world will not permit any settlement of the Indochinese war which does not agree with the basic imperatives of American policy in that area.

[23] Mutual Security Agency, *U.S. Technical and Economic Assistance in the Far East* (May 1953).

[23a] This plan for regrouping villages, inspired by the success of a similar British project in Malaya, was reported to be a special interest of Nguyen Huu Tri, Governor of North Viet Nam.

Determined to see the independence of the Associated States assured by democratic means, American officials have emphasized above all the importance of carrying on the war; they have encouraged the French and urged the Vietnamese to intensify their military effort. Despite Secretary of State Dulles' statement when he was in Paris, that the war could be won in 1954,[24] Senator Mike Mansfield reported to the United States Senate, after a trip to Indochina, that the non-Communist forces were still "a long way from the threshold of victory."[25] But that the war should go on, supported generously by the United States, influential Americans seemed agreed. The American position was summed up by Vice President Richard Nixon when he declared: "Under no circumstances could negotiations take place that would place people who want independence under bondage. It is impossible to lay down arms until victory is completely won."[26]

It does not ensue, however, that the United States is to be blamed for the continuation of the war, as a considerable body of French opinion of the Right and Center (to say nothing of the Left) seems to think. Such critics tend to take rather lightly the responsibilities that France has assumed in Indochina. It is quite true, as they argue, that the war cannot be permitted to go on indefinitely, and it is certain that if the French were compelled to increase their expeditionary force to the point where they would have to have recourse to conscripts from metropolitan France, French public opinion would force peace on any French government. However, the French cannot simply pack up and leave. Not only is there the practical problem of finding the transport to evacuate the expeditionary corps; there is the overriding and undeniable fact that any evacuation at this time would result in the speedy elimination or subjugation of all non-Communist elements in the country, and the institution of a Communist dictatorship not only in Viet Nam, but also in Laos and Cambodia, with serious and unsettling results for all of Southeast Asia.

If the British, before evacuating India in time of peace, first needed a Mountbatten to work out in detail the political structure and the alignment of forces to be left in control in India and Pakistan, similar action would seem to be an obvious prerequisite to a departure from warring Viet Nam. The United States took the French Government at its word when it assumed primary responsibility for a solution of the Vietnamese question; Frenchmen can hardly be surprised that the United States expects them to remain in the country until non-Communist nationalist elements are in a position to defend themselves, and a viable democratic national regime can be left in effective

24 *Le Monde*, December 16, 1953.
25 83d Congress, 1st Session. *Indochina. Report of Senator Mike Mansfield on a Study Mission to the Associated States of Indochina, Viet Nam, Cambodia, Laos.* October 27, 1953.
26 *New York Times*, November 8, 1953.

control. That is, after all, only what French officials professed to be aiming at when they asked, and received, American aid. To the Frenchmen who accuse the United States of undue intransigence, it is enough to recall that in 1947, when the Viet Minh had not yet sided with the Soviet bloc, Secretary of State Marshall expressed the hope of the American Government that the French could work with Viet Minh leaders for a peaceful settlement. At that time, however, French officials showed no great desire to make peace in Indochina.

Now that the Viet Minh has aligned itself with the Soviet bloc, the French Government, Vietnamese nationalist circles, and American statesmen are all agreed upon the fact that negotiations can only be undertaken from a position of strength. But wide differences exist among them as to what the word strength should mean. For the Vietnamese patriot, strength means above all political stability and that, in turn, requires in the Bao Dai zone a policy which would satisfy nationalist feelings sufficiently to free non-Communist elements now with the Viet Minh of any complex of guilt toward the nation when they break with the Communists. For the French, a position of strength *par excellence* in Viet Nam would be one of equilibrium which would allow them to keep the balance equal between the Communist Viet Minh and the nationalists, so as to enable the French to play the role of arbiter between the two sides. For American statesmen interested in this part of the world, strength seems to mean a series of military successes on the part of the French Union army to pave the way for the capitulation of the adversary.

These divergent concepts cannot be easily reconciled, but it would be unrealistic to attempt to impose any policy which ignored the Vietnamese point of view. The Vietnamese do not regard military victories, in and of themselves, as an adequate means of pacifying the country; as long as Viet Nam does not achieve full independence, a French victory over any fraction of the Vietnamese people would in some degree be resented by the rest of the population as a defeat for the whole nation. Irrational and illogical as this attitude may seem, it is nonetheless the prevailing one; for that reason, it is one that American policy-makers cannot afford to disregard.

It is a matter of record that prominent Americans have consistently insisted on the right of the Associated States to independence, as has the United States Department of State, and for that reason Indochinese nationalists have looked hopefully to the United States for help. They have not always received it. In their justifiable concern to maintain a united front between France and the Associated States, American officials came to the aid of France during its difficulties with King Norodom Sihanouk; and in Viet Nam, at the time of the Saigon nationalist congress, they went so far as to try to persuade certain of the participants to adopt a more moderate course. When Vice President Nixon arrived in Indochina during the fall of 1953, he also urged the Vietnamese to co-operate with France. Writing from Viet Nam, Max Arnaud, a French journalist in touch with Vietnamese nationalist circles, commented in an important dispatch:

> To declare, as he [Nixon] had done, that 'it is possible and necessary for Viet Nam and France to carry on, within the framework of the French Union, a common struggle in order to attain common objectives,' is to demonstrate the evolution of American policy in Indochina in the last two years. The United States continues to present itself as the defender of the independence and liberty of peoples, but it is clear that this preoccupation is now only secondary. . . .
>
> It [the American Embassy] is trying by every means to avoid a break between the Associated States and France, and each time it aligns itself on our side in order to give France no pretext for putting an end to the conflict. An American diplomat said recently with humor: 'We are the last French colonialists in Indochina.'
>
> But Vietnamese nationalist circles, particularly in Tonkin, have taken Mr. Nixon's initiative very badly. . . . Many of them feel that the support given to the French by Mr. Nixon is a new proof of the egoism of great nations. They feel that they have been deceived when they contemplate the new attitude of a country on which they thought that they could depend to obtain their total independence from France. The general feeling is that if the nationalist effervescence of the month of October has now calmed down, it is certainly not dead. If it resumes one day or another, it will be directed against the United States as well as against France. It seems that only the Communists could benefit.[27]

Strong as these words may be, they point to the basic problem confronting Vietnamese nationalists who, no matter how extreme their language may be, are rarely extremists. They have undertaken the difficult task of trying to lay down political roots in the country, to divest themselves of the charge of being identified more closely with France than with Viet Nam, to persuade the people to follow them rather than the Viet Minh. If Norodom Sihanouk was trying to secure his control over what might have developed into a popular revolutionary movement against him, so the members of the Saigon congress were trying to assert their political leadership among their compatriots. There is no reason to believe that nationalists, either in Viet Nam or Cambodia, are not aware that they will have numerous and weighty problems to deal with once they have achieved independence. That they see fit to concentrate on the independence issue to the virtual exclusion of all others, is simply their response to the temper of the country to which they are naturally more sensitive than any foreigner could be. Under these circumstances, it would seem to be in the American interest to encourage them to assume leadership, to guide them if necessary into constructive channels, and to recognize that the success of the war against Communism in Viet Nam depends upon the extent to which they can rally popular support and harness the full energies

[27] *Le Monde*, November 12, 1953.

of the nation. The aim of American policy, after all, is not to create a Vietnamese Formosa, but to build a free and independent Viet Nam.

The evolution of the Vietnamese political scene must inevitably influence the shape of any political settlement, if there is any possibility at all of achieving one. A serious problem for the many Frenchmen and Vietnamese of good will who are anxious for peace with the Viet Minh is the weakness of the non-Communist forces in Indochina. The Viet Minh still exercises nationalist appeal among its compatriots who cannot forget that Viet Nam's steady advance after the second World War in the direction of unity and independence occurred only because of the existence of the Viet Minh. No Vietnamese can forget that Ho Chi Minh was the first Vietnamese leader to declare the independence of Viet Nam, not merely in principle as did Tran Trong Kim, but in fact. He declared it an independent state in September 1945 and a free state in March 1946; the Ho Chi Minh regime was the only government of Viet Nam until 1947, and the French had been the first to recognize it as such. When Ho Chi Minh went to war, he had seemed to be the heir to the nationalist tradition of his people, the spiritual descendant of De Tham and Phan Dinh Phung, who once led guerrillas against the French, of Phan Boi Chau who had sought Chinese as well as Japanese help against them, of Nguyen Thai Hoc, leader of the anti-Communist VNQDD, who died at Yen Bay. Ho Chi Minh had also followed in the footsteps of the emperors who had fought French rule, three of whom had been in exile at the same time not so long ago. For this reason prominent anti-Communist nationalists never publicly criticized what was regarded throughout Viet Nam as "the resistance" or the *maquis,* and even several members of the royal family and of the former imperial Cabinet came out in favor of Ho during the first years of his government.

No sooner had the Viet Minh given Vietnamese new reason for confidence in the future, however, than it acted in such a way as to leave little hope that that future could be a happy one. It imposed a Communist dictatorship upon the resistance, which served to convince many nationalists that the Viet Minh was primarily concerned with consolidating Communist power at the expense of non-Communist nationalists who might possibly challenge its leadership; that is, at the expense of the nationalist movement itself. In that way it alienated many nationalists, some of whom had worked with the resistance at the start and others who had held aloof because of its Leftist leaders.

At the same time, the Viet Minh cut itself off from most of non-Communist Asia and the West; and false ideas and conceptions about the West have been generated in this closed Viet Minh world where the radio and press, and all the organs of mass propaganda speak only with the strident voice of Communism. The disastrous mistake of the Viet Minh and its leaders, whatever their provocation, was to move so blindly into the Communist camp, and this without any obvious pressure being exerted upon them from behind the Iron Curtain. It did not serve the Vietnamese struggle for independence to make the Communist leadership dictatorial and overt; it served Vietnamese independence no more for the Viet Minh to identify its struggle with the ideological aims of the Soviet bloc. These political actions have had the effect of nullifying the remarkable military accomplishments of the Viet Minh, without bringing any decisive help from abroad. The Communist policies of the Viet Minh have consistently negated its military policy; the more it fights, the more it is forced into a dead end. In the years since 1950 it appears even to have abandoned any attempt at an independent diplomacy.[28]

No less than the United States and France, however, the Viet Minh cannot disregard the evolution of the Vietnamese political scene. Despite its strongly entrenched military position, the Viet Minh cannot simply ignore the fact that the Bao Dai regime, which has been recognized by thirty-five countries (although by few Asian states), has acquired a strong international position. Nor can it ignore the fact that national consciousness has made great strides in the Bao Dai zone and that if former Bao Dai governments did not represent Vietnamese nationalist feelings, the Cabinet established in January 1954 under Prince Buu Loc, the Emperor's cousin and former Vietnamese High Commissioner in Paris, can be considered as a definite break with the past. Composed mostly of sincere and disinterested nationalists, among them several legal scholars, the Buu Loc Cabinet holds out the promise of an increase in efficiency which is essential to the future of any nationalist regime. It is a Cabinet of young men—Buu Loc himself is only thirty-nine—and with the exception of two Dai Viet members, it is a government of technicians. Nguyen Trung Vinh, chief of the Vietnamese delegation at the Pau Conference, the Vice Prime Minister and Minister of Agriculture, also has the new title of Minister of Agrarian Reform. Nguyen Dac Khe, Buu Loc's second in command in Paris, who, like the prince, played a key role in Franco-Vietnamese negotiations since the Elysée Accords, has the new post of Minister in charge of National Democratization. The new Minister of Foreign Affairs, Nguyen Quoc Dinh, was professor of international law at the University of Toulouse.

As Buu Loc assumed office, he appealed for whole-hearted support, both from the nationalists and from Bao Dai. "The first mission of my government," he said, "will be to negotiate with France for recognition of the total independence of Viet Nam." He declared his desire to make of Viet Nam a true democracy, and added, "I declare emphatically that there can be no true democratic regime without an elected national assembly."

To Bao Dai, he said: "Nothing lasting in our country can be realized

[28] In 1950 Dang Chan Lieu, press attaché of the Viet Minh delegation in Paris until the delegation was closed in August 1949, went on a mission to Indonesia to try to gain recognition for the Viet Minh government. This mission, which failed, was the last act of Viet Minh diplomacy in a non-Communist country.

without you; on the contrary, there is every hope for your government if it can count on your active support." At the same time, he urged national union upon the country, saying, "I dare to hope that the coming days will be marked by the arrival of men of all points of view who will accept responsibilities in keeping with their ability and their vocation."[29]

The task ahead was not an easy one. The years of corruption, which had weakenèd and discredited the regime, seemed to have left an indelible stamp on the Bao Dai zone. The vital forces of the population had still to be channeled behind the government, a state of affairs which both President Eisenhower and Premier Laniel publicly deplored, although the French and American Governments had not been very fortunate in the choice of the men with whom they dealt as representatives of the Vietnamese nation. From widely divergent groups came demands for free elections of a national assembly, for popular controls over the government and for representation of the various political tendencies in the country. Nationalists demanded representative government with growing intensity and with virtual unanimity, and they could hardly be ignored at a time when the Bao Dai government needed, as never before, to consolidate its strength among the people so as to be able to deal with the Viet Minh on more equal terms.

At Berlin, early in 1954, the Big Three Foreign Ministers had agreed to hold a conference in Geneva at the end of April, to try to settle the Korean question and also to discuss the problem of peace in Indochina. For a number of Frenchmen, some of them highly placed, the next step seemed simple: persuade the Chinese to end their aid to the Viet Minh and the war would be over. There was a certain degree of logic in this argument; it would be unrealistic to assume that a total identity of interests existed between China and the Viet Minh; the Chinese could be counted on to supply the Viet Minh only so long as it served their interest to do so. This time, however, when France had little to offer to China, influential Frenchmen looked to the United States to make concessions for them; they talked of recognition of Communist China, its admission to the United Nations, and Chinese trade with the West. And to encourage Washington along this road, they pointed out that the reluctance of French opinion to agree to the formation of a European army in which Germany would participate (originally a French idea), a key aim of American foreign policy, was not unrelated to the continuing drain of the war in Indochina which seriously weakened France in relation to her traditional European enemy.

But it was asking a great deal for the United States to make such concessions to the Chinese, particularly at a time when American public opinion was in no mood to soften toward the Communists. And this fact was recognized not only by Americans, but also by the considerable body of French

[29] *Le Monde,* January 18, 1954.

and Vietnamese opinion which favored negotiations with the Viet Minh without the interference of foreign powers, whether the United States or Communist China, which could not have the same interests, or the same stake, in Indochina as they.

In any case, there was no simple solution ahead. Some favored a coalition government for Viet Nam, uniting Communists and nationalists, but with the nationalists still relatively weak this prospect inevitably invoked reminders of Prague, where Communist participation in the government had led rapidly to Communist control over the country and was violently rejected by the West.

The other solution, which seemed to be favored not only by certain French government circles and by some Americans (prominent among them Walter Lippmann), but also by the Viet Minh, was some kind of partition of Viet Nam, with the northern half of the country in Viet Minh hands and the south under the nationalists. The Viet Minh seemed to have subordinated the unity and independence for which it originally went to war, and which it still found so useful as a propaganda slogan, to a determination to maintain some area of the country under Communist control even at the sacrifice of both unity and independence, to say nothing of hundreds of thousands of lives. The prospect of partition, however, would occasion grave concern on the part of a number of Vietnamese nationalists, not only because it would be counter to the historical trend toward the unification of Viet Nam, but also because of the nature of the regimes which would almost certainly take shape in a divided country. As regards the Communist zone, the more respect the Chinese would feel toward a strong united Viet Nam, the less reason they would have not to absorb completely a Vietnamese soviet republic of sharply reduced dimensions. In the south, as Buu Hoi wrote, partition "would probably lead to the indefinite maintenance of a good part of the expeditionary corps in the non-Communist zone. There would be a real danger then of seeing—as certain backward elements in French politics would like—the re-establishment of the old colonial order, where the military means would seem to permit."[30]

The immediate outook for Viet Nam was a difficult and troubled one, and many Vietnamese, and Frenchmen too, were anxious lest the solution of the struggle which concerned them both so deeply be subordinated to the solution of more general and perhaps even insoluble problems of Far Eastern and international policy. One thing, however, was clear: for Viet Nam the only alternative to chaos is a position in Southeast Asia, not as a satellite of China, whoever the rulers of that country may be, nor as a proving ground for any new form of Western colonialism, but as a fully independent nation endowed with democratic institutions. Only under such conditions

[30] L'Express, March 6, 1954.

could the dynamic abilities of the Vietnamese people be roused from a sleep of centuries to enable them to contribute anew to civilization.

The profound attachment of the Vietnamese to their independence cannot be better expressed than in the classic proclamation issued as early as the beginning of the fifteenth century by the Emperor Le Loi: "Our people long ago established Viet Nam as an independent nation with its own civilization. We have our own mountains and rivers, our own customs and traditions, and these are different from those of the foreign country to the north [China]. . . . We have sometimes been weak, and sometimes powerful, but at no time have we suffered from a lack of heroes."[31] There is no reason to believe that this spirit has changed.

[31] The proclamation *Binh Ngo Dai Cao* written by Nguyen Trai.

SELECTED BIBLIOGRAPHY

The following bibliography makes no claim to be comprehensive. For a much fuller bibliography readers should consult *Indochina: A Bibliography of the Land and the People* (Washington: Library of Congress, Reference Department, 1950) and the shorter selected bibliography, *Southeast Asia: An Annotated Bibliography of Selected Reference Sources* (Washington: Library of Congress, Orientalia Division, 1952).

GOVERNMENT PUBLICATIONS

FRANCE

Bulletin officiel du Haut-Commissariat de France en Indochine.

Délégation française auprès de la Commission allemande d'Armistice. *Recueil de Documents publiés par le Gouvernement français.* Tome premier, 29 juin 1940–29 septembre 1940 (Paris, Alfred Costes, 1949).

Direction de la Documentation. *Notes documentaires et Etudes* (this title was subsequently changed to *Notes et Etudes documentaires*):

76. *La mise en valeur de l'Indochine française.* I.
95. *La mise en valeur de l'Indochine française.* II.
120. Rapport presenté par le général Catroux. *La crise franco-japonaise de juin 1940.*
316. *Le chemin de fer du Yunnan.*
548. *Documents rélatifs aux Problèmes Indochinois*: I. *Accords entre la France et le Viet-Nam.*
554. *Ibid.* II. *Accords entre la France, le Cambodge, la Cochinchine et le Laos.*
555. *Ibid.* III. *Accords internationaux relatifs à l'Indochine.*
633. *La constitution du royaume du Cambodge.*
725. *Constitution du royaume du Laos.*
752. *Positions indochinoises: Bao Dai.*
998. *L'évolution économique de l'Indochine*: I. *Introduction du plan de modernisation et d'équipement de l'Indochine.*
999. *Ibid.* II. *Extraits du plan de modernisation et d'équipement de l'Indochine.*
1131. *Principales réalisations politiques accompliés dans les térritoires d'Outre-Mer depuis 1945.*

1295. *Actes définissants les rapports des états associés du Viet-Nam, du Cambodge et du Laos avec la France.*

1325. *Textes relatifs à l'organisation constitutionnelle du Viet-Nam.*

1355. *Discours prononcé à l'occasion de l'ouverture de la Conférence inter-états . . .* (Pau).

1425. *Conventions Inter-Etats. . . .* (novembre–decembre 1950)

1811. *Traité d'Amitié et d'Association et Conventions annexes entre la République française et Le Royaume du Laos (Paris, le 22 octobre 1953).*

Gouvernement général de l'Indochine. Direction des affaires politiques et de la sûreté générale. *Contribution à l'histoire des mouvements politiques de l'Indochine française* (Hanoi, 1933):

Vol. 1. *Le Tan-Viet Cach Menh dang (Parti révolutionnaire du Nouvel Annam).*

Vol. 2. *Le Viet-Nam Quoc-Dan dang (Parti national annamite du Tonkin).*

Vol. 4. *Le Dong-Duong Cong-San dang (Parti communiste indochinois).*

Vol. 5. *La Térreur Rouge en Annam.*

Gouvernement général de l'Indochine. Direction fédérale de l'information. *Le situation en Indochine, mars 1945–juin 1946* (Saigon, 1946).

Gouvernement général de l'Indochine. Direction des Services économiques. *Annuaire statistique de l'Indochine.*

Journal officiel de l'Indochine.

Journal officiel de la République française. Débats parlementaires. Assemblée nationale.

Journal officiel de la République française. Débats parlementaires. Conseil de la République.

Journal officiel de la République française. Débats de l'Assemblée de l'Union française.

Ministère de la France d'Outre-Mer. *Bulletin.* (Title varies. Beginning January 1951, called *Chroniques d'Outre-Mer*).

République française. Haute Cour de Justice. *Procès du Maréchal Pétain* (Paris, Imprimeries des Journaux officiels, 1945).

French Press and Information Service (New York). *News from France.*
———. *Documents.*

FRANCO-VIETNAMESE DOCUMENTS

Conférence Franco-Vietnamienne, Dalat, 1946. Occasional documents.

Conférence Franco-Vietnamienne, Fontainebleau, 1946. Proceedings and documents.

"Democratic Republic of Viet Nam," 1945—
(Ho Chi Minh Government)

Office de l'Information de la République du Viet-Nam (Hanoi). Bernard, Maurice and Yvonne, *Lettre aux Amis d'Hanoi* (1945).

——. *Les Elections Générales et l'Assemblée Nationale Constituents Vietnamienne.*

Délégation de la République démocratique du Viet-Nam en France. Service d'Information. Bureau de Paris. *Achievements of the Democratic Republic of Viet-Nam* (1948).

——. *Bulletin du Viet-Nam.*

——. *Causes of the conflict between France and Viet-Nam* (1948).

——. *The Democratic Republic of Viet-Nam* (1948).

——. *Messages.*

——. *Messages de Paix adressés par le Président Ho-Chi-Minh au People et au Gouvernement français* (1947).

——. *Le nouveau Viet-Nam en construction. Comment la Révolution a triomphé de la famine,* by Hoang-Van-Duc (1946).

——. *Le Président Ho-Chi-Minh* (1947).

——. *Quelques aspects du Viet-Nam nouveau* (1946).

——. *Six mois d'opérations militaires au Viet-Nam* (1947).

——. *Sur une lettre ouverte à Monsieur Bollaert, Haut Commissaire en Indochine* (1947).

——. *Two years' achievement of the Viet-Nam nationalist government* (1947).

——. *Viet-Nam, république démocratique* (1946).

——. *Viet-Nam's fight against Fascism (1940–1945)* (1948).

Ministère du Travail. *Législation du Travail* (Paris, 1949).

National Defense Council. *One Year of Revolutionary Achievement. Report to the Vietnam People at Hanoi by Vo-Nguyen-Giap* (Bangkok: Viet-Nam News Publication, 1946).

Vietnam News Service (Bangkok). *Ho-Chi-Minh, the "Father" of his People* (1949).

——. *Vietnam, a New Stage in Her History.*

——. *Vietnam Defeats Famine* (1951).

Vietnam News Service (Rangoon). *Viet-Nam Information* (a regular bulletin).

——. *Educational Problems in Viet-Nam,* by Nguyen Khanh Toan (1950).

Vietnam (Bao Dai Government), 1949—

Bac-Viet Hanh-Chinh Ban Nguyet San (Bulletin Administratif du Nord Viet-Nam).

Cong-Bao Viet-Nam (Journal officiel du Viet-Nam).
Cong-Van Tap-San Nam-Viet (Bulletin officiel du Sud Viet-Nam).
Viet-Nam. Bulletin d'information publié par le Haut-Commissariat du Viet Nam en France.
Viet-Nam Nien-Giam Thong-ke (Annuaire Statistique du Viet-Nam).
Vietnamese Information Bulletin (Saigon).

"Inter-State"

Conférence Inter-Etats de Pau. Proceedings.
Institut d'Emission des Etats du Cambodge, du Laos et du Vietnam. Service des Etudes Economiques et Financières. *Statistiques Economiques et Financières.*
————. *Etudes et Documents.*

United States

Department of Agriculture. Office of Foreign Agricultural Relations. *The Agriculture of French Indochina* (1950).
Department of State Bulletin.
Department of State. Office of Intelligence and Research. *Political Alignments of Vietnamese Nationalists* (1949).
Department of State. *Papers Relating to the Foreign Relations of the United States: Japan 1931–1941* (1943).
————. *United States Relations with China* (1949).
Economic Cooperation Administration (later known as Mutual Security Agency and Foreign Operations Administration). Reports to Congress.
Special Technical Economic Mission to Cambodia, Laos and Vietnam. *Quarterly Activity Report.*
Eighty-third Congress. First session. *Indochina. Report of Senator Mike Mansfield on a Study Mission to the Associated States of Indochina, Viet Nam, Cambodia, Laos.* October 27, 1953.

Great Britain

Hansard. Parliamentary Debates.
Vice Admiral the Earl Mountbatten of Burma. Report of the Combined Chiefs of Staff by the Supreme Allied Commander. *Southeast Asia 1943–1945.* (London: H. M. Stationery Office, 1951).

United Nations

Economic and Social Council. Economic Commission for Asia and the Far East. *Economic Bulletin for Asia and the Far East* (Quarterly).
————. *Economic Survey of Asia and the Far East* (Annual, 1947—).

NEWSPAPERS

Anh-Sang (Saigon).
L'Aube (Paris).
L'Aurore (Paris).
Cambodge (Nnom Penh).
Climats (Paris).
Combat (Paris).
Dan Ta (Saigon).
L'Echo du Viet-Nam (Saigon).
Franc-Tireur (Paris).
France-Soir (Paris).
Giang-Son (Hanoi).

L'Humanité (Paris).
Le Journal d'Extrême-Orient (Saigon).
La Liberté (Pnom Penh).
Le Monde (Paris).
Paris-Presse-l'Intransigent (Paris).
Le Populaire (Paris).
Saigon Moi (Saigon).
Témoignage Chrétien (Paris).
Tia-Sang (Hanoi).
Than-Chung (Saigon).
L'Union Française (Saigon).

PERIODICALS

Asia (Saigon).
Asian Horizon (London).
Asiatic Review (London).
Doi Moi (Saigon).
Eastern World (London).
Esprit (Paris).
L'Express (Paris).
Far Eastern Survey (New York).
France-Asie (Saigon).
Indochine Française (later entitled *France-Indochine*), (Paris).

Indochine Sud-est Asiatique (Paris).
Marches Coloniaux (Paris).
Moi (Saigon).
Mondes d'Orient (Paris).
L'Observateur (Paris).
Pacific (Paris).
Pacific Affairs (New York).
Politique Etrangère (Paris).
Les Temps Modernes (Paris).

BOOKS AND PAMPHLETS

Anh-Van and Jacqueline Roussel. *Mouvements nationaux et lutte de classes au Viet-Nam* (Paris: Publications de la IVe Internationale, 1947).

Association Culturelle pour le Salut du Viet-Nam. *Témoignages et Documents Français Relatifs à la Colonisation Française au Viet-Nam* (Hanoi, 1945).

Association France–Viet-Nam. *Les propositions du président Ho-Chi-Minh* (Paris, 1947).

Bauchar, René (pseud.), Jean Charbonneau. *Rafales sur l'Indochine* (Paris: Fournier, 1946).

Baudouin, Paul. *Neuf mois au Gouvernement (Avril–Décembre 1940)* (Paris: Le Table Ronde, 1948).

Bernard, Paul. *Nouveaux Aspects du Problème Economique Indochinois* (Paris: Fernand Sorlot, 1937).

Blanchet, Andre. *Au pays des ballila jaunes* (Saint-Etienne: Dorian, 1947).

Boisdon, Daniel. *Les Institutions de l'Union française* (Paris, 1949).

Brodrick, Alan H. *Little China: the Annamese Lands* (London, New York: Oxford University Press, 1942).

———. *Little Vehicle: Cambodia and Laos* (London: Hutchinson, 1949).

Cabaton, Antoine. *L'Indochine* (Paris: Laurens, 1932).

Canada, Department of Mines and Technical Surveys: Geographical Branch. *Indo-china, A Geographical Appreciation* (Ottawa, 1953).

Callis, Helmut G. *Foreign Capital in Southeast Asia* (New York: Institute of Pacific Relations, 1942).

Chaigneau, Michel Duc. *Souvenirs de Hué* (Paris, 1867).

Charles-Roux, F. *Cinq Mois Tragiques aux Affaires étrangères, 21 mai—1ᵉ novembre 1940* (Paris: Plon, 1949).

Chézal, Guy de. *Parachuté en Indochine* (Paris: Editions des deux Sirènes, 1947).

Dansette, Adrien. *Leclerc* (Paris: Flammarion, 1952).

Decoux, Jean. *A la Barre de l'Indochine* (Paris: Plon, 1949).

Delavignette, Robert and Charles-André Julien. *Les Constructeurs de la France d'Outre-Mer* (Paris: Correa, 1946).

Devillers, Philippe. *Le Viet Nam Contemporain* (Paris: Comité des Etudes des Problèmes du Pacifique, 1950).

———. *Histoire du Viet Nam de 1940 à 1952* (Paris: Editions du Seuil, 1952).

———. *Vietnamese Nationalism and French Policies,* in W. L. Holland (ed.), *Asian Nationalism and the West* (New York: Macmillan, 1953).

Dorgelès, Roland. *Sur la Route Mandarine* (Paris, 1929).

Douglas, William O. *North of Malaya* (New York: Doubleday, 1953).

Ducoroy, Maurice. *Ma trahison en Indochine* (Paris: Les Editions Internationales, 1949).

Emerson, Rupert, *et al. Government and Nationalism in Southeast Asia* (New York: Institute of Pacific Relations, 1942).

Ennis, Thomas E. *French Policy and Developments in Indochina* (Chicago: University of Chicago Press, 1936).

Ethnic Groups of Northern Southeast Asia (New Haven: Yale University, 1950).

Feis, Herbert. *The Road to Pearl Harbor* (Princeton: Princeton University Press, 1950).

Figuères, Léo. *Je Reviens du Viet-Nam libre* (Paris, 1950).

Galembert, J. de, and E. Erard. *Les Administrations et les services publics indochinois* (Hanoi, 1931).

Gaudel, André. *L'Indochine française en face du Japon* (Paris: Susse, 1947).

Gaultier, Marcel. *Gia-Long* (Saigon, 1933).

———. *Minh-Mang* (Paris: Larose, 1935).

Gauthier, Julien. *L'Indochine au travail dans la paix française* (Paris: Eyrolles, 1949).

Gobron, Gabriel. *Histoire et Philosophie du Caodaisme* (Paris: Derby, 1949).

Gosselin, Captain Ch. *L'Empire d'Annam* (Paris: Perrin, 1904).

Goudal, Jean. *Labor Conditions in Indochina* (Geneva: International Labor Office, 1938).

Gourou, Pierre. *L'Avenir de l'Indochine* (Paris: Centre d'Etudes de Politique Etrangère, 1947).

———. *Utilisation du Sol en Indochine française* (Paris: Hartmann, 1940).

———. *Land Utilization in French Indochina* (New York: Institute of Pacific Relations, 1945). Mimeographed for limited distribution.

———. *Les Paysans du delta tonkinois, étude de géographie humaine* (Paris: Editions d'Art et d'Histoire, 1936).

Hammer, Ellen J. *The Emergence of Viet-Nam* (New York: Institute of Pacific Relations, 1947).

———. "The French Empire Today," in Edward Mead Earle, *Modern France: Problems of the Third and Fourth Republics* (Princeton: Princeton University Press, 1951).

———. "Indochina," in Lawrence K. Rosinger and associates, *The State of Asia* (New York: Knopf, 1951), pp. 221–67.

———. *Politics and Parties in Viet Nam* (New Delhi: Indian Council of World Affairs and Asian Relations Organization, *Foreign Policy Reports,* 1953).

Hanh Son. *Cu Tran Cao-Van* (Paris: Minh Tan). In Vietnamese.

Hertrich, Jean-Michel. *Doc-Lap! L'indépendance ou la mort!* (Paris: Vigneau, 1946).

Hull, Cordell. *Memoirs* (New York: Macmillan, 1948).

Institut Franco-Suisse d'Etudes Coloniales. *France and Viet-Nam, the Franco-Vietnamese conflict according to official documents* (Geneva: Editions du Milieu du Monde, 1947).

Isaacs, Harold R. *New Cycle in Asia* (New York: Macmillan, 1947).

———. *No Peace for Asia* (New York: Macmillan, 1947).

Janse, Olov R. T. *The Peoples of French Indochina* (Washington: Smithsonian Institution, 1944).

Le Boulanger, Paul. *Histoire du Laos Français* (Paris, Plon, 1930).

Le Bourgeois, Jacques. *Saigon sans la France, des Japonais au Viet-Minh* (Paris: Plon, 1949).

Lévy, Roger, et al. *French Interests and Policies in the Far East* (New York: Institute of Pacific Relations, 1941).

———. *L'Indochine et ses traités, 1946* (Paris: Hartmann, 1947).

Lewis, Norman. *A Dragon Apparent* (New York: Scribners, 1951).

Mordant, General. *Au Service de la France en Indochine* (Saigon, 1950).

Mus, Paul. *Le Viet-Nam Chez Lui* (Paris: Centre d'Etudes de Politique Etrangère, 1946).

———. *Viet-Nam. Sociologie d'une Guerre* (Paris: Editions du Seuil, 1952).

Newman, Bernard. *Report on Indo-China* (London: Robert Hale, 1953).

Nguyen-Ai-Quoc (Ho Chi Minh). *Le Procès de la Colonisation française* (Paris, 1926).

Nguyen-Huu-Khang. *Le Commune Annamite: étude historique, juridique et économique* (Paris: Sirey, 1946).

Nguyen Duy Thanh. *My Four Years with the Viet Minh* (Bombay: Democratic Research Service, 1950).

Nguyen Van Huyen. *La Civilisation annamite* (Collection de la Direction de l'Instruction Publique de l'Indochine, 1944).

Pasquier, Pierre. *L'Annam d'autrefois, essai sur le constitution de l'Annam avant l'intervention française* (Paris: Société d'éditions gèographiques, 1929).

Pelzer, Karl J. *Pioneer Settlement in the Asiatic Tropics* (New York: American Geographical Society, 1945).

Pinto, Roger. *Aspects de l'évolution gouvernementale de l'Indochine française* (Paris: Sirey, 1946).

Purcell, Victor. *The Chinese in Southeast Asia* (London, New York: Oxford University Press, 1951).

Robequain, Charles. *The Economic Development of French Indo-China* (London, New York: Oxford University Press, 1944).

Roubaud, Louis. *Viet Nam* (Paris: Valois, 1931).

Sabattier, General G. *Le Destin de l'Indochine: Souvenirs et Documents, 1941–1951* (Paris: Plon, 1952).

Sainteny, Jean. *Histoire d'une Paix Manquée* (Paris: Amiot Dumont, 1953).

Sarraut, Albert. *La mise en valeur des colonies françaises* (Paris: Payot, 1923).

Sasorith, Katay D. *Le Laos* (Paris: Berger-Levrault, 1953).

Southworth, Constant. *The French Colonial Venture* (London: King, 1931).

Thompson, Virginia. *French Indo-China* (London: Allen and Unwin; New York: Macmillan 1937).

Thompson, Virginia, and Richard Adloff. *The Left Wing in Southeast Asia.* (New York: Sloane, 1950).

Tran Trong Kim. *Viet Nam Su Luoc* (Hanoi: Tan Viet, 1951, in Vietnamese).

Vietnam Cultural Association for National Liberation. *Factual Records of the Vietnam August Revolution* (Hanoi, 1946).

Viollis, Andrée (pseud.), Andrée F. C. Ardenne de Tizac. *Indochine S.O.S.* (Paris: Gallimard, 1935).

INDEX

INDEX